The Derbyshire Family Commentary

ACTS

Doug Derbyshire

To request permissions, contact the publisher at admin@TellTheKids.com

Hardcover ISBN: 978-1-953935-12-0
Paperback ISBN: 978-1-953935-14-4
Electronic Book ISBN: 978-1-953935-13-7

Library of Congress Control Number: 2022939641

First Hardback Edition October 2022
First Paperback Edition October 2022
Electronic Book October 2022

Editor: Bethany Derbyshire
Cover Design: Nick Zink

Printed by Ingram Spark in the USA

Published by Tell The KIDS® LLC
7700 Skylake Drive
Fort Worth TX 76179

TellTheKids.com

Preface

One evening as I knelt in the presence of the Lord, He moved me to pray once again for my children. Gary was maybe 6 or 7 years old at the time. I began solemnly at first, but after some time my composure left me and I began to cry out my prayer. Tears filled my eyes, my body shook, and I raised clenched fists in a battle of prayer, pleading with my Lord to fill the souls of my children with the fullness of His presence, and fill the hearts and minds of my children with a love for His Word. I don't remember how long I knelt in prayer, but I do remember when He graciously drew near. I heard in my mind God's words from Isaiah 59:21, "As for Me, this is the covenant that I will make with (you) says the Lord, My Spirit who is upon you, and My words which I have placed in your mouth, shall not depart from your mouth, nor from the mouth of your children, nor from the mouth of your children's children from this time on and forever more." I immediately rose from my place of prayer, confident that my Lord had heard my request. And for the past 20 years I have had no greater joy than seeing the Lord bring these words to pass for our family. While we were all together under the same roof in Bangkla we gathered together as a family to pore over God's Word at dinners each evening and early Sunday mornings before church each week. I kept those notes from our times together in God's Word and have written them down for us here. I have added some thoughts here and there, but the heart of these notes came from our studies together as we sought to fill our family and our minds with God's Word that He might make better use of us for His purposes. Our times together have given me notes on nearly all the Bible. I will continue to put them together into a more useful form, and pass them on to you as each section is completed.

...........to my mom whose love for God's Word overflowed into my life so that I became filled with a love for God's Word at an early age.

...........to my dad whose study on the book of Job ignited a fire in my blood to study God's Word book by book and verse by verse.

...........to my four children whose obedience to God's Word and heart to take it to the next generation has filled your mom and I with joy.

...........and to Cheryl whose love for me and tireless provision for our family has enabled me to endure. For years you woke the children and had them ready for breakfast and family Bible study at 6am every morning. May the Lord bless you for what you have done for me, for our children, and for the cause of Christ in the lives of so many others. You are the most wonderful individual I have ever met. For over 37 years you have been a continual, precious, loving, untiring blessing to me personally and to the cause of Christ. I am so deeply grateful to you, so happily in love with you, and so overwhelmingly thankful to our Lord who has given you to me as such a dear, gifted, and enthusiastically hard-working partner as we minister together to take care of God's people and bring the lost to the Savior.

Foreword to Volume 4

Walking through the book of Acts is a happy occupation for me. So much of the book is centered on new souls coming to faith in Christ and new churches rising up to bring glory to God in places where Christ's name had not been known. These centerpieces of the book have been the centerpieces of our family's ministry in Thailand for the last three decades. I find teachings and stories from every chapter that apply directly to our ministry efforts today. And so often I see modern day illustrations of the teachings and stories of Acts played out before me here on the mission field even now.

Once again, I call this a family commentary, for my thoughts on each verse flow from our experiences and discussions as a family in our service to the Lord. The missionary efforts described in Acts remind me of the missionary efforts of Becky and Sandi as they taught English and the gospel in schools across Thailand. The sermons recorded in Acts remind me of Gary and Jonathan as they preached their first sermons in Bangkla and Prajinburi. Reading of Aquila and Priscilla and their service to the Lord reminds me of how wonderful it has been to serve alongside Cheryl for more than three glorious decades.

The stories of Acts inspire me, instruct me, and remind me of our family's ministry together.

I was especially reminded of you all as I read again the description of the Bereans in Acts 17:11:

17:10-11
Then the brethren immediately sent Paul and Silas away by night to Berea. When they arrived, they went into the synagogue of the Jews. These were more fair-minded than those in Thessalonica, in that they received the word with all readiness, and searched the Scriptures daily to find out whether these things were so.

Thinking of you moved me to write:

"...The Bereans are described wonderfully. They are said to be "noble" (ESV). Literally, the word translated as "fair-minded" in the NKJV here means "well-born" – of noble birth, or in this case, noble character. The same word is used in I Corinthians 1:26 when Paul says that "not many

noble" are called into the kingdom of God. What character traits make men and women appear "noble" in the eyes of heaven? Verse 11 tells us: "They received the word with all readiness, and searched the Scriptures daily." Let us be noble believers! Let us search the Scriptures daily to see what the Lord would say to us. Let us listen to sermons, participate in Bible studies, and read God's Word "with all readiness." The "noble" believer drinks God's Word in when he hears it preached, listens to it taught, and when he reads it alone at home. He is always ready to hear God speak to him when the Bible is presented before him. Noble believers are not those who daydream of other things while God's Word is taught. They do not cynically analyze the preacher's words. They sit on the edge of their seat "with all readiness" to hear God speak to their listening soul. Such were the people of Berea. It is a dear joy to me to see all my children grow to be "noble" men and women of God. Gary, Jonathan, Becky, and Sandi, all four of you bless me with how you love to drink in God's Word with "all readiness." When you were young it was my joy to teach you God's Word, and now that you are grown it is my joy to see you reverently handle the Scriptures and pass them on to others. May our family forever prove to be "noble" in this same regard.

Thinking of my four children made writing on Acts 20:31-32 both a dear joy and a "pleasant sorrow":

20:31-32
"Therefore watch, and remember that for three years I did not cease to warn everyone night and day with tears. So now, brethren, I commend you to God and to the word of His grace, which is able to build you up and give you an inheritance among all those who are sanctified."

For three years Paul worked faithfully among the believers in Ephesus to build up their faith and "warn everyone" to look out for the "savage wolves" (verse 29) that would attack their flock of believers. He gave continual, emotional pleas to them to cling to God and cling to His Word so that they would be protected from the various enemies of the Christian life. He warned them to flee sin, turn away false teachers, and stand strong before persecution. But now he was leaving them and would no longer be able to provide the warnings and teachings and comforting friendship that he had given them for the past three years. Paul knew that the great work that was done in Ephesus through his efforts was not the result of his own personal merits. "This was the LORD's doing" and it was marvelous in his eyes (Psalm 118:23). But now, even more aware of the fact that he could do nothing more for the spiritual benefit of these saints that he loved so much, he "commends" them to God and to God's Word. Paul could not carry these believers on his back and make them mature followers of Christ. But he was fully confident that God would continue the work that he had begun in Ephesus (Philippians 1:6), and that His Word, "the word of His grace," would guide them successfully through all the trials and challenges ahead.

Paul's comfort here was a great comfort to me as my children left my home. Much of me would have preferred for us to never be apart. But I was forced to recognize that I had never been the one that had secured spiritual maturity for my children. My Lord called them to Himself, and His Word grew them in the knowledge of Him. My children did not need my constant presence, they needed my Lord's constant presence and constant access to His Word. And so, it was a pleasant sorrow to commend my children to the Lord and to His Word, just as Paul commended the saints of Ephesus to the Lord here. I cannot always be with my children. They cannot have constant access to my words of counsel and comfort. But my Lord is always with them, and they do have constant access to His words of counsel and comfort. As Paul experienced here with the leaders of Ephesus, so it is our pleasant sorrow to commend those we love to the sustaining care of our Lord when the time comes for us to be set apart.

As I wrote on Acts 21:5-6, I grinned thinking of the picture of our family:

21:5-6
When we had come to the end of those days, we departed and went on our way; and they all accompanied us, with wives and children, till we were out of the city. And we knelt down on the shore and prayed. When we had taken our leave of one another, we boarded the ship, and they returned home.

Just as the Ephesian leaders had accompanied Paul all the way to his ship to see him off (Acts 20:38), so we see the saints in Tyre accompany Paul all the way out of the city on his final day with them as well. They wanted to be with Paul as long as they possibly could. Shakespeare wrote that "parting is such sweet sorrow," and Paul's departure from both Tyre and from the Ephesians seems to indicate that this is especially true for those who are bound by the bonds of love in Christ. Parting moves us to recall our precious times together, moan over the prospect of being separated, and fill us with joy in the anticipation of being reunited – a hope that is guaranteed for all who trust in Jesus. The Derbyshire good-bye is founded on this Biblical model.

And of course, I could not help but think of our family as I wrote on Luke's description of Philip's family in Acts 21:

21:7-9
And when we had finished our voyage from Tyre, we came to Ptolemais, greeted the brethren, and stayed with them one day. On the next day we, who were Paul's companions, departed and came to Caesarea, and entered the house of Philip the evangelist, who was one of the seven, and stayed with him. Now this man had four virgin daughters who prophesied.

Philip was a man "of good reputation, full of the Holy Spirit and wisdom" (Acts 6:3-5). Acts chapter 8 is devoted to providing us with a sketch of Philip's remarkable ministry. The chapter ends with Philip coming to Caesarea, and here we find Paul joining him there and staying at his home. As foretold in Joel 2:28, Philip's four grown daughters were all known for joining in their father's work as they served God's people and "prophesied." It is a dear blessing to the church when families serve the Lord together.

Philip was used by the Holy Spirit to meet the needs of the church's poor (Acts 6:1-7), to display the miraculous power of God (Acts 8:5-7), and to lead the lost to faith in Christ (Acts 8:26-40). Men like Philip are hard to find, and are a dear blessing to the church. But men like Philip who serve the Lord and who are blessed to see their children serve Him in the same way are even harder to find and are a rich blessing to their church indeed.

God's people love to see families serving Him together. The sight moved Luke to make note of it because it is such an encouragement to see and because it is all too hard to find. Abigail was a saintly follower of God, but her husband was not. Timothy was a faithful servant of the Lord, but his father was not. Job was "blameless and upright in heart" and approved by God, but his wife was not. David's heart was knit to God's, but his sons' were not. And on and on the list goes.

It remains my prayer for our family that we might be like Philip's family – that all who take note of us (as Luke did of Philip) would have the joy of seeing not only our faith, but seeing the faith of our children as well.

I love God's Word so much. I hold it cupped in my hands each morning, drinking in the treasure that the words are to me. The very thoughts of God written down for me to bask in! Oh, how I love His Word! It is my constant meditation (Psalm 119:97). It is "my delight" (Psalm 119:174). It is a "great treasure" to me (Psalm 119:162). And the delight of this great treasure is made more precious still knowing that it is the meditation and delight and treasure of all my children as well.

I am so grateful for Cheryl and the children that God has given me. May His Word continually be the joy of our family generation after generation.

Doug Derbyshire
March 12, 2022

Acts 1

1:1-3
The former account I made, O Theophilus, of all that Jesus began both to do and teach, until the day in which He was taken up, after He through the Holy Spirit had given commandments to the apostles whom He had chosen, to whom He also presented Himself alive after His suffering by many infallible proofs, being seen by them during forty days and speaking of the things pertaining to the kingdom of God.

Luke ended his "former account" (the book of Luke), with Jesus' ascension back up into heaven, and now he picks up where he left off at the end of his "first book" (ESV). The book of Luke was intended to detail for us "all that Jesus began both to do and teach." Luke emphasized Jesus' teachings, because Jesus was "a teacher come from God" (John 3:2) and came to fulfill the prophecy of Isaiah 54:13 that God's people would have the remarkable privilege of being "taught by God" (John 6:45). But as wonderful as Jesus' teachings were, Luke did not stop there; he wrote of both the things that Jesus taught, and he wrote of the things that Jesus did – "of all that Jesus began both to do and teach." Jesus was followed and revered because of His teachings (John 6:68), but He was also revered and followed because of all the miraculous, loving, rescuing, useful things that He did. Matthew Henry wrote, "Those are the best ministers that both do and teach, whose lives are a constant sermon."

And now, it is our highest calling to do and teach that which Jesus did and taught, bolstered by Jesus' promise in John 14:12 – "Most assuredly, I say to you, he who believes in Me, the works that I do he will do also; and greater works than these he will do, because I go to My Father." Everything we do that is patterned after the works of Jesus now takes on eternal import. The work of healing the sick takes on such greater significance because we read that Jesus healed the sick. We find affirmation for our efforts when we provide food for others, seeing that Jesus fed the hungry. When we baptize new believers, forgive those who hurt us, and treat children with kindness – we do so with joy, knowing that Jesus did all these things. The actions of our Lord provide us with nearly endless examples for how to live. He paid taxes, He left home to preach the gospel, He fiercely guarded the holiness of worship gatherings, and on and on His examples go. And though the sheer number of remarkable actions carried out by Jesus made it impossible to write everything down (John 21:25), it was Luke's stated intention to narrate for us a great many of His efforts, so that we might be bettered by His example and continue His example for the next generation. And as a help to us in our effort to imitate the works of Christ and to retell the teachings of Christ, Luke will now provide us with this second narration – "The Acts of the Apostles," so that we might be blessed by reading about the first gen-eration of believers and their effort to teach and do all the things that Jesus taught and did.

When Jesus rose from the dead, Luke tells us that He came back for 40 days "speaking of the things pertaining to the kingdom of God." Life is short, and 40 days is shorter still, and Jesus exemplified for us that the proper way of "redeeming the time" (Ephesians 5:16) – making the best use of the time allotted to us on earth – is to focus our attention on "the things pertaining to the kingdom of God." People often tried to distract Jesus from the matters that pertained to the kingdom of God. In Luke 12 a man tried to wrest Jesus' attention from God's kingdom matters to handle a money dispute, but Jesus would have none of it. In Luke 12:14 He said, "Man, who made Me a judge or an arbitrator over you?" And in John 6:15 when the people tried to take Jesus and force Him to become their earthly king, He would have none of that either. Jesus was completely devoted and kept His attention riveted on "the things pertaining to the kingdom of God. Colossians 3:2 compels us to "Set your mind on things above, not on things on the earth." This was the example of our Lord. Let us, then, strive to imitate Him, expending all possible devotion to "the things pertaining to the kingdom of God."

1:4-5

And being assembled together with them, He commanded them not to depart from Jerusalem, but to wait for the Promise of the Father, "which," He said, "you have heard from Me; for John truly baptized with water, but you shall be baptized with the Holy Spirit not many days from now."

Jesus came "both to do and teach" (verse 1) "of the things pertaining to God" (verse 3). This great ministry of doing the works of God and teaching the words of God will be imparted to His disciples, but they were in no way capable of bearing the weight of such a ministry. The ministry passed on by Jesus to the disciples is the loftiest, most noble enterprise ever undertaken by men – to do the works of God and teach the words of God so that the souls of men might be saved and the Most High God would be glorified in their lives. But the greatness of the enterprise of godly service is counter-manded by the deficiencies of man. Godly service is wonderful! It delights the souls of the servants, it sees eternal destinies changed, and sees the Creator rightly praised. But our Lord makes special effort to drive the point home: "Without Me you can do nothing" (John 15:5). If we are to carry out the works of God, we must be filled with the Spirit of God. The dawn of the disciples' new ministry is upon them. But they must be filled with the power and presence of God if they are to carry out His plans. So Jesus instructs them to wait in Jerusalem for "the Promise of the Father." Joel 2:28 delivered the Father's promise that He would fill His children with His Spirit. Later, John the Baptist confirmed that Jesus would fill His followers with the Holy Spirit of the Lord (Matthew 3:11). And now, the time is close! "Not many days from now" the Spirit will fall on Jesus' disciples and they will be suddenly empowered and inspired to carry out the great works of God.

The prerequisite placed on the disciples in anticipation of the coming of the Holy Spirit was simple: "Wait." The old adage "good things come to those who wait" is never better illustrated than it is right here. Jesus promises to fill His followers with His Spirit. But first, they must wait for a time. When the time comes for us to wait for God's provision or God's direction, let us be found faithful in the call to wait. If our Lord's provision or direction seem slow in coming, so be it. Let us be resolute in our wait for His arrival, joining the psalmist in Psalm 25:21 and say, "Let integrity and uprightness preserve me, for I wait for You." Let us not think to depend on any other source of strength, but rather maintain that "Our soul waits for the LORD; He is our help and our shield" (Psalm 33:20). Saul lost a kingdom because his weak faith did not allow him to wait for God's plan to unfold (I Samuel 13). Let us find instruction in that lesson and wait with contentment should the Lord give us the command to "wait for the Promise" as He does for His disciples here.

1:6-7

Therefore, when they had come together, they asked Him, saying, "Lord, will You at this time restore the kingdom to Israel?" And He said to them, "It is not for you to know times or seasons which the Father has put in His own authority."

Our Lord has made it abundantly clear that He is returning to earth to gather His children to heaven and bring judgment on unbelievers (John 14:1-3, I Thessalonians 4:13-18, II Timothy 4:1, etc.). He has also made it just as abundantly clear, however, that He will not tell us when He is coming back. Matthew 24:36 says, "But of that day and hour no one knows, not even the angels of heaven, but My Father only." And in Matthew 24:44 Jesus emphasizes again that "the Son of Man is coming at an hour you do not expect." We are not told why the Father is keeping His timing secret, but we can guess pretty easily. Our human character is annoyingly prone to mishandling even glimpses of the future. In Jesus' parable of the evil servant in Matthew 24:45-51, as soon as the evil servant thought he knew what the coming days held, he began to "beat his fellow servants, and to eat and drink with the drunkards." If we think judgment for our sins is far in the distant future, we are prone to sin today. And if we think that judgment is imminent, we are prone to discontinue the practical matters of responsible living and forget the importance of today.

So then, since Jesus is definitely returning, and He definitely will not tell us the day of His return, how should we properly await His second coming? We find three actions outlined for us in God's Word. II Peter 3:11 (NLT) tells us first of all that "Since everything around us is going to melt away, what holy, godly lives you should be living!" Jesus is coming! He will judge the living and the dead! Therefore, let us make it our highest priority to live "holy, godly lives."

Secondly, Mark 13:33 says, "Take heed, watch and pray; for you do not know when the time is." Jesus is coming! We don't know when. But the Lord is pleased to see us live in excited anticipation of His arrival. We are to look for Him! As a child sits on the porch and scans the horizon for his dad to return from a long trip, so we are to keep our eyes fixed upward awaiting our Savior's return. Simeon exemplifies this well. In Luke 2:25 we read: "And behold, there was a man in Jerusalem whose name was Simeon, and this man was just and devout, waiting for the Consolation of Israel, and the Holy Spirit was upon him." As Simeon actively awaited Jesus' advent, so we are to actively await Jesus' second coming.

And thirdly, we are to do all that we can to hasten our Lord's return. II Peter 3:12 says that we should be "looking for and hastening the coming of the day of God." Giving perhaps the clearest clue we have regarding the Savior's return, Jesus tells us in Matthew 24:14 – "This gospel of the kingdom will be preached in all the world as a witness to all the nations, and then the end will come." Before Jesus returns, His gospel will be preached "in all the world." Tragically, His gospel is still not being preached in many places. There are still so many people in so many corners of the world that have never had anyone tell them the good news of Jesus' love for them. When horrible things happen, particularly on a grand scale, some people are prone to ask, "Why do you wait, Lord? Why will You not come today and end this suffering?" His words in Matthew 24:14 answer that question simply enough. First, His gospel will be preached "to all the nations, and then the end will come." Peter's imperative in II Peter 3:12 inspires us to "hasten" that day, to hurry that day, to rise up and rush out to make the gospel message readily available to every last person in every last village, so that we might do our part to hasten the second coming of Christ – the day we long for in such earnest.

1:8

But you shall receive power when the Holy Spirit has come upon you; and you shall be witnesses to Me in Jerusalem, and in all Judea and Samaria, and to the end of the earth."

The disciples' trust in Jesus had finally matured, but their vision for service to Him was still confined to the advancement of their own nation and the prosperity of their own people (verse 6). After His resurrection, however, Jesus repeatedly inspired His disciples to expand their outlook to include a more global vision – a vision that it is essential for all of us to keep fresh in our minds today. At about the same time that He said these words in verse 8, Jesus also said, "Go therefore and make disciples of all the nations" (Matthew 28:19).

The prospect of making a global impact for the cause of Christ would have been as ridiculous for the disciples as it would be for you and I in our era. People without unique positions of authority, or fantastic wealth, or remarkable giftedness lack the requisite capacity to have a global impact. Jesus counters that concern, however, with His promise of divine power ushered in by the abiding presence of the Holy Spirit. The Lord commanded His disciples to serve Him "to the end of the earth," but He also reassured them that He would go with them and that He would empower their service with His ever-present omnipotent strength.

Jesus further reassured them with the job description presented to this first generation of missionaries. They were to be "witnesses." All they were required to do to expand the kingdom of God on earth was to bear witness to what they saw the Lord do and what they heard the Lord teach. They were not required to conjure up a new set of quaint sayings and clever proverbs that would catch the attention of the world's greatest minds. They were not required to display feats of strength or showcase an exhibition of raw talent that would turn the heads of the world's rich and famous. They were to bear witness to what they saw the Lord say and do. This is a job we can do. We can easily, yes, easily carry out the command of our Lord to have a global impact and bring the gospel to the ends of the earth, because no unusual physical or mental abilities are required of us. We are required to give testimony to the greatness of God and repeat His truths to men. No personal greatness is required. The book of Acts will detail for us a steady procession of disciples who wonderfully obeyed the Lord's command here. In Acts 4, a great many men and women in Jerusalem began to follow Jesus because "great power" was given to the apostles when they "<u>gave witness</u> to the resurrection of the Lord Jesus" (Acts 4:33). Later, the whole family of Cornelius comes to faith when Peter travels to Caesarea and declares, "<u>we are witnesses</u> of all things which He did both in the land of the Jews and in Jerusalem, whom they killed by hanging on a tree" (Acts 10:39). And later, when Paul was saved and called to be a missionary, he was given the same instructions: "For you will be <u>His witness</u> to all men of what you have seen and heard" (Acts 22:15).

Our Lord here calls His followers to advance the kingdom of God throughout the whole earth. But He does not call them nor call us to go alone, or to go unempowered, or to go do a job that normal people can't do. We are to go to "the end of the earth" and draw people to be reconciled with their Creator. And as we go we are assured that the Spirit of God will go with us, the power of the Lord will be upon us, and all we have to do is to bear witness to that "which we have seen with our eyes, which we have looked upon, and our hands have handled, concerning the Word of life" (I John 1:1).

1:9-11
Now when He had spoken these things, while they watched, He was taken up, and a cloud received Him out of their sight. And while they looked steadfastly toward heaven as He went up, behold, two men stood by them in white apparel, who also said, "Men of Galilee, why do you stand gazing up into heaven? This same Jesus, who was taken up from you into heaven, will so come in like manner as you saw Him go into heaven."

Jesus gives His final words to His followers, and then, unbound by the forces of nature, He ascends up into the heavens right before their very eyes. They had riveted their attention on His message, and now their eyes were fixed on His face as He rose heavenward in an awe-inspiring display of peaceful power. Apparently, the apostles became lost in thought, their eyes riveted to the place in the clouds where they last saw Jesus. But soon, two angels appeared to encourage them and send them on their way to more productive efforts than stargazing. The thought that we might never see a loved one again can afflict the hearts of men and women with sadness. When the elders of Ephesus said their last good-byes to Paul, "they all wept freely, and fell on Paul's neck and kissed him, sorrowing most of all for the words which he spoke, that they would see his face no more" (Acts 20:37-38). In a great kindness, the angels came to spare the disciples this sorrow. They assured the apostles that they would see Jesus again! I Thessalonians 4 details the Lord's second coming that will be "in like manner" – in the same manner, but reverse direction of His departure from the earth.

Luke 24:52-53 tells us that the apostles responded to the angels' words wonderfully: "And they worshipped Him, and returned to Jerusalem with great joy, and were continually in the temple praising and blessing God. Amen." They could no longer see Jesus, but they worshipped Him just the same. He was out of sight, but they kept Him ever the center of their mind's eye. They continued to worship the Savior they could no longer see, and the following pages of Acts will show the remarkable events that will flow out from those worship times together. Perhaps their eyes could not see the Lord, but their spiritual insights were never better. Blessed are those who do not see and yet believe (John 20:29).

1:12-14
Then they returned to Jerusalem from the mount called Olivet, which is near Jerusalem, a Sabbath day's journey. And when they had entered, they went up into the upper room where they were staying: Peter, James, John, and Andrew; Philip and Thomas; Bartholomew and Matthew; James the

son of Alphaeus and Simon the Zealot; and Judas the son of James. These all continued with one accord in prayer and supplication, with the women and Mary the mother of Jesus, and with His brothers.

Jesus has ascended into heaven and given His followers orders to wait for the Holy Spirit to come upon them in Jerusalem. A list is provided of the names of those who awaited the outpouring of God's Spirit, and we find the characteristics of those who waited together to be noteworthy. God's Word is full of accolades for Mary, the mother of Jesus, but as for the others gathered, we find as many faults recorded as virtues. Peter denied the Lord three times (Luke 22), Thomas doubted His return (John 20:25), and His brothers scoffed at Him (John 7:5). This is hardly a gathering of all-stars. We find great comfort in this gathering of the servants of the Lord. When our church gatherings are filled with doubters, former failures, and current challenges, let us take note that these are the kind of sheep that the Lord has always called to Himself. God has not called us together because we are great, but because He is great – great in mercy, and great in kindness, inspiring us to both forgive quickly, and to see the potential in young believers rather than scorn the background of former sinners.

We are also moved by the activity that has unified the group while they wait. Jesus promised to send His Spirit on them in Jerusalem. Perhaps the apostles would have received the outpouring of the Spirit no matter how they spent their time, but we do not find them lounging or engaged in entertainment. They are praying. They have been promised the presence of the Holy Spirit, and they feel so urgently in need of the Spirit that they plead with the Lord to fill them with His presence right away. Undoubtedly, they remembered the words of the Lord in Luke 11:13 – "How much more will your heavenly Father give the Holy Spirit to those who ask Him!" They were promised the Spirit, they were desperate for the Spirit, and they were assured that praying for the Spirit would hasten the meeting of their need with the Lord's promised provision. So they prayed. Matthew Henry says, "Those are in the best frame to receive spiritual blessings that are in a praying frame." Do we have needs? Certainly, we are in no less need for the presence of the Spirit of God now as the apostles were back then. Let us pray.

And then we see how they prayed. They prayed "in one accord." With similar great insight, Matthew Henry says, "Those who so keep the unity of the Spirit in the bond of peace are best prepared to receive the comforts of the Holy Ghost." We have so many needs. The people around us have so many needs. We are desperate for the Lord to answer our many requests

– and we are reminded here that those who pray and those who build unity in the body of Christ are "best prepared" and "in the best frame" to receive powerful, timely answers from the Lord. May all who are in need of the presence, power, and provision of the Holy Spirit take note of the example provided for us here.

1:15-20

And in those days Peter stood up in the midst of the disciples (altogether the number of names was about a hundred and twenty), and said, "Men and brethren, this Scripture had to be fulfilled, which the Holy Spirit spoke before by the mouth of David concerning Judas, who became a guide to those who arrested Jesus; for he was numbered with us and obtained a part in this ministry." (Now this man purchased a field with the wages of iniquity; and falling headlong, he burst open in the middle and all his entrails gushed out. And it became known to all those dwelling in Jerusalem; so that field is called in their own language, Akel Dama, that is, Field of Blood.) "For it is written in the Book of Psalms: 'Let his dwelling place be desolate, and let no one live in it'; and, 'Let another take his office.'"

What do we do when our life is turned upside down? What do we do when we are betrayed? Peter provides for us here an excellent example. He joins together with the closest followers of Jesus, numbering 120 or so, and discusses with them the proper course of action. Peter undoubtedly found some wisdom and comfort in the counsel of the other believers, but we see that the proposal he brings before the disciples is completely rooted in Scripture. Let us take note. When betrayed by those in our inner circle, or when our ministry or efforts crash around us, let us look to God's Word for our proper response.

First, Peter notes that they should not be shocked by Judas' betrayal. David wrote of such betrayal long before. In Psalm 41:9 David wrote, "Even my own familiar friend in whom I trusted, who ate my bread, has lifted up his heel against me." As he wrote, David may have been thinking about Ahithophel's betrayal in II Samuel 15:12, but Peter rightly saw David's words as a prophecy of Judas' betrayal of Jesus, saying with certainty that David wrote those words "concerning Judas." Peter took strength and confidence in the words, seeing that if Scripture foresaw Judas' betrayal, Scripture could also foretell what the betrayed should do next.

When facing betrayal, Peter next tells the disciples that rather than lick their wounds and pity themselves, they should pity their betrayer and anticipate that this traitor will face a devastating, even violent demise. Peter then quotes Psalm 68:25 which foretells that the traitors of the Messiah will see "their dwelling place be desolate" and no one will live in their tents. Peter graphically describes how this passage applied to Judas' demise and how only the dead made their home in Judas' Akel Dama.

And finally, Peter's search of the Scriptures brought him to Psalm 109:8 where David says of the wicked, "Let his days be few, and let another take his office." So then, once again, as Peter grappled with the sorrow of Christ's death and the sting of Judas' betrayal, he found comfort and guidance in God's Word. God's Word taught him that betrayal at the hands of our friends is not shocking, for even godly King David encountered the same. God's Word granted him the satisfaction and comfort of seeing that the Lord brings judgment on those who betray His children. Furthermore, the Scriptures taught Peter that rather than feel discouraged over the loss and betrayal that he had endured, he should simply "let another take his office," he should appoint a godlier man to carry out the task that the rebel Judas had failed to accomplish. Scripture guided Peter on both how to feel and what to do, even in this unique circumstance. Let us then follow Peter's example and "search the Scriptures daily" (Acts 17:11) so that we can always know how to feel and how to act when both troubles and opportunities come our way.

1:21-26
"Therefore, of these men who have accompanied us all the time that the Lord Jesus went in and out among us, beginning from the baptism of John to that day when He was taken up from us, one of these must become a witness with us of His resurrection." And they proposed two: Joseph called Barsabbas, who was surnamed Justus, and Matthias. And they prayed and said, "You, O Lord, who know the hearts of all, show which of these two You have chosen to take part in this ministry and apostleship from which Judas by transgression fell, that he might go to his own place." And they cast their lots, and the lot fell on Matthias. And he was numbered with the eleven apostles.

Taking their marching orders from Psalm 109:8, the 120 believers set about to choose a replacement for Judas, desiring to "let another take his office" (verse 20). The qualifications for the position were extremely high. The new apostle must be a man who had followed Jesus from the day Jesus was baptized by John to the day He ascended into heaven. We see then that not just his character and faith were essential, but the length of time that he demonstrated his faith and character was also essential. Even with such high qualifications, however, not one, but two worthy candidates were found. What a blessing it is when God's people are blessed by a multitude of faithful men and women.

The two men were both so well thought of that the gathering could not discern which was the better choice. So, they took the matter directly to the Lord and cast lots, asking Him to decide Judas' replacement. The lot fell to Matthias, and though the Bible never mentions him again, we may assume that he honored the Lord as he carried out his responsibilities as the newest apostle. The Bible does not mention Matthias' contributions to the ministry, it simply re-emphasizes the disqualifying trait of the man he replaced. Matthias quietly served the Lord in the stead of Judas, who "by transgression fell." Today, Judas is still known by name by millions, whereas far fewer can identify Matthias. Judas remains famous and his actions can be recalled by many. No one today can list a single action that Matthias carried out. We are reminded that it is far, far better for us to serve the Lord in holy, faithful anonymity than to have a prominent ministry and reputation destroyed by the ravages of sin.

Acts 2

2:1

When the Day of Pentecost had fully come, they were all with one accord in one place.

It is difficult to overstate the benefits of God's people gathering together in one accord. In John 20:19 the disciples gathered together, much as they do in our verse here. As they met, Jesus appeared in their midst. Thomas missed the meeting and his absence caused him to disbelieve the resurrection of his Lord (John 20:24-25). Hebrews 10:25 grants us a simple admonition: "Let us not neglect our meeting together" (NLT). Such good things happen when God's people meet together in one accord in one place! Asaph had his doubts answered when he joined his fellow worshippers in the house of God (Psalm 73:17). Rhoda had her prayers answered when she met with her fellow believers (Acts 12:12-16). Simeon and Anna encountered Jesus when they joined with the worshippers in the Lord's house (Luke 2:25-38). And such can be the expectation of all of us when we gather with God's people, because Jesus has promised that He will join our fellowship when we gather together in His name. "For where two or three are gathered together in My name, I am there in the midst of them" (Matthew 18:20). Jesus commanded His followers to wait in Jerusalem until the Holy Spirit came upon them in power, and here we see the disciples gathered together in obedience and anticipation. And still today, we have good cause to promote and participate in the gatherings of God's people. The happy results that came about through the gathering of God's people in Scripture can still be our expectation today.

2:2-4

And suddenly there came a sound from heaven, as of a rushing mighty wind, and it filled the whole house where they were sitting. Then there appeared to them divided tongues, as of fire, and one sat upon each of them. And they were all filled with the Holy Spirit and began to speak with other tongues, as the Spirit gave them utterance.

In Mark 16:15 Jesus gave His disciples His Great Commission: "Go into all the world and preach the gospel to every creature." Carrying out this mission, however, would require so much more than devotion, hard work, and personal prowess. The disciples would be completely dependent on the presence of God Himself if they were to have a hope for changing the world. And here we see the arrival of the Help that the disciples required.

I Corinthians 12:7 says, "The manifestation of the Spirit is given to each one for the profit of all." The Spirit of the Lord comes upon us, His children, not to enhance our status, but to empower us to bless those around us for the "profit" of all. And we see here that this was true from the very onset of the Spirit's appearance. The very first manifestation of the presence of the Spirit was that the disciples "began to speak with other tongues." The following verses detail for us that the immediate result of the Spirit's arrival was that the disciples were empowered to proclaim "the wonderful works of God" (verse 11) in the language of their hearers. The clear and powerful presentation of the Good News was the initial manifestation of the presence of God's Spirit. "Suddenly" the disciples spoke with God-infused power because "the Spirit gave them utterance." "Suddenly" the disciples were able to articulate gospel truths with incredible clarity, because "the Spirit gave them utterance." And suddenly, people were drawn to listen to the disciples' teachings because they could discern that these were not the words of men, but the words of God conveyed by the Holy Spirit through the tongues of His children.

2:5-11

And there were dwelling in Jerusalem Jews, devout men, from every nation under heaven. And when this sound occurred, the multitude came together, and were confused, because everyone heard them speak in his own language. Then they were all amazed and marveled, saying to one another, "Look, are not all these who speak Galileans? And how is it that we hear each in our own language in which we were born? Parthians and Medes and Elamites, those dwelling in Mesopotamia, Judea and Cappadocia, Pontus and Asia, Phrygia and Pamphylia, Egypt and the parts of Libya adjoining Cyrene, visitors from Rome, both Jews and proselytes, Cretans and Arabs – we hear them speaking in our own tongues the wonderful works of God."

Today, our Lord summons us to take the gospel to the nations. Here, however, the arrival of the Holy Spirit summoned the nations to the gospel. "Devout men," men with a heart for holiness and a desire to please their Maker "from every nation under heaven" were drawn to come and listen to these men that were freshly filled with the power and presence of the Holy Spirit of God. We are encouraged by this reminder that "devout men," men with spiritual sensitivity, are drawn to the opportunity to listen to the Spirit speak. Let us also be reminded, however, that it is the presence of the Holy Spirit that beckons devout listeners. We should have no misconception that we can draw devout men to follow us by our own personal winsomeness. It is not the clever speech of the apostles that caused devout men to draw near; it was the manifestation of the presence of the Holy Spirit that drew them in. Today, it is no different. We must be filled with the presence of God if we are to offer anything meaningful to our listeners.

The source of the apostles' message (the Holy Spirit) called the crowd, and then the message that they presented continued to captivate their audience. They spoke to their "amazed and marveled" listeners about "the wonderful works of God." Oh how our soul loves to sit and consider "the wonderful works of God." We are awed by His creative genius and power. We are inspired and humbled by the perfection of His holiness. We are overwhelmed by His love and kindness toward us – and can hardly take it all in when we consider His Son's crucifixion on our behalf. Our spirit rises within us as we consider our Lord's resurrection and ascension, and we are filled with hope with the promise of His imminent return and His preparation of a home for us in heaven. Oh the blessed opportunity to speak of and listen to "the wonderful works of God!" And then, after the apostles spoke of the wonderful works of God in creation, election, redemption, forgiveness, sanctification, and salvation, they could each then continue to discuss the wonderful works of God in their own personal encounters with Him. Thomas could talk of doubts removed. Nathanael could speak of his omniscient Savior who saw him under a fig tree. Matthew could speak of when the Lord attended his party, John could talk of leaning on the Lord at dinner, and Peter could talk of forgiveness after failure, walking on water, catching 153 large fish, and catching one fish to pay his taxes. Goodness! It is hardly surprising to see that the gathering was riveted to the apostles' teaching, when we see the glorious subject matter of their speech: "The wonderful works of God."

The source of the message was the Holy Spirit. The subject of the message was the wonderful works of God. And so intent was our Lord to communicate His glorious truths to His creation that He made sure that the transmission of His message was similarly fantastic. "We hear them speaking in our own tongues." Let there be no mistake. God speaks our language. And here we see Him communicate His heavenly truths in the language of His earthly hearers. The whole scene was so beautiful. It amazed the crowd at the time, and amazes us today as we ponder again the magnificent efforts of God to communicate His "wonderful works" to the hearts of men in dire need.

2:12-13
So they were all amazed and perplexed, saying to one another, "Whatever could this mean?" Others mocking said, "They are full of new wine."

Man's ability, yes, man's propensity to demonstrate remarkably terrible insight is striking. Even as "devout men" (verse 5) stood mesmerized and awestruck by the disciples' public discourse on the "wonderful works of God" (verse 11), others stood on the sideline and hurled sarcastic insults at the speakers and listeners alike. Though "amazed and perplexed," devout men immediately saw that something magnificent was empowering the disciples – how else could these unlearned Galileans speak the native tongue of every person present (verse 7-8)? The mockers, however, explained it away with ease: "They are full of new wine." They did not understand the great things of God, they did not recognize the "wonderful works of God" on display before their very eyes, and their poor spiritual insights led them to a laughable, shameful demonstration of illogical nonsense. Alcohol does not endow speakers with sudden fluency in unstudied languages. But poor spiritual insights will move men to make ridiculous assumptions that lead to a host of disgraceful beliefs and actions. Poor spiritual insight moved

15

men to plot to murder Jesus after He raised Lazarus from the dead in John 11. Poor spiritual insight moved men to send Jesus away after He cast the demons from the man in Mark 5. And poor spiritual insight moved men to credit alcohol rather than the Holy Spirit with the apostles' miraculous linguistic capabilities here. Poor spiritual insights will lead to poor decisions in a host of matters. Let us be neither surprised nor discouraged when mockers deride us for our beliefs and efforts. They cannot hope to understand our efforts to obey our Lord and communicate His truths, for these things are "spiritually discerned." "The natural man does not receive the things of the Spirit of God, for they are foolishness to him; nor can he know them, because they are spiritually discerned" (I Corinthians 2:14).

2:14-15

But Peter, standing up with the eleven, raised his voice and said to them, "Men of Judea and all who dwell in Jerusalem, let this be known to you, and heed my words. For these are not drunk, as you suppose, since it is only the third hour of the day.

Hecklers from the crowd accused Peter and the disciples of being drunk and disorderly. Betrayed by their poor insights, these hecklers could not distinguish the influence of alcohol from the influence of God's Holy Spirit.

It is not always necessary to respond to our critics. Jesus demonstrated that clearly when He stood before Pilate and "answered him not one word" (Matthew 27:14). No good thing results from godly men engaging in shouting matches and hot debates with sin-loving scorners or foolish mockers. Proverbs 26:4 says, "Do not answer a fool according to his folly, lest you also be like him."

Dispelling false accusations and correcting ignorant assumptions does, however, provide thinking men with the opportunity to repent of erroneous beliefs. Proverbs 26:5 provides a caveat for the previous proverb by saying: "Answer a fool according to his folly, lest he be wise in his own eyes."

Peter's defense of his character and explanation of the current event won over many onlookers – even among the skeptics in the crowd. Verse 41 tells us that some 3,000 souls were moved to follow Christ after hearing Peter's rebuttal of his detractors. May the Lord grant us this discernment and inner strength to know when to remain silent before foolish mockers, and when to defend the faith before would-be believers.

2:16-21

But this is what was spoken by the prophet Joel: "And it shall come to pass in the last days, says God, that I will pour out of My Spirit on all flesh; your sons and your daughters shall prophesy, your young men shall see visions, your old men shall dream dreams, and on My menservants and on My maidservants I will pour out My Spirit in those days; and they shall prophesy. I will show wonders in heaven above and signs in the earth beneath: blood and fire and vapor of smoke. The sun shall be turned into darkness, and the moon into blood, before the coming of the great and awesome day of the LORD. And it shall come to pass that whoever calls on the name of the LORD shall be saved."

Peter quotes Joel 2:28-32 to explain to the "amazed and perplexed" crowd (verse 12) that the event unfolding right before them was not a mysterious occurrence, and it certainly wasn't the result of alcohol consumption (verse 13). The powerful presentation and sudden understanding of the wonderful Word of God and the "wonderful works of God" (verse 11) was the result of the fulfillment of Joel's prophecy that God would one day "pour out" His Spirit on His people.

In addition, Peter's reference to Joel's prophecy highlighted for his hearers that this prophecy foretold that God's Spirit would not only fall on prophets and priests – but "on all flesh" – on all His children – young and old, servants and masters, men and women. Recalling Joel's words was an invitation for the people to come! Come and take part in the great works of God to redeem the world from sin and to fill the redeemed with the comforts, guidance, and power of His Holy Spirit. "Whoever" desires to be filled with the Spirit of God can now fulfill their heart's desire! "Whoever calls on the name of the LORD shall be saved!" Judgment is coming! One day "the sun shall be turned into darkness, and the moon into blood, before the coming of the great and awesome day of the LORD." But there is rescue available from that day of judgment that even now is on the horizon! The way of salvation is available to all! "Whoever" calls on the Lord to save them from sin and judgment will be emptied of sin and filled with God's Spirit, just as the crowd has witnessed exemplified before them.

It is noteworthy to see that one of the outflows of being filled with the Holy Spirit is that Peter bases his discourse with the people on God's Word. He quotes Joel here, and in a moment, he will quote David in verses 25-28. When the Spirit of God fills us, we are moved to speak more and more of God's words and are content to use fewer and fewer of our own. We have here perhaps the first sermon of the New Testament. It is a sermon delivered by a man freshly filled with the Spirit of God. It is a sermon filled with the Word of God from the Scriptures. The two will always go hand in hand. The Spirit will always direct our attention to the message that He has already documented for us in His Word. May we always mirror Peter's example by having our sermons, our teachings, and even our daily conversations be infused by the Spirit of God and focused on the Word of God.

2:22-24

Men of Israel, hear these words: Jesus of Nazareth, a Man attested by God to you by miracles, wonders, and signs which God did through Him in your midst, as you yourselves also know – Him, being delivered by the determined purpose and foreknowledge of God, you have taken by lawless hands, have crucified, and put to death; whom God raised up, having loosed the pains of death, because it was not possible that He should be held by it.

The evidence of the presence and power of the Holy Spirit was set squarely before the people (verses 2:1-12), but they were "perplexed" (verse 12) and "confused" (verse 6), because their spiritual understanding was darkened by "ignorance" and "blindness of heart" (Ephesians 4:18). This same ignorance and blindness of heart had caused them to utterly fail to recognize the deity of Christ and rightly respond to His instruction regarding the Kingdom of God. And seeing that the people were prone to miss the Spirit's call, just as they had missed Jesus' call, Peter smoothly transitions from his introduction of the Holy Spirit to teach them again the essential truths of Jesus of Nazareth. Peter pleads with his listeners – do not miss what the Spirit is saying to you as you missed what Jesus was saying to you! You should have known who Jesus was! He was "attested by God to you by miracles, wonders, and signs which God did through Him in your midst!" It was inexcusable to miss who Jesus was. Nicodemus saw it plainly enough. In John 3:2 he said to Jesus, "Rabbi, we know that You are a teacher come from God; for no one can do these signs that You do unless God is with him." It was and is inexcusable to miss who Jesus is.

Peter's listeners not only missed who Jesus was, they took "lawless hands" and crucified Him on the cross. But Peter is careful to point out that their evil act did not thwart the purposes of God. The people did not murder Jesus because they overpowered Him, but rather His death was according to the "determined purpose and foreknowledge of God." The people had crucified Jesus with evil hearts of unbelief – and it was essential that they repent of that. But even as the crucifixion of Jesus put the people's evil hearts on full display, His death also put His "eternal power and divine nature" (Romans 1:20 ESV) on full display as well.

Through Jesus' death and resurrection, our Lord "loosed the pains of death." The gospel writers record for us the physical agony that Jesus endured on the cross. The scourging, the crown of thorns, the beating, and the nails all gripped our Lord in torment. But on the third day, our Lord returned to life, He was "loosed" from the pains that accompanied His death!

The gospel writers also record for us the "pangs" (ESV) of death that gripped the Lord in the garden the night before His crucifixion. Like the pangs of childbirth, the pangs of delivering us from sin seared through Jesus the night before He died, gripping Him "in agony" (Luke 22:44). The painful weight of bearing our sin, the dreadful anticipation of death at the hand of sinners "put Him to grief" (Isaiah 53:10). But these pains and pangs of death were temporary. Our Lord resurrected on the third day and wonderfully, eternally "loosed the pains of death."

And, too, Peter's words remind us that the effects of the Lord's resurrection not only loosed the pains of death in His mind and body, Jesus' conquest of death has "loosed the pains of death" in our soul as well. We need no longer fear the permanence of death – for Jesus has loosed us from that dark prospect and declared for us that death is not permanent. "(For) if the Spirit of Him who raised Jesus from the dead dwells in you, He who raised Christ from the dead will also give life to your mortal bodies through His Spirit who dwells in you" (Romans 8:11). Because we know that Jesus rose from the dead, we know that since He lives in us, we will rise too! He has loosed the pains of death!

Since the day when Abel became the first man to die, death has been associated with pain and grief, suffering and mourning. Death causes us to mourn the loss of time with loved ones. The sick and injured carry pains to their last moments. We are saddened when the lives of good men and women are cut short. But the resurrection from the dead of Jesus of Nazareth allows us to overcome all these many "pains of death." His life bestows life to our mortal bodies. His life grants peace to our troubled minds. Because Jesus rose from the grave, "Death no longer has dominion over Him" (Romans 6:9). And because He lives in us, we have been granted this precious cure for death's sting. Jesus has "loosed the pains of death."

2:25-28

For David says concerning Him: "I foresaw the LORD always before my face, for He is at my right hand, that I may not be shaken. Therefore my heart rejoiced, and my tongue was glad; moreover my flesh also will rest

in hope. **For You will not leave my soul in Hades, nor will You allow Your Holy One to see corruption. You have made known to me the ways of life; You will make me full of joy in Your presence."**

Once again, just as he quoted Joel earlier, Peter now quotes David for his listeners. Jesus told the crowd that the Old Testament Scriptures were written about Him (John 5:39), and Peter here provides his hearers an example from David's Michtam in Psalm 16. Peter declares that David was speaking specifically of the resurrection of Jesus when he wrote in Psalm 16:10, "For You will not leave my soul in Hades, nor will You allow Your Holy One to see corruption." Peter's hearers had failed to recognize that Jesus was Immanuel, but they did revere Scripture as The Word of God, so Peter had good cause to be hopeful that he could inspire his listeners to follow Jesus by simply re-presenting references to Jesus in the writings of these Old Testament saints.

There is much to glean from Peter's quote from Psalm 16:8-11. I find every line inspiring. Because the Father is at our right hand, we, like Jesus, can face the storms of life and "not be shaken" (verse 25). We are amazed that even though Jesus faced the torment of the cross, His "heart rejoiced" and His "tongue was glad" (verse 26). In fact, it was this joy of His Father's presence, and the joy of taking part in His Father's mission that allowed Jesus to "endure the cross" (Hebrews 12:2). I am greatly inspired by Jesus' example in verse 25 which Peter quotes from Psalm 16:8, stating, "I have set the Lord always before me." Ah, let us set our Lord always before us. Let us set His love for us before us in times of worry. Let us set His mission before us lest we grow complacent. Let us set His nearness before us to dispel our loneliness. Let us set His Word before us that we might know how best to serve Him. Ah, let us set His radiant glory ever before us in our daily times of prayer that we might be blessed by His attentiveness toward us. Let us set our Lord before us that we might reflect His glory to those around us. And let us set the Lord before us that we might enjoy fellowship with our Creator today and forever. What a blessed thought.

As if all that were not enough, verse 28 finishes with "You have made known to me the ways of life; You will make me full of joy in Your presence." Jesus' joy was in His Father's presence. The people loved Jesus and wanted to make Him their king, but He left the crowd and went up into the mountain to pray, because His joy came from His Father's presence, not from the accolades of men (John 6:15). When His popularity rose and His ministry expanded, Jesus again left the crowd and went up to the mountain to pray (Mark 1:35), because the source of His joy was His Father, not the successes of His ministry. Peter's reminder of David's description of Jesus provides great inspiration for us. In the presence of our Father there is fullness of joy. Let us ever, always crave our Father's presence as Jesus so wonderfully demonstrated. Let us respond to our Father's remarkable invitation just as David wrote: "When You said, 'Seek My face,' my heart said to You, 'Your face, LORD, I will seek'" (Psalm 27:8).

2:29-31

Men and brethren, let me speak freely to you of the patriarch David, that he is both dead and buried, and his tomb is with us to this day. Therefore, being a prophet, and knowing that God had sworn with an oath to him that of the fruit of his body, according to the flesh, He would raise up the Christ to sit on his throne, he, foreseeing this, spoke concerning the resurrection of Christ, that His soul was not left in Hades, nor did His flesh see corruption.

Preachers and teachers of God's Word can take much comfort in the fact that it is not our responsibility to preach the gospel cleverly. We are merely required to preach it clearly. It is not necessary that we come up with new truths to share, we can simply share with passion and clarity the same truths that our Father has been teaching His people since the beginning. Here, Peter recites for his listeners Psalm 16:10 – "You will not leave my soul in Hades, nor will You allow Your Holy One to see corruption." He then recites Psalm 132:11, "The LORD has sworn in truth to David; He will not turn from it: 'I will set upon your throne the fruit of your body.'" The crowd listening to Peter had read those passages many, many times before. They had read those words and they had seen Jesus walk among them – but to this point, they had never considered that these Psalms were talking about Jesus. But suddenly, when Peter brings his point home, 3,000 people will instantly believe (verse 41). Peter merely recited the simple truth: David could not have been talking about himself in Psalm 16, for David did die and his body certainly did "experience decay" (CSB). Peter tells the crowd that David was talking about Jesus, the Christ, who died on the cross right in front of them, but then rose from the dead right in front of them, just as David said He would.

It is so uplifting to me to picture this scene when Peter simply recited God's Word and the Spirit compelled 3,000 listeners to believe. "The word of God is living and powerful" (Hebrews 4:12). Let us handle it with trembling hands (Isaiah 66:2) and sure hearts (Romans 1:16). Let us handle it skillfully and faithfully (II Timothy 2:15). Let us not imagine that we must improve upon it, embellish it, or replace it with a timelier message. Let us simply repeat the great words of God to the spiritual ears of our listeners and watch with joy and awe as the Spirit moves the hearts of our hearers to believe and to respond. Peter's means of calling the crowd to Jesus was simply presenting the Word of God to them with boldness and clarity. He will never stop using this means of reaching his hearers. In II Peter 1:12-13 he says, "Therefore, I will always remind you about these things—even though you already know them and are standing firm in the truth you have been taught. And it is only right that I should keep on reminding you as long as I live."

2:32
This Jesus God has raised up, of which we are all witnesses.

"We are all witnesses." Our role in teaching God's people and calling the lost to reconcile with our Creator is not complex. Peter has already demon-strated our first responsibility, which is simply to present God's Word clearly. Peter's sermon here in Acts 2 is not a clever collection of witty sayings that he conjured up in his own head. He simply quotes Joel 2, Psalm 16, Psalm 132, (and in a moment he will quote Psalm 110:1). And in this verse here, Peter demonstrates our second responsibility: We are to be "witnesses." Once again, we see that nothing exceptional about us is necessary before we can become a spokesperson for Christ. We are merely called upon to be "witnesses." We declare to others what we have seen God do. John said the same thing: "(That) which we have heard, which we have seen with our eyes, which we have looked upon, and our hands have handled, concerning the Word of life...that which we have seen and heard we declare to you, that you also may have fellowship with us" (I John 1:1, 1:3). Our role as servants of God is to declare to others what He teaches in His Word, and to state for others what we have seen Him do. We declare that once we were doomed by sin, but now we are witnesses to how He took away our sin and healed our guilty conscience. We are witnesses to the life that God has given to us in Christ. Peter's sermon illustration is simple. "I saw Jesus die on the cross. And I saw Jesus come back from the dead. We all saw it. We are all witnesses to this remarkable, miraculous event." There is no age requirement, no academic constraint, no level of personal genius that is re-quired before we can be ambassadors for Christ. We simply tell others what we have seen God do for us, in us, and around us. After Paul was converted on the Damascus road, Ananias healed his blind eyes and called him to this very thing: "The God of our fathers has chosen you that you should know

His will, and see the Just One, and hear the voice of His mouth. *For you will be His witness* to all men of what you have seen and heard" (Acts 22:14-15).

2:33

Therefore being exalted to the right hand of God, and having received from the Father the promise of the Holy Spirit, He poured out this which you now see and hear.

Peter was there when Jesus passed on to the disciples the Father's "promise of the Holy Spirit" in John 14:26. Now, Peter attests before his attentive crowd that the Holy Spirit of God is the source of the power of his words, and the source of the disciples' ability to communicate in multiple languages "the wonderful works of God" (verse 11). It is the Holy Spirit that compelled men and women from all over the city to rush to the disciples and listen to their message. It was the Holy Spirit that confirmed in the hearers' hearts the truth of Peter's words. And it was the Holy Spirit that compelled the listeners to cry out in verse 37 "what shall we do?" after they were "cut to the heart" by the Spirit-infused power of Peter's words. Peter did not misinterpret the reason behind the crowd's sudden interest in him. It is the Spirit who compels men to listen. It is the Spirit who compels listeners to repent. And it is the Spirit who compels the repentant to live by faith and serve with vigor. 3,000 souls will be saved on this day, and Peter rightly declares that this is because the Spirit was "poured out," not because they found Peter impressive. Today, let us share Peter's insight and acknowledge that the spiritual victories we see are the result of the work of the Holy Spirit, and not the result of our own gifted endeavors.

2:34-37

For David did not ascend into the heavens, but he says himself: "The LORD said to my Lord, 'Sit at My right hand, till I make Your enemies Your footstool.'" Therefore let all the house of Israel know assuredly that God has made this Jesus, whom you crucified, both Lord and Christ. Now when they heard this, they were cut to the heart, and said to Peter and the rest of the apostles, "Men and brethren, what shall we do?"

Having already quoted three Old Testament passages (Joel 2 and two other Psalms), Peter now quotes Psalm 110:1 to add further weight to his message calling his hearers to repent of their sin and unbelief. Peter warns the crowd that the "Lord" in David's psalm referred to Christ, the Messiah, and that the LORD God would cast down the enemies of Christ and make them His footstool. Peter then powerfully carried his message home – "God has made this Jesus, whom you crucified, both Lord and Christ." In effect, Peter is warning the crowd that they have made themselves the enemies of the Christ, and are thus doomed to incur the punishment that has long been prepared for those who fail to honor the One who entered the world as "both Lord and Christ."

The indictment stung their conscience and cut them to the heart. Their conscience now awakened, the people suddenly knew that Peter's words were all true. Jesus is the Christ, the Savior of the world, and rather than trust Him and obey Him, they had rejected Him and murdered Him. The sudden impact of the weight of their guilt was overwhelming and they spontaneously cried out for help. All at once their soul knew that they had no merit to warrant forgiveness, but with great awareness of their need they cried out, "Men and brethren, what shall we do?" This is, perhaps, the best possible question that can be asked by those suddenly aware of their sin. What must I do to be forgiven and be reconciled to my Creator? For 3 years the unbelievers in the crowd had asked imperfect questions (as did the priests, Pharisees, and then the Sadducees in Luke 20), or had responded poorly to Jesus' perfect answers (as did the rich man in Luke 18:18-23 and Pilate in Luke 23). But here we see the crowd ask the right question. "Our sin is great, what can we possibly do to take this sin away?" And the verses following will tell us that they not only asked the right question, but they responded rightly to the answer as well.

Acts 2:38-39

Then Peter said to them, "Repent, and let every one of you be baptized in the name of Jesus Christ for the remission of sins; and you shall receive the gift of the Holy Spirit. For the promise is to you and to your children, and to all who are afar off, as many as the Lord our God will call."

In verse 37 the crowd asked, "What shall we do?" What can we do to correct our past misdeeds and unbelief? Peter answers them here: "Repent." We cannot be right with God and continue in the same lifestyle we have always lived. We must turn from sin. We must turn from dependence on empty religious rituals. We must stop trusting in any other god but the One who created us and died on the cross for us. Some in Peter's day would try to continue trusting in their own works even after coming to know that Jesus is the Son of God who takes away the sins of the world. This is not acceptable. We must repent of all allegiances and all dependencies on all gods and all rituals apart from trust in the Savior-Creator Jesus. Some in our day would try to continue living in sin and immorality even after coming to know that Jesus is the Son of God who takes away the sins of the world. This also is not acceptable. We must repent of all sins. We must turn away from all actions and attitudes that God's Word calls sin – regardless of how acceptable these things may seem to the world at large.

If we are to receive God's offer of salvation, we must repent of all things which displease our God, and then "be baptized in the name of Jesus Christ" to openly declare our repentance and celebrate that we have received "the remission of sins." The reward for repentance and obedience through baptism is of inestimable value. "You shall receive the gift of the Holy Spirit." The same Spirit which blew upon the apostles like a mighty wind and burned brightly upon them like holy fire will also fall in like fashion on all those who repent of sin and trust in Jesus from that time on and forevermore. The gift of the Holy Spirit was not given only to the apostles; He was promised to all our children and all our children's children. He is promised to all in our nation and to all "who are afar off" as well. God is calling the people of the world to Himself, and "as many as the Lord our God will call" will have opportunity to be filled with the Holy Spirit just as Peter is here. It is a joy to the soul just to glance at the wonders experienced by those filled with the Holy Spirit. Those filled with the Spirit of God can be filled with the expectation that they can speak God's Word in a way that their hearers can understand it as exemplified in our passage here. Those filled with God's Spirit can be filled with the anticipation of being enabled to speak God's Word to God's people as Jahaziel does in II Chronicles 20:14. Those filled with God's Spirit will be granted the joy of seeing their godly efforts prosper and be fruitful as in Isaiah 32:15. The Spirit of the Lord allows us to find rest in tumultuous times as stated in Isaiah 63:14. God's Spirit empowers us to walk in His statutes (Ezekiel 36:27), to be filled with "excellent wisdom" (Daniel 5:14), to see visions (Joel 2:28), to be filled with the power to execute justice (Micah 3:8), and to be filled with the power to lead men and conquer enemies (Judges 6:34). Such is the precious promise given to those that the Lord our God will call! God does not save us and then leave us to our own devices. He saves us, and then fills us with His Spirit, who empowers, instructs, and comforts all those who will repent and come to the God who calls us to Himself.

2:40
And with many other words he testified and exhorted them, saying, "Be saved from this perverse generation."

As the angel cried out to Lot to save himself and his family from the perverse Sodomites, Peter now urges his listeners to save themselves from the doom that was fast approaching their evil company. Genesis 19:15 says, "The angels urged Lot to hurry, saying, 'Arise, take your wife and your two daughters who are here, lest you be consumed in the punishment of the city.'" With this same urgent concern Peter "testified" to the truth. He taught the gospel truth that God reigns, God judges, and unbelief and disobedience to His Lordship will lead to certain and eternal calamity. He "exhorted" his hearers to heed his warnings, repent of sin, comply with God's commands, and flee the company and destiny of those that are hellbent on rebellion against their Creator.

Let us emulate the urgency of Peter and the earnestness of the angels in Genesis 15 when we share the gospel today. The old adage that says "there is strength in numbers" betrays those who feel secure in the company of sinners. We must summon our hearers to repentant action! We must warn those who stroll in sin on the beach of life, not yet concerned that the tsunami of God's judgment is coming! This "perverse generation" has twisted God's daily demonstration of mercy to deceive themselves into thinking that heaven can be reached without holiness. This "crooked" (ESV) generation has warped the understanding of its constituents leading them to believe that God can be replaced by self without consequence. Peter warns the crowd in his day as we must warn the crowd in our day to "repent" (verse 38) of their sin, repent of their lack of faith in Christ, repent of their misdirected priorities, and "be saved" by the only One who has the power to save: "the Lamb of God who takes away the sin of the world" (John 1:29).

2:41
Then those who gladly received his word were baptized; and that day about three thousand souls were added to them.

All at once, three thousand souls were saved. It is hard to imagine a happier event. Luke 15:10 tells us that the angels rejoice when a single sinner repents and reconciles with the Lord, and here we find cause to rejoice 3,000 times over. I am struck by Peter's message which God used to save 3,000 souls. Peter pointed squarely at the sin of his listeners, incriminating them in the murder of Jesus (verse 36), and then called on them to repent of that and all other sins (verse 38). We might be tempted to think that talking of the goodness of God rather than the sinfulness of man would gain us more ready hearers. It might seem that demanding repentance rather than simply promising forgiveness would be a less popular preaching style, and yet we see that the result of Peter's Spirit-empowered, straightforward sermon was that 3,000 people "received his word." They believed Peter's words, they were cut to the heart with the sting of a guilty conscience, and they were overwhelmed with the need to turn from sin and seek to reconcile with the same Jesus that they had once killed on the cross. The response to Peter's call for repentance was wonderful, and today, if we would seek the same results from our preaching, let us not seek a different method of communicating. Let us seek the outpouring of the Holy Spirit as encouraged to do in Luke 11:13. Let us not weaken our message with fluff and feathers, which tickle the ear, but permit the conscience to go on sleeping. Let us teach our hearers the sacred truth that God is holy and demands that we repent of our lack of holiness. The salvation of thousands of souls can be seen when God's people preach the message of repentance of sins under the power and presence of God's Holy Spirit.

2:42

And they continued steadfastly in the apostles' doctrine and fellowship, in the breaking of bread, and in prayers.

The formation of the church begins with the salvation of souls (verse 41). As wonderful as that is, however, conversion of a heart to faith in Christ is not the end point of Christian service. Immediately, we find these brand-new believers in this brand-new church "steadfastly" engaged in four prime activities.

First, we see that the church of Jerusalem "continued steadfastly in the apostles' doctrine." Steadfast instruction in the doctrine of Jesus Christ and steadfast adherence to the doctrine of Jesus Christ (that was passed on through the apostles) was of foundational importance to the world's first believers. We must give the highest possible priority to teaching the doctrines that our Lord has taught us in His Word. Paul gives this very exhortation to Timothy, calling on him to "give attention to reading, to exhortation, to doctrine" (I Timothy 4:13). And then, emphasizing this need even further, I Timothy 4:16 adds, "Take heed to yourself and to the doctrine. Continue in them, for in doing this you will save both yourself and those who hear you." II John 1:9 says, "Whoever transgresses and does not abide in the doctrine of Christ does not have God. He who abides in the doctrine of Christ has both the Father and the Son." The doctrine of Jesus Christ, who He is, as well as the doctrine from Jesus Christ, what He taught, must forever remain the primary focus of the church. Without proper doctrine, our fellowship easily erodes into a Spirit-less social gathering and then erodes further still to acceptance of immoral relationships. Without proper doctrine, the breaking of bread erodes into a picnic without any thought at all given to Jesus' sacrifice, torment, and death. And without proper doctrine, even prayer becomes dishonoring to God as prayers begin to be offered to mortal men (perhaps called saints) or to a vast array of other gods who cannot answer our deepest needs.

Secondly, the people "continued steadfastly" in fellowship. Christ-followers are not encouraged to become monks, and they certainly are not to become hermits. One of the foundational pillars of the early church was the fellowship that was promoted and enjoyed by the new believers. Virtually all of life's godly pleasures are enhanced in the company of God's people. Birthdays, holidays, and Saturdays are all made holy and joyous events when enjoyed in the company of God's people. Graduations, promotions, weddings, and similar causes for observance also have their importance enhanced and their celebrations improved upon when enjoyed in the fellowship of God's people. Happy events are made happier and sorrows are better endured when godly people are blessed with the fellowship of other godly people. Such was the example provided us in the early church and such is our blessed privilege to enjoy still today.

Thirdly, the early church was known for their commitment to "the breaking of bread," which many acknowledge is a reference to the observance of Communion. Jesus commanded us to remember His sacrifice, torment, and death on the cross (Luke 22:19), and the early church did just that. Without the death of Jesus on the cross, every single human being would live and die and go to hell. So, we find it right for us to gratefully, solemnly think of the torment that He endured on our behalf, and the love that He demonstrated for us though we were undeserving. His command to "do this in remembrance of Me" compels us to faithfully, gratefully, reverently observe Communion in our churches still today.

And fourthly, believers in the early church "steadfastly" devoted themselves to prayer. I Thessalonians 5:17 stirs us to "pray without ceasing." We must pray alone with God in a quiet setting. We must pray with our family and our friends in our homes. And with our attentions focused on the presence of our Savior, we must pray in gatherings with the saints in His house. Jesus emphasized His Father's words in Isaiah 56:7 when He delivered His firm announcement, "My house shall be called a house of prayer" (Matthew 21:13). When we attend church, it is common for us to sing in worship, and well we should. We listen to a sermon, and this is also good and proper. But let us not forget that our Lord forcefully dismissed those in His house of worship when they failed to make it a house of prayer. Hebrews 10:25 calls on us to not forsake the assembling of ourselves to-gether. And when we assemble together, we must pray. The people in our church have many needs. The lost around our church desperately need to know the Savior. Failure to pray for these matters is to infer that we do not care if the lost are doomed to hell, we do not care if the saints find provision for their needs, and we do not care if God's will is done on earth as it is done in heaven. And since we absolutely do care for these things, let us follow the example of Jerusalem's very first church and pray with one another when we gather with one another.

2:43

Then fear came upon every soul, and many wonders and signs were done through the apostles.

Through the power and presence of the Holy Spirit, the apostles carried out "many wonders and signs." The sick were healed, demons were cast out, and the gospel truth of Jesus Christ was presented powerfully. And as the apostles carried out the works of God in the power of God "fear came upon every soul." There is a kind of fear that rises up with the threat of personal danger. This is not that kind of fear. This is the fear of the soul, the awe and fear that overcomes the souls of men and women when they see the hand of God on holy men. Jude 1:5-12 describes the gross depravity of "brute beasts" who demonstrate one depraved attitude after another "without fear." But people with a working conscience will be shaken with fear by the demonstration of the power of God in the lives of holy men. Such is the case here. Jerusalem's onlookers saw the power of God revealed, and they feared lest that power be moved in judgment against them. New believers saw the power of God revealed, and they feared, struck by how long they had been blind to the truth, and mortified by how close they came to missing the Way to God altogether. And godly men and women saw the power of God revealed, and they, too, were filled with fear. For those closest to God are the first to fall to their knees in reverent awe and fear in the presence of the One whose greatness surpasses all possible description.

The fear of the Lord is the beginning of wisdom. And here we see that the fear of the Lord was the beginning of the church as well. God is great and we are not. His love powerfully draws us to Him, but His greatness moves us to bow in godly fear as we hold His feet in grateful adoration. God is so great that even the reflection of His majesty in the works of His servants is enough to bring holy fear to the souls of everyone still blessed with a working conscience.

Good deeds stir men to praise men. Works of God carried out by the hands of men stir men to fear God as exemplified here.

2:44-45
Now all who believed were together, and had all things in common, and sold their possessions and goods, and divided them among all, as anyone had need.

When the Holy Spirit falls on His people, we are filled with a consuming drive to take care of one another. Before His ascension, Jesus repeated three times His command for Peter to feed His sheep (John 21:15-17), and after His ascension, the Holy Spirit continues to repeat that command in the spiritual ear of His servants. The early church did not coddle the lazy. Paul gave specific instructions for those who could provide for themselves but did not – "when we were with you, we commanded you this: if anyone will not work, neither shall he eat" (II Thessalonians 3:10). Neither is this inspiration from the Spirit intended to over-burden a few to provide everything possible for the many. Paul says in II Corinthians 8:13-14, "For I do not mean that others should be eased and you burdened; but by an equality, that now at this time your abundance may supply their lack, that their abundance also may supply your lack – that there may be equality." The early church was not a commune where no one worked, and everyone lived off the savings of the rich. But the people of the first church were so consumed with nourishing the body of Christ, that their former concern of gaining personal profit was replaced with the godly concern of providing for the needs of God's people. Ephesians 4:28 calls on us to work hard so that we "may have something to give him who has need."

The needs of the body of Christ are many and varied. Blessedly, God's provisions for the body of Christ are also many and varied. Some may have money, but others may have a room that might bless someone in the church (II Kings 4:8-11). Some fight to protect God's people (I Samuel 23:1-2), and others provide food for the fighters (I Samuel 25:18). Sometimes the person providing for the church today, is the one that the church must rise up to provide for tomorrow. In II Samuel 17:27-29, we see several men from several places find themselves inspired by the Lord to provide for David, the king that had provided so much for them in the past. They traveled good distances to bring David beds, basins, barley, and beans, among a bunch of other things in an Old Testament example of God's people taking care of God's people.

Today, when we are drawn to provide for the needs of God's people in our church, let us take delight in knowing that this is a sign of the Spirit's working within us. And when we see everyone in our church rushing to find the needs and meet the needs of all the saints near and far, let us especially take humble joy in seeing that the Holy Spirit is moving in our church just as He did here in the first church of Jerusalem.

2:46-47

So continuing daily with one accord in the temple, and breaking bread from house to house, they ate their food with gladness and simplicity of heart, praising God and having favor with all the people. And the Lord added to the church daily those who were being saved.

Luke ends the chapter with a happy summary of the joys of the early church. Far from dreading the drudgery of church meetings, the people loved their meetings together. They met in worship every day! And not content with that, they met together for fellowship "from house to house" as well! Worshiping God in the company of God's people was a delight to their soul. Their friendships with God's people as they carried out God's purposes further delighted their soul. Gladness permeated their worship meetings and gladness permeated their friendly gatherings outside of church. Worldly concerns had little opportunity to distract them because the joys of walking closely with God in happy fellowship with His people gave them "simplicity of heart." Their heart desired very little beyond meeting with God and meeting the needs of His people. Worship of God and fellowship with His people consumed their interests, and when God's name, God's Word and God's people captivate our attentions, gladness of heart and spiritual prosperity will be the happy result.

Acts 3

3:1-6

Now Peter and John went up together to the temple at the hour of prayer, the ninth hour. And a certain man lame from his mother's womb was carried, whom they laid daily at the gate of the temple which is called Beautiful, to ask alms from those who entered the temple; who, seeing Peter and John about to go into the temple, asked for alms. And fixing his eyes on him, with John, Peter said, "Look at us." So he gave them his attention, expecting to receive something from them. Then Peter said, "Silver and gold I do not have, but what I do have I give you: in the name of Jesus Christ of Nazareth, rise up and walk."

Psalm 55:17 says, "Evening and morning and at noon I will pray, and cry aloud, and He shall hear my voice." With that same devotion to prayer, in that spirit of hungering for prayer, with a craving for regular, even frequent times of prayer, Peter and John arrive together at the temple to pray. And here we find that a miracle will take place, even before the prayer meeting begins. Such is often the case. Just setting our hearts on godly pursuits, simply setting our eyes on holy goals, and setting our feet on walking toward those goals will often move us to the vicinity where God intends to move in power. Peter and John are walking to the house of prayer. They have not prayed yet. But their heart is in the right place, and, not coincidentally, so is their body, which grants them the blessed opportunity for God to use them to see a life changed.

Let us pray. Let us crave prayer. Let us pray often and regularly. And let us always be where we should be at the hour we should be there. At the hour of prayer, may God find us praying. At the hour of worship, may God find us in His house of worship. At the hour of service, may the Lord find us serving His people. At "the hour of prayer" Peter and John are found going together to pray, and a miracle ensues. May their experience act as an invitation to follow their example.

The lame man asks for money, but the apostles are not blessed with these things. Their heart to "give to him who asks" (Matthew 5:42), however, is undaunted by their poverty. Money would help him make it through the day, but the power to walk would help him much more, and the opportunity to encounter the God who wields that power would bless him greater still.

Let us make appropriate effort to work hard in life that we may earn an honest wage in order that we might "have something to give him who has need" (Ephesians 4:28). But let us make all the more effort to walk closely and obediently to Jesus Christ of Nazareth, so that we might be best positioned to intercede with compassion and power on behalf of those in need.

3:7-10
And he took him by the right hand and lifted him up, and immediately his feet and ankle bones received strength. So he, leaping up, stood and walked and entered the temple with them – walking, leaping, and praising God. And all the people saw him walking and praising God. Then they knew that it was he who sat begging alms at the Beautiful Gate of the temple; and they were filled with wonder and amazement at what had happened to him.

Peter healed the man, not by his own power, but "in the name of Jesus Christ of Nazareth," and so it follows that after being healed, the man is found "praising God" not praising Peter. John the Baptist noted that "He (Jesus) must increase, but I must decrease" (John 3:30), and so all who share John's longing to carry out the great works of God will affirm that the sought-after outcome of Christian service is that God is praised, not His servants. Peter heals in Jesus' name for Jesus' sake, and the healed man goes on to praise God, and the onlookers are "filled with wonder and amazement" at the presentation of the power of God before them. In Acts 14 the exact same miracle is carried out by Paul. A lame man is healed in Lystra. In contrast to the storyline here, however, the crowd mistakenly praises Paul and Barnabas rather than praise the Lord. In verse 18 the people try to offer sacrifices in worship of Paul. *And in the very next verse*, the crowd stones Paul and drags his body outside the city. Let us take proper notice. Moving men to praise the Lord leads to all manner of wonderful outcomes. Letting our guard down and relishing the praise of men, however, leads to nothing good for anyone. Let us walk with God and show compassion on His people. Let us devote our lives to God's name, God's Word, and God's people. But when the Lord uses our devotion to carry out remarkable achievements, let us divert all accolades misdirected in our direction and reflect them back on our Master. When God is praised today, the echo of that praise rings out forever! If we are praised, however, the tinny sound will likely annoy some, and may even prove dangerous as hinted at in Paul's experience in Lystra, and as clearly shown in the story of Herod and the worms in Acts 12:23.

The effects of God's healing through Peter are immediate. There is no gradual improvement in strength that might confuse onlookers into thinking that natural causes brought about the man's cure. The picture presented is a happy one. The lame man is instantly cured in Jesus' name. He leaps up and rushes into the temple praising God. We may assume that his vocal praises are loud and catch the ears of everyone in the temple, and that his skipping up and down in the house of worship catches their notice as well. It is good and proper to display enthusiastic praise for the greatness of God and wholehearted thanks for His kindness to us. Let us take proper note of the lame man's response to God's gift to him. For our part, let us remember that our God has saved our soul! Sullen, occasional, muffled acknowledgements of half-hearted gratitude fail to properly showcase the goodness of God. Once cured, the man is immediately found walking, and leaping, and praising God. May our praise and thanks for all that God has done for us be found no less enthusiastic.

3:11-16

Now as the lame man who was healed held on to Peter and John, all the people ran together to them in the porch which is called Solomon's, greatly amazed. So when Peter saw it, he responded to the people: "Men of Israel, why do you marvel at this? Or why look so intently at us, as though by our own power or godliness we had made this man walk? The

God of Abraham, Isaac, and Jacob, the God of our fathers, glorified His Servant Jesus, whom you delivered up and denied in the presence of Pilate, when he was determined to let Him go. But you denied the Holy One and the Just, and asked for a murderer to be granted to you, and killed the Prince of life, whom God raised from the dead, of which we are witnesses. And His name, through faith in His name, has made this man strong, whom you see and know. Yes, the faith which comes through Him has given him this perfect soundness in the presence of you all."

Now healed of the disease that had crippled him since birth, after jumping in excitement and shouting his uncontainable praise, the man stops his jubilant show of thanks for a moment, and we see him as he "held on to Peter and John." His praise was Heavenward, but that made him no less grateful for the servants of God who allowed him to experience the power of God. Pastors and church leaders are moved by the Spirit within them to love God's children. Peter and John healed the man in a spontaneous display of Spirit-directed compassion. And the man now healed is then drawn to hold Peter and John in a tight embrace of Spirit-directed gratitude. Leaders in the church care for the flock, and the children of God overflow with love for their leaders in return. Such is the happy and mutually uplifting state of the healthy church that is demonstrated here.

Onlookers to the miracle are "greatly amazed" and "ran together" to set their gaze on both the healed and the healers. Unlike the healed man, however, they do not spontaneously break out in praise to God, giving unwarranted and unwanted attention to Peter and John instead. Seeing the crowd gawk at men rather than give their praise to God, Peter gives another extemporaneous sermon much as he did in chapter 2. Weak faith in God and overconfidence in man are two common character flaws that Peter seeks to remedy in his short sermon on Solomon's porch. "Why do you marvel at this?" Peter asks. God created the worlds with the power of His Word – how much easier is it for Him to heal a crippled man? And why are you looking "so intently" at John and me? No "power" or "godliness" of mortal man could possibly carry out the miracle you have just witnessed. Then, after placing the credit where the credit was due, Peter quickly moves to address the sin of his listeners (just as he did in chapter 2). Peter explained that the Father sent Jesus His Son as Savior of the world – but rather than embrace Him "you denied the Holy One and the Just" and "killed the Prince of life." We are again reminded that repentance is at the core of the Christian message. We cannot be reconciled to God without first admitting and repenting of our sin. Peter does not dangle a tantalizing message to the eager crowd: "Believe in Jesus and be healed of all your pains." No, he addresses their sin and calls on them to repent. Once we repent of our sin and unbelief, however, the joys of Jesus' forgiveness and healing can fully be brought to bear.

After addressing their need for repentance, Peter then addresses their need for faith: "Faith in (Jesus') name has made this man strong." The truth is so wonderful that Peter says it again, stating, "The faith that is through Jesus has given the man this perfect health" (ESV). Despite all our observable capabilities, the human race is completely helpless in scenarios that really matter. Our conscience demands that we be good, but no one is good (Matthew 19:17). We desire to be spiritually pure and to do all we can to assure that our soul has a place reserved in heaven, but in the spiritual realm, Jesus is clear that "you can do nothing" (John 15:5). On our own, we can do nothing to heal the incurable; we are unable to cleanse the guilty of their sin, and we are incapable of taking anyone to heaven. Blessedly, we are not required to do these things. We are required to have faith in the One who can. Simple, unwavering faith in the name of Jesus is all that we need to experience "perfect soundness" in our body, our mind, and our soul.

Peter's short sermon includes a three-point summary description of this Jesus that has just healed a man born lame. First, He is "the Holy One." God is holy (Leviticus 11:44). He is perfect in thought, in motivation, and in deed. Everything about Him is good, and everything He makes and everything He does is good. God alone is perfectly holy. And Jesus, God-in-flesh, is the Holy One come down to earth. Everything Jesus does is holy. Everything He says is perfectly holy. What a blessing it is for us to have Jesus' life recorded for us in Matthew, Mark, Luke, and John. The pages of those Gospels provide us with the depiction of what a holy life looks like. We are commanded to be holy (I Peter 1:15), and Jesus exemplifies for us the holy life that He requires. So then, let us pattern our life, our speech, and our priorities after those displayed by Jesus, the Holy One come down to earth.

Verse 14 also says that Jesus is "the Just." Psalm 7:11 says, "God is a just judge, and God is angry with the wicked every day." Jesus is perfectly holy and so godly men and women strive to imitate Him. But Jesus is also just, so wicked men and women have cause to fear Him. Those with their wits about them will take note that Jesus is just, and they will rush to repent of the sin in their heart that is certain to incur the wrath of a holy and just judge. Jesus is holy. Let us imitate Him. Jesus is also just. We must bow before Him in humble repentance, acknowledging that our imitation of His holiness is imperfect.

And thirdly, verse 15 says that Jesus is the "Prince of life." The phrase seizes our attention and beckons us to roll it over in our mind. The verse in the Christian Standard Bible translation says that Jesus is the "source of life." The ESV translates the phrase as Jesus is the "Author of life," reinforcing the powerful impact of Peter's words when he looked his listeners in the eye and said, "You killed the Author of life." It is Jesus, the Prince of life that gives us life and breath and everything we see around us (Acts 17:25). Man did not spontaneously appear. As the Author of life, it was Jesus who breathed life into mankind. "And the LORD God formed man of the dust of the ground, and breathed into his nostrils the breath of life; and man became a living being" (Genesis 2:7). And at the end of our life on earth, it is this same Jesus who will breathe into us the breath of eternal life so that we will live in heaven with Him forever (John 10:28, I Thessalonians 4:17).

Oh, such a rich description of our Lord is given to us by Peter in so few words. Jesus is the Holy One. Jesus is the Just. And Jesus is the Prince of life. As the crowd listened intently to Peter's sermon, let us listen carefully to all the words in Scripture, seeing again that Jesus is the source of life for all that lives. "I am the Lord God. I created the heavens like an open tent above. I made the earth and everything that grows on it. I am the source of life for all who live on this earth, so listen to what I say" (Isaiah 42:5 CEV).

3:17-21

Yet now, brethren, I know that you did it in ignorance, as did also your rulers. But those things which God foretold by the mouth of all His prophets, that the Christ would suffer, He has thus fulfilled. Repent therefore and be converted, that your sins may be blotted out, so that times of refreshing may come from the presence of the Lord, and that He may send Jesus Christ, who was preached to you before, whom heaven must receive until the times of restoration of all things, which God has spoken by the mouth of all His holy prophets since the world began.

Peter had just leveled against his listeners the harshest charge imaginable, confronting them with the fact that they had "killed the Prince of life" (verse 15). Here, Peter salves the sting of his indictment by acknowledging that his "brethren" had crucified Jesus "in ignorance." The sin of the crowd must be addressed, but Peter wished to communicate that he bore them no malice and wanted the best for them. He was gentle and empathetic as he confronted them with their sin, not vindictive or harsh. Hebrews 5:2 teaches us that Jesus "has compassion on those who are ignorant" and

Peter displays that compassion by wrapping the conscience-stinging truths of the gospel in tenderness and understanding.

Peter's tenderness toward the crowd, however, in no way allows him to skirt the crowd's painful yet essential obligation. They must repent. They must repent of their sin of unbelief. They must repent of cruelly crucifying the Prince of life. They must repent of their mishandling of the Scriptures and writings "of all His prophets" which clearly foretold for them of the suffering and salvation that would come to and through Jesus. Their sin was horrifying. Can any sin be more vile? They had "killed the Prince of life." Yet Peter blesses them with the news that if they will repent of their past sins and be "converted" to faith in Jesus, that their sins will be "blotted out" and that "times of refreshing may come from the presence of the Lord." Our soul savors the phrase: "so that times of refreshing may come from the presence of the Lord." The searing pain of a guilty conscience can be torment. The ache of guilt can cripple even the strongest. Vision for the future, hope for happiness today, and motivation to attempt new things for God can all be drained away from us by the smothering pall of guilt. But when Jesus draws near, when we are granted access to "the presence of the Lord," our soul is revived by the "refreshing" presence of our Savior. The sin and guilt that once crushed our spirits are now crushed instead by "the presence of the Lord." Similarly, sometimes in the service of the Lord we find that the weight of the work and the physical strain of our responsibilities exhaust our bodies and fray our emotions. Peter's words again remind us of the cure: exhausted and worn down by the work at hand, we find times of refreshing in the presence of our Lord. And, too, the loss of loved ones, the death of dreams, and griefs of all kinds can sap us of our joy and dim the horizon so deeply that we hardly find strength for today and little hope that tomorrow will be better. But then, oh the joy of the arrival of the presence of our Savior! Times of refreshing come from the presence of the Lord. Often, I have been asked how I was able to continue the work in our early days on the field when the weight of the responsibilities was seemingly overwhelming. When questioned, my thoughts turn inward, my soul smiles again, and a deep, pervading joy of remembrance wells over me as I think again of the presence of my Lord that refreshed my soul day after day. Peter's listeners had murdered the Prince of life, but repentance and conversion would be rewarded with forgiveness and acceptance, and the unsurpassable privilege of being ushered into the very presence of the Prince of life. Heaven is heaven because Jesus is there. So God's people are granted something very much like heaven on earth – the times of refreshing that are enjoyed by all those who are blessed to welcome the coming of the presence of the Lord.

The joy that Peter spoke of in our verses here, God's Word invites all of us to enjoy today. James 4:8 says, "Draw near to God and He will draw near to you." And as He draws near, times of refreshing once again revive our soul.

Jesus had been crucified, resurrected, and had returned to heaven – for "heaven must receive (Him) until the times of restoration of all things." But though Jesus left the world to return to His heavenly home, Peter delights to inform his listeners that they still have opportunity to enjoy fellowship with Him on earth. If they will repent of their sins and be converted to faith in God's Son, the Father will "send Jesus Christ" to everyone who trusts in His name. In Revelation 3:20 we see Jesus carrying out His mission to fellowship with His children, having been sent from the Father for this good purpose. "Behold, I stand at the door and knock. If anyone hears My voice and opens the door, I will come in to him and dine with him, and he with Me." "The Father has sent the Son as Savior of the world" (I John 4:14). But the Father has also sent His Son to be our Friend and dearest Companion through the journey of life. He is our lofty Savior, but He has been "sent" by the Father to be our ever-present help as well. What a blessed thought.

3:22-23

For Moses truly said to the fathers, "The LORD your God will raise up for you a Prophet like me from your brethren. Him you shall hear in all things, whatever He says to you. And it shall be that every soul who will not hear that Prophet shall be utterly destroyed from among the people."

Peter continues his discourse aimed at calling his listeners to place their faith in Jesus. He recalls for them Deuteronomy 18:15-18 when God promised to send the people another "Prophet" like Moses. Hebrews 3 provides a number of comparisons between Moses and Jesus, and it is not difficult to think of many more. Deuteronomy 18:18 says that both Jesus and Moses were granted the responsibility of taking the Father's words and passing them on to the people. Both Jesus and Moses interceded on behalf of sinful, unworthy people (Numbers 14:19, John 17, Hebrews 7:25). Both Jesus and Moses delivered the people from bondage (Exodus 3:7-10, John 8:36). Both Jesus and Moses communed with the Father directly (Exodus 33:11, John 12:28). And both were said to be the humblest of all men (Numbers 12:3, Matthew 11:29). Perhaps there were many in the crowd who were either unfamiliar with the prophecy of Deuteronomy 18 or unfamiliar with Jesus, so, up to that point, they had rejected Jesus' sovereignty. Perhaps before Jesus' resurrection, the connection between Deuteronomy 18:15-18 and the glory of Jesus was easier to miss. But now, with this prophecy presented clearly before them and the life and power of Jesus and His disciples again displayed before their eyes, many in the crowd were suddenly compelled to believe.

The belief that all religions are good is held by many. But the fact remains that "every soul who will not hear that Prophet shall be utterly destroyed." Every soul that does not elevate Jesus as Lord of all shall be "utterly destroyed." Every soul that exalts the teachings of any other religious leader over the teachings of Jesus "shall be utterly destroyed." "He who believes in the Son has everlasting life; and he who does not believe the Son shall not see life, but the wrath of God abides on him" (John 3:36). It is neither loving nor kindhearted to avoid the tension and confrontation that may be necessary to call people to place their faith in Jesus. With grave concern, Peter calls his hearers to turn from their sin and unbelief and trust in the "Prophet" sent to them by the Lord God. Peter's compassion for the crowd will allow him to do nothing less than compel all his listeners to follow Jesus, because all who fail to believe and obey "that Prophet," Jesus, the Son of God, "shall be utterly destroyed."

3:24-26

Yes, and all the prophets, from Samuel and those who follow, as many as have spoken, have also foretold these days. You are sons of the prophets, and of the covenant which God made with our fathers, saying to Abraham, "And in your seed all the families of the earth shall be blessed." To you first, God, having raised up His Servant Jesus, sent Him to bless you, in turning away every one of you from your iniquities.

Having already established that his hearers had "denied the Holy One" and "killed the Prince of life" (verses 14 and 15), Peter chooses not to continue to berate them for their sin, but to give them good cause for turning from it. All of the prophets, from Samuel to Malachi had spoken of Jesus. They had "foretold these days" when Jesus would be born, heal the sick, preach to the poor, suffer, die, and rise again. All of the prophets spoke with clarity and faith of the coming of the Savior Jesus – and "you are sons of the prophets." Peter's words were both kind and compelling. As children of Abraham, they were children of the faithful prophets of God and were thus heirs of all that God had promised. They were beneficiaries of God's promise to bless the seed of Abraham. Their sin was great, but God's intention to forgive and bless them was greater still, and Peter did not want them to miss out on God's gifts of grace that were there for the taking. Their sin was great, but it was God's merciful intention to overcome their sin. Despite their many flaws, God "raised up His Servant Jesus" in order to bless them and turn "every one of you from your iniquities."

The gifts of God's grace are many. These gifts include healing for the lame (verses 1-10) and "times of refreshing" in the "presence of the Lord" (verse 20), but this blessing from God to turn us away from our iniquities is certainly not inferior to any of His other gifts to man. Our Lord turns us away from our iniquities so that we abhor the very sins we once enjoyed. He turns the atheist from his unbelief. He turns the adulterer from his perverted love. He turns old sinners from their self-centeredness and arrogant cynicism, and He turns young sinners from all sorts of mischief. But more blessed still is the fact that the Lord not only turns us away from sinning, He turns away from us the guilt and punishment for our sins. Jeremiah 36:3 points out both of these aspects: "It may be that the house of Judah will hear all the adversities which I purpose to bring upon them, that everyone may turn from his evil way, that I may forgive their iniquity and their sin." And perhaps more famously, II Chronicles 7:14 says, "If My people who are called by My name will humble themselves, and pray and seek My face, and turn from their wicked ways, then I will hear from heaven, and will forgive their sin and heal their land." God turns us away from sinning, and He turns away from us the devastating eternal consequences of sin. What a blessed thought.

Acts 4

4:1-4
Now as they spoke to the people, the priests, the captain of the temple, and the Sadducees came upon them, being greatly disturbed that they taught the people and preached in Jesus the resurrection from the dead. And they laid hands on them, and put them in custody until the next day, for it was already evening. However, many of those who heard the word believed; and the number of the men came to be about five thousand.

Several matters of interest attract our attention here. Though a great many listeners were captivated by Peter's message, others were "greatly disturbed." Let us not be surprised when our presentation of the gospel angers some hearers. It has been this way from the beginning. The Sadducees claimed that there was no afterlife and no heaven to go to, so the disciples' eyewitness account of the resurrection of Jesus was certain to catch their vehement opposition. We must not be surprised, and we certainly must not be intimidated by angry responses. The message of the gospel stings the conscience, and a stung conscience will often lash out in a reflex impulse of anger. Let us take these angry outbursts patiently and with understanding.

Quick anger may yet evolve into later repentance, even among the angriest of critics, and the anger of the unrepentant can hardly interfere with the faith of the elect as we see in verse 4.

We see that the Sadducees were enraged and the disciples were arrested, but in the meantime, some 5,000 men came to faith in the Jesus that the disciples preached. We are reminded that God's glory is not dependent on our comfort. It is quite possible for us to make people very angry with us, be arrested, get sick, fail a test, lose our job, have a bad back, remain poor, AND see God glorified in the process. The disciples were arrested, but thousands of souls were reconciled with their Creator. God could have easily prevented the former while still assuring the latter, but He did not, because not only does He see physical trials hardly worth comparing to spiritual victories, but those close to Him feel that way as well! After enduring many trials and pains even worse than what the disciples endured here, Paul writes in II Corinthians 4:17, "For this light momentary affliction is preparing for us an eternal weight of glory beyond all comparison" (ESV). May the Lord grant us this joy of seeing present, personal pains as "light" and "momentary" when compared to the eternal overriding satisfaction of carrying out our Master's work.

4:5-10

And it came to pass, on the next day, that their rulers, elders, and scribes, as well as Annas the high priest, Caiaphas, John, and Alexander, and as many as were of the family of the high priest, were gathered together at Jerusalem. And when they had set them in the midst, they asked, "By what power or by what name have you done this?" Then Peter, filled with the Holy Spirit, said to them, "Rulers of the people and elders of Israel: If we this day are judged for a good deed done to a helpless man, by what means he has been made well, let it be known to you all, and to all the people of Israel, that by the name of Jesus Christ of Nazareth, whom you crucified, whom God raised from the dead, by Him this man stands here before you whole."

We take much proper comfort in knowing that our Lord records the names of those who are His so that our place in heaven is secured. Our name is written in the Book of Life and Jesus our Lord will announce us by name before the presence of the Father and the holy angels (Revelation 3:5). And as for those who mock us and seek our hurt, we have no need to wonder if they will get away with their misdeeds. Our Lord knows them by name as well. Here we see perpetrator after perpetrator, persecutor after persecutor recorded by name for their opposition to the servants of Christ.

God knows those who are His (II Timothy 2:19), and He also knows very well those who are not. Their names are also recorded. Their comeuppance awaits. Let us treat them with proper respect, as Peter does here, knowing that the Lord will deal with them soon enough.

The prosecutors of Peter and the apostles are not men of no means. They are "rulers, elders, and scribes." They are men of power, at least of an earthly sort, the kind of power that made the parents of the blind man in John 9 fear to stand up for their own son. But Peter does not fear to stand up for His Savior, because he was "filled with the Holy Spirit" (verse 8). Let us respect all men, but let us fear no man as long as we, too, are filled with God's Holy Spirit. As the courtroom scene unfolded, Peter's accusers sat semi-circled around him. They "surrounded (him) like bees" (Psalm 118:12). Jesus taught His disciples that the world would do to them just as they had done to Him – "If they persecuted Me, they will also persecute you" (John 15:20). And now, just as they had tried Jesus in fulfillment of the Scriptures, they do the same to Peter. Psalm 22:16 foretold the event in Jesus' life that is now being replayed in His disciples' life: "Dogs have surrounded Me; the congregation of the wicked has enclosed Me" (Psalm 22:16). But those surrounded by the protective love of Christ do not need to fear being surrounded by enemies. In II Kings 6, the young man fears because he sees an army of enemies around him. He fears, until Elisha asks the Lord to open his spiritual eyes. "And Elisha prayed, and said, 'LORD, I pray, open his eyes that he may see.' Then the LORD opened the eyes of the young man, and he saw. And behold, the mountain was full of horses and chariots of fire all around Elisha" (II Kings 6:17). Such is our opportunity today. Psalm 5:12 reminds us even now, "You bless the godly, O Lord; you surround them with your shield of love" (NLT).

The trial begins with a question: "By what power or by what name have you done this?" And since a trial should begin with a charge against the defendant, and since the accusers failed to state the charge, Peter reminds all in attendance of the "crime" that he was accused of. He was accused of "a good deed done for a helpless man." The evil enemies of Christ intended to quell the momentum of the Spirit-led revival sweeping Jerusalem, but their opposition only served to put on public display the power of God, the loving compassion of His people, and the mean-spirited, self-serving designs of their detractors. Through the healing of the lame man, the glory of God was manifested, and the good deeds of God's people were witnessed – and all this was placed on a public stage by the trial that was set up by the Jewish leaders. God used their heart to oppose Jesus to actually glorify Jesus and increase His visibility and renown. Peter may have been thinking of this very event when he wrote in I Peter 4:14, "If you are reproached for the name of Christ, blessed are you, for the Spirit of glory and of God rests upon you. On their part He is blasphemed, but on your part He is glorified."

And now, for the third time in three chapters, Peter charges his hearers with murdering Jesus. As we share the wonderful gospel and freely give away healing acts of compassion to those around us, we are once again reminded by Peter's persistent example that we cannot simply tell nice stories and do good deeds if we are to see people reconciled with the Creator. We must call people to repent of all that God calls sin. Jesus Christ of Nazareth died to save men from their sins, He was raised from the dead by God the Father, He healed a helpless, crippled man, and He ever lives to rescue the perishing, restore the rebelling, and to save and soothe troubled souls. But if the people were to gain all that Jesus was offering to provide them, they must first confess and repent of their sinful unbelief that once caused them to murder the Prince of life (Acts 3:15), and now leads them to oppress His servants. The Jewish leaders had rejected Jesus, but the healing of the lame man provided yet another piece of evidence that this Jesus that they had rejected was "the chief cornerstone" (verse 11) and they would surely fall in ruin if they refused to build and base their lives on Him as their foundation.

4:11-12
This is the stone which was rejected by you builders, which has become the chief cornerstone. Nor is there salvation in any other, for there is no other name under heaven given among men by which we must be saved.

The rulers, elders, and scribes (verse 5) who gathered to oppress the apostles were supposed to be "builders" of the Kingdom of God. But they had "rejected" the "chief cornerstone" of that kingdom and in so doing they had rejected the only means of securing their eternal salvation. Old Testament writers wrote of this cornerstone. Psalm 118:22 speaks of Him. Isaiah 28:16 speaks of Him and calls Him "precious" and "a sure foundation." Ephesians 2:20 removes all doubt regarding the stone's identity: "Jesus Christ Himself being the chief cornerstone." But Jesus had already made it clear by referring to the term while chiding the chief priests and scribes for rejecting Him (Luke 19:17).

Jesus is the cornerstone. The existence of the universe is founded on Him. "All things were created through Him." Jesus is the cornerstone. Our purpose for living is founded on Him. All things were created "for Him" (Colossians 1:16). Jesus is the cornerstone. There is no other means by which we can build a life that is pleasing to our Creator, and no other means by which we can leave earth and enter heaven except through Jesus. "He who believes in the Son has everlasting life; and he who does not believe the Son shall not see life, but the wrath of God abides on Him" (John 3:36).

Verse 12 continues that train of thought, stating, "Nor is there salvation in any other (name)." If we are to be saved from sin, we must stand on the cornerstone, Jesus, as the Savior from that sin. As much as the world would like to disbelieve them, Peter's words could hardly be clearer. "There is no other name under heaven given among men by which we must be saved." There is no other religion that can save a man from the guilt of his sin and grant him access to heaven. There is no good deed, or series of good deeds, or lifetime of good deeds that can save a man from the punishment for his sins and grant him access to heaven.

The cost of redeeming a life from the penalty of sin is a life (Hebrews 9:22). No lesser sacrifice than a life, and no lesser sacrificer than the perfect Jesus will suffice. If there was any other way to erase sin and grant men and women access to heaven, why would Jesus be willing to be tortured and die on our behalf? If being a good Buddhist, earnest Muslim, or sincere atheist could still qualify a human being to leave earth and enter heaven, why would Jesus find it necessary to die for us? Jesus made this very point on the eve of His crucifixion. In Matthew 26:39 Jesus prayed, "O My Father, if it is possible, let this cup pass from Me." If there was any other possible means to save the souls of men, Jesus pleaded the Father to use that means instead. But no, there is no other way to save a sinful soul other than by Jesus, the Son of God, dying to pay man's punishment, and rising again to conquer the death that would otherwise doom man's eternity. Jesus Christ died and rose from the dead, and there "is no other name under heaven given among men by which we must be saved." Peter addressed a crowd that was in desperate need of understanding the eternal peril of rejecting Jesus. Today, we, too, address a world that is in desperate need of understanding this same essential truth.

4:13

Now when they saw the boldness of Peter and John, and perceived that they were uneducated and untrained men, they marveled. And they realized that they had been with Jesus.

The great men who stood in judgment of Peter and John are said to have "marveled" at them. They oppressed Peter and John with the full power of their position, and they marveled at how John and Peter stood their ground with confidence and an amazing air of authority. They cross examined the two men with withering questions made razor sharp by their high education and brilliant intellect – and then "marveled" at how these "uneducated and untrained men" answered them so insightfully and skillfully. These "rulers and elders" were accustomed to being able to bully their opposition into submission with threats and shows of power, but once again they had to "marvel" at the "boldness" that Peter and John demonstrated in a setting that would have certainly intimidated anyone else. The manner in which Peter and John presented themselves, having nerves of steel and brilliant answers to challenging questions, was astounding. Peter and John amazed their enemies. Their critics marveled at how such unremarkable men could come across so remarkably. Stunned by the disparity between the natural inadequacies of Peter and John and the supernatural presence of Peter and John, the elders and rulers sought for an explanation. At last, they found one: "They had been with Jesus."

There could not possibly be a wider disparity than who we are without Christ and who we are in Christ. "The weapons of our warfare are not carnal" (II Corinthians 10:4), and the source of our wisdom and strength in serving our Lord is not derived from natural elements. It is God's wonderful intent to communicate His truths and display His greatness for the benefit of the men and women He has created. By nature, however, mankind is a terrible conduit for communicating God's truths and displaying His greatness. So then, our Lord does not leave us alone to stumble along and try to represent Him the best we can. No, God does not rely on man to carry out His great works. God amazes people like the elders and leaders in our story here by revealing His truths through "Christ in you, the hope of glory" (Colossians 1:27). Christ lives in us! Christ radiates the glory of the Father! And we, as the trembling body of Christ, become His "earthen vessels," His "jars of clay" (ESV) which hold the excellence of the power of God (II Corinthians 4:7). God's excellence, however, is neither limited by, nor enhanced by our personal attributes. Peter and John amazed the great men around them, not because of any personal abilities (in fact, the rulers scorned their personal qualities), but because "they had been with Jesus."

By all means, let us be diligent in our effort to enhance our personal capabilities in serving our Father. Let us value education and all kinds of special training. But let us be keenly aware that our weaknesses do not limit God's power to use us, nor does any personal prowess on our part in any way enable God to use us. "God has chosen the foolish things of the world to put to shame the wise, and God has chosen the weak things of the world to put to shame the things which are mighty; and the base things of the world and the things which are despised God has chosen, and the things which are not, to bring to nothing the things that are, that no flesh should glory in His presence" (I Corinthians 1:27-29).

The elders marveled at Peter and John because the two of them had been with Jesus. If we are to carry out the great works of God, we must be with Jesus. If we are to communicate the great truths of God, we must be with Jesus. Apart from Jesus, we can do nothing of significance. But when Christ is in us, we provide the world good cause to marvel.

4:14-17

And seeing the man who had been healed standing with them, they could say nothing against it. But when they had commanded them to go aside out of the council, they conferred among themselves, saying, "What shall we do to these men? For, indeed, that a notable miracle has been done through them is evident to all who dwell in Jerusalem, and we cannot deny it. But so that it spreads no further among the people, let us severely threaten them, that from now on they speak to no man in this name."

When Jesus brought Lazarus back from the dead, John records a similar reaction from the unbelieving leaders. John states, "Then the chief priests and Pharisees gathered a council and said, 'What shall we do? For this Man works many signs. If we let Him alone like this, everyone will believe in Him, and the Romans will come and take away both our place and nation'" (John 11:47-48). Such is the horrible state of mind that comes over men and women when personal comfort and personal pride take precedence over reverence for the truth. The religious leaders saw the miracle at the hands of Peter and John done in the name of Jesus. The evidence of the power of Jesus was not only right in front of their faces, but His power had also become "evident to all who dwell in Jerusalem." The truth and evidence of Jesus' power to save was plainly seen. They did not deny it, they simply did not want it.

What can be done for those who do not want the truth? John 14:6 says that Jesus is the way, the truth and the life. All who believe in Him are granted admission to the Father's presence in heaven. But if men despise that truth, rather than embrace that truth, what hope do they have? John 8:32 says the truth will set us free from the guilt and punishment of sin. But if we reject the truth rather than depend on the truth, we will gain no benefit from the truth.

In John 18:38 Pilate asked, "What is truth?" And then he acquiesced to the crowd and allowed Jesus to be murdered. Pilate's actions demonstrate that we cannot make good decisions if the truth is not known. Ignorance of the truth condemns us to fail. Even more culpable, however, are those who know the truth, and yet refuse to submit to it. They exchange the truth of

God for a lie (Romans 1:25) that is more convenient, more to their personal liking, or more likely to grant them personal gain. Those who know the truth, as the leaders do in our story here, but ignore that truth, seek to hide that truth, or wish to "suppress" that truth are particularly odious in God's sight. "For the wrath of God is revealed from heaven against all ungodliness and unrighteousness of men, who <u>suppress the truth in unrighteousness</u>" (Romans 1:18). The rulers, elders, and scribes in Jerusalem were granted a personal view of clear evidence upholding the truth that the power of God is in the name of Jesus. Tragically, the truth did not help them at all, "not being mixed with faith in those who heard it" (Hebrews 4:2).

4:18-20

So they called them and commanded them not to speak at all nor teach in the name of Jesus. But Peter and John answered and said to them, "Whether it is right in the sight of God to listen to you more than to God, you judge. For we cannot but speak the things which we have seen and heard."

The Lord commanded Peter and John and the apostles to "go into all the world and preach the gospel to every creature" (Mark 16:15), but the leaders now command them to stop preaching Jesus' gospel (verse 17). We are commanded to obey those in authority (Hebrews 13:17), but when the commands of men conflict with the commands of God, Peter and John matter-of-factly state for the council that God's commands take precedence. Peter and John are not modeling noncompliance; they are not championing rebellion from authority. They are demonstrating that Christians need not feel even a twinge of hesitation if we see that obeying God's law will require us to violate a law of man's making. <u>Submission to the call and commands of God overrides all other obligations</u>.

Obeying God's commands rather than man's commands is made even less difficult because "his commandments are not burdensome" (I John 5:3). Obedience to our Lord does not require remarkable skills or strengths. The burdens placed on us by human authorities can be extremely taxing, but the burdens placed on us by the commands of Jesus are described as "easy" and "light" (Matthew 11:30). In response to the civic authorities' ban on speaking in Jesus' name, John says in verse 20, "We cannot but speak the things which we have seen and heard." Later, when writing his first epistle, John said the same thing again, stating, "That which we have seen and heard we declare to you" (I John 1:3). John was not asked by the Lord to wage an intellectual battle with the highly educated scribes before him. He was simply commanded to tell others what he had seen Jesus do and heard Jesus say. Peter was not asked to out-wrestle the power and authority of his accusers. He, too, was simply commanded by the Lord to tell what he had seen Jesus do and what he had heard Jesus say.

We must obey God rather than man – and blessedly, contrary to what might seem to be the case, obeying God is less taxing, requires less personal giftedness, and yields far greater long-term dividends.

4:21-22

So when they had further threatened them, they let them go, finding no way of punishing them, because of the people, since they all glorified God for what had been done. For the man was over forty years old on whom this miracle of healing had been performed.

Those who opposed Jesus also opposed His followers. But here we find that their opposition was made impotent by the holy lives and powerful ministry of God's servants. Let there be no mistake, those who fought against Peter and the apostles were powerful, influential men, who held a vehement hatred for everything that the apostles taught and did. But their determination to do injury to the apostles' ministry was reduced to empty threats out of deference for "the people" – the great crowd of witnesses who "glorified God" when they saw with their own eyes the works of compassion and power carried out by Jesus' followers.

In Matthew 5:16 Jesus said, "Let your light so shine before men, that they may see your good works and glorify your Father in heaven." Here, we see that the apostles' works did exactly that. Seeing the apostles' works, the people "glorified God." It is instructive to see that the same works which glorified God were also the works which protected God's servants. The leaders could find "no way of punishing them" because the apostles were holy and compassionate in all their dealings with men. Titus 2:6-8 calls on godly men to "be sober-minded, in all things showing yourself to be a pattern of good works; in doctrine showing integrity, reverence, incorruptibility, sound speech that cannot be condemned, that one who is an opponent may be ashamed, having nothing evil to say of you." Such is the case in our story here. As opposed as they were to the doctrine and actions of the Christians before them, the leaders could find "nothing evil to say" against them. Today, if we should find ourselves under personal attack, may our personal holiness and public shows of compassion be our preferred method of self-preservation as well.

4:23-26
And being let go, they went to their own companions and reported all that the chief priests and elders had said to them. So when they heard that, they raised their voice to God with one accord and said: "Lord, You are God, who made heaven and earth and the sea, and all that is in them, who by the mouth of Your servant David have said: 'Why did the nations rage, and the people plot vain things? The kings of the earth took their stand, and the rulers were gathered together against the LORD and against His Christ.'"

Having at last been released from their unlawful capture, Peter and John immediately returned to the company of their fellow believers and "reported all that the chief priests and elders had said to them." The chief priests and elders were well known for abusing their power and sorely oppressing their enemies, so the apostles' testimony of how the leaders had suddenly released them without injury made all the apostles' listeners instantly recognize that the entire event had been orchestrated by God. The event moves them, not only to thank God for rescuing His people, but to praise God for His power that created all things: "Lord, You are God, who made heaven and earth and the sea, and all that is in them." It is good to remember that God is not simply to be praised for the small acts of kindness that He lovingly pours out on us personally, but for His omniscient genius and omnipotent power by which He created all things. The believers were not distracted by the personal benefits that trust in God had brought them. No, they were re-overwhelmed with the Spirit-directed drive to offer awe-filled worship and praise toward the One who not only works to provide for His people, but works to sustain the life and breath of all living things as He "upholds the universe by the word of his power" (Hebrews 1:3 ESV).

Remembering the power of God that created the world and sustains the galaxies reminded them of Psalm 2. "Why did the nations rage, and the people plot vain things?" Of course Peter and John were rescued from the opposition of the leaders! All those who gather together "against the LORD and against His Christ" (Psalm 2:2) must certainly fail! Their "plot" to oppose God's people will be a "vain" pursuit. They cannot succeed against us! Our God created the heavens and the earth and the sea and all that is in them! Surely, He has the power to protect His people! See how faith in God's power to create the world gives us peace and confidence as we face the trials of today and see how our experience with God's loving provision for us today reminds us of the greatness of His limitless power and majesty that set creation in motion since the dawn of time.

Rather than exalt the apostles, those who heard their testimony were powerfully moved to praise the Lord who made heaven and earth. May all of our Lord's many kindnesses toward us yield a similar outcome in the hearts of those who witness His blessings on us.

4:27-30

For truly against Your holy Servant Jesus, whom You anointed, both Herod and Pontius Pilate, with the Gentiles and the people of Israel, were gathered together to do whatever Your hand and Your purpose determined before to be done. Now, Lord, look on their threats, and grant to Your servants that with all boldness they may speak Your word, by stretching out Your hand to heal, and that signs and wonders may be done through the name of Your holy Servant Jesus."

Peter and John had just been arrested, interrogated, and threatened by a hostile group of city leaders. As they considered their proper response, they were reminded of the fact that the Lord Jesus endured the same thing. He, too, was arrested and interrogated by both Pilate and Herod, and was harassed by both "the Gentiles and the people of Israel." But this fierce opposition from such a battery of enemies did not hinder God's purposes in the least! Herod, Pontius Pilate, Gentiles from foreign nations, and His fellow countrymen in Israel all rose up to oppose and oppress the holy Servant Jesus. The combined efforts of all these powerful enemies, however, served only to carry out the opposite of their intent. Their determined efforts to oppose Jesus actually worked to accomplish the "purpose" of Jesus that He had "determined before to be done."

Since, then, their Lord had demonstrated for them that opposition was more apt to further God's purposes than impede God's purposes, the disciples lifted up their prayer that the Lord would use all present and future persecution for His glory. Rather than ask to be protected from persecution, they asked for courage in the face of persecution. They prayed for the ability to "speak Your word" with "all boldness." They also prayed for continued empowerment in their service to the Lord in the face of opposition. They asked that they might be enabled to heal the hurting and demonstrate "signs and wonders" that would be done both through and for the name of Jesus. Their heart was to see that the threats of the enemy would simply provide a backdrop for the mighty acts of God and provide a stage that would allow witnesses to see all the amazing things that God does for His people. David's prayer in Psalm 64 desired the same thing: "O God, listen to my complaint. Protect my life from my enemies' threats...Then they will proclaim the mighty acts of God and realize all the amazing things he does. The godly will rejoice in the Lord and find shelter in him. And those who do what is right will praise him" (Psalm 64:1,9-10 NLT).

4:31
And when they had prayed, the place where they were assembled together was shaken; and they were all filled with the Holy Spirit, and they spoke the word of God with boldness.

In verse 29 the disciples prayed that the Lord would fill them with boldness to preach His word, and God quickly demonstrated His answer. The house was physically shaken, which must have filled the disciples with holy fear and awe. They had asked for boldness, and were quickly rewarded with the empowering, indwelling presence of the Holy Spirit. Matthew Henry points out that "nothing emboldens faithful ministers more in their work than the tokens of God's presence with them, and a divine power going along with them." The power of the Spirit's presence shook the foundations of the building, filling the disciples with certainty that God was with them and that His power has no limit. The disciples' response to the Lord's presence is instructive: "They spoke the word of God with boldness." They asked for boldness to speak His word, He answered their prayer, and they immediately made good use of His answer to carry out His purposes.

Let us be faithful to our Lord's desires when He answers our prayerful requests. When the Spirit draws near to bless our soul and when the kindness of our Lord answers our prayers, let us speak "the word of God with boldness." Boldly speaking the words of God is a manifestation of the presence of God in the life of a believer. "God has not given us a spirit of fear" (II Timothy 1:7). He gives His people the spirit of boldness to speak His Word in the power of His presence. Timidity and a hesitation to speak God's Word to those who need it is an indication that we are not filled with the Spirit, which should drive all godly souls to pray as the apostles do in our verses here.

4:32
Now the multitude of those who believed were of one heart and one soul; neither did anyone say that any of the things he possessed was his own, but they had all things in common.

In John 17:11 Jesus prayed for His disciples, "Holy Father, keep through Your name those whom You have given Me, that they may be one as We are." And here we see the record of the Father's answer to the Son's request. All the followers of Christ "were of one heart and one soul." David wrote 1,000 years before this day, "Behold, how good and how pleasant it is for brethren to dwell together in unity!" (Psalm 133:1). And from David's day to ours, God's people have been granted access to the deep, abiding joy of experiencing unity in the body of Christ.

The Spirit of God has fallen on His disciples, and the immediate result was the rise of a unified spirit of love for one another. The Spirit's presence moved everyone in the church to view everyone else in the church as members of their own immediate family. Every burden of every member was considered a personal need by everyone else. Suddenly, personal gain lost all significant value. The body of Christ, infused by the presence of the Spirit, had one mind – their thoughts were unified by the mind of Christ (I Corinthians 2:16). They had "one heart and one soul" – their motives, vision, purposes, concerns, heartbreaks, and joys were all commonly felt and bound them all together. Such is the case when the Spirit comes in power upon His people.

When our church is blessed with loving unity, we can rightly kneel in gratitude and praise to our Lord, knowing that it is His Spirit that allows such unity to bind us together. Left alone, men and women will be self-centered and self-seeking. And "where envy and self-seeking exist, confusion and every evil thing are there" (James 3:16). But when the Spirit arrives to bind our hearts and minds and souls in the unified body of Christ, "confusion" is replaced with clarity, and the "evil things" of the world are replaced with the holy purposes of God. And the nearly unsurpassable joy of serving and relating rightly with the Creator of the universe is then surpassed by the joy of doing so in the company of like-minded saints who serve Him and love Him just as we do.

4:33

And with great power the apostles gave witness to the resurrection of the Lord Jesus. And great grace was upon them all.

So much of our faith and message depends on the "resurrection of the Lord Jesus." If Jesus did, indeed, rise from the dead, all His teachings are immediately confirmed, His deity is established, and the necessity of man's submission to His authority is made plain. The apostles, therefore, centered their messages around this theme, confirming their claim with many eye-witness accounts of their Lord's resurrection.

The people spent their time attesting to the resurrection of Jesus (verse 33) and caring for one another's needs (verse 32, 34-35), and as they did so "great grace was upon them all." As they gave themselves to His purposes, they were upheld by an abundant supply of the grace and mercies of God. Often men give great effort to a task but have little to show for it – but not here. Here, everything the apostles set their mind to do was met with great success, because "great grace was upon them all." Sometimes good deeds are sullied by ingratitude, well-meaning partners are separated by misunderstandings, hard work goes unrewarded, and feelings are hurt by unintended offenses – but not here. "Great grace was upon them all." The Spirit blessed their efforts, invigorated their spirits, uplifted their souls, and filled their hearts with joy. Their sails were constantly filled with the winds of His blessings. Oh, how we are in need of strength and wisdom and insight in our service to the Lord and His people. It is right to pray for these things. But God's grace is what we chiefly need. God's grace can fill us with strength and make our weaknesses of no disadvantage. And blessedly, our Lord is pleased to freely bestow this grace, this "great grace" on His children.

Recognizing our need for God's grace as our chief need, let us "come boldly to the throne of grace, that we may obtain mercy and find grace to help in time of need" (Hebrews 4:16). Our Lord gives grace to those who approach Him and boldly ask for it before His throne. So let us pray for His grace. And the Lord gives grace to those who walk uprightly, so let us walk in obedience before Him, for He gives grace to those who do. Psalm 84:11 says, "For the LORD God is a sun and shield; the LORD will give grace and glory; no good thing will He withhold from those who walk uprightly." Grace, this "great grace" that empowered the work of the apostles is our greatest need in life, and prayer and purity are the keys to obtaining it from our Lord. Let us kneel in prayer and let us walk in holiness, for when we do, we, too, may experience this "great grace" that was upon God's people here in Acts chapter 4.

Acts 4:34-37

Nor was there anyone among them who lacked; for all who were possessors of lands or houses sold them, and brought the proceeds of the things that were sold, and laid them at the apostles' feet; and they distributed to each as anyone had need. And Joses, who was also named Barnabas by the apostles (which is translated Son of Encouragement), a Levite of the country of Cyprus, having land, sold it, and brought the money and laid it at the apostles' feet.

The fact that "great grace was upon them all" (verse 33) did not mean that the people did not suffer the pains of poverty. Jesus taught us that "the poor you will always have with you" (Matthew 26:11 NIV), for though God's grace fills us with "the unsearchable riches of Christ" (Ephesians 3:8), eternal riches do not protect us from temporal poverty. In fact, Proverbs 13:7 points out that the sure inheritance of "great riches" to come may well move a man to happily "make himself poor."

In Hebrews 11:26 Moses was commended for "esteeming the reproach of Christ greater riches than the treasures in Egypt." And here, we see Barnabas similarly commended for esteeming the care of the body of Christ greater riches than the silver in his hand. He sold his property, and rather than using the money for his own profit, he offered it as a sacrifice to the Lord to take care of the needs of the saints. His name was recorded because his sacrifice for the church was noteworthy and inspiring to all who witnessed his gift, and to all who had their needs met through his gift. In Acts 13:2 Barnabas and Saul are called by the Holy Spirit to begin the great work of taking the gospel to the Gentile world. Let all of us who long to do great things for God not miss the fact that Barnabas' sacrifice for the church was the precursor for the Spirit calling him to carry out God's great work to come. Just as the rich man's attachment to his money disqualified him from service to the Lord in Matthew 19, so Barnabas' sacrifice became a qualifying feature for his world changing work to come. Let us be ever mindful of the call to sacrifice for the sake of the people and purposes of God. For just as our Lord's sacrifice for us qualified Him to be our Great High Priest, so our sacrifices for Him work to make us eligible to be His faithful ministers in return.

Acts 5

5:1-5

But a certain man named Ananias, with Sapphira his wife, sold a possession. And he kept back part of the proceeds, his wife also being aware of it, and brought a certain part and laid it at the apostles' feet. But Peter said, "Ananias, why has Satan filled your heart to lie to the Holy Spirit and keep back part of the price of the land for yourself? While it remained, was it not your own? And after it was sold, was it not in your own control? Why have you conceived this thing in your heart? You have not lied to men but to God." Then Ananias, hearing these words, fell down and breathed his last. So great fear came upon all those who heard these things.

Having seen Barnabas and others sell lands and homes and bring the money to the apostles for the benefit of needy believers, Ananias and his wife Sapphira look to follow this godly example. They sold their land and brought money from the sale to the apostles. But here is where they strayed from the example set before them. Wanting the praise of men, they claimed that they were giving away the entirety of their profits, but wanting the personal benefit of the money as well, they kept back part of the money for themselves.

Matthew Henry writes concerning this passage: "Those that boast of good works they never did, or promise good works they never do, or make the good works they do more or better than really they are, come under the guilt of Ananias's lie, which it concerns us all to dread the thought of." *"It concerns us all to dread the thought of."* The dreadful thoughts presented in this passage concern me very much. It seems to me that I have done far worse things than Ananias. I am ashamed to consider it, but I am certain that I have. I think that I understand verse 5: "So great fear came upon all those who heard these things." I feel their fear and dread. I suspect they felt as I do, that I am worthy of the punishment meted out on Ananias. May the holy fear that this story evokes cause us to consider this sin which moves God to respond so severely.

Peter rebukes Ananias, stating, "You have not lied to men, but to God." Ananias sold his land and brought some of the money, perhaps most of the money and donated it to a good cause. No one would have disapproved of his withholding some of his own money to use on his own needs. Ananias' lie was not to men, for men would not have cared. Even if they knew of the disparity, it is likely that most men would have regarded his generosity as outweighing his mild dishonesty and given little more than a mild exhortation to be honest and forthright in the future. We are reminded, however, that "the LORD does not see as man sees" (I Samuel 16:7). Onlookers at the time might well have considered Ananias to be a good man who mildly exaggerated his generosity. The Lord, however, found his sin to be a capital offense. Let us take the lesson to heart – for I fear Ananias' sin may not be far from any of us.

It seems that the sin of Ananias that the Lord found so repulsive was the sin of lying – perhaps a certain type of lying, perhaps a lie in a specific situation. He hatched a plot, at Satan's temptation, to "lie to the Holy Spirit" (verse 3). He premeditated a plot to lie "to God" (verse 4). In II Kings 5 we find a story that presents some similarities. God demonstrates His power and grace to Naaman – and Gehazi lies in an effort to personally benefit from God's great work before them. Gehazi gets his money, but his act is not hidden from the Lord, and in II Kings 5:26-27 Elisha says to him, "Is it time to receive money and vineyards, sheep and oxen, male and female servants? Therefore the leprosy of Naaman shall cling to you and your descendants forever." Profiting from the works of God is repulsive in heaven's eyes. And using deception to steal from God's glory for the sake of personal gain is even worse. I Timothy 6:5 speaks of "men of corrupt minds and destitute of the truth, who suppose that godliness is a means of gain. From such withdraw yourself." We see from our story here that God hates lying. Proverbs 6:17 verifies for us that one of the six things God hates the most is a "lying tongue." But this story also shows us that another thing that God hates is when men try to gain personal profit from His work or from their work done in His name. If God should use us for His glory, let us tremble in fear of allowing pride or deception to divert God's due praise into our personal account. The outcome that befalls those who do so is frightful to consider.

5:6-11

And the young men arose and wrapped him up, carried him out, and buried him. Now it was about three hours later when his wife came in, not knowing what had happened. And Peter answered her, "Tell me whether you sold the land for so much?" She said, "Yes, for so much." Then Peter said to her, "How is it that you have agreed together to test the Spirit of the Lord? Look, the feet of those who have buried your husband are at the door, and they will carry you out." Then immediately she fell down at his feet and breathed her last. And the young men came in and found her dead, and carrying her out, buried her by her husband. So great fear came upon all the church and upon all who heard these things.

Sapphira was granted a chance to repent: "Tell me whether you sold the land for so much?" She could still save herself with prompt repentance. But no, she added lie upon lie, and squandered her opportunity. Let us be sure to repent when time is provided for us to repent, or when our conscience stings over the wound of unrepented guilt, or when a fellow believer calls our sin to our attention. It is one thing to sin, but it is far worse to sin without remorse, or to sin and then protect your reputation with man rather than guard your relationship with God.

Peter had preached many sermons and his words had brought his hearers life. But here, his words bring death to Sapphira. Though we desire the salvation of all our hearers, we cannot be certain how our presentation of Christ's message will ultimately affect them. Some will believe and be saved, but sadly, others will refuse to repent and be condemned, as it is written, "To the one we are the aroma of death leading to death, and to the other the aroma of life leading to life. And who is sufficient for these things?" (II Corinthians 2:16).

At the news of these two deaths, "great fear" fell over both the believers in the church and also on "all who heard these things." When God is

THE DERBYSHIRE FAMILY COMMENTARY

forgotten, men and women are emboldened to sin. But when the presence and power and holiness of God are demonstrated, as in the story here, the fear of being a sinful man in the presence of a holy God can overflow from the church and bring the fear of sin even on unbelievers outside the church. It is this fear that moves unbelievers to be suddenly ashamed of their sin when in the presence of one of God's people. Unbelievers who proudly brandish their impure relationships, addictions, and unholy practices before their unbelieving friends are moved to hide these sins from the eyes of believers. They are often ashamed to speak of them in the presence of godly men and women, and are suddenly moved to apologize for vulgar speech said in the presence of a child of God, even though they speak crudely without conscience when with baser friends. May God's presence in us and our holy example lived out before them continue to move people to fear their sin rather than bask in it.

5:12-13
And through the hands of the apostles many signs and wonders were done among the people. And they were all with one accord in Solomon's porch. Yet none of the rest dared join them, but the people esteemed them highly.

Look at the remarkable effect of the Christ-empowered, Christ honoring church on the community at large: "The people esteemed them highly." The followers of Christ demonstrated His virtues so admirably that all who took notice of them were impressed by them. Their integrity in the marketplace and acts of charity on behalf of the needy quickly moved the community at large to appreciate them and hold the Christ-followers in high regard.

The people deeply respected the virtues of the believers, but after hearing what happened to Ananias and Sapphira, unbelievers dared not join in the Christians' worship meetings, their guilty conscience warning them that they were surely worthy of the same judgment that befell Ananias. In our day, I fear there may be too much emphasis placed on making our worship gatherings "seeker friendly." The presence of the Spirit of God here in Acts chapter 5 caused unbelievers to fear joining with those who were entering the presence of God. I am afraid that if there is no such fear, it is because they do not sense that God is near. The presence of God evokes the fear of God – if unbelievers are happy to attend worship services and feel no conviction over their sin, it may indicate that the Spirit of God is absent from the meeting. By all means, let us lovingly invite unbelievers to come to God, but let us by no means make our worship hour a time when sinners feel more welcome than the Holy Spirit.

5:14-16

And believers were increasingly added to the Lord, multitudes of both men and women, so that they brought the sick out into the streets and laid them on beds and couches, that at least the shadow of Peter passing by might fall on some of them. Also a multitude gathered from the surrounding cities to Jerusalem, bringing sick people and those who were tormented by unclean spirits, and they were all healed.

"Believers were increasingly added to the Lord." "Multitudes of men and women" were saved (verse 14). The judgment of God on Ananias and Sapphira deterred sinners who loved their sin from joining the family of faith (verse 13). But others, who preferred to be freed from sin rather than free to sin, were drawn in large numbers to worship the God who heals those who are "tormented" by sin and sickness and unclean spirits. Saving souls and healing sickness was the hallmark of the early church in Jerusalem in accordance with the ministry that the apostles had received from the Lord in Luke 9 (Luke 9:2), and again in Luke 10 (Luke 10:9).

God demands that we walk before Him in holiness. Surely, we cannot deny this lesson from the story of Ananias and Sapphira. Let us not dilute this truth, shirk this truth, or in any way fail to communicate this truth as we teach. But the Holy God who executes judgment on sinners is also the God who heals those who come to Him seeking His cure. He heals *everyone* who seeks His prescription for renewal. "...and they were *all* healed." Our Lord heals the sick. He healed withered hands, lame feet, bent backs, deaf ears, and blind eyes. Our Lord heals hearts when they are broken and our inner core when we are troubled. Knowing this, David prayed in Psalm 6:2, "Have mercy on me, O LORD, for I am weak; O LORD, heal me, for my bones are troubled." Our Lord even heals our soul and spirit when we sin against Him. Knowing this, David also prayed, "I said, 'LORD, be merciful to me; heal my soul, for I have sinned against You'" (Psalm 41:4). And even if our world should fall apart, God stands ready to heal that too. Psalm 60:2 says, "You have made the earth tremble; You have broken it; heal its breaches, for it is shaking."

"...And they were all healed." What a wonderful picture. Sickness, sin, emotional trauma, and all manner of catastrophe – all healed by the power of Christ through His church. Our Lord is the Great Physician "who forgives all your iniquities, who heals all your diseases" (Psalm 103:3). There is nothing He cannot cure.

5:17-20

Then the high priest rose up, and all those who were with him (which is the sect of the Sadducees), and they were filled with indignation, and laid their hands on the apostles and put them in the common prison. But at night an angel of the Lord opened the prison doors and brought them out, and said, "Go, stand in the temple and speak to the people all the words of this life."

In Acts 4:18 the authorities demanded that Peter and the apostles discontinue preaching in the name of Jesus. Peter and John told them up front that they could not submit to this God-defying demand, and now, one chapter later, seeing that the apostles truly had no intention of discontinuing their commitment to teach and heal in the name of Jesus, the high priest and "all those who were with him" had the apostles arrested once again. We are reminded that godly service does not protect us from ungodly persecutors. Jesus taught us that "if they persecuted Me, they will also persecute you" (John 15:20).

We are not told how many hours the apostles were behind bars, just as we are not told today how long present trials will last, but we are told that that very night an angel of the Lord opened the prison doors and instructed the apostles to return to the temple and "speak to the people all the words of this life." The NLT renders the angel's instruction as: "give the people this message of life!" The apostles were rescued by the angel – but not so that they could protect their own safety or to enjoy the comforts of life, no, they were freed in order to teach to all people "the words of this life." They were to teach of the eternal life that comes only through faith in Jesus (John 3:36). They were to teach on the abundant life that only Jesus gives (John 10:10). Oh, what a great message we have been given to share! Eternal, abundant living! How many people despair because the specter of death haunts their days and deprives them of peace? We have for them the words of life! How many others live with the nagging sense that their life is hollow and meaningless, endured rather than enjoyed because they have not found the purpose and promise of a life in and through Christ? We have for them the words of life! Jesus taught us what real living is – what it's like to live a fulfilling, joy-filled, meaningful life that never ends (John 6:63). Blessed with the opportunity to hear Jesus articulate "the message of life," Peter never wanted to leave the Lord's side. When asked if Peter wanted to turn back from following after Jesus, Peter replied, "Lord, to whom shall we go? You have the words of eternal life." Yes, the words of fulfilling, joy-filled, meaningful life that never ends have been given to us by Jesus. What else can we do but agree with Peter and follow Him with total devotion? Let us rise with excitement to join the apostles' work and teach to all people "the words of this life."

Growing up, I loved to sing the old hymn by Philip Bliss:

Sing them over again to me
Wonderful words of life
Let me more of their beauty see
Wonderful words of life
Words of life and beauty teach me faith and duty
Beautiful words, wonderful words
Wonderful words of life
Beautiful words, wonderful words
Wonderful words of life
Christ the blessed One, gives to all wonderful words of life
Sinner, list to the loving call
Wonderful words of life
Oh, so freely given, wooing us to heaven
Beautiful words, wonderful words
Wonderful words of life
Beautiful words, wonderful words
Wonderful words of life
Sweetly echo the Gospel call
Wonderful words of life
Offer pardon and peace to all
Wonderful words of life
Jesus, only Saviour, sanctifying forever
Beautiful words, wonderful words
Wonderful words of life
Beautiful words, wonderful words
Wonderful words of life

5:21-26

And when they heard that, they entered the temple early in the morning and taught. But the high priest and those with him came and called the council together, with all the elders of the children of Israel, and sent to the prison to have them brought. But when the officers came and did not find them in the prison, they returned and reported, saying, "Indeed we found the prison shut securely, and the guards standing outside before the doors; but when we opened them, we found no one inside!" Now when

the high priest, the captain of the temple, and the chief priests heard these things, they wondered what the outcome would be. So one came and told them saying, "Look, the men whom you put in prison are standing in the temple and teaching the people!" Then the captain went with the officers and brought them without violence, for they feared the people, lest they should be stoned.

The angel freed the apostles from jail and gave them the mission to return to the temple and resume the work of preaching the good news of life in Christ. We are impressed to see that they lost no time in obeying the angel's instructions and "entered the temple early in the morning and taught." Having so recently been arrested, we might have expected the apostles to be understandably concerned for their safety, but it seems they were more concerned with obeying the Lord than they were concerned with protecting themselves, providing for us an excellent example to follow.

In II Kings 1 we see Elijah being summoned by the ruling authorities, just as the apostles are summoned by the council of priests here. After 100 men tried to arrest Elijah and were consumed by fire from heaven, a third captain of fifty approached him. "And the third captain of fifty went up, and came and fell on his knees before Elijah, and pleaded with him, and said to him: 'Man of God, please let my life and the life of these fifty servants of yours be precious in your sight. Look, fire has come down from heaven and burned up the first two captains of fifties with their fifties. But let my life now be precious in your sight.' And the angel of the LORD said to Elijah, 'Go down with him; do not be afraid of him.' So he arose and went down with him to the king" (II Kings 1:13-15). The officers of the priests in our story here show a similar fear in carrying out their assigned task to summon Peter and the apostles to return for questioning. Like the third captain in II Kings 1, they approach God's servants peacefully, without threats or coercion, because they, too, feared for their lives if they treated God's servants irreverently. "They feared the people, lest they should be stoned." Such is often the blessed state of God's obedient servants. But when the Lord grants us protection like this and fills our detractors and enemies with fear like this, let us not think for a moment that these times of special protection are simply for our safe passage. His protection is provided to assure that His name is exalted, and His message is proclaimed. When we find ourselves unusually protected by the Lord's hand and see people of power demonstrate that they fear us, let us take that as a Spirit-directed opportunity to exalt God's name, proclaim His Good News publicly, and call on sinners to repent, as the apostles will nicely illustrate in the verses to come.

5:27-28
And when they had brought them, they set them before the council. And the high priest asked them, saying, "Did we not strictly command you not to teach in this name? And look, you have filled Jerusalem with your doctrine, and intend to bring this Man's blood on us!"

Once again, we find Peter and the apostles standing before the council of priests as men accused. The priests quickly voice the accusation made against God's servants, "Did we not strictly command you not to teach in this name? And look, you have filled Jerusalem with your doctrine!" The priests had scorned the commands of Jesus, but they were quick to demand that others obey their own commands. And so we find it still today that those most guilty of rebellion against God are often those most insistent that their own demands be met.

We are intrigued to see the convicting power of the broken conscience, even in the hearts of those most ferociously opposed to the Lord's authority. In Matthew 27:25 these same men, in the heat of their aggravated assault on Jesus, cried out, "His blood be on us and on our children." So driven by rebellion and hate, they felt, for a moment, that their sin of murder was justified. Now, however, the accusation brought from the lips of Jesus' righteous servants stung their conscience so badly that the council vehemently denied any culpability in Jesus' death. What they had been so proud of, and so vehemently in favor of just weeks before, they now could not bear to admit. Matthew Henry writes: "Thus are they convicted and condemned by their own consciences, and dread lying under that guilt in which they were not afraid to involve themselves."

We need not be harsh or mean-spirited when presenting the Gospel truth that "all have sinned and fall short of the glory of God" (Romans 3:23). Let us tenderly, powerfully present the truth that all men and women are sinners, and all sin leads to death. The Holy Spirit speaking to our hearers' God-given conscience brings the souls of the spiritually attuned to quick conviction. Hearing the "doctrine" of the apostles, the council members were cut to the heart over their role in Jesus' murder. Let us take confidence that the Spirit of the Lord can bring that same conviction for sin on hearers of the "doctrine" of Christ today.

5:29
But Peter and the other apostles answered and said: "We ought to obey God rather than men."

The council demands to know why the apostles defied their command to discontinue preaching the doctrine of Jesus, and in response, Peter repeats his statement from Acts 4:19. God instructs us to obey the ordinances of men. I Peter 2:13 says, "Submit yourselves to every ordinance of man for the Lord's sake." But if the laws of man conflict with the laws of God, the laws of God must take precedence. The apostles might have chosen a number of different avenues in their defense. They were doing good deeds for their community, and the power of God was working miracles through them. But rather than use these methods of self-defense, they simply went to the heart of the matter. God had commanded them to preach the gospel and make disciples of all the world, and they must obey this edict from God, regardless of the opposition. "We ought to obey God." We must obey God. We may incur the wrath of God-haters, we may be enticed by bad examples, we may find God's ways more difficult than the ways of others, but we must, above all things, follow the example of the apostles here and "obey God." If we find ourselves harassed by oppressors, tempters, scorners, or villains of any kind, let us hold fast to the example of the apostles and the battle cry of David in Psalm 119:115, "Depart from me, you evildoers, for I will keep the commandments of my God!"

5:30-32

The God of our fathers raised up Jesus whom you murdered by hanging on a tree. Him God has exalted to His right hand to be Prince and Savior, to give repentance to Israel and forgiveness of sins. And we are His witnesses to these things, and so also is the Holy Spirit whom God has given to those who obey Him.

With Spirit-infused boldness, Peter preaches to his accusers. He is more concerned with exalting the name of Jesus and calling his listeners to repentance than he is with self-defense. Though the council members did not revere Jesus, yet they claimed to revere God, so Peter uses their professed allegiance to God as a bridge to trusting in Jesus. "The God of our fathers raised up Jesus." The very God that they claimed to believe in is the very God who raised Jesus from the dead. Just as Jesus called on His God-fearing followers: "You believe in God, believe also in Me" (John 14:1), so Peter now urges the council to believe in Jesus because it was the God who they revered that raised Jesus from the dead.

If the leaders needed evidence to believe these things, Peter offered the testimony of the 12 men standing before them: "We are His witnesses to these things." Peter and the apostles saw Jesus alive after God resurrected

Him from the dead! They saw Him with their own eyes! And as further evidence, Peter says that the Holy Spirit also attests to the veracity of their testimony. The miraculous signs and wonders done by the apostles through the empowerment of the Spirit substantiated their message that Jesus is both "Prince and Savior."

All men and women must recognize that Jesus is "Prince." He is sovereign over all creation. His commands must be obeyed; His truths must be upheld; His purposes must be carried out. Jesus is also "Savior." The council members were guilty of murdering Jesus by hanging Him on a tree. And this sin, and all lesser sins, must be atoned for. The wages of sin is death and hell. All sinners need a Savior to rescue them from the penalty of their sin. And Jesus is the world's one and only Savior from sin. "Nor is there salvation in any other, for there is no other name under heaven given among men by which we must be saved" (Acts 4:12).

Some might pretend to think of Jesus as their Savior while denying that He is sovereign Prince. They happily take comfort in the thought of Jesus saving them from sin and admitting them into heaven, but they refuse to submit to Him as Sovereign Lord. But God has exalted Jesus to be "Prince" *and* "Savior." If we do not submit to Him as our Prince, we simultaneously reject Him as our Savior as well.

5:33
When they heard this, they were furious and plotted to kill them.

The words here are upsetting. These deeply religious men are proven to be nothing more than cold-blooded murderers. See how religion does nothing to curb evil dispositions. The elders and priests on this "council" (verse 21) plotted to kill these men who were "guilty" of preaching the gospel of Jesus, healing sick people, and delivering those who were "tormented by evil spirits" (verse 16). As we read the words from these sinister men plotting to murder the apostles, we want to cry out as Pilate cried out to the murderous crowd in Matthew 27:23, "Why, what evil has He done?" How can preaching the words of Jesus and healing the sick be grounds for execution? The old King James Version says that when the council heard Peter's words, "they were cut to the heart." They were "diaprio," which literally translated would mean they were sawn in two with a saw. Perhaps this wording helps us understand the viciousness of their attack. Peter's sermon cut to their heart; his words stung their conscience like a jagged saw. The Lord has made our conscience an extremely sensitive organ. When it is stung, the conscience brings exquisite pain. It is reflexive, defensive pain, similar to the pain that causes us to take our fingers off a hot stove with lightning speed. Peter's words stung the already bruised conscience of the elders, and the ensuing spiritual pain caused them to lash out reflexively as if stabbed with a knife. There is no reasonable justification for calling for the death of good men who heal the sick and religiously love God and love their neighbors as Jesus instructed them to do. But the wounded conscience is severely painful. As soon as it begins to sting us, we must rush to repent and receive our Lord's balm of forgiveness. An untreated stinging conscience will plague us with a constant painful impulse to commit further wrongs, just as the council members demonstrate here.

5:34-39

Then one in the council stood up, a Pharisee named Gamaliel, a teacher of the law held in respect by all the people, and commanded them to put the apostles outside for a little while. And he said to them: "Men of Israel, take heed to yourselves what you intend to do regarding these men. For some time ago Theudas rose up, claiming to be somebody. A number of men, about four hundred, joined him. He was slain, and all who obeyed him were scattered and came to nothing. After this man, Judas of Galilee rose up in the days of the census, and drew away many people after him. He also perished, and all who obeyed him were dispersed. And now I say to you, keep away from these men and let them alone; for if this plan or this work is of men, it will come to nothing; but if it is of God, you cannot overthrow it – lest you even be found to fight against God."

The council began open discussion regarding the immediate execution of Peter and the apostles (verse 33). With their lives seemingly in the balance, help arrived from an unexpected source. Gamaliel, a highly respected Pharisee and member of the council stood up in the meeting and advised his fellow countrymen to "take heed to yourselves what you intend to do regarding these men." The committee had long stopped listening to the whispers of the Holy Spirit, but apparently, their carnal mind was still open to the persuasions of sound logic. Gamaliel argued that if the apostles came from God, the committee could never defeat them, and if the apostles did not come from God, they would soon enough disappear and "come to nothing." At best, rash acts of violence against the apostles would prove to be unnecessary, and at worst, if these men did come from God, violence against them would turn out to be a fight against God Himself.

The council's response to Gamaliel's presentation reminds us that some men may be moved by rational arguments and sound logic even when they have barricaded themselves from listening to spiritual truths. May the Lord give us wisdom and insight to present truths in the manner that is most likely to favorably move our listeners. Let us always be ready to provide spiritual food for the spiritually hungry, but for those who cannot yet stomach a spiritual discussion, let us prepare light snacks of rational logic that may yet stimulate an appetite for soul food.

5:40-42

And they agreed with him, and when they had called for the apostles and beaten them, they commanded that they should not speak in the name of Jesus, and let them go. So they departed from the presence of the council, rejoicing that they were counted worthy to suffer shame for His name. And daily in the temple, and in every house, they did not cease teaching and preaching Jesus as the Christ.

Having decided already to let the apostles go, the council decided to beat them before they left. And once again they commanded the apostles to discontinue speaking "in the name of Jesus" even though the disciples had already openly stated their intention to continue preaching in Jesus' name despite these demands. Far from intimidating the apostles, the beatings they received caused them to rejoice! They found it an honor to be "counted worthy to suffer shame for His name." We are inspired by their response and are reminded that when glorifying the name of Jesus is our chief priority, the fear of physical pain is reduced, and the body's cry to flee discomfort is drowned out by the joyful song of the soul that finds such great delight in honoring the God who saved us.

Peter may well have been thinking of this event when he wrote in I Peter 4:13-14, "But rejoice to the extent that you partake of Christ's sufferings, that when His glory is revealed, you may also be glad with exceeding joy. If you are reproached for the name of Christ, blessed are you, for the Spirit of glory and of God rests upon you. On their part He is blasphemed, but on your part He is glorified." In Matthew 5:11-12 Jesus said, "Blessed are you when they revile and persecute you, and say all kinds of evil against you falsely for My sake. Rejoice and be exceedingly glad, for great is your reward in heaven, for so they persecuted the prophets who were before you." When we are persecuted for the cause of Christ, Jesus tells us that we are "blessed" and that we have cause to "rejoice" – and apparently the apostles felt blessed, because they were filled with joy, yes, *joy* because they were beaten. The joy of sharing in Christ's sufferings is a perfect antidote for the poison of persecution. The thrill that overtakes the soul while serving the

Lord's purposes is the perfect remedy for all physical discomfort, especially the discomfort that comes from persecution. Look at what is provided for the servants of Christ who suffer personal pain in His service: "The Spirit of glory and of God rests upon you" (I Peter 4:14). The disciples were able to rejoice in their sufferings because "the Spirit of glory" and the Spirit of God rests on those who endure persecution for the sake of the Kingdom of God. And we see here that the presence of the Spirit of God is enough to overcome the shame of public ridicule and the pain of cruel punishment. Our Lord does not promise to protect us all from persecution. But He does repeatedly remind us that if we do suffer persecution, that He will bless us with immeasurable joys.

Acts 6

6:1
Now in those days, when the number of the disciples was multiplying, there arose a complaint against the Hebrews by the Hellenists, because their widows were neglected in the daily distribution.

In the midst of the wonderful expansion of the early church, even as "the number of the disciples was multiplying" and the power and presence of the Holy Spirit was openly blessing the body of Christ, even in this blessed state, problems arose in the fellowship. We are reminded that problems are likely to arise even in the best of churches, among even the godliest saints. The complaint was made that the Greek speaking widows were "neglected" in the "daily distribution," while the Hebrew speaking widows were given some manner of daily provisions. In a demonstration of remarkable love and generosity, the church had sold possessions and donated from their means for the sake of the church widows who had difficulty providing for them-selves. The heart behind the program was praiseworthy, but the practical administration of the program proved complex. Perhaps the oversight was not accidental, but rooted in the deplorable sin of prejudice – a sin which still merits determination to purge from our church today. Or perhaps the oversight was unintentional and arose because some of the Greek speaking widows were not as well connected with those who were carrying out the daily distribution. Sin and self-centeredness are certainly at the core of many troubles in the church, but faultless people and faultless efforts are by no means immune from complaints just the same. Let us not feel defensive when criticism is leveled at us or at our church, for not all criticism signifies that actual wrongs have been committed. Let us rather examine the complaint with a sensitive spirit and then respond as best we can as the apostles demonstrate in the verses to follow.

6:2-4

Then the twelve summoned the multitude of the disciples and said, it is not desirable that we should leave the word of God and serve tables. Therefore, brethren, seek out from among you seven men of good reputation, full of the Holy Spirit and wisdom, whom we may appoint over this business; but we will give ourselves continually to prayer and to the ministry of the word.

After examining the problem at hand, the apostles concluded that the matter of care for the widows must be addressed. But they also saw that administration of this great work would require significant time and energy, which would diminish the time they could spend on studying and teaching the Word of God. As Moses was advised to delegate some of his responsibilities to the elders of Israel in Exodus 18, so the apostles now see the same need to delegate responsibility to others in the church. Teaching the words of God to the people of God is among the highest work given by God to man. II Timothy 3:17 tells us that it is through the instruction of the Word of God that the men of God become "complete." It is through the instruction of the Word of God that the men of God become "thoroughly equipped for every good work." Since, then, teaching God's Word is so foundational for the making and equipping of disciples, the apostles could not turn from this responsibility for the sake of any lesser task. Committing themselves anew to the great work of prayer and the ministry of the Word, the apostles initiated the process for establishing new leaders in the church who would oversee this important ministry of caring for needy widows.

Under the direction of the apostles, the church body was to select seven men who would direct the distribution of funds to the needy. This ministry of benevolence may be a lesser work than that of teaching God's Word, but that fact by no means demeans its importance. Just look at the qualifications required to carry out this role! The men must have a "good reputation." They must have proven themselves to be "full of the Holy

Spirit." And since discernment was needed to assure that the funds were rightly handled and the right people were helped in the right way, the men appointed must be filled with "wisdom" as well. Perhaps these men would be called upon to do little more than "serve tables," but every work carried out in care of God's people is of the utmost importance and requires godly men enabled by the gifts of the Holy Spirit to do the work in a way that glorifies the Father.

As for the apostles, after delegating the benevolence ministry to others, they reiterated their commitment to "give ourselves continually to prayer and to the ministry of the word." Should the Lord continue to call members of our family to this blessed work of shepherding the saints, may the apostles' example be the hallmark of our life of ministry. Let us give ourselves *continually* to prayer. Let us give ourselves *continually* to the study and teaching of God's Word. May all those closest to us testify to the hours we spend in prayer interceding on behalf of the lost and the saved alike, pleading that our Lord's will might be done here on earth just as it is in heaven. And may our ministry not be limited to a sermon or two each week, but be filled with constant devotion to the intense study of God's Word and an abundance of meetings with God's people where we are found discoursing with person after person, group after group on the great treasures contained in the pages of the Scriptures. May David's cry in Psalm 119:97 be our heart's cry as well: "Oh, how I love Your law! It is my meditation all the day." And then, let us rise from our meditation and memorization of God's Word and give the highest possible priority to teaching the words of God to the people of God so that the men and women of God "may be complete, thoroughly equipped for every good work."

6:5-7

And the saying pleased the whole multitude. And they chose Stephen, a man full of faith and the Holy Spirit, and Philip, Prochorus, Nicanor, Timon, Parmenas, and Nicolas, a proselyte from Antioch, whom they set before the apostles; and when they had prayed, they laid hands on them. Then the word of God spread, and the number of the disciples multiplied greatly in Jerusalem, and a great many of the priests were obedient to the faith.

It is difficult to please people. People come to us from so many backgrounds and have such widely varying past experiences and current opinions that if we do anything or say anything to please one person, it will almost necessarily mean that we will displease someone else. But here we see that in the midst of a heated controversy, where two sides clearly held different viewpoints, "the whole multitude" was "pleased" with the apostles' response to the conflict in the church. "The whole multitude" was "pleased." After decades in the Lord's service and dealing with countless controversies great and small, this almost parenthetical statement rivets my attention. "The saying pleased the whole multitude." "Behold, how good and how pleasant it is for brethren to dwell together in unity!" (Psalm 133:1). And oh, how elusive perfect unity can be. Ten men will rarely be in perfect unity in any matter. Unity among 100 men is rarer still. And for "the whole multitude" to see eye-to-eye on this controversy, the Spirit of God must draw near to guide and guard the hearts and tongues of men. If at any time we are blessed to enjoy the "multitude" of our church family enjoying unity and agreement for a time, we can lift up our hearts in joy-filled praise, knowing that our Lord has graciously drawn near to us to bless us like this.

Since the day people stopped working on Babel (Genesis 11), men and women have been filled with a divisive spirit of dis-union. If we say anything in our church or do anything in our church that proves to "please the whole multitude" let us not deceive ourselves into thinking that our winsome personality has brought this to pass. It is the Lord who builds the house (Psalm 127:1), and it is the Lord who builds unity in His people. In the early days of David's reign in Hebron, the nation was on the brink of all out civil war. Abner, the commander of Israel's army, was murdered while attempting to unite Israel and Judah together. But just as civil war seemed inevitable, David's actions saved the day. II Samuel 3:36 says, "Now all the people took note of (what the king had done), and it pleased them, *since whatever the king did pleased all the people*." May this type of pleasant unity permeate all our ministries, when everything that one saint does is pleasing in the eyes of all the rest of God's people.

Attempting to please people is a fool's errand. The old adage "you can't please everyone" is proven and re-proven by everyone who ever tries. In Galatians 1:10 Paul said that as a bondservant of Christ, he did not seek to please men. His heart was to please God, not people. But in a wonderful paradox, the godly man's pursuit of pleasing his Savior will often be blessed with unity among his fellow believers as well. And this unity yields such wonderful results! The apostles responded to the complaint, all the people were pleased with their response, and then "the word of God spread." Unity in the body of Christ was the forerunner for the addition of many souls into the kingdom of heaven. If disunity haunts our church, let us treat disharmony as an emergency, "endeavoring to keep the unity of the Spirit in the bond of peace" (Ephesians 4:3). Disharmony must be defeated before the Word of God will spread. But when perfect unity permeates our church, and when all our church members are "pleased," let our praise be lifted to the Lord who alone is the One who knits our hearts together (Colossians 2:2).

6:8-10

And Stephen, full of faith and power, did great wonders and signs among the people. Then there arose some from what is called the Synagogue of the Freedmen (Cyrenians, Alexandrians, and those from Cilicia and Asia), disputing with Stephen. And they were not able to resist the wisdom and the Spirit by which he spoke.

Stephen was not numbered among the 12 apostles. He was one of the seven deacons, entrusted with the responsibility of taking care of the poor. His role in the church was that of a servant. Peter compared his role to "serv(ing) tables" (verse 2). And yet, as he carried out his work as a servant of the church, we find him not only distributing donations to the poor, but preaching with so much power and wisdom that the religious scholars could not hold their ground in their spiritual discussions with him. We find him so filled with power that "great wonders" and miraculous signs were accomplished through him. Stephen provided food, money, and clothing for those who needed those things. But many people have needs that money cannot provide, and for those needs Stephen was endowed with remarkable "faith and power" through which God used him to miraculously provide for those whose needs could not be met by earthly means. Stephen did not hold the office of a preacher in the church, and yet his handling of the Scriptures overwhelmed the unbelieving scholars. Stephen was not an apostle, and yet, like the apostles, he was empowered by the Spirit to do "great wonders." We are reminded that children of God do not require special titles or special recognition before they can carry out the special works of God. Stephen was asked to "serve tables," and being found faithful in that task, the Lord called Him and equipped Him for higher service.

Gary preached on this concept beautifully in his sermon on II Samuel 5. II Samuel 5:2 says, "In time past, when Saul was king over us, you were the one who led Israel out and brought them in; and the LORD said to you, 'You shall shepherd My people Israel, and be ruler over Israel.'" Saul was king. David was not. But in his sermon, Gary said, "You do not have to wait for a different title to perform higher service." David did not wait to be crowned king before he cared for and protected his people. He was called to higher service and he did so even without a kingly title. Stephen's life mirrored

David's in this respect. He was not an apostle, but he was called to higher service for the Savior's causes, and his lack of a special title neither disqualified him from that service nor handicapped his ministry in any way.

In Stephen's case, he was deeply respected by his fellow believers. They recognized that he was "full of faith and power" (verse 8) and filled with the Holy Spirit (verse 5). In David's case, however, this was not always true. Nabal in I Samuel 25 and a host of others before and after Nabal gave David no respect at all. Gary's insights on this were excellent once again when he said, "You do not have to be appreciated or recognized to be called to higher service." Gary went on to say, "It is God alone who calls us to higher service, it is God alone who sustains us in higher service, and it is God alone who prospers us in higher service." All of these points are clearly demonstrated in the life of Stephen, who had no apostolic title, but was clearly equipped with the power of the Holy Spirit just as the apostles were.

Should the Lord call us to higher service, let us not seek titles, recognition, or appreciation from men. Instead, let us draw near to the throne of grace that we might continually kneel in the presence of God. For it is the presence and power of His Spirit which sustains us and equips us for the work at hand, not the titles and accolades of men.

6:11-15

Then they secretly induced men to say, "We have heard him speak blasphemous words against Moses and God." And they stirred up the people, the elders, and the scribes; and they came upon him, seized him, and brought him to the council. They also set up false witnesses who said, "This man does not cease to speak blasphemous words against this holy place and the law; for we have heard him say that this Jesus of Nazareth will destroy this place and change the customs which Moses delivered to us." And all who sat in the council, looking steadfastly at him, saw his face as the face of an angel.

I Peter 4:14 says that those who are "reproached for the name of Christ" are blessed, "for the Spirit of glory and of God rests upon you." We are here provided a glimpse of what it looks like to have the "Spirit of glory" rest upon us. As Stephen was falsely accused, and as his death sentence approached, he sat before his hate-filled, lying accusers in complete peace. His face shone "as the face of an angel." Psalm 46:1 says that "God is our refuge and strength, a very present help in trouble." And here we see that in Stephen's trouble, the Lord was "very present." Stephen's loving Savior drew very near, and his countenance reflected the glorious nearness of

His Lord. Matthew Henry writes of Stephen: "Such an undisturbed serenity, such an undaunted courage, and such an unaccountable mixture of mildness and majesty, there was in his countenance, that every one said he looked like an angel." Lange says in his commentary, "God manifest(s) his glory in his servants, especially when they suffer," for when they suffer, "'the Spirit of glory' (I Peter 4:14) rests upon them." In his wonderfully titled commentary, Lange's Commentary on the Holy Scriptures: Critical, Doctrinal, and Homiletical, he gives an insightful discourse on the angelic face of Stephen. He writes that Stephen's face shone like an angel because 1) His countenance reflected the face of Jesus who says to His servants, "In the world you shall have tribulation, but be of good cheer: I have overcome the world" (John 16:33). 2) The glow of his countenance was "the radiance of his inward assurance of faith, which exclaimed: 'If God be for us, who can be against us?'" (Romans 8:31). 3) Stephen's angelic countenance "was the effulgence (radiance) of that future glory with which 'the sufferings of this present time are not worthy to be compared'" (Romans 8:18). It was "the serenity that appears on the countenance of a believer who has fallen asleep in the Lord." 4) Stephen's face shone with "the departing light of an earthly existence that closes in peace in God." And 5) The glow on his face "is the dawning light of eternity approaching with the (radiance) of heaven."

Let us be reminded that our glory does not depend on our level of comfort, and, more importantly, the glory of God that is reflected and radiated by us is not dependent on our comfort level either. With Stephen's example painted so vividly before us, let us strive to flee temptation rather than flee trouble, and let us fear sin so much more than we fear suffering. For the glory of God is obscured by our sin, but may be wonderfully illuminated in our suffering.

Acts 7

7:1-8

Then the high priest said, "Are these things so?" And he said, "Brethren and fathers, listen: The God of glory appeared to our father Abraham when he was in Mesopotamia, before he dwelt in Haran, and said to him, 'Get out of your country and from your relatives, and come to a land that I will show you.' Then he came out of the land of the Chaldeans and dwelt in Haran. And from there, when his father was dead, He moved him to this land in which you now dwell. And God gave him no inheritance in it, not even enough to set his foot on. But even when Abraham had no child, He promised to give it to him for a possession, and to his descendants after him. But God spoke in this way: that his descendants would dwell in a foreign land, and that they would bring them into bondage and oppress them four hundred years. 'And the nation to whom they will be in bondage I will judge,' said God, 'and after that they shall come out and serve Me in this place.' Then He gave him the covenant of circumcision; and so Abraham begot Isaac and circumcised him on the eighth day; and Isaac begot Jacob, and Jacob begot the twelve patriarchs."

Stephen is on trial. It is an illegitimate trial with false charges, false witnesses, and corrupt judges, and his life hangs in the balance. Yet when the high priest gives Stephen the floor, we are amazed to see that he does not speak a single word in his own defense. Rather than provide evidence of his innocence, Stephen preaches a spontaneous sermon, walking through God's covenant-centered relationship with His people (verses 5,8,17), His peoples' deplorable response (verses 39,52), and the need for his listeners to repent of resisting the Holy Spirit (verse 51), murdering Jesus (verse 52), and failure to keep God's law (verse 53). Stephen appears to have no regard for his personal well-being. He is completely consumed with his desire to see God exalted and see men repent of their sin and reconcile with Jesus.

Following Jesus' example when facing a similar trial, Stephen does not waste even a single word talking about himself. He speaks, instead, of "the God of glory." He is accused of blasphemy, but this reverent, exalting title for God shows plainly that Stephen was no blasphemer. He revered the Lord as "the God of glory." Stephen reminded his listeners, and reminds us, his readers, that our God is "the God of glory," and "great is the glory of the Lord" (Psalm 138:5). His glory is "above the heavens" (Psalm 8:1). The glory of our God "was like a consuming fire on top of the mountain" in Exodus 24:17. And in heaven, the glory of God will shine like the sun (Revelation 21:23). The glorious splendor of our holy, omnipotent God is overwhelming to consider. The glory of the Lord caused John to fall before him "as dead" in Revelation 1:17 and caused all the people to tremble before Mt. Sinai in Exodus 19. After God's victory at the Red Sea, Moses sang of the incomparable glory of God: "Who is like You, O LORD, among the gods? Who is like You, glorious in holiness, fearful in praises, doing wonders?" (Exodus 15:11). When given the opportunity, Stephen chose to speak of the glory of God rather than speak on his own behalf. May it be that way for all of us when we happily take our eyes off our own paltry importance and set our gaze on the God of amazing, incomparable, unsurpassable glory.

7:9-16

"And the patriarchs, becoming envious, sold Joseph into Egypt. But God was with him and delivered him out of all his troubles, and gave him favor and wisdom in the presence of Pharaoh, king of Egypt; and he made him governor over Egypt and all his house. Now a famine and great trouble came over all the land of Egypt and Canaan, and our fathers found no sustenance. But when Jacob heard that there was grain in Egypt, he sent out our fathers first. And the second time Joseph was made known to his brothers, and Joseph's family became known to the Pharaoh. Then

Joseph sent and called his father Jacob and all his relatives to him, seventy-five people. So Jacob went down to Egypt; and he died, he and our fathers. And they were carried back to Shechem and laid in the tomb that Abraham bought for a sum of money from the sons of Hamor, the father of Shechem."

Stephen continues his sermon to the extremely hostile crowd. He summarizes the life of Joseph, reminding his listeners that the reason Joseph was delivered out of all his troubles was that "God was with him." The priests and scribes and religious leaders were convinced that they were destined to receive the blessings of God because they were descendants of Abraham. But Stephen reminds them that Joseph's blessings did not arise simply from his relation to Abraham, but because "God was with him." Our bloodline cannot save us. Religion alone cannot save us. If we are to receive the blessings that granted Joseph success, if we are to obtain rescue from the penalty of sin, we must cling to Immanuel, God with us. If God is with us, the destiny of our soul is secure. If God is not with us as He was with Joseph, however, we have little hope for this life, and no hope at all for the life to come.

7:17-28

"But when the time of the promise drew near which God had sworn to Abraham, the people grew and multiplied in Egypt till another king arose who did not know Joseph. This man dealt treacherously with our people, and oppressed our forefathers, making them expose their babies, so that they might not live. At this time Moses was born, and was well pleasing to God; and he was brought up in his father's house for three months. But when he was set out, Pharaoh's daughter took him away and brought him up as her own son. And Moses was learned in all the wisdom of the Egyptians, and was mighty in words and deeds. Now when he was forty years old, it came into his heart to visit his brethren, the children of Israel. And seeing one of them suffer wrong, he defended and avenged him who was oppressed, and struck down the Egyptian. For he supposed that his brethren would have understood that God would deliver them by his hand, but they did not understand. And the next day he appeared to two of them as they were fighting, and tried to reconcile them, saying, 'Men, you are brethren; why do you wrong one another?' But he who did his neighbor wrong pushed him away, saying, 'Who made you a ruler and a judge over us? Do you want to kill me as you did the Egyptian yesterday?'

Stephen continues his sermon, giving further confirmation that his heart's desire is not to defend his innocence but to awaken his listeners to their need to reconcile with God. He began with Abraham, proceeded with Joseph and the "patriarchs," and now he continues the narrative with a discussion of the early life of Moses. Stephen intentionally mentions the Egyptians' violent oppression of the people of Israel by "making them expose their babies" – killing the infants of the infant Hebrew nation. In striking similarity to the Egyptian oppressors, Stephen's hearers were actively seeking to oppress and destroy the infant believers of the early church in Jerusalem. But both efforts would fail. Just as the Lord protected His people from the Egyptian tormentors, so He will now protect His church from their present-day persecutors.

Stephen is also intentional in pointing out to his hearers that Moses defended his fellow Israelite because he "supposed that his brethren would have understood that God would deliver them by his hand, but they did not understand." In a clear parallel, Jesus came to save the lost (Luke 19:10), with good cause to expect that His people would understand. But just like the uninsightful Israelites did not understand Moses' role to rescue them, so Stephen's accusers "did not understand" that Jesus came to save them from their sins. The brutish ignorance of the Israelites who opposed Moses are re-exemplified in the brutish ignorance of Jesus' and now Stephen's accusers. The striking similarity between how the early Israelites treated Moses and how Stephen's accusers treated Jesus and His followers will quickly overwhelm Stephen with righteous indignation and lead to the sudden, powerful indictment of his hearers that is fast approaching in verses 51-53.

7:29-35

"Then, at this saying, Moses fled and became a dweller in the land of Midian, where he had two sons. And when forty years had passed, an Angel of the Lord appeared to him in a flame of fire in a bush, in the wilderness of Mount Sinai. When Moses saw it, he marveled at the sight; and as he drew near to observe, the voice of the Lord came to him, saying, 'I am the God of your fathers – the God of Abraham, the God of Isaac, and the God of Jacob.' And Moses trembled and dared not look. Then the LORD said to him, 'Take your sandals off your feet, for the place where you stand is holy ground. I have surely seen the oppression of my people who are in Egypt; I have heard their groaning and have come down to deliver them. And now come, I will send you to Egypt.' This Moses whom they rejected, saying, 'Who made you a ruler and a judge?' is the one God

sent *to be* a ruler and a deliverer by the hand of the Angel who appeared to him in the bush."

Stephen continues his powerful discourse drawing an unmissable comparison between the ancient Jews' rejection of Moses and Stephen's contemporaries who rejected Jesus. "The one God sent to be a ruler and a deliverer" was the one that "they rejected." As slaves in Egypt, God's people were desperately in need of a deliverer. But when the Lord raised up Moses to rescue them, their evil pride and lack of spiritual insight moved them to ask their sneering question, "Who made you a ruler and a judge?" In the same way, the Jews listening to Stephen were in desperate need of a Savior. But when God sent Jesus to save His own people, "His own did not receive Him" (John 1:11). Isaiah 53:3 prophesied that Jesus would be "despised and rejected by men," and Jesus confirmed that He must be "rejected by this generation" (Luke 17:25). But though He was despised and rejected by men, Jesus was "chosen by God and precious" (I Peter 2:4). The leaders' rejection of Jesus in no way diminished His authority or the fact that the foundation of man's salvation rests completely in Him. Psalm 118:22 foretold, "The stone which the builders rejected has become the chief cornerstone," and in Mark 12:10 Jesus confirmed that this Psalm spoke of Him. As Moses came to deliver his people from Egypt, so Jesus came to deliver His people from sin. Sadly, just as the people of Israel had once rejected Moses, now they had rejected Jesus just the same.

Stephen was on trial, charged with blasphemy against Moses (Acts 6:11). But the Jews' rejection of Jesus mirrored their ancestors' contempt for Moses, and Stephen powerfully demonstrates that, in fact, it was his accusers who were the ones guilty of rejecting and blaspheming their deliverer. This counter accusation by Stephen will cut his hearers to the heart (verse 54), but rather than repent of their guilt, they will deepen their guilt as we will soon see.

7:36-43

"He brought them out, after he had shown wonders and signs in the land of Egypt, and in the Red Sea, and in the wilderness forty years. This is that Moses who said to the children of Israel, 'The LORD your God will raise up for you a Prophet like me from your brethren. Him you shall hear.' This is he who was in the congregation in the wilderness with the Angel who spoke to him on Mount Sinai, and with our fathers, the one who received the living oracles to give to us, whom our fathers would not obey, but rejected. And in their hearts they turned back to Egypt, saying to Aaron,

'Make us gods to go before us; as for this Moses who brought us out of the land of Egypt, we do not know what has become of him.' And they made a calf in those days, offered sacrifices to the idol, and rejoiced in the works of their own hands. Then God turned and gave them up to worship the host of heaven, as it is written in the book of the Prophets: 'Did you offer Me slaughtered animals and sacrifices during forty years in the wilderness, O house of Israel? You also took up the tabernacle of Moloch, and the star of your god Remphan, images which you made to worship; and I will carry you away beyond Babylon.'"

The charge against Stephen that he had spoken blasphemous words against Moses (Acts 6:11) appears more and more ridiculous as Stephen's Moses-honoring discourse continues. And once again, he subtly and smoothly, yet powerfully delivers the counter accusation that it was his accusers who were the ones guilty of following in the path of those who despised Moses. Stephen quotes Moses' words from Deuteronomy 18:15, "The LORD your God will raise up for you a Prophet like me from your brethren. Him you shall hear." The Prophet that Moses spoke of, of course, is Jesus. Moses taught the people that God the Father would put His words in the mouth of the Prophet (Deuteronomy 18:18), and that the people must listen to and obey all that He says, stating, "Him you shall hear."

Stephen does not yet outright accuse his listeners of rejecting the Prophet that Moses commanded them to obey (he will soon enough), but he does remind them that when the people rejected Moses that "God turned" (verse 42). When the people despised Moses' teachings, "God turned away from them" (NLT) – a horrifying prospect. God had given Moses "the living oracles," the words of life, and Moses was faithful in communicating the "living and powerful" word of God (Hebrews 4:12) to His people. Tragically, however, the people "would not obey" God's word and they "would not obey" Moses, the one God sent to them as both deliverer and prophet, rescuer and messenger from heaven. Oh, the love of God which moves Him to rescue His people and communicate to them His heart. Certainly, anyone who would scorn God's merciful provision through the leadership of Moses would be worthy of severe punishment – and so no one could be surprised that the Lord destroyed their nation for their rejection of His prophet and carried them "away beyond Babylon" as captives in a foreign land.

Stephen is preparing his audience for his scathing accusation that is just a few verses away. God entrusted Moses with His "living oracles," His life-giving words, and called Moses to deliver His message of hope and deliver His people from their humiliation in Egypt. But the people shamefully rejected the prophet-deliverer Moses — and their rejection of their Heaven-sent rescuer brought calamity "beyond Babylon" upon them. Now, just as Moses prophesied, God sent Jesus to His people to deliver them from sin. Stephen's message is ominous. If God punished His people for rejecting Moses, how much more will He punish those who reject His Son? Stephen's time on earth is drawing to a close. His martyrdom is at hand. But his final words are a powerful call for his listeners not to repeat the sins of Israel's past, but to rush to embrace the Savior-Prophet sent by God. May we respond better to Stephen's message than his original hearers did.

7:44-53

"Our fathers had the tabernacle of witness in the wilderness, as he appointed, instructing Moses to make it according to the pattern that he had seen, which our fathers, having received it in turn, also brought with Joshua into the land possessed by the Gentiles, whom God drove out before the face of our fathers until the days of David, who found favor before God and asked to find a dwelling for the God of Jacob. But Solomon built Him a house. However, the Most High does not dwell in temples made with hands, as the prophet says: "Heaven is My throne, and earth is My footstool. What house will you build for Me? Says the LORD, or what is the place of My rest? Has My hand not made all these things?" You stiff-necked and uncircumcised in heart and ears! You always resist the Holy Spirit; as your fathers did, so do you. Which of the prophets did your fathers not persecute? And they killed those who foretold the coming of the Just One, of whom you now have become the betrayers and murders, who have received the law by the direction of angels and have not kept it."

Stephen was abducted and forced to endure a sham trial, accused of blaspheming Moses and God (6:11) and speaking blasphemous words against the temple and the law (6:13). He was given the floor to make his defense (7:1), and his opening comments demonstrated his deep reverence for God and his high respect for Moses, clearly refuting the first two charges of blasphemy. He now moves to answer the charge of speaking blasphemous words against the temple. Stephen reminds his audience of the prophet's words in Isaiah 66:1, "Heaven is My throne, and earth is My footstool. Where is the house that you will build Me?" In some ways, yes, the temple was the dwelling place of God. But in reality, the temple could not pretend to contain the limitless majesty of the eternal Creator. But what the temple could not do, Christ Himself did by sending His people the Holy Spirit to dwell in the hearts of His children in a way the temple could not equal. The temple, which was wonderful in its depiction of the dwelling place of God, was properly held dear by God's people. But it brought no disrespect to the temple to say that the temple's days were past, for now God dwells in the hearts of those who trust Him. Just as the tabernacle was once revered as God's resting place but was shown no disrespect when it was replaced with Solomon's temple, so now, Stephen refutes the claim that he has blasphemed the temple by teaching that the Lord now dwells in His people.

Stephen's sermon is complete. He has walked through the history of God's dealings with Israel from Abraham to Solomon, and in doing so he exonerated himself of holding any blasphemous beliefs toward God. His sermon also highlighted Israel's repetitive acts of rebellion against God and persecution of God's servants. And now, suddenly, "with irrepressible indignation and a flaming zeal" (Lange Commentary on the Holy Scriptures), Stephen lashes out at his accusers for following in the footsteps of their "fathers" as "betrayers and murderers" of Jesus, "the Just One," and persecuting and killing those who served Him. They were without excuse! They could not claim ignorance! They had "received the law by the direction of angels" and they had "not kept it." The Scriptures foretold the coming of Jesus, and they missed His arrival. The prophets named His birthplace, described His ministry, and even pictured the donkey that He would ride on into Jerusalem. But Stephen's audience had rebelled against God, disobeyed His laws, and oppressed those sent to call them to repentance – just as their fathers had done. As Jesus called the Pharisees sons of the Devil in John 8:44, so Stephen now calls his accusers sons of the murderous rebels in Israel's past. Tragically, when Jesus spoke those words in John 8, His enraged hearers picked up stones to stone Him (John 8:59), and they will respond in the exact same way to Stephen's conscience-wounding accusation now.

7:54
When they heard these things they were cut to the heart, and they gnashed at him with their teeth.

Stephen's powerful sermon has ended, and his words stabbed the conscience of his accusers like a knife. Everything that Stephen said was true, but the truth often hurts, especially when the light of the truth burns an open wound on a stinging conscience. They could not refute Stephen's words, but that did not lessen their seething hatred for his words, and they "gnashed at him with their teeth." Our eyes are drawn to the phrase, "When they heard these things they were cut to the heart." In Acts 2:37, after Peter's sermon, the Word preached yielded the same effect on the hearts of the hearers: "They were cut to the heart." In Acts 2, however, after being "cut to the heart," the people repented of their sin and rushed to reconcile with God and place their faith in Jesus. Here, after being cut to the heart by Stephen's sermon, Stephen's hearers "gnashed at him with their teeth" and rather than repent, they were sent into a rage that would cause them to murder Stephen. Both crowds were "cut to the heart" by the sermons they heard. In the instance in Acts 2, the people were overwhelmed with sorrow and cried out, "What shall we do?" Here in Acts 7, however, the crowd gnashed at Stephen with their teeth and murdered him.

Two sermons were delivered by holy men of God. Two messages calling on the hearers to repent were communicated. But in one instance people responded to God's Word with repentance, and in the other instance the people responded with loathing and anger and murder. What made the difference? Both Peter in Acts 2 and Stephen in Acts 7 were holy servants of God who demonstrated the power of the Spirit's presence. Both men spoke boldly and brought the sins of their hearers to the front of their attention. The difference did not lie in the speaker. The difference did not lie in the message or the presentation of the message. The difference was in the hearts of the hearers. All men are sinners. But some men hate their sin and long to be holy, while others delight in their sin and take offense at any urging to change. All of us are estranged from our Creator because of our sin, but some long to be right with God, while others demand to be their own god, or at least demand the right to tell their god what he can and cannot require of them. Such is the case here. The word was preached in Acts 2 and the hearers were convicted of sin and clung to the opportunity to have that sin forgiven. Here, the word was also preached, and the hearers were also convicted of sin. But they preferred pretended autonomy to reconciliation with God. And they scorned forgiveness for the sake of holding on to their pet sin.

7:55-56

But he, being full of the Holy Spirit, gazed into heaven and saw the glory of God, and Jesus standing at the right hand of God, and said, "Look! I see the heavens opened and the Son of Man standing at the right hand of God!"

Stephen was surrounded by enemies, but they did not trouble him much, because his gaze was concentrated on heaven. There was a look of hatred on the faces of the powerful group around him, but their hateful glares did not trouble him either, because he was gazing into heaven. If at any time we find ourselves paralyzed by fear or crippled with anxiety, perhaps the problem is not with the trouble that surrounds us, but on the focal point of our gaze. If our gaze is on our troubles, we will likely find cause to worry. But if our gaze is on the "glory of God" we will be hard pressed to concern ourselves with matters of personal discomfort. Peter's walk on the water pictures this for us nicely. Jesus invited Peter to walk with him on the sea, and Peter finds himself capable of walking on water! – as long as his gaze was on the Son of Man. But as soon as Peter took his gaze off of Jesus and looked at the wind whipping the waves around him, he became afraid and began to sink. Our Lord assures us that no matter what dangers or troubles or failures or pains surround us, He will grant perfect peace to all those who fix their gaze on Him (Isaiah 26:3). When battered by trouble, let us follow the example of Stephen and make our prayer the prayer of Jehoshaphat in II Chronicles 20:12, "We have no power against this great multitude that is coming against us; nor do we know what to do, but our eyes are upon You."

7:57-58
Then they cried out with a loud voice, stopped their ears, and ran at him with one accord; and they cast him out of the city and stoned him. And the witnesses laid down their clothes at the feet of a young man named Saul.

The world is at its worst when wicked people take the life of godly men and women. Stephen's caring ministry and noble character were well described in chapter 6. He possessed a kind heart, a sharp intellect, and a powerful presence. But these qualities do not endear God's people to evil men. Let us not mistakenly believe that being right with God will make us popular with people. Stephen's last work on earth was to deliver a sermon which walked through the Bible's account of God's dealings with His people, and His people's repeatedly poor response. Rather than be cut to the heart and repent of their sin, they murdered the messenger in an effort to silence the accusing voice in their head. Stephen's listeners rushed on him, shouting out loud from the intense, searing pain of a guilty conscience.

We read this account of Stephen's murder, his martyrdom at the hands of religious evil people, and we are moved to pause in silence for a moment, desiring to give Stephen the honor that was denied him by this hostile crowd of wretches. And yet, at the same time, we realize that we cannot begin to honor him as Jesus did, rising from His throne in heaven to stand in Stephen's honor and welcome him into paradise (verse 56). Godliness may not grant us popularity with men, but it does grant us favor with our Creator, who assures us that He will not forget our efforts done on His behalf (Hebrews 6:10). Let us not be disheartened by Stephen's violent murder.

Verses 57-58 trouble our soul. But verse 56 reminds us that God will honor His faithful servants when the world treats them poorly. He will not allow his servants to be denied the honor due them, nor will He leave His people leaderless. When Moses passed away, the Lord raised up Joshua in his place. When Joshua passed away, the Lord raised up judges to take his place (Judges 2:16). And when Jesus returned to the Father in heaven, He sent His Spirit to guide us in His absence. Sometimes there is a clear heir to carry on the ministry of godly men – as Elisha carried on in Elijah's stead. But sometimes, the Lord raises up His choicest servants from the most unlikely of places. And so it is here, as the writer of Acts gives us this prescient picture "of a young man named Saul." Stephen is here taken from his glorious ministry on earth to receive his glorious reward in heaven. And quite unpredictably, rising up in his place, this murderous young Saul will soon pick up Stephen's gauntlet and become a Spirit-filled, powerful articulator of the wonderful truths of God.

7:59-60

And they stoned Stephen as he was calling on God and saying, "Lord Jesus, receive my spirit." Then he knelt down and cried out with a loud voice, "Lord, do not charge them with this sin." And when he had said this, he fell asleep.

Stephen's body is being stoned. It will soon pass away and be of no further use to him. But he will not miss it. The eyes of his spirit are on the Lord Jesus, and the sight of the Lord makes him unmindful of his physical well-being. His prayer and his anticipation is that his spirit will be received into the presence of the Lord. Oh, the wonder of the Christian's expectation. Stephen here displays that which all God's children are allowed to experience – that our soul lives even as our body dies. Our spirit can be refreshed even when fatigue wears our body down. Our soul can be full and fulfilled even when our body hungers and thirsts. Our body may be in pain, or wracked with illness, or surrounded by danger. But our spirit can be safe and secure and in comfort in the Savior's arms. Stephen's prayer, "Lord

Jesus, receive my spirit," reminds us that blows to our body cannot touch our soul. Our spirit is safe in the arms of the Savior who has promised us that He will do just as Stephen asks: He will "receive" us unto Himself that where He is, we shall be also (John 14:3).

Stephen's final moments on earth are recorded to inspire us by his remarkable example. As children of God, we are called upon to live like Jesus. We are to "walk just as He walked" (I John 2:6). And here we are granted this picture of a godly man who lived like Jesus, and then, when sudden death overtook him, we find that he was ready to die like Jesus too. In Luke 23:46, as Jesus laid down His life, He spoke from Psalm 31:5, "Into Your hands I commit My spirit." And in keeping with his Lord's example, Stephen does the same by stating, "Lord Jesus, receive my spirit." Jesus, suffering the agonizing death of crucifixion, looked down on His murderers and cried out in Luke 23:34, "Father, forgive them, for they do not know what they do." And Stephen, suffering an agonizing death by stoning, again follows his Lord's example and cries out with a loud voice, "Lord, do not charge them with this sin." Like Jesus in life, like Jesus in death, and like Jesus in resurrection. May our future hope of resurrection allow us to imitate Christ today, regardless of the setting.

Acts 8

8:1-4

Now Saul was consenting to his death. At that time a great persecution arose against the church which was at Jerusalem; and they were all scattered throughout the regions of Judea and Samaria, except the apostles. And devout men carried Stephen to his burial, and made great lamentation over him. As for Saul, he made havoc of the church, entering every house, and dragging off men and women, committing them to prison. Therefore those who were scattered went everywhere preaching the word.

We find here the church troubled by much sorrow and persecution-induced scattering. "Devout men" who loved the Lord "made great lamentation" over the loss of such a beloved leader in the church. Their sorrow was deepened by the "great persecution" which became more and more widespread following Stephen's death. Good men and women whose only crime was their faith in Jesus were dragged from their homes and imprisoned. Saul "made havoc of the church." Fellowships that met together in homes were raided and members dragged away from their family. Meeting together became increasingly dangerous. Perhaps some became disillusioned, perhaps some despaired that the world would soon over-power God's people. But even in this unhappy narrative we find evidence that God is in control and that He is protecting His church. The violent per-secution of the church drove many believers away. In fact, the persecution drove almost everyone away – "except the apostles." Usually, persecution affects church leaders first. Pastors and Christians in the public eye are far more vulnerable to persecution than the quieter, less conspicuous followers of Christ. But the Lord's hand was on His church. The members were scat-tered, but the key leaders, the apostles, were not scattered. They were protected by the Lord so that they could continue to care for the spiritual needs of the young believers. Perhaps it appeared to some that the church was being destroyed, but the Lord was providing His people what they needed even more than safety – the presence of His Spirit and the blessing of godly leadership. Equipped with these gifts, the early church continued to thrive despite the persecution.

The apostles were not scattered, and perhaps providing an even clearer sign that the Lord was moving even in the midst of the persecution, people who fled from the persecution "went everywhere preaching the word." They did not flee persecution and hide out in anonymity. They fled Jerusalem and promptly preached the Good News in their new haven. In Matthew 10:23, Jesus gave this instruction to His followers: "When they persecute you in this city, flee to another." And in obedience to that di-rective, His people fled Jerusalem to other cities. But persecution did not turn God's people into fugitives, it turned them into missionaries. Gary says, "There is no evil that God cannot redeem for His purposes," and we can hardly find that statement more vividly displayed than in this story here. It is not that the persecution had no effect on God's people. A great many godly men and women "made great lamentation" over the death of their brothers and sisters and the evil treatment shown to the church. But despite these reasons to lament, the early church could also take much comfort in knowing that the Lord was using the persecution to fulfill His intention to expand His Kingdom.

Some early believers were martyred, and the early church was sorely wounded by this severe persecution. But "there is no evil that God cannot redeem for His purposes." This understanding can provide much comfort in difficult times.

8:5-8

Then Philip went down to the city of Samaria and preached Christ to them. And the multitudes with one accord heeded the things spoken by

Philip, hearing and seeing the miracles which he did. For unclean spirits, crying with a loud voice, came out of many who were possessed; and many who were paralyzed and lame were healed. And there was great joy in that city.

Acts 6:5 lists the names of the seven men who were chosen to oversee the church's benevolence ministry. Stephen is listed first, and the story of his remarkable power in the Spirit and ultimate martyrdom is recorded in chapter 7. The second person listed among these special seven is Philip. And here we are granted a glimpse of his ministry. Philip was called to higher service by the church. He was specifically given a leadership role in the matter of distributing provisions for the needy widows among the believers. But just as we saw that Stephen's ministry was much larger than simply helping "serve tables" (Acts 6:2), so we now see that Philip's ministry also extended far beyond the confines of care for widows.

Philip traveled cross-culturally to Samaria and "preached Christ." Jesus is the very center, the very heart of the gospel, so much so that to preach the gospel is to "preach Christ." To preach the great things of God is to "preach Christ." May this short summary-description of Philip's preaching ministry not be lost on us. If we are preaching exegetical sermons through the Old Testament, or preaching verse by verse through the New Testament, or even if we are preaching a topical sermon on a matter of contemporary relevance, let us follow Philip's example and "preach Christ."

We find here that the effect of Philip's ministry was that "there was great joy in that city." God's word, rightly delivered and rightly received, brings joy to the recipients. The word preached may bring "godly sorrow" (II Corinthians 7:10) for a time as the hearers cry over the stain of their sins. But godly sorrow turns to repentance that leads to salvation (II Corinthians 7:10) and our salvation fills God's people with joy as we rejoice in the God of that salvation (Habakkuk 3:18). The preacher of the gospel is entrusted with distributing to his listeners "the oil of joy" (Isaiah 61:3) so that we may be "clothed with gladness" (Psalm 31:10). As Philip "preached Christ," people were delivered from unclean spirits, they were healed of disease, and they were filled with the joy of knowing God and experiencing His forgiveness.

The world is filled with lost souls who struggle against the throes of mourning and sorrow and depression. Let us "preach Christ" for them, for it is Christ alone who can heal all sorrows and replace the "spirit of heaviness" with the "garment of praise" and the "oil of joy."

8:9-13

But there was a certain man called Simon, who previously practiced sorcery in the city and astonished the people of Samaria, claiming that he was someone great, to whom they all gave heed, from the least to the greatest, saying, "This man is the great power of God." And they heeded him because he had astonished them with his sorceries for a long time. But when they believed Philip as he preached the things concerning the kingdom of God and the name of Jesus Christ, both men and women were baptized. Then Simon himself also believed; and when he was baptized he continued with Philip, and was amazed, seeing the miracles and signs which were done.

Philip's sermons in Samaria fell on the ears of people that had long been under the influence of a sorcerer named Simon. Philip came to "preach Christ," to preach on the greatness of Jesus, which was a striking contrast to Simon's messages which claimed that "he (himself) was someone great." Simon held significant sway in the community. Everyone "gave heed" to his recommendations. If we were in Philip's shoes, we might be tempted to view Simon as an enemy, a rival spiritual influence who was respected by many as "the great power of God." But Simon was not an enemy, he was a lost unbeliever who needed to know "the things concerning the kingdom of God." He needed to be introduced to the "name of Jesus Christ." For when he was introduced to Jesus, Simon promptly put his faith in Him. Philip taught Simon the things concerning the kingdom of God. He taught him how sin bars us entry from the kingdom of God. Philip taught how Jesus' death on the cross grants us access to the kingdom of God. He taught how the kingdom of God includes both His kingdom in heaven, and His kingdom which resides in the heart of the believer (Luke 17:21). He taught who is great in the kingdom of God (Matthew 18:4), and he taught who is least in the kingdom of God (Matthew 5:19). Philip likely taught on who is permitted to enter the kingdom of God (Matthew 7:21), and likely included the difficulties that some must overcome in order to enter the kingdom of God (Luke 18:24). He taught that we must all "seek the kingdom of God" above all other pursuits (Luke 12:31). And he likely taught on the many descriptions of the kingdom of God that Jesus provided in Luke 13. Simon thought highly of himself, and the people who knew him felt the same, believing that "the great power of God" resided in him. But when Philip "preached Christ" (verse 5) and preached on the wonders of the kingdom of God, even Simon the sorcerer was "amazed" by the weight of Philip's message and by the power manifested in the miracles that accompanied Philip's ministry. Let us respect all men and women. But let us not be intimidated by anyone, nor fear that the gospel may be inadequate to convert some hardened sinners. The gospel is powerful (Romans 1:16, Hebrews 4:14). It is sufficient to turn even hardened sinners like Simon to repentance and saving faith in Jesus.

8:14-17

Now when the apostles who were at Jerusalem heard that Samaria had received the word of God, they sent Peter and John to them, who, when they had come down, prayed for them that they might receive the Holy Spirit. For as yet He had fallen upon none of them. They had only been baptized in the name of the Lord Jesus. Then they laid hands on them, and they received the Holy Spirit.

Philip's work among the people of Samaria quickly gained the attention of the believers in Jerusalem, and Peter and John, the church's preeminent leaders, were sent to pray for the new believers (verse 15) and extend to them the right hand of Christian fellowship. Upon their arrival, the apostles found that the Holy Spirit had not yet fallen upon any of them. Soon, believers would be filled with the Holy Spirit at the moment they placed saving faith in Jesus. When Peter preached Christ for Cornelius' household, Cornelius' family was saved and suddenly filled with the Spirit of God. Acts 10:44 says, "While Peter was still speaking these words, the Holy Spirit fell upon all those who heard the word." And when Paul and Barnabas preached the gospel in Antioch in Pisidia the new believers were "filled with joy and with the Holy Spirit" (Acts 13:52). But here, just as with the early believers at Ephesus that were spoken of in Acts 19:2, saving faith was embraced by these Samaritan believers, but the Holy Spirit had not yet "fallen" upon them. Blessedly, Jesus had promised in Luke 11:13 that the Father would "give the Holy Spirit to those who ask Him," so Peter and John could pray in confidence that the Lord would answer their request to pour out His Spirit on these new believers.

The picture here reminds us of the importance of welcoming new believers into the family of faith, the essentialness of being filled with the Holy Spirit, and the prominent place of prayer in the ministry of leaders in the church. May our efforts in our churches today be similarly uplifting to other believers, focused on and dependent on the Holy Spirit, and may our hearts continually be at the ready to kneel in the work of intercessory prayer.

8:18-21

And when Simon saw that through the laying on of the apostles' hands the

Holy Spirit was given, he offered them money, saying, "Give me this power also, that anyone on whom I lay hands may receive the Holy Spirit." But Peter said to him, "Your money perish with you, because you thought that the gift of God could be purchased with money! You have neither part nor portion in this matter, for your heart is not right in the sight of God."

In the world of the ungodly, power and virtue are independent qualities. Power can be bought and sold, bartered or commandeered at the discretion of the power brokers. Virtue is not required, and may even be a liability in the quest to gain further power. In the kingdom of God, however, the power of God is unobtainable by those who do not walk with Him in holiness. Simon's heart "is not right in the sight of God" and his unholy motives disqualify him from the very thing he seeks. Simon's desire is to wield God's power. But God's power is not made available to those who seek personal gain. John the Baptist came in the "power of Elijah," and he was given this power for holy purposes, not personal advancement. God's power in John the Baptist served to "turn the hearts of the fathers to the children, and the disobedient to the wisdom of the just, to make ready a people prepared for the Lord" (Luke 1:17). God's power revealed through John the Baptist moved people to be obedient, to be just, and to prepare their hearts to enter and enjoy the presence of their Savior. None of these matters were priorities to Simon. He simply desired to maintain his place of power and influence in the community. Peter's rebuke is scathing. You and your money will die together! You have no "part" in the kingdom of God and you will receive no "portion" of the power of God.

Simon's error is terribly serious. He had put his faith in Jesus (verse 13), but he had not yet been discipled, and his spiritual understanding was still dangerously tied to his pagan belief that money and influence with man were preferable to holiness and the approval of God. We are reminded of the necessity of discipleship. Simon was converted to faith in Christ, but his spiritual misunderstandings were not cured all at once. New believers cannot be left to their own devices. They must be discipled, sometimes with terse tones. When Titus was making disciples on the island of Crete, Paul instructed him to "rebuke them sharply, that they may be sound in the faith" (Titus 1:13). Here, Peter rebukes Simon "sharply" so that his faith might be sound. "Power belongs to God" (Psalm 62:11). It is not the possession of man that can be bought and sold. It is proper to be in awe of God's power and filled with gratitude and praise when He reveals His power through His children. Psalm 68:35 says, "O God, You are more awesome than Your holy places. The God of Israel is He who gives strength and power to His people. Blessed be God!" Simon was not wrong to hold in wonder the sight of the power of God in the hands of His people, but Simon's mistake was in thinking that the Holy God's power could be obtained by unholy means to carry out unholy purposes. This is a deeply pagan thought unfit for a child of God to even consider. Let us take proper warning any time we are tempted by the sin of Simon to twist godly service into a pursuit of personal glory.

8:22-24

"Repent therefore of this your wickedness, and pray God if perhaps the thought of your heart may be forgiven you. For I see that you are poisoned by bitterness and bound by iniquity." Then Simon answered and said, "Pray to the Lord for me, that none of the things which you have spoken may come upon me."

Peter continues his extremely stern rebuke of Simon after he tried to buy "the gift of God" with money (verse 20). He calls on Simon to immediately repent of his "wickedness" and "pray" for forgiveness. Simon's request to buy the Holy Spirit for the sake of his own reputation revealed that his heart was very far from God. Peter is so appalled by Simon's request that he warns Simon that "perhaps" his sin "may be forgiven" – not that God does not forgive those who repent, but that Simon's thoughts had become so corrupt that Peter feared he had become too blind to his sin to repent. Simon was "poisoned by bitterness." Self-centeredness is a bitter poison. It is a venom that creates toxic relationships with those around us. It is a toxin that kills our relationship with God. "Your money perish with you," was Peter's immediate response in verse 20. For if Simon would not repent, he would poison himself to death with his self-centeredness, and his money would die with him. Peter's strong reaction stirs us to recognize the need to give stern warnings to those who are "poisoned by bitterness."

Peter is further disturbed by Simon's request, discerning that in addition to being "poisoned by bitterness," Simon was also "bound by iniquity." Simon has put his faith in Jesus (verse 13), but he has not yet broken the shackles of sin that have bound him for so long. Simon embraced Christianity. But his previous religion did not forbid sin, especially secret sin, and Simon mistakenly believed that he could advance in his new religion and remain chained to his sinful desires that had held him in bondage as long as he could remember. We must call children of God away from sin as Peter does with Simon here. We love sinners and call them to repent, we cannot coddle sinners and allow them to continue to coddle their sin. In Genesis 4:7 the Lord warns Cain, "Sin is crouching at (your) door" (ESV).

This is Peter's warning to Simon here. Simon is "bound by iniquity." He has not allowed Jesus to release him from the shackles of his sin, and that sin is crouching at his heart's door, seeking to control his attitudes and seeking to control his destiny. Simon must quickly repent, or risk suffering the consequences of Cain.

Peter's rebuke was scathing, but it may have been lifesaving. Peter's words move Simon to repent and express proper fear of the Lord's judgment. Simon was a sorcerer (verse 9). He was guilty of willingly working as a conduit for the devil's powers and masquerading as a wielder of the power of God (verse 10). He further incriminated himself by trying to buy the Holy Spirit with money, reflecting the gross state of his soul which was "poisoned by bitterness and bound by iniquity" (verse 23). His evil deeds in the past and the persistence of wicked thoughts even after professing faith in Jesus might give us little hope for Simon. But throughout the centuries, our Lord continually amazes us with His kindness and gentleness toward the repentance of horrid people. Perhaps no one illustrates this better than King Ahab. Ahab rejected God and became a Baal worshiper (I Kings 16:32). He and his wife massacred the prophets of the Lord (I Kings 18:4). He murdered Naboth in I Kings 21. In fact, I Kings 21:25 says that "there was no one like Ahab who sold himself to do wickedness in the sight of the Lord." But after hearing Elijah's condemnation, Ahab fasted in fear of the Lord's judgment and "went about mourning" (I Kings 21:27). And despite a lifetime of evil acts, the Lord showed gentle mercy toward Ahab in response to his humble demonstration of fear of God's judgment (I Kings 21:29). No matter how evil men and women can be, they are always only one step of repentant contrition away from evoking God's tender mercies. Sin and self-centeredness were crouching at Simon's door, just as they crouched at the door of Cain's heart in Genesis 4:7. Cain did not heed the Lord's warnings and suffered terrible consequences. Simon, however, feared the Lord. And we have good cause to hope that Peter's efforts to exhort and disciple him led to a blessed outcome.

8:25
So when they had testified and preached the word of the Lord, they returned to Jerusalem, preaching the gospel in many villages of the Samaritans.

Through Peter's visit to the new believers in Samaria, the Holy Spirit fell on them in power, Simon the sorcerer was brought to a fuller understanding of the heart of God, and we may suppose that the visit by Peter and John brought many other blessings to the fledgling church in Samaria as well. But Philip and the new church in Samaria also deeply blessed Peter and John in return. Peter and John were now suddenly inspired to preach the gospel "in many villages of the Samaritans." It seems they had never before felt led to preach in Samaria. Before being inspired by Philip's example, John was more prone to pray that God would rain fire on the Samaritans than he was to preach the gospel to them (Luke 9:54). But as is still the case in the church today, God's people are designed to be mutually encouraged by one another. Peter and John richly blessed the new church – and they in return were blessed and bettered by Philip and the church in Samaria. In the body of Christ, leaders and new believers, teachers and learners, givers and receivers are all wonderfully mutually blessed by one another. This blessed aspect of Christian life was a joy to Paul, and he looked forward to visiting the church in Rome so that "we may be mutually encouraged by each other's faith, both yours and mine" (Romans 1:12 ESV).

8:26

Now an angel of the Lord spoke to Philip, saying, "Arise and go toward the south along the road which goes down from Jerusalem to Gaza." This is desert.

Philip was already hard at work for Kingdom purposes in Samaria. He had a vibrant ministry that certainly depended on him for leadership. And in the midst of this blessed, blossoming work the Lord called him to a new task. This is often God's way with His people. The Lord chooses people at work to add work to. He is far less likely to call people to work that are presently doing nothing. He often chooses His busiest servants with the least amount of free time on their hands to carry out new assignments of service. In the kingdom of God, the reward for a job well done is more work. In Luke 19:26 Jesus said, "To everyone who has will be given." We find that this not only applies to rewards, it also applies to assignments. Those, like Philip, who are faithful in service to the Lord in one arena, will often find themselves called to serve the Lord in other areas as well. And so we find Philip called by the Lord to distant service even as his present efforts were yielding so much fruit.

We are struck by the fact that God calls Philip to the desert. Almost by definition, very little grows in a desert. Very few people live in the desert. Laborers there are almost certain to bear little fruit. Yet the Spirit called Philip to leave his thriving metropolitan ministry to embark on a spiritual venture in the desert. In Mark 4:36 Jesus "left the multitude." He left thousands of people who were hanging on His every word in order to cross a sea and minister to one, solitary, out-of-his-mind, demon-possessed, homeless man. And as soon as Jesus finished His encounter with the man, He returned to the boats and crossed back over the sea to return to the crowds again. Jesus' example in Mark 4 and 5 tells us that God's call to Philip to leave the crowd in order to minister to one man in the desert is by no means an isolated incident. In God's spiritual economy, it is right to leave the crowds for the sake of one. In Barnes' Notes on the Bible, the author explains Philip's call to leave the crowds to trek into the desert: "The salvation of a single sinner is an object worthy (of) the attention of God." We might all agree that saving one soul would be worth a trip into the desert, but we must remember that Philip did not know in advance what he would find when he arrived in the desert. He was leaving a thriving ministry, and did not know what God would use him to do instead. The Jamieson-Fausset-Brown Commentary praises Philip's obedience, saying that God called Philip to the desert, and like Paul, he "was not disobedient to the heavenly vision" (Acts 26:19), and like Abram, he "went out, not knowing where he was going" (Hebrews 11:8).

8:27-28

So he arose and went. And behold, a man of Ethiopia, a eunuch of great authority under Candace the queen of the Ethiopians, who had charge of all her treasury, and had come to Jerusalem to worship, was returning. And sitting in his chariot, he was reading Isaiah the prophet.

Philip obeyed the Spirit's call to leave his thriving ministry in Samaria and travel to the desert. On his arrival, we have no indication that he knew what to expect or what he would find. But we may suppose that he arrived prayerfully, obediently, and expectantly. And as he stood in active anticipation of what the Lord would do through him, a high official "of great authority" from Ethiopia passed by him – and he was "reading Isaiah the prophet!" What a blessing this must have been to Philip, seeing that the Lord had prepared this encounter long in advance, confirming that he had not come to the desert by mistake, but rather that the Lord had prepared a divine appointment for him.

Up until very recently, the apostles and leaders of the church, including Philip, had only preached among the Jews, and had confined the vast majority of their efforts to Jerusalem. Persecution was steadily moving God's people and the gospel message further and further out from Jerusalem, but now Philip could see that the gospel was not just spreading accidentally, as a side effect of persecution. God was calling the world to Himself – as He had always said He would. Zephaniah prophesied of this day when he spoke of the plan of God to call all peoples to Himself: "I will restore to the peoples a pure language, that they all may call on the name of the LORD, to serve Him with one accord. From beyond the rivers of Ethiopia My worshipers, the daughter of My dispersed ones, shall bring My offering" (Zephaniah 3:9-10). David prophesied of this day as well, writing in Psalm 68:31, "Envoys will come out of Egypt; Ethiopia will quickly stretch out her hand to God." This man of "great authority" had come from Ethiopia to "stretch out his hand" to worship the Lord from Ethiopia, and Philip was called to welcome him into God's kingdom. What a blessed encounter it is when the Lord brings us to meet with those that He has called to Himself. So often, people that are called by God do not need us to demonstrate powerful verbal skills to draw them to Christ. They simply need us to be at the God-appointed place at the God-appointed time. It is our readiness to share the gospel, not our skill in sharing the gospel that people chiefly need. The Spirit of God had perfectly prepared the heart of this Ethiopian official to believe the gospel, and blessedly, Philip "arose and went," not knowing what he would encounter in the desert, but spiritually ready for whatever the Lord would have him do.

8:29-30

Then the Spirit said to Philip, "Go near and overtake this chariot." So Philip ran to him, and heard him reading the prophet Isaiah, and said, "Do you understand what you are reading?"

The Spirit of God had whisked Philip off into the desert, and as he stood beside the road, awaiting, as we may suppose, further instructions from the Lord, a foreigner drove by in his chariot reading the book of Isaiah. The Spirit immediately confirmed what Philip must have already surmised, that the Lord would have him teach this man the truths of God. But we find wisdom in Philip's greeting. It was clear that the Lord had appointed this meeting, but Philip does not presume to know what the Ethiopian official needed from him. He does not launch into a sermon. He asks a question. "Do you understand what you are reading?" We must know our audience if we are to best present the gospel to them. We must not give meat to those who need milk (I Corinthians 3:2, Hebrews 5:12) and vice versa. We should not teach advanced, hard-to-grasp concepts to those who are not even born again yet. And it is of little benefit to speak of subtle nuances in the Greek or Hebrew text when our listeners are illiterate. In Acts 22:2 Paul preached in Hebrew. In Acts 23:6 Paul spoke on the resurrection of the dead. In

Acts 17:29 Paul preached on idolatry. And in each instance, Paul chose the content and/or the language of his message after discerning the needs and background of his listeners. Philip's initial question provides us with an excellent example. Our ministry to God's people and our presentation of the gospel will be enhanced if we have a good grasp on what our hearers already do and do not "understand."

8:31-35

And he said, "How can I, unless someone guides me?" And he asked Philip to come up and sit with him. The place in the Scripture which he read was this: "He was led as a sheep to the slaughter; and as a lamb before its shearer is silent, so He opened not His mouth. In His humiliation His justice was taken away, and who will declare His generation? For His life is taken from the earth." So the eunuch answered Philip and said, "I ask you, of whom does the prophet say this, of himself or of some other man?" Then Philip opened his mouth, and beginning at this Scripture, preached Jesus to him.

The Ethiopian official was reading Isaiah 53. He had a heart for the things of God, he had traveled far and long to worship the one true God, and yet he humbly admitted that he could not understand this passage of Scripture without help. So, beginning at Isaiah 53, Philip "preached Jesus to him." We can surmise that Philip taught him the Old Testament passages that foretold the coming of the Messiah, of Jesus' birth in Bethlehem, and of Jesus' sinless life and powerful ministry. The passage that the Ethiopian official was reading was a clear prophetic depiction of the sufferings of Jesus, and Philip would have walked him through Jesus' trial, crucifixion, resurrection, and ascension. In verse 5, Philip traveled to Samaria and "preached Christ," and here we see him climb into a foreigner's chariot, and once again he "preached Jesus." When Philip preached, he preached Jesus. Paul said that when he preached, Jesus was not only the main subject he preached on, Jesus was the only subject he preached on! In I Corinthians 2:2 Paul wrote, "For I determined not to know anything among you except Jesus Christ and Him crucified." Paul also wrote that nothing in life can compare to "the excellence of the knowledge of Christ Jesus my Lord" (Philippians 3:8). If knowing Jesus is the believer's greatest joy in life, our second greatest joy must be in helping others know Him too. And so we find Philip engaged in the great work of preaching Jesus, so that this stranger on a desert road might be allowed to know the excellence of the knowledge of Christ Jesus our Lord.

8:36-38

Now as they went down the road, they came to some water. And the eunuch said, "See, here is water, what hinders me from being baptized?" Then Philip said, "If you believe with all your heart, you may." And he answered and said, "I believe that Jesus Christ is the Son of God." So he commanded the chariot to stand still. And both Philip and the eunuch went down into the water, and he baptized him.

Philip had "preached Jesus" to this official from Ethiopia, and so enthused by what he heard, and so intent on obeying all that Jesus taught, the man sprang forward to be baptized as soon as they saw water. Psalm 119:60 says, "I made haste, and did not delay to keep Your commandments." The Ethiopian eunuch followed that example well in pleading to be baptized as soon as occasion allowed. As soon as we know the will of God, we must urgently obey the will of God. Delayed obedience is sin – in the matter of baptism and in all other matters as well.

Philip taught the Ethiopian (and us) the essential prerequisite for baptism: we must "believe with all (our) heart." Jesus taught us, "You shall love the LORD your God with <u>all your heart</u>, with <u>all your soul</u>, and with <u>all your mind</u>. This is the first and great commandment" (Matthew 22:37-38). This is Jesus' summary statement of that which defines a Christian, and Philip uses this same idea of whole-hearted, "all your heart" belief and devotion as his summary statement of that which is required for baptism. Half-hearted devotion and half-hearted faith have no place in the kingdom of God. James says that a "double-minded man" (James 1:8), a man made up of half-faith, half-doubt is denied assurance of answered prayer, and here, Philip teaches that half-heartedness disqualifies from baptism as well.

8:39-40

Now when they came up out of the water, the Spirit of the Lord caught Philip away, so that the eunuch saw him no more; and he went on his way rejoicing. But Philip was found at Azotus. And passing through, he preached in all the cities till he came to Caesarea.

Seeing exuberant faith in the face of new believers is a great reward for those who preach God's Word. Philip must have felt drawn to stay with this man for a while longer to nurture him in the faith. But "the Spirit of the Lord caught Philip away, so that the eunuch saw him no more." In Acts 17, Paul was only given three weeks to preach the gospel in Thessalonica before he was forced to leave the fledgling believers there. He then preached in Berea, but was once again forced to leave them after a short time. Here, Philip was only allowed a few hours with the eunuch before the Spirit caught him away to preach in the cities from Azotus to Caesarea. It is a blessing to know that the Lord is faithful to His children and can care for them so much better than we can. We must intercede before the Lord for the sake of new believers, but let us be heartened by the fact that the eunuch never again saw his father in the faith, but even so, "he went on his way rejoicing." The Holy Spirit guides and guards and upholds His children even when fellowship with those dearest to us in the family of faith is denied for a time. They were denied the joy of one another's company, but Philip continued preaching and the official from Ethiopia continued rejoicing in the Lord. When we are separated from those we love, let us not be paralyzed with sorrow, but follow these examples and continue to serve the Lord and continue to rejoice in His goodness.

Acts 9

9:1-5

**Then Saul, still breathing threats and murder against the disciples of the
Lord, went to the high priest and asked letters from him to the synagogues
of Damascus, so that if he found any who were of the Way, whether men
or women, he might bring them bound to Jerusalem. As he journeyed
he came near Damascus, and suddenly a light shone around him from
heaven. Then he fell to the ground, and heard a voice saying to him, "Saul,
Saul, why are you persecuting Me?" And he said, "Who are You, Lord?"
Then the Lord said, "I am Jesus, whom you are persecuting. It is hard for
you to kick against the goads."**

In John 16 Jesus warned His followers that the time was coming when
they would be severely mistreated by the world. John 16:2 says, "Yes, the
time is coming that whoever kills you will think that he offers God service."
How could anyone be cruel to his fellow man and think that his actions were
pleasing to God? And especially, how could anyone be cruel to those devoted to God and yet twist their logic so badly that they could believe that
God would be pleased with those who persecuted His own children? Jesus

answers this question for us, "And these things they will do to you because they have not known the Father nor Me" (John 16:3). Here, in fulfillment of Jesus' prophecy, we see Saul threatening, imprisoning, and murdering innocent men and women when he found them walking in the Way of Jesus. And in further fulfillment of Jesus' words, when Jesus appears to him on the Damascus road, Saul asks, "Who are You, Lord?" Saul threatened, imprisoned, and murdered Jesus' followers because he did not know Jesus.

Let us bring people to Jesus! A single introduction to Jesus was all that it took to cause a sudden, total transformation in the life of Saul. Let us not doubt that anyone can be saved. Let us not think that anyone is too evil or too blind, too obstinate or too ignorant. Let us bring them to the knowledge of Christ. There is no manner of evil that a man cannot stoop to if he does not know Jesus; and there is no depth of evil that a man cannot rise out of if he is brought to the knowledge of Christ.

In Matthew 25:40 Jesus said, "inasmuch as you did it to one of the least of these My brethren, you did it to Me." And here we see that Jesus meant His words to be more literal than figurative when He says to Saul, "Saul, Saul, why are you persecuting Me?" Saul was persecuting Christians. But Jesus felt the pain of Saul's persecution. When believers suffer persecution, we "partake of Christ's sufferings" (I Peter 4:13), or as the HCS puts it, we "share in the sufferings of the Messiah." We share in His sufferings, and He shares in our pain. Jesus did not say, "Why are you persecuting My people?" He asked, "Why are you persecuting Me?" – because Jesus is "very present" (Psalm 46:1) with His children when they suffer. Saul was waging a war on the followers of Jesus, but the presence of Jesus in and among His disciples meant that Saul was actually fighting God Himself, the very thing that Gamaliel warned against in Acts 5:39. Saul thought that he was waging a war against Christians too weak to defend themselves. But from Jesus' viewpoint, Saul was throwing himself against His Maker. Though many translations do not include the final phrase, it seems to picture Jesus' message to Saul well: "It is hard for you to kick against the goads." It is a painful, hopeless effort to persist in kicking a firmly emplaced sharpened goad. Ellicott's Commentary for English Readers sums up the meaning of the phrase quickly, stating, "To resist a power altogether superior to our own is a profitless and perilous experiment." Saul's persecution of the children of God was a "profitless and perilous experiment." Those he martyred were carried to the arms of Jesus in paradise, and those he threatened were sustained by those same arms as Jesus drew near to those He loved.

9:6

So he, trembling and astonished, said, "Lord, what do You want me to do?" Then the Lord said to him, "Arise and go into the city, and you will be told what you must do."

Saul's worldview was suddenly turned upside down. He had thought that persecuting the Way of Jesus was a service to God, but now, as Jesus stood in blazing glory before him, Saul was confronted with the revelation that his whole life's work was actually an evil, misguided, vain pursuit. He had repeatedly blasphemed Jesus' name, scoffed at Jesus' teachings, and tormented Jesus' followers. But now, this same Jesus that he had so vehemently opposed stood in blazing glory before him. The sudden realization of the supremacy of Christ caused Saul to collapse "trembling and astonished." He had thrown all of his energies into the enterprise of stamping out Jesus' disciples, but now he suddenly understood that everything he had been doing was wrong – everything! What do we do when our life's course requires, not a subtle redirection, but a total overhaul? Saul is a man of action; he is driven to act on his newfound understanding. But he has no idea what he should do next.

"Lord, what do You want me to do?" Let us be quick to ask our Lord this question both when the trials of life darken our path and when the glory of our Savior shines brightly before us. David was well known for asking this question frequently. In I Samuel 23:2 he asked God if he should go save the city of Keilah. In I Samuel 30:8 he asked God if he should pursue the Amalekites. And in II Samuel 5, David twice asks God what he should do in his war with the Philistines. Unless the matter is clearly presented in Scripture, let us be supremely cautious before assuming God's will, and let us outright reject our flesh's desire to replace God's will with our own.

The Lord's answer to Saul's question is instructive. "Arise and go into the city, and you will be told what you must do." Jesus could have given His full instructions to Saul right there. But it is His will to use His people to present His will and ways. We do not serve the Lord as independent ministers. We are mutually encouraged by one another and interdependent on one another in the body of Christ. God has not deemed it best for any one person to know all His will. Saul would grow to become one of the Lord's choicest servants. But he will need Ananias' instruction and prayer support before he can grow in his new walk of faith with the Lord. God spoke to David through Nathan (I Chronicles 17), He spoke to Peter through Paul (Galatians 2:11), and here He will speak to Paul through Ananias. Let us cultivate a heightened readiness to listen to God's people when they speak, for when our Lord moves to tell us what He would have us do, He often speaks to us through His children, our fellow believers.

9:7-9

And the men who journeyed with him stood speechless, hearing a voice but seeing no one. Then Saul arose from the ground, and when his eyes were opened he saw no one. But they led him by the hand and brought him into Damascus. And he was three days without sight, and neither ate nor drank.

Saul had traveled to Damascus, consumed with the desire to oppress those who followed Jesus. Now, all prior commitments and cravings were forgotten. He was consumed with knowing Christ and knowing His will. On the Damascus road, Jesus told Saul that after he arrived in the city, he would be told what to do – and Paul is intent on setting his full attention on being prepared to hear from the Lord. Saul's eyes were blinded by the glory of the Lord, but for the first time, he could see his sin with absolute clarity. His previous disdain for Jesus was now wholly replaced with an all-consuming need for Jesus. If Jesus did not forgive him, his soul was doomed. If Jesus did not instruct him, he was at a loss with what to do next. If Jesus did not heal his eyes, he would be unable to serve Him. In John 15:5 Jesus said, "Without Me you can do nothing." Saul appears to understand that here. He kneels in his darkness and waits for the Lord to come. He neither eats nor drinks, for his soul is consumed with his need for the forgiveness, instruction, and presence of Jesus Christ, the very One he had so recently, so vehemently opposed. Saul's situation was desperate. He knew he needed Jesus, and determined to do nothing else but kneel in pursuit of Him.

9:10-14

Now there was a certain disciple at Damascus named Ananias; and to him the Lord said in a vision, "Ananias." And he said, "Here I am Lord." So the Lord said to him, "Arise and go to the street called Straight, and inquire at the house of Judas for one called Saul of Tarsus, for behold, he is praying. And in a vision he has seen a man named Ananias coming in and putting his hand on him, so that he might receive his sight." Then Ananias answered, "Lord, I have heard from many about this man, how much harm he has done to Your saints in Jerusalem. And here he has authority from the chief priest to bind all who call on Your name."

Ananias knows a good number of reasons why Saul should not be admitted into the fellowship of faith. Saul has done much harm to God's people in the past, and has the authority even now to "bind all who call on Your name." Ananias' talk with the Lord is similar to Samuel's discussion with God in I Samuel 16. In verse 6 of that chapter, Samuel looked at the impressive appearance of Eliab and said, "Surely the LORD's anointed is before Him!" But God's famous reply comes in verse 7, "Do not look at his appearance or at his physical stature, because I have refused him. For the LORD does not see as man sees; for man looks at the outward appearance, but the LORD looks at the heart." Here, Ananias looked at the reputation of Saul and with Samuel's same certainty he replied to the Lord, "Lord, I have heard from many about this man." He is not safe! He is not fit for Christian service! He does not deserve your kindness! Just as Samuel was convinced by external evidence that Eliab was fit for higher service, Ananias was convinced for similar reasons that Saul was unfit for higher service.

Outward appearance holds very little importance in the kingdom of God. It was said of Jesus Himself, "There was nothing beautiful or majestic about his appearance, nothing to attract us to him" (Isaiah 53:2 NLT). Even past good deeds or past misdeeds have little impact on determining who God will call to higher service. Let there be no mistake. We are qualified to be adopted as the children of God and we are qualified to take part in the high call of Christian service, not by our personal merits, but by "the washing of regeneration and renewing of the Holy Spirit" (Titus 3:5). Saul's reputation was frightful, and Ananias felt he had cause for concern. But the "washing" and the "renewing" work of the Lord will make Saul a "new creation" (II Corinthians 5:17) and thus fit for whatever the Lord will call him to do.

9:15-16
But the Lord said to him, "Go, for he is a chosen vessel of Mine to bear My name before Gentiles, kings, and the children of Israel. For I will show him how many things he must suffer for My name's sake."

Ananias hesitates to visit Saul, because he has done so much to harm God's people. Ananias saw Paul as an enemy. The Lord, however, saw Saul as "a chosen vessel." Oh, that we may be granted the vantage point of God when assessing how best to respond to the people around us! When James and John saw the Samaritans treat Jesus rudely, they asked His permission to call down fire from heaven and wipe them all out (Luke 9:54). But Jesus rebuked James and John and he corrected Ananias here, reminding them and us that it is His heart to save sinners, not ignore them or destroy them. Ananias saw absolutely no potential for good in Saul, but in the words of Matthew Henry, "It is the Lord's glory to surpass our scanty expectations, and show that those are vessels of his mercy whom we are apt to consider as objects of his vengeance."

Jesus calls Saul a "chosen vessel." He has chosen Saul to be His standard bearer before kings and nations. This same Saul who now kneels blind and broken on Straight Street will be elevated by the Lord so that he will become "not at all inferior to the most eminent apostles" (II Corinthians 11:5). He will do more for the Kingdom of God than anyone he will ever know. But he will also "suffer for (Christ's) name's sake." Saul will accomplish much, and he will suffer much. And we are inspired to read that, of the two, Saul will boast more in his sufferings than in his successes. Years later, he will write in II Corinthians 12:9, "Therefore most gladly I will rather boast in my infirmities, that the power of Christ may rest upon me."

9:17-19
And Ananias went his way and entered the house; and laying his hands on him he said, "Brother Saul, the Lord Jesus, who appeared to you on the road as you came, has sent me that you may receive your sight and be filled with the Holy Spirit." Immediately there fell from his eyes something like scales, and he received his sight at once; and he arose and was baptized. So when he had received food, he was strengthened. Then Saul spent some days with the disciples at Damascus.

Moments before, Ananias considered Saul an enemy. Now he calls him "brother." The Lord called Saul to be His own, and all that God delights to call sons, we must delight to call brothers. We must put aside all that we have known of people before they come to the cross. We must forgive as Christ forgives, accept all that He accepts, and welcome into the kingdom all that He welcomes in.

Through Ananias' visit, Paul's blindness was healed, and he was filled with the Holy Spirit. In verse 6, Jesus instructed Saul to enter Damascus, "and you will be told what you must do." And so we find Saul spending several days in the city being instructed by the disciples and preaching what he was learning to others (verse 20). We may suppose that this fellowship in Damascus was very sweet. The instruction of mature believers sounds wonderful in the ears of new, hungry believers, and the testimony of new believers sounds equally wonderful in the ears of those who have followed the Lord for a long time.

9:20-22
Immediately he preached the Christ in the synagogues, that He is the Son

of God. Then all who heard were amazed, and said, "Is this not he who destroyed those who called on this name in Jerusalem, and has come here for that purpose, so that he might bring them bound to the chief priests?" But Saul increased all the more in strength, and confounded the Jews who dwelt in Damascus, proving that this Jesus is the Christ.

Galatians 1:17 says that Saul went to Arabia for a while for a concentrated time of prayer and study with the Lord, and then returned to preach in Damascus. But here, Luke tells us that Saul also "immediately" preached about Jesus in the synagogues. It is a sure sign of the Spirit's work in new believers when they not only rejoice in their new found salvation, but "immediately" teach what they are learning to others.

In Acts 8:5 Philip went to Samaria and "preached Christ," and here Saul is found doing the very thing he once vehemently, violently opposed. Just as Philip did, Paul centered his message on Jesus. "He is the Son of God." If Jesus is the Son of God, then He is our Creator, we must honor Him. He is the redemption for our sins, we must place our dependence on Him. He is our Judge, we must reconcile with Him. As the Son of God, Jesus knows how we came into existence, why we came into existence, how we should best spend our days on earth, and how we can safeguard our eternal soul. The fact that Jesus is the Son of God is at the core of the answer to all of life's most pressing questions, so it is not surprising that the preaching ministry of both Philip and now Saul is summarized with the same two words, they "preached Christ."

Saul immediately began to preach Christ, and he immediately faced opposition. Far from being discouraged by the opposition, however, verse 22 says that "Saul increased all the more in strength." Matthew Poole's Commentary says, "True grace thrives by exercise and opposition," and Saul illustrates both, as he immediately set out to exercise his new faith through preaching the gospel message and was provided an opportunity to further strengthen his faith by defending that faith in the face of opposition.

Our soul is like a muscle. It is strengthened when exercised, and is even further strengthened when exercised against resistance. Let us guard against flabbiness of the soul. Let us consistently, even religiously exercise our faith with godly service and declaration of the Truth. And let us not faint when we are opposed. Bearing up in the face of opposition not only proves our faith, it also strengthens our faith, and strengthens the faith of those who are watching us as well.

9:23-25

Now after many days were past, the Jews plotted to kill him. But their plot became known to Saul. And they watched the gates day and night, to kill him. Then the disciples took him by night and let him down through the wall in a large basket.

Saul, the great persecutor of the church, was now a transformed follower of Jesus. Sadly, persecution of the church did not end when Saul was converted. The world is full of evil men, fully ready to rise in the place of any sinner who chooses to turn to repent and walk with God. Let us not be fooled into thinking that our life will be set at ease if any one evil man or woman is taken away. We see that even without Saul's leadership, opposition to the Way of Jesus continued. See how quickly evil men turn on one another. So recently, these Jews had applauded Saul and cheered his exploits against the Christians. Now they "plotted to kill him." Rather than respond with repentance to the message, the Jews opted to kill the messenger. Their plan failed, however. The very disciples that Saul once sought to put to death, now save his life by secretly lowering him down the city wall in the dark of night.

9:26-28

And when Saul had come to Jerusalem, he tried to join the disciples; but they were all afraid of him, and did not believe that he was a disciple. But Barnabas took him and brought him to the apostles. And he declared to them how he had seen the Lord on the road, and that He had spoken to him, and how he had preached boldly at Damascus in the name of Jesus. So he was with them at Jerusalem, coming in and going out.

Saul's life was changed. He once sought to destroy all who followed Jesus, but now he was filled with the Spirit-led longing to "join" with Jesus' disciples in fellowship, worship, and prayer. Understandably, however, the believers "were all afraid of him, and did not believe that he was a disciple." Undoubtedly, they suspected his intentions, fearing that he sought to spy them out so that he could arrest them all after learning who all the Christians were. The distrust may have continued much longer if Barnabas had not arrived, took Saul under his wing and vouched for the authenticity of his faith. He brought Saul to Peter and James (Galatians 1:18-19), allowed Saul to give his testimony of conversion, and relayed how Saul had "preached boldly at Damascus." Saul's testimony and the assurance of Barnabas were enough to convince Peter and James of the genuineness of Saul's faith, and soon Saul was accepted into the family of faith in Jerusalem "coming in and going out" with all the disciples in fellowship and service. What a blessing it is when the bond of love in the Spirit of Christ dissolves all former fears and prejudices.

9:29-30
And he spoke boldly in the name of the Lord Jesus and disputed against the Hellenists, but they attempted to kill him. When the brethren found out, they brought him down to Caesarea and sent him out to Tarsus.

Whatever the early believers thought about Saul before his conversion, we can see that his bold proclamation of the gospel and the persecution he suffered at the hands of unbelievers were enough to win over his fellow believers. As soon as they "found out" that evil men were intent on taking Saul's life, they banded together to protect Saul and provide safe passage for him out of Jerusalem. We may suppose that their assistance was not without personal risk, but once Saul had proven to possess true faith in Christ, everyone in the church was willing to risk much for the sake of one of their own. Let us be quick to defend all who "speak boldly in the name of the Lord Jesus." In our day, perhaps, bold witnesses of the gospel may not risk death at the hands of unbelievers, but they do make themselves vulnerable to all manner of criticism. Let us rush to the defense of bold preachers and proclaimers of the gospel. Saul faced death, yet his brothers and sisters in the faith were willing to face the same outcome to defend him. Let there be no cowardice in us. Let us defend our brothers and sisters who faithfully teach God's Word, regardless of the personal risk.

9:31
Then the churches throughout all Judea, Galilee, and Samaria had peace and were edified. And walking in the fear of the Lord and in the comfort of the Holy Spirit, they were multiplied.

Following a prolonged period of persecution, the church now enjoyed a time of "peace." The people in the churches all across the region were being "edified," they were being "built up" (ESV) by their fellowship, by the manifestations of the power and presence of the Spirit, and by their study of God's Word. The churches multiplied, and their members multiplied. It was not the disappearance of persecution that caused the churches to grow, however, it was "the comfort of the Holy Spirit." The church does not require sunny skies and painless living to grow. Even in the absence of violent persecution, the early church, like our church today, still encountered the death of loved ones, hardships in the workplace, and troubles of various kinds. But "the comfort of the Holy Spirit" allows us to bear all these things with a deep, abiding sense of contentment, fulfillment, and even joy. We cannot promise new believers that their life in Christ will be free of difficulties. We can, however, assure them that our God is the "God of all comfort" (II Corinthians 1:3), and He will "comfort (us) on every side" (Psalm 71:21).

The churches also multiplied, because her members were "walking in the fear of the Lord." God's judgment on Ananias and Sapphira taught the people that God is holy, that He demands holiness in His children, and that He pronounces judgment on hypocrisy and secret sin. This instilled a holy fear of the Lord in the church. Fear of heights causes us to avoid heights, but fear of the Lord draws us to Him. We fear Him for His holiness, and His greatness, and we love Him for these same things. We draw near to Him with a holy fear that dreads doing anything that might injure our precious relationship with such a wonderful Savior. Those who fear the Lord seek to draw ever closer to Him, and the closer we draw to Him, the more we seek to draw closer still – and invite others to join us in our blessed, joy-filled, holy quest. And so, when God's people fear Him, the church prospers, for "He will bless those who fear the LORD, both small and great" (Psalm 115:13).

9:32-35

Now it came to pass, as Peter went through all parts of the country, that he also came down to the saints who dwelt in Lydda. There he found a certain man named Aeneas, who had been bedridden eight years and was paralyzed. And Peter said to him, "Aeneas, Jesus the Christ heals you. Arise and make your bed." Then he arose immediately. So all who dwelt at Lydda and Sharon saw him and turned to the Lord.

One man was healed, and a multitude repented of their sins and "turned to the Lord." Oh, how good it is when the great acts of God in the life of one person awaken the conscience of those who witness the power of His hand. Jesus saved the Samaritan woman, and many men and women in the city of Sychar were saved (John 4). The sight of Jesus healing bodies and purifying corrupted souls should convict witnesses of their own need and their privilege to know their Creator. Each of God's blessings granted each of His children is intended to draw many hearts to God. When people see the power of God manifest in the life of someone near, they are held accountable for how they respond. Matthew 11:20-22 records: "Then He began to rebuke the cities in which most of His mighty works had been done, because they did not repent: 'Woe to you, Chorazin! Woe to you, Bethsaida! For if the mighty works which were done in you had been done in Tyre and Sidon, they would have repented long ago in sackcloth and ashes. But I say to you, it will be more tolerable for Tyre and Sidon in the day of judgment than for you.'"

9:36-38

At Joppa there was a certain disciple named Tabitha, which is translated Dorcas. This woman was full of good works and charitable deeds which she did. But it happened in those days that she became sick and died. When they had washed her, they laid her in an upper room. And since Lydda was near Joppa, and the disciples had heard that Peter was there, they sent two men to him, imploring him not to delay in coming to them.

In Joppa, the city where Jonah once went to flee from the Lord (Jonah 1:3), this woman, called Tabitha by some, and Dorcas by others, spent her days doing "charitable deeds." Her life was "full of good works" which endeared her to the community of faith there. But death comes to the godly and the ungodly – as a reward to one and a judgment on the other – and we are told that while Peter was in the next town over, Tabitha became sick and passed away. Tabitha's life and death might not have come to the attention of anyone outside their little group, except for the remarkable faith of these disciples in Joppa. Hearing that Peter was ministering in Lydda, just 6 miles away, the church sent two men to Peter "imploring him not to delay in coming to them." The story seems to infer that the church was asking Peter to come and bring Tabitha back to life. If so, their faith truly matched Tabitha's works in greatness.

On May 30, 1792, William Carey, reverently called "the father of modern missions" preached his well-known sermon "Expect great things from God. Attempt great things for God." The church in Joppa certainly embodies that spirit in our story here.

9:39-43

Then Peter arose and went with them. When he had come, they brought him to the upper room. And all the widows stood by him weeping, showing the tunics and garments which Dorcas had made while she was with them. But Peter put them all out, and knelt down and prayed. And turning to the body he said, "Tabitha, arise." And she opened her eyes, and when she saw Peter she sat up. Then he gave her his hand and lifted her up; and when he had called the saints and widows, he presented her alive. And

it became known throughout all Joppa, and many believed on the Lord. So it was that he stayed many days in Joppa with Simon, a tanner.

Walking with Jesus is wonderfully, remarkably preparatory for confronting any challenge that we may face. Here, the saints of Joppa ask Peter to do the unthinkable – restore life to their dear sister in Christ. But even in this most unique of circumstances, Peter finds himself well prepared. He had seen Jesus do this very thing. And so we find Peter providing us with an excellent example of how to handle challenges – he did exactly what he saw Jesus do. In Mark 5, Jesus arrived at Jairus' house to revive his daughter. And in Mark 5:40 Jesus sent everyone out of the room before he restored the girl to life. Peter saw Jesus do that, and so, in this most unusual of circumstances, Peter does not hesitate to imitate exactly what he saw Jesus do in that situation. In Acts 9:40, Peter "put them all out." He sent everyone out of the room. Why? Because that's what Jesus did when He raised a girl from the dead. In Mark 5:41, Peter saw Jesus as He "took the child by the hand." And in Acts 9:41 Peter "gave her his hand and lifted her up." In Mark 5:41, Jesus said, "Little girl, I say to you, arise." And in Acts 9:41 Peter continues his imitation of Jesus and says, "Tabitha, arise." Peter's imitation of Jesus saw a dear saint of the Lord restored to life. Let us follow his example and imitate Jesus in all circumstances great and small. Let us study the life and teachings of Jesus, and be so well versed in them, that we are ready to do and say all that Jesus did and said in similar situations. Such great outcomes may be experienced by the church if we will imitate our Savior.

Acts 10

10:1-4

There was a certain man in Caesarea called Cornelius, a centurion of what was called the Italian Regiment, a devout man and one who feared God with all his household, who gave alms generously to the people, and prayed to God always. About the ninth hour of the day he saw clearly in a vision an angel of God coming in and saying to him, "Cornelius!" And when he observed him, he was afraid, and said, "What is it, lord?" So he said to him, "Your prayers and your alms have come up for a memorial before God."

The story of Cornelius is a joy to read. It seems that the sad majority of the world's people turn their backs on their conscience, ignore their need for God, ignore the glory of God that deserves our praise and devotion, and ignore the needs of their fellow man. But then we come upon men like Cornelius. Men who were not blessed with godly families or an early introduction to the truths about their Creator, and yet follow the guidance of their conscience to not sin, kindly care for the needs of others, and revere God, even though they may not know Him well. It is a blessing to meet people like Cornelius, people that God has called to Himself from families and from nations that do not know Him well.

We are granted a summary picture of Cornelius. He was "devout." He carefully guarded his personal purity and faithfully sought to please God in all he did. He "feared God." He kept God in proper awe and revered Him as all-powerful and ever present. He "gave alms generously" to the poor and needy around him. And he "prayed to God always," obeying the edict to "pray without ceasing" (I Thessalonians 5:17), even though he had not yet had the privilege of hearing that taught. And at three in the afternoon, during the observed hour of prayer, an angel from heaven approached him as he prayed before the Lord. Let us be reminded that the most likely time to hear from God is while He has our rapt attention in prayer.

The angel brings Cornelius an uplifting word: "Your prayers and your alms have come up for a memorial before God." The message must have caused the heart of Cornelius to soar, and provides similar inspiration to us. God remembered every penny that Cornelius gave away, and God remembered every prayer that Cornelius had ever lifted up. When God considers us, He does not consult a list of our faults. He "does not keep a record of wrongs" (I Corinthians 13:5 CSB). Instead, with great grace, He sets our prayers and service to Him before His eyes as a memorial to us. Goodness, what a blessed thought. In Numbers 10:10 God said, "Also in the day of your gladness, in your appointed feasts, and at the beginning of your months, you shall blow the trumpets over your burnt offerings and over the sacrifices of your peace offerings; and they shall be a memorial for you before your God: I am the LORD your God." From Heaven's perspective, our worship, our prayers, and our acts of godly service are memorable events! They are fit to be memorialized, and are placed prominently before the Lord, perpetually pleasing Him and stirring His heart to bless us. Revelation 8 pictures for us our prayers continually rising before the Lord like incense. And Revelation 5:8 directly compares our prayers to incense: "Now when He had taken the scroll, the four living creatures and the twenty-four elders fell down before the Lamb, each having a harp, and golden bowls full of incense, which are the prayers of the saints." When we pray, our prayers do not evaporate into thin air. Every word is heard by the Lord, and we are overwhelmed with the thought that our prayers are pleasing to Him – like sweet smelling incense they rise before Him, not to be overlooked or forgotten, but to be memorialized before Him, and moving Him to show us His amazing compassion, just as we will see in this story of Cornelius in the verses to come.

With this thought before us, let us forever put behind us half-hearted and dispassionate prayers over menial matters. Let us cry out our prayers for the lost, groan out our prayers for our personal holiness, plead with the Lord to bless His people, and praise our God with proper exuberance. The prayers of God's people rise up before the Lord as a memorial to the one who prays. Let us pray with intensity so that this memorial might shine brightly and pleasingly before Him.

10:5-8

"Now send men to Joppa, and send for Simon whose surname is Peter. He is lodging with Simon, a tanner, whose house is by the sea. He will tell you what you must do." And when the angel who spoke to him had departed, Cornelius called two of his household servants and a devout soldier from among those who waited on him continually. So when he had explained all these things to them, he sent them to Joppa.

The role of man in the plans of God is little less than astounding. An angel from heaven comes to Cornelius and speaks with him face to face. What better explainer of the great things of God could there be than an angel from heaven? But remarkably, he <u>does not</u> explain to Cornelius the great truths of God. He sends him to Peter, so that Peter can share the gospel of Jesus with him. We found the same to be true with Saul. Jesus met him on the road to Damascus and stopped his caravan to confront him over his sin. But Jesus <u>does not</u> explain the great truths of the gospel to Saul, He sends Saul to Ananias who will teach him these things. In Acts 8:26, we saw an angel of the Lord appear to Philip and command him to go south, and then we see the angel coordinate a miraculously timed meeting in the desert so that Philip could share the gospel with a traveling Ethiopian. We surmise that angels are perfectly suited to explain spiritual truths to men. They are sinless, unencumbered by ego, and are eyewitnesses of His glory. Why doesn't God convey His truths through angels? The question is interesting, but the answer is clear: it is the will of God that His eternal truths be taught to men and women by men and women, as both teacher and listener are empowered by the Holy Spirit.

Let us rise up and take our appointed role as preachers of the gospel of peace (Romans 10:15). Angels protect us (Psalm 91:11, Acts 5:19), angels may guide us (Acts 8:26), and they may bring down God's hand of judgment on sinners (Acts 12:23). In heaven, angels may join us in praising the Father (Revelation 16:5), but on earth it is our work, it is our responsibility, and ours alone to "go into all the world and preach the gospel to every creature"

(Mark 16:15). The angel of the Lord visits Cornelius, not to share the gospel with him, but to send him to a man who will. Let us "sanctify the Lord God in our hearts" so that we will "always be ready" (I Peter 3:15) to share the wonderful gospel at these divine appointments.

10:9

The next day, as they went on their journey and drew near the city, Peter went up on the housetop to pray, about the sixth hour.

Here we find Peter praying at noon, just as we found Cornelius praying at three the day before. And just as God spoke to Cornelius as he prayed, He now speaks to Peter in a vision during Peter's time of prayer. Let us pray! Let all who seek vision and long to hear the voice of God devote themselves to prayer.

Perhaps we have no commandment from the Lord to pray at noon, but we have the record of a godly example. In Psalm 55:17 David writes, "Evening and morning and at noon I will pray, and cry aloud, and He shall hear my voice." David found assurance of God's rescue, Peter was granted a heavenly vision, and we are likely to be similarly blessed if we will join these men in devoting ourselves to multiple moments of daily prayer.

10:10-16

Then he became very hungry and wanted to eat; but while they made ready, he fell into a trance and saw heaven opened and an object like a great sheet bound at the four corners, descending to him and let down to the earth. In it were all kinds of four-footed animals of the earth, wild beasts, creeping things, and birds of the air. And a voice came to him, "Rise, Peter; kill and eat." But Peter said, "Not so, Lord! For I have never eaten anything common or unclean." And a voice spoke to him again the second time, "What God has cleansed you must not call common." This was done three times. And the object was taken up into heaven again.

The Lord was calling Cornelius to Himself, and He was to use Peter as His ambassador to explain the Way to him more fully. But Peter's background would have made it virtually impossible for him to carry out God's plan to bring salvation and discipleship to Cornelius' family. As far as Peter knew, all unbelievers were unclean and all Gentiles were unbelievers, which meant that all Gentiles were unclean. And his godly desire to guard his cleanliness before the Lord moved him to shun all Gentiles. He could not imagine that the time for the Lord to call all the world to Himself was now upon them. Oh, how kind our Lord is when He prepares us for future service with lessons in advance. Leviticus 11 gave clear instructions that some meat must not be eaten by God's people because it was considered unclean. Jesus said that He came to fulfill the law (Matthew 5:17), but Peter certainly could not yet appreciate all that this meant, and continued to hold that there were foods, and people, and many other matters that were inherently unclean. But now, Peter's understanding is suddenly upended with the voice of the Lord saying, "What God has cleansed you must not call common." With great kindness, the Lord spoke this message to Peter in advance, preparing him for a brand-new facet of ministry that He had already set in motion.

10:17-20
Now while Peter wondered within himself what this vision which he had seen meant, behold, the men who had been sent from Cornelius had made inquiry for Simon's house, and stood before the gate. And they called and asked whether Simon, whose surname was Peter, was lodging there. While Peter thought about the vision, the Spirit said to him, "Behold, three men are seeking you. Arise therefore, go down and go with them, doubting nothing; for I have sent them."

It is one of God's many kindnesses to us that He prepares us in advance for matters of greatest importance. Some opportunities must be seized quickly, and without the Lord's preparations in our hearts, we would be likely to act too slowly or miss opportunities altogether. The Lord grants Peter a vision, and a voice saying, "What God has cleansed you must not call common." The vision caught Peter's full attention and caused him to ponder the matter. He "wondered within himself what this vision which he had seen meant." And while the Lord had Peter's attention, He sent him another word, "Go down and go with them, doubting nothing; for I have sent them."

Peter did not immediately understand the vision. The vision caused him to be "deeply perplexed" (CSB). And because of his lack of clarity, he "doubted in himself" (KJV). Peter had doubts about the reliability of the vision. He doubted his understanding of what the vision was telling him. He likely doubted that this vision applied to people. But, blessedly, the Lord knew Peter would have these doubts. So, He gave Peter a clear message: "Go with them, doubting nothing." As Abraham left Ur "not knowing where he was going" (Hebrews 11:8), as Esther went before the king, not knowing if she would live or die (Ester 4:16), so Peter goes down to see the visitors from Cornelius, not knowing what would come of it. Let us obey our Lord's directives to us, doubting nothing, even when the outcome of our efforts is still unknown.

10:21-23
Then Peter went down to the men who had been sent to him from Cornelius, and said, "Yes, I am he whom you seek. For what reason have you come?" And they said, "Cornelius the centurion, a just man, one who fears God and has a good reputation among all the nation of the Jews was divinely instructed by a holy angel to summon you to his house, and to hear words from you." Then he invited them in and lodged them. On the next day Peter went away with them, and some brethren from Joppa accompanied him.

Peter hears the testimony of his visitors and immediately "invited them in and lodged them" even though they were Gentiles. Peter was initially perplexed by his vision, but he quickly applies his vision to the setting before him and then just as quickly puts into practice what he has learned – that he should no longer consider Gentiles unclean. We are impressed that Peter is able to put aside a lifetime of prejudice after a single word from the Lord. May we be equally as sensitive to the Spirit's instruction.

The next day Peter "went away with them." But he did not travel alone. "Some brethren from Joppa accompanied him." Peter must obey the Lord's directive, but he also desires to protect his reputation and relation with his fellow Jewish believers, and so he invites "some brethren from Joppa" to accompany him on the trip. Their eyewitness account of the event would help corroborate Peter's story, affirm that the Spirit directed Peter to enter the company of these Gentiles, and provide helpful witness of the fruit of their venture – whatever that fruit might prove to be.

Peter does not serve the Lord on his own. He is careful to keep in the company of the saints as he goes about the Father's work. Doing so allows him to further disciple the believers who are with him, and provides prudent protection from false accusations that may well arise later from those who might doubt the holiness of Peter's dealings with these foreigners. Peter's actions provide us an excellent example of obedience entwined with prudence. As strange as it may sound, it is often not enough to be holy. We must be able to prove that we are walking with the Lord in holiness, lest the good things that we do "be spoken of as evil" (Romans 14:16).

10:24-26
And the following day they entered Caesarea. Now Cornelius was waiting for them, and had called together his relatives and close friends. As Peter

was coming in, Cornelius met him and fell down at his feet and worshiped him. But Peter lifted him up, saying, "Stand up; I myself am also a man."

After a day and a half on the road, Peter and his little band arrived at Caesarea. They found Cornelius awaiting their arrival with much anticipation. Not content with hearing the message from God by himself, he had "called together his relatives and close friends" as well. It is not reasonable to hear a message from God and feel no impulse to pass His words on to others.

God's messengers are precious to us. They handle the very words of God and represent His love and His glory as His ambassadors. The sight of the highly anticipated arrival of the man of God overwhelmed Cornelius and he "fell down at his feet and worshiped him." We might think that Cornelius' actions came out of ignorance, not realizing that men should not be worshiped. But then we see that John had a similar reaction when standing in the presence of God's messenger. In Revelation 19:10, John falls down and begins to worship his angelic guide. Perhaps Cornelius' understanding was clouded, but John knew very well that God is to be worshiped and God alone. And yet, though he knew this, the glory of the Lord was so reflected in the presence of His angelic ambassador that John was overwhelmed with reverential awe of this angel who knew the heart of God, had stood in the presence of God, and came bearing the words of God. Oh, how beautiful (Isaiah 52:7) are the feet of those who bring the good news of God's truths! Their feet are beautiful, and their countenance radiates the glory of God that they are on mission to serve. Ambassadors of Christ are endowed with the words of God, and sometimes the glory of the Word of God in the heart of the presenter is so great that their hearers are filled with an intense appreciation for them. This appreciation is here improperly manifested by an act of worship which Peter quickly refuses. "Stand up; I myself am also a man." Those who walk in the presence of God and speak the words of God may endure high praise from God's people. But like Peter here, and like the angel in Revelation 19, those who stand in the presence of God are little moved by the praises of men. The greatness of God is always displayed in glory before their mind's eye, and so they discourage personal praise. It is hard to think too highly of yourself when God is in your view.

10:27-33
And as he talked with him, he went in and found many who had come together. Then he said to them, "You know how unlawful it is for a Jewish man to keep company with or go to one of another nation. But God has

shown me that I should not call any man common or unclean. Therefore I came without objection as soon as I was sent for. I ask, then, for what reason have you sent for me?" So Cornelius said, "Four days ago I was fasting until this hour; and at the ninth hour I prayed in my house, and behold, a man stood before me in bright clothing, and said, 'Cornelius, your prayer has been heard, and your alms are remembered in the sight of God. Send therefore to Joppa and call Simon here, whose surname is Peter. He is lodging in the house of Simon, a tanner, by the sea. When he comes, he will speak to you.' So I sent to you immediately, and you have done well to come. Now therefore, we are all present before God, to hear all the things commanded you by God."

Cornelius and Peter are granted their first meeting together. They have nothing in common except for their devotion to God and God's love for them, so their self-introductions have nothing to do with their personal position, and solely focus on what God has spoken to them. Perhaps we would do well to introduce ourselves with a similar focus on our Lord's works and a similar silence regarding our own.

Peter begins by saying that unless the Lord had spoken to him, he would have never agreed to meet with Cornelius. And Cornelius follows by saying that unless the Lord had spoken to him, he would have never even known who Peter was. And then, with their short introductions behind them, Cornelius invites Peter to attend to the matter at hand, stating, "We are all present before God, to hear all the things commanded you by God."

Peter preached to a crowd of mockers in Acts 2:13-39. He preached to a crowd of gawkers in Acts 3:11-26. He preached to the angry, unbelieving Sanhedrin in Acts 4:1-12. But for all his preaching, it may be that Peter had never preached to a thirstier, more eager crowd than the one he faced here in Cornelius' house. It is a joyful opportunity to preach God's words even to unbelieving ears that do not care for our message. But it is a dear, soul-uplifting joy to preach to God's people who hang on every word and who will excitedly rise up and glorify God in response.

By divine appointment, Peter is asked to teach the words of God to devoted followers of God. Let us happily embrace each opportunity to teach and preach God's words to God's people in God's house each week. And let us never lose our proper excitement for what a delightful, wonderful, God-orchestrated and God-honoring event that is.

10:34-35
Then Peter opened his mouth and said: "In truth I perceive that God

shows no partiality. But in every nation whoever fears Him and works righteousness is accepted by Him."

"God shows no partiality." Our God taught this to His people long before Peter's time. Deuteronomy 10:17 says, "For the LORD your God is God of gods and Lord of lords, the great God, mighty and awesome, who shows no partiality nor takes a bribe." The Lord revealed this same truth to Paul: "There is no partiality with God" (Romans 2:11). Observers noticed this about Jesus, noting in Luke 20:21 that "You are not partial to any, but teach the way of God in truth." God will not save a man or a woman just because they are Jewish, and He will not condemn anyone just because they are not Jewish. The wonderful truth that must be presented to all peoples in every nation is that the God who created us is ready even now to cleanse us of our sins and take us as His child. He does not play favorites. All nations under heaven are granted an open path to knowing God and enjoying Him forever.

People of every tribe and tongue and nationality can come to God. This is not, however, saying that all roads lead to God or that all religions are good or that sinners can continue sinning and still be accepted by God. Not all religious people are pleasing to God, only "whoever fears Him." Those who revere God, love God, and shun all other gods are "accepted by Him" regardless of their ethnic background. This is wonderful news! But it is only wonderful news for those who revere God and for those who take the gospel of God to those who need Him. It provides no hope at all to those who trust in any other god but our Creator, and who trust in any savior other than Jesus, the Son of the living God.

The Lord God is ready to cleanse the sins of men and women in every nation under the sun. He does not show partiality. This is wonderful news! But it is not wonderful news for those who refuse to repent of their sin. Only the man and the woman who "works righteousness" is "accepted by Him." Those who persist in their sin, who cling to their sin rather than cling to their Savior can find no hope in these words at all. Psalm 15:1-2 reminds us that we are invited to come to God, but we are not invited to come to God and drag our sins with us. "LORD, who may abide in Your tabernacle? Who may dwell in Your holy hill? He who walks uprightly, and works righteousness, and speaks the truth in his heart."

Peter's words do not apply to those who worship hand-made gods or man-made religions. They do not apply to those who seek to be spiritual, but refuse to repent of their sin. But for those of us who take the gospel to distant lands, and for those in distant lands who have their hearts stirred by the message and mercy of their Creator, these words of Peter are a blessed encouragement.

10:36-38

The word which God sent to the children of Israel, preaching peace through Jesus Christ – He is Lord of all – that word you know, which was proclaimed throughout all Judea, and began from Galilee after the baptism which John preached: how God anointed Jesus of Nazareth with the Holy Spirit and with power, who went about doing good and healing all who were oppressed by the devil, for God was with Him.

Cornelius and his family and friends are all seated before Peter, intent on listening to "all the things commanded you by God" (verse 33). And so Peter begins to teach his captivated audience "the word which God sent to the children of Israel." God's Word to His people says, "You shall be holy; for I am holy" (Leviticus 11:44). God's Word to His people says, "The soul who sins shall die" (Ezekiel 18:20). God's Word to His people says that because of their rebellion, and their "wickedness," and because they have "multiplied disobedience," that God is at war with them. "I, even I, am against you and will execute judgments among you" (Ezekiel 5:6-8). Blessedly, God's Word also says that there is a way to peace with God "through Jesus Christ." He is the "Prince of Peace" (Isaiah 9:6). He will grant peace "to His people and to His saints" (Psalm 85:8). He will make peace "through the blood of His cross" (Colossians 1:20) for both the Jews and the Gentiles, providing peace to both "him who is far off and peace to him who is near" (Isaiah 57:19).

Peter tells Cornelius' family "the word which God sent to the children of Israel." It is a word that fills us with awe at God's greatness, sorrow over our sinfulness, and fear of His judgments. But His Word to us is a word of "peace." It is a peace brought to us by Jesus our Savior who was anointed by God "with the Holy Spirit and with power" and who "went about doing good and healing all who were oppressed by the devil."

Oh, what a wonderful message we have to bring to both those far off and those who are near. Our sin has caused us to be at enmity with God. But Jesus' death on the cross has put to death the enmity between the Creator and His children. Ephesians 2:15 says that Jesus "abolished in His flesh the enmity...thus making peace."

10:39-43

"And we are witnesses of all things which He did both in the land of the Jews and in Jerusalem, whom they killed by hanging on a tree. Him God

raised up on the third day, and showed Him openly, not to all the people, but to witnesses chosen before by God, even to us who ate and drank with Him after He arose from the dead. And He commanded us to preach to the people, and to testify that it is He who was ordained by God to be Judge of the living and the dead. To Him all the prophets witness that, through His name, whoever believes in Him will receive remission of sins."

Peter declares that he and the apostles "are witnesses of all things which (Jesus) did." We who are children of God by faith can take much comfort in knowing that we do not follow "cunningly devised fables." We have put our trust in Jesus. And our trust in Him is justified by the testimony of people who saw His great works, saw Him die, and saw Him risen from the dead with their own eyes. Peter relayed this same message in his second letter: "We do not follow cunningly devised fables when we made known to you the power and coming of our Lord Jesus Christ, but were eyewitnesses of His majesty" (II Peter 1:16). John gave the same affirmation. "That which we have seen and heard we declare to you, that you also may have fellowship with us" (I John 1:3). Let us recall that even today the Lord can use our personal testimony to good effect. First and foremost, we must teach the world the words of God. But in drawing people to the Savior, it is also often useful to give them our own eye-witness account of what our Lord has done in us and around us.

It is our joy to know Jesus and then to preach Jesus (Acts 11:20). We do not simply preach that Jesus is one choice out of many viable religious options. We preach that Jesus is the "Judge of the living and the dead." There is a judgment day awaiting all people. We do not have a choice regarding who judges us. Jesus is the One who will judge us and decide the eternal destiny of everyone on the planet. Blessedly, there is a way for us to pass His judgment, for He is not only Judge, but He is also Forgiver and Savior, and "whoever believes in Him will receive remission of sins."

10:44-48
While Peter was still speaking these words, the Holy Spirit fell upon all those who heard the word. And those of the circumcision who believed were astonished, as many as came with Peter, because the gift of the Holy Spirit had been poured out on the Gentiles also. For they heard them speak with tongues and magnify God. Then Peter answered, "Can anyone forbid water, that these should not be baptized who have received the

Holy Spirit just as we have?" And he commanded them to be baptized in the name of the Lord. Then they asked him to stay a few days.

In Acts 2:38 Peter told the crowd, "Repent, and let everyone of you be baptized in the name of Jesus Christ for the remission of sins; and you shall receive the gift of the Holy Spirit." In Peter's mind, if his listeners would confirm their faith with baptism, God would confirm His presence in them through the Holy Spirit. Here, however, God already confirmed His presence in this family of Gentile believers, so Peter quickly assessed that they were ready to be baptized in obedience to the Lord's command.

Acts 10 records for us a blessed event! The record of the first souls saved and the first people baptized in a non-Jewish family. In Matthew 28:19 Jesus commanded Peter and the apostles to "make disciples of all the nations." And here we see the great work of the Great Commission being carried out. Peter heard these Gentiles "speak with tongues and magnify God." And so it was his joy to baptize this family "in the name of the Lord." It was the first time Peter had ever seen the Holy Spirit poured out on the Gentiles. It was his first moment witnessing a Gentile being baptized. The event was historical and recorded in Scripture to provide eternal commemoration of salvation arriving to a brand-new people group. I read this passage and my heart leaps with the joy of so many happy memories. I have seen the Spirit of the Lord fall on believers from communities that have never worshiped God before. I have witnessed the baptism of believers in villages that had never before worshiped God since the dawn of time. Peter's joy is a joy still treasured by missionaries today. It is God's heart to save souls from every "tribe and tongue and people and nation" (Revelation 5:9). And the work that He did through Peter in the family of Cornelius, He continues to do through His servants in the nations of the world today.

Acts 11

11:1-3
Now the apostles and brethren who were in Judea heard that the Gentiles had also received the word of God. And when Peter came up to Jerusalem, those of the circumcision contended with him, saying, "You went in to uncircumcised men and ate with them!"

We would like to believe that when the lost have the gospel preached to them and when the saints are strengthened in their faith that all of God's people would rise up to thank and encourage God's servants who were used to bring such things to pass. We might think that when souls are saved, and devoted disciples are made that all of God's people would rejoice. Sadly, Peter finds that this is not necessarily the case. It may be that the church will always have some who will oppose even the godliest of efforts if those efforts do not conform to their preferred systems and strategies.

The Holy Spirit put His stamp of approval on the Gentiles' faith and on Peter's efforts when He fell on Cornelius' household (Acts 10:44). It is shameful when God's people disapprove of that which the Lord clearly approves of. To be fair, these brethren were voicing a complaint that Peter himself would have voiced before he saw the vision granted him in Acts 10:9-16. Let us be patient with the concerns and complaints of our fellow believers who have not enjoyed the same vantage points that we have been granted.

We take note of the fact that these complaining criticizers were not enemies of the faith. They were "apostles and brethren." It is further instructive to see that they did not consider Peter infallible or too exalted to be chastised. Peter was in the inner circle of Jesus. He was granted a special visit with the Lord after His resurrection (Luke 24:34). And yet, Peter's fellow believers did not assume his actions were best, nor did they believe he was entitled to any preferential treatment. If Peter's fellow believers did not give him the benefit of the doubt and did not think that he was above criticism, how can we imagine that we are worthy of any better treatment from those around us today? Let us take criticism patiently and respectfully, humbly changing our course when the complaints have merit and humbly providing answers to our critics when their complaints are errantly placed.

11:4-12
But Peter explained it to them in order from the beginning, saying: "I was in the city of Joppa praying; and in a trance I saw a vision, an object descending like a great sheet, let down from heaven by four corners; and it came to me. When I observed it intently and considered, I saw four-footed animals of the earth, wild beasts, creeping things, and birds of the air. And I heard a voice saying to me, 'Rise, Peter; kill and eat.' But I said, 'Not so, Lord! For nothing common or unclean has at any time entered my mouth.' But the voice answered me again from heaven, 'What God has cleansed you must not call common.' Now this was done three times, and all were drawn up again into heaven. At that very moment, three men stood before the house where I was, having been sent to me from Caesarea. Then the Spirit told me to go with them, doubting nothing. Moreover these six brethren accompanied me, and we entered the man's house.

Peter is called on the carpet to answer for his actions at the home of a Gentile. Rather than dismiss the criticism with a curt "God told me to do it, this is none of your business," Peter "explained it to them in order from the beginning." "A soft answer turns away wrath" (Proverbs 15:1), and a thorough, well-spoken answer can turn away criticism. Peter's first helpful response to the criticism was a humble, yet confident, orderly testimony of the events that had recently transpired. Peter's second helpful response was referring to his many witnesses that he had wisely taken with him to Cornelius' house. In his testimony, Peter tells his detractors, "These six brethren accompanied me." Peter was not acting as a lone ranger. He remained in the fellowship of other believers and kept himself accountable to the family of faith throughout his interactions with the Gentile believers. And these two actions will prove to completely win over his attackers and move them to retract their complaints and glorify God in verse 18.

11:13-18

"And he told us how he had seen an angel standing in his house, who said to him, 'Send men to Joppa, and call for Simon whose surname is Peter, who will tell you words by which you and all your household will be saved.' And as I began to speak, the Holy Spirit fell upon them, as upon us at the beginning. Then I remembered the word of the Lord, how He said, 'John indeed baptized with water, but you shall be baptized with the Holy Spirit.' If therefore God gave them the same gift as He gave us when we believed on the Lord Jesus Christ, who was I that I could withstand God?" When they heard these things they became silent; and they glorified God, saying, "then God has also granted to the Gentiles repentance to life."

Peter's testimony rocked his hearers' understanding. Not without reason, they had understood from their childhood that the Jews were the only people on earth destined to receive God's eternal blessings. But the angel's appearance to Cornelius, the vision given to Peter, and the fact that the Holy Spirit fell on these Gentiles turned this understanding upside down. And then, Peter's remembrance of the words of Jesus foretelling that all those that He would call His own "shall be baptized with the Holy Spirit" left them speechless. "They became silent." Their critiques of Peter's actions were suddenly dismissed, and they were forced to ponder, instead, the full impact of Peter's insights regarding the matter at hand. How long each man sat in silence is not stated, but at last they all came to a wonderful conclusion: "God has also granted to the Gentiles repentance to life." And happily, this conclusion moved them to "(glorify) God."

When the Gadarenes saw Jesus save Legion, they chased Him away (Mark 5:1-17). When the Jews saw Jesus save Lazarus, they plotted to kill Him (John 11:45-53); and when Jesus saved a lame man from his sins, the scribes were infuriated (Mark 2:1-7). But here, after much deliberation, the brethren in Jerusalem chose to react differently. They rejoiced and glorified God for the salvation He brought to man. The Gadarenes valued their money greater than they valued the salvation of men. The scribes in Mark 2 valued their traditions and their theology greater than the salvation of men. And the Jews valued their "place and nation" (John 11:48) more than they valued the rescue of a life from the grave. Let us join the brethren in this passage and find the salvation of a soul very precious to us.

Peter's encounter with Cornelius was very difficult for the brethren in Jerusalem to accept, but in the end, their devotion to the kingdom of God and their heart for the salvation of man won the day. May we be found to be like them, and hold that the glory of God and the salvation of man are matters of far greater importance to us than any matter of personal preference or prejudice.

11:19-21

Now those who were scattered after the persecution that arose over Stephen traveled as far as Phoenicia, Cyprus, and Antioch, preaching the word to no one but the Jews only. But some of them were men from Cyprus and Cyrene, who, when they had come to Antioch, spoke to the Hellenists, preaching the Lord Jesus. And the hand of the Lord was with them, and a great number believed and turned to the Lord.

To this point we have been granted the remarkable testimony of remarkable men who carried out the remarkable works of God. The powerful preaching ministries of Peter, Stephen, Philip, and Paul have been described and the great numbers of those who came to faith in Christ through their preaching have been recorded. Here, however, we find no names of powerful preachers. The subject of their sermons did not change, they continued "preaching the Lord Jesus" just as the famous apostles and evangelists did (Acts 5:42, 8:5, 9:20). The results of their preaching did not change: "A great number believed and turned to the Lord." One difference we do find, however, is the anonymity of those who spread the gospel. Rather than finding the names of famous men like Peter, Paul, Philip, and Stephen preaching the gospel, we are told only that "those who were scattered" preached the word of truth everywhere they went. No names are provided. No central figure riveted the attention of the crowds or the notice of Luke as he wrote. God's Word spread, and it spread through the witness of men and women whose names are not recorded and who gained no earthly fame. We do not have to be great men to spread the gospel. We must "preach the Lord Jesus." We must preach that He is Creator and Lord, that all things were made by Him and for Him (Colossians 1:16). We must preach that He died on the cross to pay the penalty for our sins; and we must preach that He rose from the dead. We must preach that He ascended into heaven, that

He will return again to earth, and that He will judge the living and the dead. Let us not seek a name for ourselves. That is obviously unnecessary. Let us seek only to preach the Lord Jesus and make His name great.

Chapter 11 provides a great turning point in the narrative of Acts. Before Peter's visit to Cornelius, the Word of God was preached "to no one but the Jews only." But now we find that the target audience of the ministries recorded in Acts will shift to Gentile listeners. Here we find these devoted followers of Christ taking the gospel to a brand-new people group. They did so without any apostolic leadership. They received their inspiration directly from the Holy Spirit. The New King James Version here says that the believers began preaching to "the Hellenists" – who were Greek-speaking Jews. But the context is clearly indicating that they were preaching to Gentiles, not just the Jews, and some translations employ that thinking and translate "Gentiles" into the narrative rather than "Hellenists." They were so invigorated by the gospel message, so driven to see God glorified, and so concerned for the eternal well-being of their fellow man that they crossed the dividing line of race and culture to carry the gospel truths to the Gentiles. This same enthusiasm for the gospel, this same devotion to our Creator, and this same love for humanity continue to fuel the fires of missions endeavors to this very day.

The apostles did not reinforce the ranks of "those who were scattered" preaching the Good News (Acts 8:1). But those who preached were blessed with even better company. "The hand of the Lord was with them." Psalm 98 speaks of the glorious times when the hand of the Lord does "marvelous things" to convey His salvation to the nations of the world. "Oh, sing to the LORD a new song! For He has done marvelous things; His right hand and His holy arm have gained Him the victory. The LORD has made known His salvation; His righteousness He has revealed in the sight of the nations" (Psalm 98:1-2). The hand of Saul and the hands of evil men and unbelievers may have been against them, but "the hand of the Lord was with them" and so their mission flourished. For if the hand of God is for us, what does it matter whose hands are against us?

11:22-23
Then news of these things came to the ears of the church in Jerusalem, and they sent out Barnabas to go as far as Antioch. When he came and had seen the grace of God, he was glad, and encouraged them all that with purpose of heart they should continue with the Lord.

News of the salvation of non-Jews in Antioch "came to the ears of the church in Jerusalem," and Barnabas was sent to assess the genuineness of their faith. If Barnabas carried with him any doubts or misgivings regarding the prospect of Gentiles entering the Kingdom of God, his doubts dissipated quickly when he saw "the grace of God" upon the believers there. Titus 2:11-14 tells us what it looks like when the "grace of God" falls upon us: The grace of God "teaches" us, it compels us to turn away from ungodliness and worldly lusts, to live "soberly, righteously, and godly in the present age." The grace of God moves us to look forward to the return of our Lord and Savior Jesus Christ, to purify ourselves, and to be "zealous for good works." When Barnabas arrived and found all of these unnatural, Spirit-given traits thriving among the Gentile believers, he was quickly convinced that "the grace of God" had fallen upon them. Blessed by the wonderful evidence of their new life in Christ, Barnabas encouraged the believers in Antioch to live with "purpose of heart" and to "continue with the Lord."

There are two general ways of living. We can live for the moment, do what seems best to us as opportunities arise and fall, and follow the feelings and leanings of our flesh. Or we can live "with purpose of heart." We arise in the morning driven with "steadfast purpose" (ESV) to carry out the desires of our Lord. Our own cravings become less important to us and we are undistracted by passing diversions regardless of whether they cause us pain or pleasure. Barnabas encourages the people to choose this second way of living. Dogs and cats and hoot owls live without "purpose of heart." They live to carry out the desires of their flesh. When they're hungry, they eat. When they're thirsty, they drink. When they're tired, they rest. There is no overriding purpose that takes precedence over their physical desires and trivial opportunities. We are not to live that way. We are called to live "with purpose of heart." The driving force behind all that we do is not to be food, or rest, or entertainment, but to carry out the purposes of God.

Barnabas also encouraged the believers to "continue with the Lord," to "cleave" (KJV) to the Lord continually. Paul encouraged the church in Colossae, "As you therefore have received Christ Jesus the Lord, so walk in Him" (Colossians 2:6). Good starts in Christ are wonderful, but we must ever, always "continue" with Him, "cleave" to Him. We must rise up early with our eyes on His face. We must set our minds on the mind of Christ that we might be like Him, represent Him, and care for His people as He does. We must "continue with the Lord." We must cling to Him for comfort, rely on Him for strength, look to Him for guidance, stand with Him in controversy, walk in His ways, speak His words, and do His works. We must "continue with the Lord." We must cling to His feet, cling to His promises, cling to His truths, and cling to our hope in Him. The beginning of a new life in Christ is glorious. But even better still is the life that never stops growing in "the grace of God" and constantly, unfailingly seeks to "continue with the Lord." Barnabas encouraged the early believers in Antioch and His encouragements stir us still today to "Seek the LORD and His strength; seek His face evermore!" (Psalm 105:4), and to follow the Lord's call in Psalm 27:8, "When You said, 'Seek My face,' my heart said to You, 'Your face, LORD, I will seek.'"

11:24
For he was a good man, full of the Holy Spirit and of faith. And a great many people were added to the Lord.

The work in Antioch was flourishing. Men and women fled the persecution in Jerusalem and carried the Good News there, where the Holy Spirit caused it to take root in good soil. The church was thriving, the ministry was expanding, and disciples were being made. Yet when Barnabas arrived, the work was blessed even more. "A great many people were added to the Lord." Oh, how good it is when the Lord sends His precious saints to bless the lives of other precious saints. Unhealthy churches embroiled in squabbles, jealousies, and unholy living may not always welcome the arrival of godly men. But good churches with godly members who are filled with the Spirit and fully occupied with doing good works will always welcome the arrival of heaven-sent reinforcements.

The ministry of Barnabas saw "a great many people" won to faith in Christ. If it were possible, all of us who desire to be used of God for His great purposes would be blessed by the opportunity to sit under his tutelage and have him mentor us in Christian ministry. Although that is not possible, we can seek to imitate the traits of Barnabas that Luke tells us God used to reap much spiritual fruit. First, Barnabas was "a good man." In Barnes' Notes on the Bible, he comments on this trait of Barnabas: "We should not undervalue talent, eloquence, or learning in the ministry, but we may remark that humble piety will often do more in the conversion of souls than the most splendid talents." The Bible does not indicate that Barnabas was a gifted preacher or possessed a sharp intellect. But those around him said that "he was a good man." As Barnes notes, it is not improper to thank the Lord for the special talents that He bestows on His ministers. But in our imitation of Christ, let us seek to be good men and feel no need to envy the gifts of talented men.

Barnabas was also recognized as a man "full of the Holy Spirit." The godly man longs for the Lord to use him to carry out works that he simply cannot do on his own. He desires to see souls saved – but it is obvious to all that only God can save a soul. If we would see the Lord use us to see the lost saved, it must be He who does the work in us. No number of talents can make up for the absence of the Holy Spirit. But the presence of the Holy Spirit in a man makes his lack of talent of no consequence at all. Do we long to be filled with the Spirit of God as Barnabas was? Luke 11:13 grants us this promise: "If you then, being evil, know how to give good gifts to your children, how much more will your heavenly Father give the Holy Spirit to those who ask Him!"

And thirdly, Barnabas is said to be a man full of faith. Oh, how often a ministry is stunted by insufficient faith! Once again, we find that it is not courage or giftedness that we need to carry out the works of Christ. We need faith. Our weaknesses are hardly detrimental to our ministry when we have faith that God can do all things. Let us have faith in God's sustaining hand, trust in His unfailing love, and have unwavering confidence that His counsel to us in the Scriptures provides the wisest course of action. If we would see the Lord use us for His great purposes we must trust in His word, in His power, and in His character. Psalm 4:5 says, "Offer the sacrifices of righteousness, and put your trust in the LORD." Psalm 37:3 says, "Trust in the LORD, and do good." This is what Barnabas was known for. May our lives be saturated with these same traits.

11:25-26
Then Barnabas departed for Tarsus to seek Saul. And when he had found him, he brought him to Antioch. So it was that for a whole year they assembled with the church and taught a great many people. And the disciples were first called Christians in Antioch.

Seeing the hand of God on Saul, Barnabas first befriended him in Acts 9:27. In Acts 9:30, the believers sent Saul to Tarsus to rescue him from the hand of the murderous Hellenists in Jerusalem. Now, seeing that the thriving work in Antioch needed godly leadership, Barnabas sought Saul out and brought him to help with the work there. The two of them proved to be a powerful team, and they "taught a great many people."

The new believers in Antioch grew "strong in the Lord and in the power of His might" (Ephesians 6:10). In fact, they grew so strong in the Lord, they spoke so powerfully in His name, they imitated His life so closely, obeyed His commands so faithfully, and taught His message so diligently that they began to be called "Christians," meaning followers of Jesus Christ, or little Christs. The name is a wonderful name. It is a dear privilege to be called "Christian." We belong to Jesus Christ. We imitate Christ. We serve Christ. We stand for what Christ stood for, and we long for what Christ longed for. We have the mind of Christ (I Corinthians 2:16). We adopt the attitude of Christ (Philippians 2:5 NLT). And we do the works of Christ (John 14:12). Believers in the Son of God were first called Christians in Antioch, and we delight to receive their name passed on to us. Having their name, then, let us have their attributes as well, so that anyone who has any significant interaction with us at all will be sure to associate our name with the name of our Lord and Savior Jesus Christ.

11:27-30

And in these days prophets came from Jerusalem to Antioch. Then one of them, named Agabus, stood up and showed by the Spirit that there was going to be a great famine throughout all the world, which also happened in the days of Claudius Caesar. Then the disciples, each according to his ability, determined to send relief to the brethren dwelling in Judea. This they also did, and sent it to the elders by the hands of Barnabas and Saul.

Following Barnabas' favorable visit to Antioch, a loving camaraderie grew between the believers in the church in Jerusalem and those in Antioch. Visits between the two congregations became more frequent, and "prophets came from Jerusalem to Antioch" to encourage the saints there. One such visit was by Agabus, who prophesied of an approaching famine. We are blessed as we read the response of the church in Antioch. In antici-pation that the famine would cause much hardship to their fellow believers in Jerusalem, the church in Antioch "determined" to do all that they could to take care of the saints there – most of whom they had never even met. Their sensitivity to the needs of other believers, and their prompt and generous response exemplifies for us what it looks like when God's people are Spirit-led to take care of God's people. Loving God supremely will always move us to delight in loving His children sacrificially.

It is His love for us and His Spirit in us which compel us to love all of His children and leap toward any opportunity to show them kindness. Most of the church in Antioch did not know most of the church in Jerusalem. But that proved no hindrance to their generosity. Both churches knew their Father, and that was enough to bind them together. The church in Antioch could not know the specific needs that the saints in Jerusalem would incur, but that also proved to be no hindrance to their generosity. They did not need to know the extent of Jerusalem's need. They knew very well the extent of Christ's kindness to them, and gave their gifts based on the level of His generosity. "Let us love one another, for love is of God; and everyone who loves is born of God and knows God. He who does not love does not know God, for God is love. Beloved, if God so loved us, we also ought to love one another" (I John 4:7,8,11). The church in Antioch provides us with a wonderful example of what it looks like when believers love one another well.

Acts 12

12:1-2
Now about that time Herod the king stretched out his hand to harass some from the church. Then he killed James the brother of John with the sword.

"Now about that time..." At the same time that the church was enjoying such wonderful growth, at the same time that the churches in Antioch and Jerusalem were enjoying such blessed fellowship, Herod "stretched out his hand" to "harass" them. "Friendship with the world is enmity with God" (James 4:4), and friendship with God may well lead to enmity with the world as well. Such is the case here, as we find that although the believers in Jerusalem enjoyed great favor with God and great favor in the eyes of their fellow believers, that favor did not extend to the wicked King Herod. Let us not expect unbelievers and wicked men to treat us as godly brothers in Christ do.

It is noteworthy that so little detail is dedicated to this heartbreaking event in the life of the early church. This marks the first time in history that an apostle was martyred, and yet so little was said about it. How could the martyrdom of James garner so little attention from the narrative of the Spirit-breathed Scriptures? We are reminded that we are at our best when we exalt God. It is man's highest work of significance to bring glory to God. We are not to make it our highest aim to see God glorify us. We need feel no offense for James' sake. He feels no slight. Today he exalts the Lord in glory before the throne of grace, just as he exalted the Lord in glory when Herod killed him with the sword. For James, death brought very little significant change. On earth, he lived to worship and exalt his Lord, and in heaven he continues to do the same.

II Timothy was Paul's final epistle. And as he came to the end of his last recorded words, he wrote, "No one stood with me, but all forsook me" (II Timothy 4:16). In verse 11 of that chapter he also wrote, "Only Luke is with me." How could the Apostle Paul, the one that God used to bring the Gospel to so much of the known world, come to the end of his life and find himself alone? The answer is similar to our question regarding James. We are to live our life to exalt our Creator. He is great. We are not. Let the rewards of fame be given to others. It is enough for us to be "found in Him" (Philippians 3:9). For then, when Christ is exalted, our eternal glory is assured, regardless of how much or how little the world makes of our time on earth. For if we die with Him, we shall also live with Him. If we endure, we shall also reign with Him (II Timothy 2:11-12).

12:3-4
And because he saw that it pleased the Jews, he proceeded further to seize Peter also. Now it was during the Days of Unleavened Bread. So when he had arrested him, he put him in prison, and delivered him to four squads of soldiers to keep him, intending to bring him before the people after Passover.

In Acts 8:1 we saw the great persecution of the church begin. Initially, the apostles were protected from this oppression, but now we see that the apostles are suddenly the prime targets of Herod's harassment. After murdering James, Herod quickly moved to imprison Peter as well, intending to kill him as soon as the Passover observances were complete. Luke does not bother telling us what the pretended charges were that Herod used to arrest Peter. It was clear that Herod arrested Peter and planned to put him to death because his evil efforts "pleased the Jews." Herod's desire to please wicked people moved him to murder an innocent man, and plot to kill another. Let Herod's example remind us that we must be carefully selective regarding the company we keep. "Do not be deceived: 'Evil company corrupts good habits'" (I Corinthians 15:33). Herod's desire to court the favor of the wicked Jews has already made him a murderer, and now moves him to further pervert justice and prepare to murder Peter. Let there be no mistake, friendships with wicked people will invariably heap guilt upon us. This understanding moved David to say, "I have hated the assembly of evildoers, and will not sit with the wicked" (Psalm 26:5).

12:5
Peter was therefore kept in prison, but constant prayer was offered to God for him by the church.

Peter was imprisoned by an evil, powerful king. 16 Roman guards watched over him to prevent his escape. James had just recently been martyred under similar circumstances. Peter's situation could not have been more perilous. "But constant prayer was offered to God for him by the church." We are led to believe that without prayer, Peter's execution was certain. Perhaps James was arrested and executed before any prayer defense could be raised, but the Passover afforded God's people time to erect a fortress of prayer around Peter, and they were faithful to the task. With Peter's life on the line, God's people prayed as if their prayers were Peter's only line of defense. They prayed as David prayed in Psalm 86:2, "Save Your servant who trusts in You!" In II Thessalonians 3:1-2, Paul asked this of his fellow believers: "Finally, brethren, pray for us, that the word of the Lord may run swiftly and be glorified, just as it is with you, and that we may be delivered from unreasonable and wicked men; for not all have faith." And here, the church does just that for Peter. They pray that Peter will be "delivered from unreasonable and wicked men." In Philippians 1:19, Paul says that he is confident that he will be delivered from his enemies because the church is praying for him, and here we see that Paul's confidence is well placed, seeing that Peter was, indeed, rescued because God's people were praying.

May all those whose rescue is dependent on our prayers be equally secure.

12:6-10
And when Herod was about to bring him out, that night Peter was sleeping, bound with two chains between two soldiers; and the guards before the door were keeping the prison. Now behold, an angel of the Lord stood by him, and a light shone in the prison; and he struck Peter on the side and raised him up, saying, "Arise quickly!" And his chains fell

off his hands. Then the angel said to him, "Gird yourself and tie on your sandals"; and so he did. And he said to him, "Put on your garment and follow me." So he went out and followed him, and did not know that what was done by the angel was real, but thought he was seeing a vision. When they were past the first and the second guard posts, they came to the iron gate that leads to the city, which opened to them of its own accord; and they went out and went down one street, and immediately the angel departed from him.

The night before Peter was to be killed, we found him sleeping. Others are pleading with the Lord for his rescue, crying out to the Lord in an all-night vigil. But Peter is peacefully asleep, fully confident in the Lord's protection. The church is doing their job of fervently praying, and Peter is doing his job of quietly resting in the presence of his Savior. When David fled from Absalom he wrote, "I lay down and slept; I awoke, for the LORD sustained me" (Psalm 3:5). David wrote again in Psalm 4:8, "I will both lie down in peace, and sleep; for You alone, O LORD, make me dwell in safety." Restful sleep in the midst of tumult is a gift from the Lord. A clear conscience under the watchful care of Immanuel yields a unique serenity that makes you feel very good when you close your eyes.

Peter is sleeping so soundly, so peacefully, that the angel had to strike him on the side to wake him up. Apparently, the Lord had not given Peter any advance assurances of rescue, for even as he walked out of the prison, he still "did not know that what was done by the angel was real, but thought he was seeing a vision." Sometimes the Lord gives us a clear vision of His sure protection, as when David faced Goliath and boldly declared, "This day the LORD will deliver you into my hand, and I will strike you and take your head from you. And this day I will give the carcasses of the camp of the Philistines to the birds of the air and the wild beasts of the earth, so that all the earth may know that there is a God in Israel" (I Samuel 17:46). But sometimes the Lord simply gives us a clear vision of His greatness and that our ultimate destiny is secure, though we may not survive the peril at hand. Such was the case for Shadrach and friends, who declared to King Nebuchadnezzar, "Our God whom we serve is able to deliver us from the burning fiery furnace, and He will deliver us from your hand, O king. But if not, let it be known to you, O king, that we do not serve your gods, nor will we worship the gold image which you have set up" (Daniel 3:17-18). May our confidence in Christ not be dependent on our physical security. God is great. Our God loves us completely. And the eternal destiny of our souls is completely assured by Christ's death, resurrection, and promise of heaven

(John 14:1-4). May these assurances grant us the same composure, the same restful sleep enjoyed by Peter 2,000 years ago, and enjoyed by David, 1,000 years before that.

12:11-12
And when Peter had come to himself, he said, "Now I know for certain that the Lord has sent His angel, and has delivered me from the hand of Herod and from all the expectation of the Jewish people." So, when he had considered this, he came to the house of Mary, the mother of John whose surname was Mark, where many were gathered together praying.

While in the glow of the angel's presence, Peter thought that he was seeing a vision. It was only after the angel departed and the chill of the air and the darkness of night enveloped him did he recognize that he had, indeed, been rescued. Knowing that a group of believers had gathered to pray for him, Peter sets out to tell them with rejoicing that their prayers on his behalf had been answered. Peter had many enemies – he notes that "the Jewish people" were those that sought his execution, as if the majority of the entire nation was against him. Peter's enemies were powerful: the hand of Herod, himself, was raised against him. But Peter also had friends who were praying for him, and it is to those friends in the faith that he turns for shelter against his enemies. Praying friends make excellent havens. When enemies and troubles assail us, let us follow Peter's footsteps to the door of those who pray for us. Their prayers provide protection, and stresses and dangers are happily lessened when in the company of praying saints.

12:13-15
And as Peter knocked at the door of the gate, a girl named Rhoda came to answer. When she recognized Peter's voice, because of her gladness she did not open the gate, but ran in and announced that Peter stood before the gate. But they said to her, "You are beside yourself!" Yet she kept insisting that it was so. So they said, "It is his angel."

Let us be enthused about praying for our fellow believers seeing that such great victories can be experienced by the church when we pray for one another. And let us be heartened by this example of weak faith finding favor with God. Peter's friends were praying that he might be rescued from his death sentence. They were in "constant" prayer for him (verse 5). But when Peter arrived in direct answer to their prayers, their faith proved to be so weak that they did not believe Rhoda's testimony even when Peter arrived at their doorstep! Their prayers were lifted up to heaven with weak faith but filled with powerful passion. And blessedly, the Lord is pleased to answer compassionate prayers and passionate prayers even when they are not mixed with great faith (Matthew 17:20, Mark 9:24).

12:16-17

Now Peter continued knocking and when they opened the door and saw him, they were astonished. But motioning to them with his hand to keep silent, he declared to them how the Lord had brought him out of the prison. And he said, "Go, tell these things to James and to the brethren." And he departed and went to another place.

Peter provides here a practical guide for how we should respond when the Lord miraculously intervenes to save us from a disaster. First, Peter motions the people with his hand to keep quiet. He does not become presumptuous. He does not throw away prudence or proper caution assuming that God's past kindness assures immunity from future dangers. Let us not think that faith in God or past provisions from God indicate that we should no longer exercise wise discretion regarding personal provision and protection. Secondly, Peter immediately gives full credit to God for his deliverance. "He declared to them how the Lord had brought him out of the prison." He does not try to divert praise to himself. He does not talk of personal courage, his powerful prayers, or his oneness with God. He gives all glory to God for his rescue, taking no credit at all for himself. Thirdly, he multiplies those who bear witness to the Lord's great work. He immediately sends his listeners off to share the wonderful news with "James and the brethren." It is good for us to preach the gospel. It is even better for us to multiply disciples who will join their voices with ours in spreading the great news entrusted to us.

12:18-19

Then, as soon as it was day, there was no small stir among the soldiers about what had become of Peter. But when Herod had searched for him and not found him, he examined the guards and commanded that they should be put to death. And he went down from Judea to Caesarea, and stayed there.

Herod's plans to execute Peter now thwarted, he immediately set out to find someone to blame. It was God's doing, and God's alone that allowed Peter to escape, but unable to exact vengeance on God, Herod chose to abuse the authority given him and execute the (somewhat) innocent guards instead. The execution of Peter's guards moves us to remember the comparable death of the guards who burned to death when they threw Shadrach, Meshach, and Abednego into the fiery furnace in Daniel 3:22. In both instances the guards were not negligent in their duty. But in both instances, they died because of the sin of their leader. Proverbs 11:9 says that "he who pursues evil pursues it to his own death," and here we see that the king's pursuit of evil resulted in the death of others as well. May this warning not be lost on us. Associations with rich and powerful men may provide temporary profit, but sooner or later, as in the sad case of these soldiers under Herod's command, associations with wicked men, and especially wicked rulers, will predictably lead to the eventual demise of those who follow them.

12:20-23

Now Herod had been very angry with the people of Tyre and Sidon; but they came to him with one accord, and having made Blastus the king's personal aide their friend, they asked for peace, because their country was supplied with food by the king's country. So on a set day Herod, arrayed in royal apparel, sat on his throne and gave an oration to them. And the people kept shouting, "The voice of a god and not of a man!" Then immediately an angel of the Lord struck him, because he did not give glory to God. And he was eaten by worms and died.

Psalm 115:1 says, "Not unto us, O LORD, not unto us, but to Your name give glory." Our greatest achievement in life is to give glory to our Creator. Psalm 96:8 calls on us to "give to the LORD the glory due His name." Here, the people of Tyre and Sidon steal from God's glory and give it to Herod, and Herod steals from God's glory in a vain attempt to keep it for himself. This, certainly, is the basest crime we can commit – to try to steal God's glory for ourselves. Proverbs 25:27 says, "To seek one's own glory is not glory." It is deception, it is theft, it is criminal arrogance, and it incurs the death penalty as we see here. Matthew Henry says, "God is very jealous for his own honour, and will be glorified upon those whom he is not glorified by." We can choose to glorify God with praise and obedience, or we can bring glory to God, as Herod did, when our wickedness is destroyed, but God will not be denied the glory due His name.

The Lord seeks the glory due His name. And we are innately endowed with the desire to surrender to Him that glory which He so richly deserves. But, like Herod, we are also prone to twist our highest calling into a pursuit of glory for ourselves. Blessedly, we are provided with a healthy outlet for this human longing to take pride and joy in our personal glory. Herod succumbed to the temptation to revel in his (supposed) glory. But for those of us who seek to live on a higher plane than Herod did (and those who would prefer to live longer than Herod did), Jeremiah 9:23-24 grants us this instruction: "'Let not the wise man glory in his wisdom, let not the mighty man glory in his might, nor let the rich man glory in his riches; but let him who glories glory in this, that he understands and knows Me, that I am the LORD, exercising lovingkindness, judgment, and righteousness in the earth. For in these I delight,' says the LORD."

12:24-25
But the word of God grew and multiplied. And Barnabas and Saul returned from Jerusalem when they had fulfilled their ministry, and they also took with them John whose surname was Mark.

"The word of God grew and multiplied." What an exciting picture. Despite persecution of the church, despite the death of James and the threats directed at God's people, God's Word "grew and multiplied." God's Word was preached by more emissaries than ever before, and the Word of God yielded greater effect on the hearts of its hearers than ever before. The number of people who believed in the Word of God "multiplied" and their reverence for God's Word "grew." This advancement of the Word of God would soon turn the world upside down (Acts 17:6), and the prominent men who will soon prove to be key instruments in the propagation of God's Word are here re-introduced. The remaining 16 chapters of the book of Acts will detail Paul's efforts in this great ministry to see the Word of God continue to grow and multiply, a ministry that has persisted throughout the ages. Today, it is our happy responsibility to join the work begun by Paul and Barnabas to see the Word of God grow and multiply. Let us preach God's Word to the lost. Let us teach God's Word to the saints. For it is in seeing the lost saved, seeing the saved discipled, and seeing the church prosper through the works of Spirit-empowered disciples that we are allowed to take part in this supreme effort to see the Word of God grow and multiply and have its blessed effect on all that it touches.

Acts 13

13:1-3

Now in the church that was at Antioch there were certain prophets and teachers: Barnabas, Simeon who was called Niger, Lucius of Cyrene, Manaen who had been brought up with Herod the tetrarch, and Saul. As they ministered to the Lord and fasted, the Holy Spirit said, "Now separate to Me Barnabas and Saul for the work to which I have called them." Then, having fasted and prayed, and laid hands on them, they sent them away.

The names of the first five prominent leaders of the church at Antioch are listed for us. As these five men "ministered to the Lord and fasted," the Holy Spirit spoke to them all in unison, instructing them to set Saul and Barnabas apart for "the work to which I have called them." This commissioning of Saul and Barnabas to take the gospel to distant lands marked the beginning of a new era. Saul and Barnabas become the first missionaries of the church, exemplifying for us the heart of the healthy church to see the kingdom of God expand in distant lands even as exuberant dedication to the work of saving souls and discipling new believers is carried out locally.

We are provided with a simple pattern for sending out missionaries. The missionary serves the Lord in his home church. As he ministers in his church, the Holy Spirit calls him to special service in distant missions. The local church affirms the Spirit's calling, commissioning the missionary to carry out the work as an emissary of the church. And finally, with prayer and fasting and good will, the church sends the missionary out to carry out their Spirit-directed call.

The matter of sending out missionaries from the church is presented as a weighty matter. Fasting and prayer are repeatedly mentioned as integral parts of the process of calling, preparing, and sending the missionaries out. The Holy Spirit called Saul and Barnabas, but He did not speak to them alone. The Spirit spoke to the entire church, and especially the leading prophets and teachers of the church so that they might verify the qualifications of the missionaries, affirm the validity of the Spirit's call, and attest to the church's intent to continue supporting the missionary's efforts through prayer. Antioch's process for sending out missionaries remains the ideal framework to guide churches still today.

Acts 13:4-8

So, being sent out by the Holy Spirit, they went down to Seleucia, and from there they sailed to Cyprus. And when they arrived in Salamis, they preached the word of God in the synagogues of the Jews. They also had John as their assistant. Now when they had gone through the island to Paphos, they found a certain sorcerer, a false prophet, a Jew whose name was Bar-Jesus, who was with the proconsul, Sergius Paulus, an intelligent man. This man called for Barnabas and Saul and sought to hear the word of God. But Elymas the sorcerer (for so his name is translated) withstood them, seeking to turn the proconsul away from the faith.

Saul and Barnabas set out as the first missionaries of the church at Antioch. We can imagine that their excitement was hardly containable. The early days of missionaries on their field of service are customarily filled with glorious opportunities to share the gospel, Spirit-led encounters with lost men and women needing a Savior, and confrontations with adversaries who seek to hinder the missionary's efforts. Here, we see all three of these common experiences of the missionary clearly illustrated.

Promptly upon their arrival in Salamis we find Saul and Barnabas preaching the Word of God in the synagogues of the Jews. One of the first orders of business for the missionary is finding a bridge to the gospel – finding a platform that will generate opportunity to present the gospel to the lost. In this case, the bridge came quickly – the synagogues were filled with religious men and women with a knowledge of God, but no knowledge of Jesus Christ. Saul and Barnabas leapt to this opportunity, utilizing this easy-to-reach bridge to share the Good News.

In addition to the joy of finding a bridge to share the gospel with the lost, another of the great joys of the missionary comes when the Lord brings to us those He has prepared to receive the Good News. No bridge is required! God brings prepared souls directly to His servants! Here, just as when the angel brought the Ethiopian eunuch to Philip in Acts chapter 8, the Spirit now brings Sergius Paulus to Saul and Barnabas, prepared to "hear the word of God" from them.

By no means are all missionary experiences positive, however. Opposition often comes quickly. Elymas the sorcerer not only rejected the Good News, but he actively sought to keep others from hearing the gospel as well. Jesus faced this same type of opposition and pronounced woe on those who obstruct the path of truth-seekers. In Luke 11:52 Jesus said, "Woe to you lawyers! For you have taken away the key of knowledge. You did not enter in yourselves, and those who were entering in you hindered." Again, in Matthew 23:13 Jesus said, "Woe to you, scribes and Pharisees, hypocrites! For you shut up the kingdom of heaven against men; for you neither go in yourselves, nor do you allow those who are entering to go in." Since both Jesus and Paul faced these men who actively seek to prevent people from reconciling with God, we are likely to face them too. Let us be undaunted by their opposition and unintimidated by the fierceness of their attacks, knowing that the gates of hell cannot prevail (Matthew 16:18) against our offense. The weapons of our warfare are no ordinary weapons. They are "mighty in God" for pulling down the strongholds (II Corinthians 10:4) that people like Elymas the sorcerer think to construct to hinder God's kingdom advances.

13:9-12

Then Saul, who also is called Paul, filled with the Holy Spirit, looked intently at him and said, "O full of all deceit and all fraud, you son of the devil, you enemy of all righteousness, will you not cease perverting the straight ways of the Lord? And now, indeed, the hand of the Lord is upon you, and you shall be blind, not seeing the sun for a time." And immediately a dark mist fell on him, and he went around seeking someone to lead him by the hand. Then the proconsul believed, when he saw what had been done, being astonished at the teaching of the Lord.

The ways of the Lord are "straight." His ways are straightforward. His teachings are honest, direct, and sincere. Those who join Elymas in opposing God seek to 'pervert' His ways. They make it seem that God is not the only god. They make it appear that holiness is not necessary, or even that evil is preferable. They pervert truth to make it seem that all religions are good. They pervert the love of God into an acceptance of immorality. They pervert His blessings and deceive men into feeling entitled. And they pervert His patience and His mercy making it appear that there is no judgment for the wicked. Paul has preached the gospel clearly, in a straightforward manner, but Elymas rushes in with a perverted twist on Paul's message, seeking to divert the proconsul's attention. Paul will have none of it. Filled with the power of the Holy Spirit, with Sergius Paulus' eternity hanging in the balance, Paul rebukes Elymas. But it is not the power of Paul that overcomes Elymas' deceptions. "The hand of the Lord" fell upon Elymas to blind his eyes and shut his mouth. The manifestation of the Spirit's power has its desired effect. Elymas slinks away and the proconsul's soul is saved.

Verse 12 says that Sergius Paulus believed the gospel "being astonished" by the teachings of the Lord. Yes, the power of the Holy Spirit that blinded the eyes of Elymas was astonishing. But "the teaching of the Lord" is even more remarkable. The gospel is astonishing. His creation of the world stretches our imagination. His standard for holiness is far beyond our expectation. Christ's willingness to suffer and die for us on the cross is truly nothing less than astonishing. His resurrection story is amazing, and His offer to us to allow our entry into heaven is astounding. So begins the missionary ministry of Paul and Barnabas. They walked in the power of the Spirit and they presented the gospel message, and Sergius Paulus was astonished by what he saw and heard. Let all missionaries in modern times take heart. The salvation of Sergius Paulus required no special attributes of Paul and Barnabas. They were "filled with the Holy Spirit." "The hand of the Lord" fell upon their enemies. And "the teaching of the Lord" astonished their hearers. The salvation of the proconsul was brought about by the filling of the Holy Spirit, by the hand of the Lord, and by His teaching. Nothing extraordinary was required of the missionary duo. Let us walk with the Lord in holiness. Let us pray that His hand will move among us. And let us pass on to others the astonishing teachings of the Lord. Ah, such blessed results await us when we do.

13:13
Now when Paul and his party set sail from Paphos, they came to Perga in Pamphylia; and John, departing from them, returned to Jerusalem.

We might miss the significance of this seemingly parenthetical statement if it were not for the serious repercussions that will arise from John Mark's departure in Pamphylia. Acts 15:36-41 tells of the break in relationship between Paul and Barnabas that arose because of John Mark's failure to complete his mission. We are not told why John Mark departed from Paul and Barnabas, but we can see from Paul's reaction that he not did feel that John Mark's abandonment of the work was justifiable. Let us loathe the idea of quitting. In John 17:4 Jesus prays, "I have finished the work which You have given me to do." In II Timothy 4:7 Paul finds comfort in the fact that he has "finished the race." Let us have a mind to follow these examples. When the Lord grants us a task, any task, let us "not lose heart" (Galatians 6:9) until our assignment is complete. Perseverance is an essential character quality of the Christian (II Peter 1:6). Quitting our post before the work is done is a discouragement to the body of Christ and will often lead to disharmony and disunity just as it does here in the case of Paul and Barnabas.

13:14-15
But when they departed from Perga, they came to Antioch in Pisidia, and went into the synagogue on the Sabbath day and sat down. And after the reading of the Law and the Prophets, the rulers of the synagogue sent to them, saying, "Men and brethren, if you have any word of exhortation for the people, say on."

John Mark abandoned them in the work, but Paul and Barnabas are found here pressing on. It seems that nothing changed from their ministry efforts, even with the loss of a key companion. In verse 5, Paul and Barnabas are seen preaching in the synagogues in Salamis, and here we find them continuing that same ministry. We must not allow the work of the Lord to be hindered. The church will always face the loss of key spiritual leaders, and the loss of these fellow laborers can cause those with weak faith to lose heart. But like Paul and Barnabas, we must be undeterred and undistracted when fellow believers are taken from us, whatever the reason.

13:16-23
Then Paul stood up, and motioning with his hand said, "Men of Israel, and you who fear God, listen: the God of this people Israel chose our fathers, and exalted the people when they dwelt as strangers in the land

of Egypt, and with an uplifted arm He brought them out of it. Now for a time of about forty years He put up with their ways in the wilderness. And when He had destroyed seven nations in the land of Canaan, He distributed their land to them by allotment. After that He gave them judges for about four hundred and fifty years, until Samuel the prophet. And afterward they asked for a king; so God gave them Saul the son of Kish, a man of the tribe of Benjamin, for forty years. And when He had removed him, He raised up for them David as king, to whom also He gave testimony and said, 'I have found David the son of Jesse, a man after My own heart, who will do all My will.' From this man's seed, according to the promise, God raised up for Israel a Savior – Jesus –

If the role of the missionary was to approach strangers and suddenly announce to them that they have believed wrongly all their life, our work would be difficult indeed. Blessedly, our Lord has called the peoples of the earth to Himself long before our arrival on the scene. The role of the missionary, then, is much easier. We simply are required to point out how the Lord has been revealing truth to them all their lives, and that we have come to call our listeners to respond to what the Lord has already revealed to their minds and conscience. In Acts 17, Paul pointed out the Athenians' reverence for "the unknown god," and here, Paul discusses his hearers' reverence for the God they know very well. Paul pointed out how their ancestors were chosen by God to receive His mercies. He reminds them of their need for a Savior in the wilderness and their need for a judge and a king to provide for their nation after their deliverance from the wilderness. God chose Israel as His own special people to receive His rescue and promised that He would one day raise up Israel's ultimate deliverer from the line of David. And now, it is Paul's happy duty to announce that this Deliverer that God had promised and that His people had expectantly awaited for generations had at last come in the flesh. God has raised up for Israel a Savior – Jesus. Paul takes the truths that God had already revealed to His people and seamlessly moves them from these accepted core beliefs to see their need to embrace Jesus as their Savior.

Paul's sermon illustrates for us a helpful way to share the gospel with those who have never heard it. Begin with truths that our listeners know and accept, and then show how those truths compel them to embrace Jesus as the Savior from their sin. Whether talking to postmodern agnostic physicians in the U.S, or to illiterate Buddhists in rural Thailand, to polytheists in ancient Greece, or to God-fearing Jews in first century Pisidia, this means of sharing the Good News continues to beckon hearers to reconcile with Jesus. When we teach the gospel to the lost, we can do so boldly and with holy optimism, knowing that the conscience of man will confirm in their heart that what we are saying is true. Even if they have never heard the full gospel before, we can know that "they know the truth about God because he has made it obvious to them" (Romans 1:19 NLT).

13:24-30

"...after John had first preached, before His coming, the baptism of repentance to all the people of Israel. And as John was finishing his course, he said, 'Who do you think I am? I am not He. But behold, there comes One after me, the sandals of whose feet I am not worthy to loose.' Men and brethren, sons of the family of Abraham, and those among you who fear God, to you the word of this salvation has been sent. For those who dwell in Jerusalem, and their rulers, because they did not know Him, nor even the voices of the Prophets which are read every Sabbath, have fulfilled them in condemning Him. And though they found no cause for death in Him, they asked Pilate that He should be put to death. Now when they had fulfilled all that was written concerning Him, they took Him down from the tree and laid Him in a tomb. But God raised Him from the dead."

Paul's listeners were "sons of the family of Abraham." They were known for their fear of God (verse 26). Paul highlights these traits and stirs them to excitement with the news that it is to them specifically that "the word of this salvation has been sent." Paul's hearers could personally apply the promises that God made to Abraham. The promises of salvation given in the Old Testament were directly given to those "who fear God." Their relation to Abraham and their fear of God had placed Paul's listeners in a very good place. Paul highlights this good place they are in so that they might see that theirs was the perfect vantage point from which to see the glorious truth that Jesus is the Messiah, come to save His people from their sin. The life, death, and resurrection of Jesus "fulfilled" all the prophecies made through the "voices of the Prophets" which they had listened to "every Sabbath." Paul invites them to take full advantage of their superb vantage point and embrace Jesus as their Lord. Paul talks of this advantage granted the Jewish people in Romans 3:1-2. "What advantage then has the Jew, or what is the profit of circumcision? Much in every way! Chiefly because to them were committed the oracles of God." The chance to study "the oracles of God" in the Scriptures provides us all with the greatest possible opportunity to rightly grasp and respond to the truths of the lordship of Christ. Jesus died to save the souls of sinful men, and He rose again as evidence of His power over death and sin, and those with access to the oracles of God, as these who listened to Paul in Pisidia, are best primed to put their faith in Jesus to the saving of their souls.

13:31-37

He was seen for many days by those who came up with Him from Galilee to Jerusalem, who are His witnesses to the people. And we declare to you glad tidings – that promise which was made to the fathers. God has fulfilled this for us their children, in that He has raised up Jesus. As it is also written in the second Psalm: 'You are My Son, today I have begotten You.' And that He raised Him from the dead, no more to return to corruption, He has spoken thus: 'I will give you the sure mercies of David.' Therefore He also says in another Psalm: 'You will not allow Your Holy One to see corruption.' For David, after he had served his own generation by the will of God, fell asleep, was buried with his fathers, and saw corruption; but He whom God raised up saw no corruption.

Paul continues his Pisidian sermon with the words of angels: "We declare to you glad tidings." In Luke 2:10 the angel announces to the frightened shepherds, "I bring you good tidings of great joy which will be to all people." In a way, Paul is here announcing the arrival of Jesus just as the angel was doing with the shepherds, so it is not surprising that he used the same words. The birth and resurrection of Jesus is good news! It is very "glad tidings" that should be passed on to the Jews in Pisidia and to "all people" everywhere. Paul emphasizes the resurrection because it was the single clearest substantiation that Jesus was the Son of God, deserving of their devotion, and able to take away their sins. Romans 1:4 says that Jesus was "declared to be the Son of God with power according to the Spirit of holiness, by the resurrection from the dead." Paul's report of Jesus' resurrection would certainly astound his hearers, and some would be tempted to doubt, so Paul provides them with two great helps to their belief. First, Paul gives them evidence. Verse 31 says that Jesus was seen "for many days" by many people, who became His "witnesses to the people." And secondly, Paul reminds them that this fantastic, super-natural resurrection of Jesus was actually foretold in the Scriptures that Paul's audience knew so well. He quotes Psalm 2, Psalm 16, and Isaiah 55 – passages that would help the crowd see that Jesus' resurrection was not beyond belief, but was the fulfillment of their beloved Scriptures, Scriptures that God had provided to prepare their hearts for this very day when the news of their Messiah's victory over death would come to their ears.

13:38-41

"Therefore let it be known to you, brethren, that through this Man is preached to you the forgiveness of sins; and by Him everyone who believes is justified from all things from which you could not be justified by the law of Moses. Beware therefore, lest what has been spoken in the prophets come upon you: 'Behold, you despisers, marvel and perish! For I work a work in your days, a work which you will by no means believe, though one were to declare it to you.'"

Having established for his listeners that Jesus is the Son of God, Paul then explains that Jesus' conquest of death provides for us "glad tidings" indeed. Through this Jesus that Paul preached, we are granted "the forgiveness of sins." This forgiveness is the very thing our souls have longed for since our conscience was first awakened to our guilt. Paul's audience had sought forgiveness in "the law of Moses," but they "could not be justified" by that means. Thai Buddhists seek to find forgiveness of sins through merit, but their own religion also teaches that merit can never take away sins. Sinners with an intact conscience long for forgiveness, so Paul was so right when he said that he came with "glad tidings!" Because it is "through this Man" – Jesus – that forgiveness and freedom from sin is finally attainable.

The forgiveness of sin is "glad tidings." The eternal destiny of all men and women is contingent on this single matter – the presence of sin versus the forgiveness of sin. The presence of sin causes the present and eternal estrangement from the presence and favor of God. The forgiveness of sin permits present and eternal fellowship with God. The attainment of the forgiveness of sin could not be more essential to the soul! This forgiveness is unavailable through any earthly means. Neither religion, nor meritorious efforts, nor virtuous behavior, nor any self-based good work can procure forgiveness of sin for us. Nothing but the sacrificed life of Jesus holds enough value to redeem a man's life from the penalty of sin. Since then, the eternal state of the soul depends completely on having sins forgiven, and since Jesus is the only possible Provider of that forgiveness, Paul warns his hearers to "beware" so that they will not miss this once-in-an-eternity opportunity to have their sins forgiven. "Despisers" of Jesus will "marvel and perish" if they refuse to "believe" in the work of Jesus that He carried out to take away their sin. Paul's message is life-changing, and it is simple. Jesus Christ died on the cross to take away our sins. He arose from the dead to prove His power over death and sin. And we must put our faith in Him, or we will "marvel and perish." Let all thinking men take note.

13:42
So when the Jews went out of the synagogue, the Gentiles begged that these words might be preached to them the next Sabbath.

Paul finished preaching Jesus, and as soon as the Jews left, the Gentiles flocked upon him and "begged" him to speak to them about Jesus again. It is a joy to speak of the deep truths of God even when the heart of the hearer is hardened. But the opportunity to preach Jesus to avid listeners is a delight. Paul's experience foreshadows the experiences of missionaries still today. We preach Jesus to the lost. Some will scoff, some will oppose, and some will not care. But the elect of God with an awakened conscience beg us to tell them more. "These words" of Jesus' life and death and resurrection stir our listeners with a hunger to listen longer. "These words" of the forgiveness that is found in Jesus ignite a fire in the souls of those who crave a clean conscience. In Romans 1:16 Paul wrote that the gospel of Jesus Christ "is the power of God to salvation." Paul's words in that verse were born out of his experiences like this, seeing the words of the gospel captivate listeners and compel them to reconcile with Jesus the Savior. God's Word beckons the human heart to strain listening ears to drink in His message again and again and again. We need not concern ourselves with the pursuit of methods to cleverly communicate God's Word. We need only to communicate "these words" of the gospel message faithfully and clearly. The power of the message itself stimulates a hunger in our hearers to hear the words again and again.

13:43
Now when the congregation had broken up, many of the Jews and devout proselytes followed Paul and Barnabas, who, speaking to them, persuaded them to continue in the grace of God.

The message that describes "the grace of God" delights the soul. The sudden understanding that guilt can be pardoned, and the stain of sin cleansed, ignites an immediate enthusiasm. The message of the grace of God often moves listeners to "immediately receive it with gladness" (Mark 4:16). But later, and sometimes sooner rather than later, troubles or persecution arise (Mark 4:17) and those who do not keep their guard up may fall away from their faith "in the grace of God." Paul's desire is to make disciples of Christ, not simply temporary admirers of Christ, so he exhorts them right from the onset of their faith to "continue in the grace of God." He desires them to continue trusting in the grace of God when memories of their guilt plague them. He exhorts them to continue trusting in the grace of God when they are distressed by anxieties, plagued with pain, and confused by troublesome events. The gospel of the grace of God urges us to respond with immediate faith. Sadly, Paul knows that "some will depart from the faith, giving heed to deceiving spirits and doctrines of demons" (I Timothy 4:1). He, therefore, warns these new believers to guard their faith carefully so that when troubles come they can "continue in the grace of God."

13:44-45
On the next Sabbath almost the whole city came together to hear the word of God. But when the Jews saw the multitudes, they were filled with envy; and contradicting and blaspheming, they opposed the things spoken by Paul.

The Word of God sparks interest! Thinkers hear the gospel's explanation of the origins of the universe and the purpose of life, and they rush to listen. Sinners hear the gospel's provision for forgiveness, and they rush to hear more. Good men with a heart for the pursuit of holiness love to drink in the commandments of the Lord. The friendless and lonely hear the gospel's description of the love of Christ, and they, too, delight to embrace the truth.

But the world is filled with men and women of a baser sort as well. Some may turn away and refuse to hear it, but others, as seen here in verse 45, do not run away, they attack the words with "envy," "contradicting," "blaspheming," and opposition. They do not believe the gospel, but are not content with simply rejecting it for themselves. They insist on preventing others from believing it as well, just as Jesus condemned the Pharisees in Matthew 23:13: "Woe to you, scribes and Pharisees, hypocrites! For you shut up the kingdom of heaven against men; for you neither go in your-selves, nor do you allow those who are entering to go in."

13:46-47
Then Paul and Barnabas grew bold and said, "It was necessary that the word of God should be spoken to you first; but since you reject it, and judge yourselves unworthy of everlasting life, behold, we turn to the Gentiles. For so the Lord has commanded us: 'I have set you as a light to the Gentiles, that you should be for salvation to the ends of the earth.'"

God's offer of salvation from sin was first given to the Jews (Romans 1:16). But as wonderful as it is to see God reach through the evil nations of the world to rescue the people of Israel, the salvation of a single nation is far too small a work for such a great Savior. Isaiah 49:6 prophesied long before Paul rebuked the Jews of Pisidia: "It is too small a thing that You should be My Servant to raise up the tribes of Jacob, and to restore the preserved ones of Israel; I will also give You as a light to the Gentiles, that You should be My salvation to the ends of the earth." God did not send His Son into the world because He loved Israel. God sent His Son to save because He "so loved the world" (John 3:16). The thought is breathtaking. God's heart is to save the world from their sins. God's heart is to send "a light" to the depraved sinners of the world who wander in spiritual darkness so that they might see how they might escape the stain, the pain, and the penalty of sin. God's design for His creation is intensely awe-inspiring. His plan is to shine light on every nation, on every village in every nation. His plan is to send "salvation to the ends of the earth." But even as we shake our heads in wonder at the staggering heart of God to save all the peoples of the world, we are further overwhelmed at God's intended <u>means</u> of saving the world. God intends to save the world. And He intends to light the way to that salvation through us! It is not through the arrival of an army of angels nor from the Spirit's sudden communication to a billion consciences that God will bring His salvation to the nations of the earth. He sent Paul and Barnabas and now sends you and I, intending to use His saved servants to carry the light of His saving truth into every dark crevice of the earth, so that everyone, everywhere can be saved. Our Lord began His saving work in Israel, but He did not stop there. He will continue to work until "all the ends of the earth have seen the salvation of our God" (Psalm 98:3).

13:48
Now when the Gentiles heard this, they were glad and glorified the word of the Lord. And as many as had been appointed to eternal life believed.

For just over a week, the Gentiles here in Antioch of Pisidia had been blessed with a taste of the great things of God. They had been introduced to the truths of Jesus the Savior and they had been spellbound by them. Now, Paul says that he intends to "turn to the Gentiles" and focus his preaching efforts on them rather than concentrating only on the Jews. The news thrills his Gentile listeners. "They were glad" and rushed to take full advantage of the opportunity to drink in "the word of the Lord." The Word of God summoned their soul to embrace the gospel truths, and all those that the Lord called to Himself, all those that He "appointed" to gain eternal life, believed the words that Paul delivered to them. What a deep joy to receive this divine appointment to eternal life. The wages of our sin means death – eternal death! But praise the Lord, through Jesus we have been provided a completely different destiny than that which we deserved because of our sin. We have been "appointed to eternal life." Let us not be over-moved or over-saddened by temporary troubles. We have been "appointed to eternal life." For us, the temporary is eclipsed by the eternal, and the fear of death is washed away by the promise of life. Let us join these Gentiles and be "glad" and glorify the Word of the Lord which brings us such life-changing news of forgiveness and eternal life in Jesus.

13:49

And the word of the Lord was being spread throughout all the region.

See what a holy fire the gospel flame kindles! The missionary task is not daunting. We go in the power of God, by the command of God, to teach the words of God. If we take the gospel to the darkest of communities, the light of God's Word is able to illuminate the hearts of the people there in an instant. If we aim to take the gospel to great nations with millions in need, we still need not fear. The fire of the Word of God can spread from heart to heart with blazing speed. Paul and Barnabas spoke to perhaps dozens of people in a handful of synagogues. How could encounters with such a limited number of people lead to revival "throughout all the region?" The gospel flame kindles a holy fire! The gospel is filled with the power of God that saves souls, transforms lives, and summons those transformed lives to pass on to others the gospel of the power of God that breathed new life into their soul. Paul and Barnabas taught perhaps dozens of people in a handful of synagogues – hardly enough contacts to make a significant impact on society it would seem. And yet, God's message "spread throughout all the region." No wonder Paul wrote that he happily, boldly taught the gospel of Christ (Romans 1:16). He had witnessed firsthand the power of Christ's gospel, not only to transform people, but to transform peoples!

13:50-52

But the Jews stirred up the devout and prominent women and the chief men of the city, raised up persecution against Paul and Barnabas, and expelled them from their region. But they shook off the dust from their feet against them, and came to Iconium. And the disciples were filled with joy and with the Holy Spirit.

God's Word was spreading and His purposes were being carried out throughout the entire region. But just as the Gadarenes banished Jesus from their region in Mark 5, so the socially privileged but spiritually destitute men and women of Pisidia "expelled" Paul and Barnabas from theirs. Those who are rich toward God are often treated poorly by those who do not want their conscience pricked. When our listeners respond to the gospel we preach, we are given many instructions on how to disciple them. We are to urge them to imitate God (Ephesians 5:1) and urge them to imitate us as we imitate God (I Corinthians 11:1). We are to spur them on to love and good works (Hebrews 10:24). We are to teach them to obey all the commandments of Jesus (Matthew 28:20). But when people reject us, we are provided specific instructions for how to respond to them as well. In Mark 6:11 Jesus says, "And whoever will not receive you nor hear you, when you depart from there, shake off the dust under your feet as a testimony against them. Assuredly, I say to you, it will be more tolerable for Sodom and Gomorrah in the day of judgment than for that city!" So, having been well prepared by Jesus to face opposition, Paul and Barnabas follow the Lord's commands. "They shook off the dust from their feet against them," and then they arose, undiscouraged, and took the gospel to others.

This first chapter of Paul's first missionary journey draws to a close, and we are blessed by the final line. "The disciples were filled with joy and with the Holy Spirit." Persecution was leveled against these new followers of Jesus. Their fathers in the faith were driven from them. Certainly, they had good cause to be anxious and filled with doubt. But, no, instead, we find that they were filled with joy. Psalm 16:11 tells us why: "In Your presence is fullness of joy." The disciples were filled with joy because they were filled with the Holy Spirit, and in His presence there is fullness of joy. Joy is a fruit of the Spirit (Galatians 5:22), it is a necessary, natural, blessed consequence of the presence of the Spirit of God within us. These men and women were brand new believers. Blessedly, the joy of the believer is not dependent on the longevity of our faith or on the fund of knowledge that we accrue. Joy is a fruit of the Spirit. His presence within His people fills us with joy regardless of outward circumstance. Joy in the midst of trial is manifest evidence of the presence of God in the life of the believer. Happily, we see that this joy is abundantly supplied even to believers that are very young in their faith.

Acts 14

14:1-3
Now it happened in Iconium that they went together to the synagogue of the Jews, and so spoke that a great multitude both of the Jews and of the Greeks believed. But the unbelieving Jews stirred up the Gentiles and poisoned their minds against the brethren. Therefore they stayed there a long time, speaking boldly in the Lord, who was bearing witness to the word of His grace, granting signs and wonders to be done by their hands.

Just as before, upon arrival in their new city, Paul and Barnabas began preaching the gospel in the synagogue. But unlike before, they remain in Iconium for "a long time." In Cyprus, it seems that they moved to a new place to preach every week. They remained in Antioch of Pisidia only a couple weeks. But here in Iconium the Spirit directed them to stay "a long time," perhaps several months. May our methods in ministry always be submissive to the Spirit's direction as demonstrated here. The method we use to access a community with the gospel may or may not need to remain constant. Our length of stay in a community presenting the gospel may range from days to years. But our dependence on the Spirit's direction and power never changes.

As they had encountered before, "a great multitude both of the Jews and of the Greeks believed." The wonderful response to the gospel was encouraging, but it also led to further persecution. Rather than fleeing the persecution, however, Paul and Barnabas remained a long time, "speaking boldly in the Lord." Matthew Henry reminds us that "Perseverance in doing good, amidst dangers and hardships, is a blessed evidence of grace." If so, Paul and Barnabas demonstrated the presence of God's grace in them as they endured harassment and poor treatment for the cause of Christ. On the one hand they faced the poison of the unbelieving Jews and Gentiles, but on the other hand they were able to see God do incredible "signs and wonders" through them which was more than adequate to embolden then to continue in the work of the Lord.

14:4-7
But the multitude of the city was divided: part sided with the Jews, and part with the apostles. And when a violent attempt was made by both the Gentiles and Jews, with their rulers, to abuse and stone them, they became aware of it and fled to Lystra and Derbe, cities of Lycaonia, and to the surrounding region. And they were preaching the gospel there.

When Paul and Barnabas were verbally abused and annoyingly harassed, they endured the trouble patiently. But when news reached their ears that "a violent attempt" was being planned to "abuse and stone them" the two men departed for Lystra and Derbe. Gill's Exposition of the Entire Bible says that the two men fled the city "not so much to save their lives, as to spread the Gospel in other parts." They did so in accordance with the Lord's command in Matthew 10:23, "When they persecute you in this city, flee to another." Arriving in Lystra and Derbe, we find that Paul and Barnabas lost no courage in their flight from persecution. As soon as they arrived in the new area, we found that they were "preaching the gospel there" just as they had been preaching in every city prior to that time. Matthew Poole, in his commentary writes, "Thus was verified what St. Paul observed (in Philippians 1:12), that all those things fell out *unto the furtherance of the gospel*, which spread the further for the scattering of the apostles and preachers of it; and thousands had not heard of Christ, if persecution had not driven the ministers of the gospel unto them: God working good out of evil, and causing the sun, when it leaves one part, to shine upon another." As it was for Paul and Barnabas, may it always be the same for us, that whenever we leave one place, it is simply so that we may serve the Lord in another – just as the sun only leaves one place so that it may "shine upon another."

14:8-10

And in Lystra a certain man without strength in his feet was sitting, a cripple from his mother's womb, who had never walked. This man heard Paul speaking. Paul, observing him intently and seeing that he had faith to be healed said with a loud voice, "Stand up straight on your feet!" And he leaped and walked.

The man listening to Paul was lame since birth. He was unhelpable. One look at his feet would tell any observer that this man had no potential for useful service. But Paul did not look at his feet. He looked at his eyes. And in his eyes, Paul could see that "he had faith." Suddenly, the man's potential for godly service skyrocketed. If Paul had only casually observed the man, he would have missed the work of God going on in his heart. But Paul was "observing him intently," and his intense observation allowed him to see what the casual observer would easily miss. May the Lord do this work in me so that I might observe those brought to me "intently." May the Lord help me not to look only on their diseases and limitations and frailties, but to look intently in their eyes and see the work of God going on in their soul. Here, we see a great work of God flow, not from Paul's boldness, his giftedness, or even his proclamation of the gospel. This great work of God ensued from Paul's intense observation of the people before him. May I go and do likewise.

14:11-18

Now when the people saw what Paul had done, they raised their voices, saying in the Lycaonian language, "The gods have come down to us in the likeness of men!" And Barnabas they called Zeus, and Paul, Hermes, because he was the chief speaker. Then the priest of Zeus, whose temple was in front of their city, brought oxen and garlands to the gates, intending to sacrifice with the multitudes. But when the apostles Barnabas and Paul heard this, they tore their clothes and ran in among the multitude, crying out and saying, "Men, why are you doing these things? We also are men with the same nature as you, and preach to you that you should turn from these useless things to the living God, who made the heaven, the earth, the sea, and all things that are in them, who in bygone generations allowed all nations to walk in their own ways. Nevertheless He did

not leave Himself without witness, in that He did good, gave us rain from heaven and fruitful seasons, filling our hearts with food and gladness." And with these sayings they could scarcely restrain the multitudes from sacrificing to them.

If we are ever prone to wonder why God does not do more miracles to convince the hearts of unbelievers, our story here provides some suggestions. Miracles often do not elicit the godly responses that God intends. Even as God revealed His power on Mount Sinai as Moses went up to receive His commandments, the people of Israel — while seeing the power of God manifested in front of them — made a golden calf to worship instead! Here — right after hearing Paul preach to them about "the living God" — the people choose to worship Paul and Barnabas instead. God has instilled in us all a heart to worship our Creator, but men and women tend to prefer gods that they can touch and see and manipulate.

Seeing the people bring them offerings of reverence, Paul and Barnabas were greatly troubled. They were quite content to be reviled by unbelievers, but they could not tolerate being worshiped by unbelievers. God can be honored when His servants are scorned, but God is not honored when His servants are worshiped. Though our inclination may be the very opposite, let us be more tolerant of people belittling us and much less tolerant of people making too much of us.

Paul vehemently rejected the offerings of his would-be worshipers. Didn't I just preach to you to "turn from these useless things?" Didn't I just tell you not to worship that which is not truly God? God is the One who created all things, and He is the One who has been "filling our hearts with food and gladness." Do not take the honor that God deserves and give it to mortal men or hand-made idols!

Interestingly, Paul did not use the healing of the lame man as his evidence for who God is. He used the creation story. He did this for good reason. God's power to heal is significant. His power to create the universe, however, is much more significant. Because God is our Creator, He is also our Judge. We must reconcile with Him. Because God is Creator and Sustainer of the universe, He is the One who provides for us "rain from heaven and fruitful seasons." He is, therefore, worthy of our worship and praise and gratitude whether He heals our diseases or not.

Jonathan is writing a remarkable doctoral thesis on this very matter — the importance of emphasizing the creation story when sharing the gospel with Buddhist background unbelievers. Jonathan's insights line up wonderfully with Paul's example (that he demonstrates again in Acts 17). May the Lord empower us as we seek to make Him known among unbelieving peoples. But let us recognize that the proclamation of the gospel reveals that God is the Creator of the universe and thus deserving of all the praise and worship of mankind. And this power of the gospel will have a greater impact on the souls of the lost than even the most remarkable demonstrations of miraculous healing power.

14:19-20

Then Jews from Antioch and Iconium came there; and having persuaded the multitudes, they stoned Paul and dragged him out of the city, supposing him to be dead. However, when the disciples gathered around him, he rose up and went into the city. And the next day he departed with Barnabas to Derbe.

How can so little be written about this incredible event? The very people who could hardly be dissuaded from worshipping Paul and Barnabas as gods were now easily persuaded to murder them without justification, "being moved with equal ease either to adore or murder them. So short-lived are human passions not governed by reason and principle!" (Benson Commentary). We find these citizens of Lystra grotesquely evil. They murder a man without remorse, and then throw his (seemingly) dead body outside the city, apparently fearing no legal response to their evil act from the civic authorities. The people were overwhelmed with respect for Paul one day, and yet their hearts were so inclined toward evil that they were able to forget Paul's goodness in a heartbeat and murder him the next day! The Benson Commentary writes that Paul could hardly "expect any better treatment, when he considered that the same multitude who applauded Christ as king of the Jews, and followed him with their acclamations, about six days after, petitioned Pilate that he might be crucified!" Barnes' Notes on the Bible says of this story, "What a striking instance of the instability and uselessness of mere popularity!" Let us be reminded that godly living and loving acts of kindness toward our fellow man may bring us into favor with God, but they will not often protect us from vile men.

This remarkable (and remarkably abbreviated) story tells that the disciples gathered around Paul's body in the field where the violent men of Lystra had dragged him. Apparently, they had followed the crowd from a distance and came to pay their last respects after the crowd dispersed. But as they stood around him, Paul suddenly "rose up" and seemingly without hesitation or much discussion, went right back into the city! We are inspired by Paul's boldness in serving the Lord. Our heart cries with sympathy as we imagine the pain he endured for the cause of Christ. And then we are overjoyed to see him instantly healed by the Lord and strengthened to return immediately to the work. The story fills us with wonder and joy and emotion. Certainly, the event elicited the same emotions in those who witnessed it! And yet so little detail is provided, and no details at all are granted regarding Paul's words at the time. How could so little be written about such a remarkable event? Truly, the Bible is uninterested in exalting men – no matter how deserving of admiration they appear to be in our eyes.

14:21-22

And when they had preached the gospel to that city and made many disciples, they returned to Lystra, Iconium, and Antioch, strengthening the souls of the disciples, exhorting them to continue in the faith, and saying, "We must through many tribulations enter the kingdom of God."

Paul and Barnabas had been in these cities once, preaching the gospel and calling people to be reconciled with Jesus the Savior. Now, they revisit those cities "strengthening the souls of the disciples." Babies are a delight to their parents, but they have very little muscle. Similarly, these babes in Christ were wonderfully born again, but needed nourishment from the Word of God and nurture from their tender, loving fathers in the faith. They needed fellowship with strong believers, so that their spiritual strength could rub off on them. They needed the intercessory prayers of Paul and Barnabas so that their souls could be strengthened. As an athlete benefits from a strength and conditioning coach, new believers are blessed by the counsel and encouragement of those who are strong in the faith, who can guide them in spiritual disciplines that will develop their spiritual vigor.

These young believers had experienced a wonderful new beginning in the Lord, but they needed encouragement to "continue in the faith." Jesus warned in His parable of the four soils (Mark 4:1-20) that "tribulation" and "persecution," as well as "cares of this world, the deceitfulness of riches, and the desires for other things" can all cause new believers to stumble and fall away. Paul and Barnabas sought to prepare the young believers to face these matters so that they might handle them successfully and maintain their faith even when facing opposing forces. Paul and Barnabas went so far as to say that tribulations "must" be endured on the way to entering the kingdom of God. "It is necessary to pass through many troubles on our way into the kingdom of God" (CSB). Matthew Henry says that troubles anticipated are more easily endured, and so Paul and Barnabas sought to warn these fledgling believers that troubles were certainly on the horizon, that they needed to steel their nerves, ready themselves, and strengthen their souls that they might meet these approaching tribulations with the power of the Holy Spirit and the armor of God (Ephesians 6:10-18).

14:23
So when they had appointed elders in every church, and prayed with fasting, they commended them to the Lord in whom they had believed.

Three things are desperately needed by a church. A church family needs godly leaders, vibrant prayer, and the presence and favor of the Lord. These matters are here addressed by Paul and Barnabas on their return visit to the churches that they had only so recently started. The church needed leadership, but there was no way that Paul and Barnabas could shepherd so many congregations, so they "appointed elders in every church." Titus 1:5-9 provides a picture of the qualifications of an elder that Paul was looking for. Jesus compared his followers to sheep (John 10, etc.), and just as sheep need a shepherd, so young believers will best thrive under the watch of caring, capable shepherds who will nurture them and teach them. The church also needs prayer, and so Paul and Barnabas "prayed with fasting" for the newly appointed elders and for the needs of the church at large. The needs of the church are never ending, so we are exhorted to pray without ceasing (I Thessalonians 5:17). Skilled and caring shepherds to lead the church are essential. Prayer on behalf of the church is desperately needed. But Paul and Barnabas saw clearly that these new believers were most urgently in need of the presence and favor of the Lord. So, after appointing leaders and praying and fasting for the churches, Paul and Barnabas "commended" these young congregations to the Lord. No matter how much we give of ourselves to our church, our abilities will never be sufficient to take care of every need. But it is of great comfort to us to know that we can commit God's people to the Lord Himself and trust that He will provide for, nurture, protect, and instruct His people so much better than we can. Just as Paul and Barnabas could not continually be present in each of the churches that they started, we cannot continually walk side by side with our beloved church members as they encounter life's daily struggles. We must commit those we bring to Christ to Him and diligently pray that He will take care of His children in all the ways that we cannot. In Barnes' Notes on the Bible, he writes, "They (Paul and Barnabas) committed the infant church to the guardianship of the Lord. They were feeble, inexperienced, and exposed to dangers; but in his hands they were safe."

14:24-26
And after they had passed through Pisidia, they came to Pamphylia. Now when they had preached the word in Perga, they went down to Attalia. From there they sailed to Antioch, where they had been commended to the grace of God for the work which they had completed.

Paul and Barnabas returned to their home church after they "had completed" the work God gave them to do (II Timothy 4:7). Completing the work that God had entrusted to them was no small accomplishment. They were run out of many towns. They were opposed by powerful people. Paul was nearly stoned to death. But the church had commissioned them to carry out the work of making disciples among foreign nations. The "grace of God" had sustained and empowered them for the great work entrusted to them. And they had proven faithful in keeping their hand to the plow (Luke 9:62) until the work was "completed." This was John Mark's flaw, he did not finish what God gave him to do, and his failure to finish his spiritual assignment would have long lasting repercussions (Acts 15:36-41).

Let us carry out to completion the tasks assigned to us by the Lord. Perseverance to complete the work set before us is the furnace in which Christian character is forged within us; it is the kiln in which Christ-like character in us is refined (Romans 5:4). Perseverance produces character in us, ignites faith in the lost, and inspires hope in the saints – "the end intended by the Lord" (James 5:11). If we quit our work before it is finished, we will stunt God's work in our inner being. May we be enabled to come to the end of our mission and say, it is "complete." Let us come to the end of our service and be able to say, "I have finished the work which You have given me to do" (John 17:4). And when our days come to an end may we be able to say, with deep godly contentment, "It is finished" (John 19:30).

14:27-28
Now when they had come and gathered the church together, they reported all that God had done with them, and that He had opened the door of faith to the Gentiles. So they stayed there a long time with the disciples.

Exemplifying for us the missionary's prime responsibility when returning home, Paul and Barnabas "reported all that God had done with them." They "gathered the church together" and reported "all that God had done." It is through the church that God proclaims His message to the world, and the members are blessed when they can have a part in sending missionaries, praying for missionary efforts, and hearing the testimony of missionaries who tell of the great works of God among the nations that He called them to reach. Missionaries are sent, but it is God who does the work, and it is the missionary's joy to recount for devoted saints all the works of God that they saw Him do in them, through them, and sometimes despite them. The "door of faith" had been opened to the Gentiles! What a joyous event to describe for eager listeners! Families and communities and nations that had been in darkness, "having no hope and without God in the world" (Ephesians 2:12) had now been brought to the light, and they had embraced the light of the world (John 8:12) as their Lord and Savior!

Still today, it remains the missionary's joyous duty to report to the churches all that God has done to open the door of faith to peoples in darkness. Seeing God save a soul makes angels rejoice (Luke 15:7). Seeing God save souls in places where no one has ever worshiped Him before is cause for all the saints to join with all the angels in rejoicing for "a long time."

Acts 15

15:1
And certain men came down from Judea and taught the brethren, "Unless you are circumcised according to the custom of Moses, you cannot be saved."

The church at Antioch was filled with godly men and women who had yielded their hearts and lives to the purposes of Christ. The presence and power of the Holy Spirit was on manifest display in them. They did miracles, taught God's word, demonstrated God's love, and sent missionaries to call people to repentance in distant lands. These "certain men" are here shown to be guilty of the same sin as that of the Pharisees that opposed Jesus. The Pharisees saw Jesus' miracles, heard His teachings, and yet refused to believe in Him. Jesus found this culpable. In John 15:22 Jesus said of them, "If I had not come and spoken to them, they would have no sin, but now they have no excuse for their sin." Then in 15:24 He continued, "If I had not done among them the works which no one else did, they would have no sin." But they did see Jesus do miracles, and so their refusal to accept Him as Lord was blameworthy. Such is the case here. These "certain men" told the

Antioch Christians that if they did not become circumcised, they "cannot be saved." Their knowledge of the Old Testament law was commendable, but their willful ignorance of the works of God before their eyes was deplorable. You cannot say that saints cannot be saved unless they do this or that, when they are obviously saved already! The Christians in Antioch demonstrated the fruits of the Spirit. Their transformed lives gave evidence of the presence of God in their souls. Their testimony of their repentance and the miracles performed by the Lord's power all affirmed that "the salvation of God" (Luke 3:6) had come upon them already. But these "certain men" opposed rather than embraced the Antioch Christians because, as Matthew Henry says, "There is a strange proneness in us to think that all do wrong who do not just as we do."

15:2

Therefore, when Paul and Barnabas had no small dissension and dispute with them, they determined that Paul and Barnabas and certain others of them should go up to Jerusalem, to the apostles and elders, about this question.

We see here the great tension between maintaining Christian unity and maintaining pure doctrine in the church. The church of Antioch could not simply split off from the Jerusalem church, for that would be a break in unity. But neither could they stay quiet about this false teaching that was being propagated by these Judean followers, for that would allow false doctrine to go unopposed. So, in a demonstration of godly passionate resolve to preserve both doctrinal soundness and Christian unity, the church in Antioch sent a group of envoys to discuss "this question" with the elders and apostles in Jerusalem.

15:3

So, being sent on their way by the church, they passed through Phoenicia and Samaria, describing the conversion of the Gentiles; and they caused great joy to all the brethren.

The ambassadors from Antioch traveled directly through Samaria on their way to Jerusalem. Jews had scorned this route for years, having no desire to interact with anyone in the region. Their scorn was stirred by their mistaken notion that the people there were inherently unfit to come to God simply on the basis of their race. By taking the way through Samaria, Paul and Barnabas openly acknowledged God's acceptance of non-Jews into the household of faith. Ellicott's Commentary for English Readers says, "The very journey was, therefore, an assertion of the principles for which they were contending."

The team from Antioch apparently encountered no small number of congregations of believers along the way and blessed them with testimonies of "the conversion of the Gentiles" in distant lands. The reports "caused great joy to all the brethren." Godly men rejoice when God's grace is extended to others. The souls of men who love the Lord are filled with joy when they hear that God has saved another soul. This continues to be demonstrated today as missionaries bring back to their home churches the testimony of those that God has rescued in their fields of service. It is a great encouragement to the missionary to see so many people rejoice over the fruit of their efforts overseas, and it is a great encouragement to the hearts of godly men and women to hear the stories of Christ saving souls in areas they cannot go themselves. The faithfulness and fruitfulness of the missionary encourages the body of Christ, and the joyous support of the church encourages the missionary, so that they all are "mutually encouraged by each other's faith" (Romans 1:12 ESV).

15:4-5

And when they had come to Jerusalem, they were received by the church and the apostles and the elders; and they reported all things that God had done with them. But some of the sect of the Pharisees who believed rose up, saying, "It is necessary to circumcise them, and to command them to keep the law of Moses."

Paul and the entourage from Antioch "were received by the church and the apostles and the elders." The implication is that they were received cordially, drawn together by the bonds of Christian fellowship. III John 1:8 says that when missionaries and servants of the Lord come our way "we therefore ought to receive such, that we may become fellow workers for the truth." Or, as the CEV says nicely, "We must support people like them, so that we can take part in what they are doing to spread the truth." The church in Jerusalem carried out this instruction from John nicely, receiving the group from Antioch warmly, and eagerly granting them a forum to report on "all things that God had done with them."

Most of the leaders of the church in Jerusalem were overjoyed by the news of the works of God being carried out by the church in Antioch, and they fully supported all that they were doing. But there were some who were unmoved by the wonderful testimonies of the Spirit's works among them. "Some of the sect of the Pharisees who believed rose up" and demanded that all these new non-Jewish believers be circumcised and follow the law of Moses. Like so many people we have met on the mission field, these Pharisees wanted the forgiveness of sins made available through Jesus, but they wanted their old religion too. Their reticence to discontinue adherence to laws that God Himself had given them is understandable, but the signs and wonders and transformed lives manifest in these new believers was proof that God had already accepted them into the household of faith. This group's refusal to accept those that God had accepted was, therefore, a serious error.

15:6-9

Now the apostles and elders came together to consider this matter. And when there had been much dispute, Peter rose up and said to them: "Men and brethren, you know that a good while ago God chose among us, that by my mouth the Gentiles should hear the word of the gospel and believe. So God, who knows the heart, acknowledged them by giving them the Holy Spirit, just as he did to us, and made no distinction between us and them, purifying their hearts by faith."

The matter at hand brought "much dispute" to the church. It is good to work diligently to maintain unity in the church. We must overlook small offenses, deal tenderly with weaknesses in our fellow believers, and be quick to yield to the opinions of others when differences of opinion are over nondoctrinal issues. But some disputes cannot be avoided, and we must not shirk our responsibility to disallow false teachings from entering our church.

The matter raged between the two factions, with neither side willing to concede their point. The Pharisee believers contended that the church of Antioch had strayed from God's ways by accepting non-Jewish believers into the household of faith. Finally, however, Peter's argument prevailed. It was not an isolated opinion of the church of Antioch that maintained that salvation came "by faith apart from the deeds of the law" (Romans 3:28). Peter had also witnessed God's acceptance of the Gentiles when the Holy Spirit fell on the household of Cornelius (Acts 10). God had obviously accepted uncircumcised, non-Jewish believers into His household of faith. It was imperative, therefore, that the church not scorn those that God had embraced. The church must not turn away those that God has welcomed in.

15:10-11

"Now therefore, why do you test God by putting a yoke on the neck of the disciples which neither our fathers nor we were able to bear? But we

believe that through the grace of the Lord Jesus Christ we shall be saved in the same manner as they."

Peter continues his argument against the Pharisee believers. His first argument, in verses 7-9, centered on Cornelius' conversion and the fact that the Holy Spirit fell on his whole family even though they were not circumcised and did not follow the laws of Moses. Now, Peter delivers an even more powerful statement. The Pharisee believers contended that the Gentiles must obey the laws of Moses just like the Jews did in order to be saved (verse 5). Here, Peter powerfully asserts that no one is saved by obeying the laws of Moses! No one has ever been saved by obeying the laws of Moses! Peter says, "Neither our fathers nor we were able to bear" the weight of obeying the laws of Moses. If obeying the Old Testament law is required to be saved, then no one will ever be saved! Jews and Gentiles "shall be saved in the same manner." We are saved "through the grace of the Lord Jesus Christ" and any attempt to demand that certain works or rites or ceremonies are required to make us fit for salvation in heaven is to desecrate the blood of Jesus Christ and say that His blood alone is not sufficient to cleanse us from our sins. The Holy Spirit's words through Peter won the day. The Pharisee believers were silenced (verse 12), as each man remembered his own rebirth when the grace of God streamed into his soul and washed him and saved him without any help from any acts of his own.

15:12
Then all the multitude kept silent and listened to Barnabas and Paul declaring how many miracles and wonders God had worked through them among the Gentiles.

The matter being settled, the church sat once more and listened to Barnabas and Paul declare their testimony of what they had seen God do among the Gentiles. Suddenly, the words of Paul and Barnabas were able to bless and inspire their listeners. Previously, the congregation had listened to Paul's words with scrutiny, and doubt, and with a critical eye, and the majesty and wonder of what God had done was lost on them. We miss the opportunity to be inspired and blessed by the testimony of God's people when we look on them with distrust and criticism. Those who critique sermons are rarely bettered by them. But at last, the people put aside their critical spirit, and their heart of acceptance granted them ears of discernment that found great delight in listening to the "wonders" that God performed among the Gentiles. One good insight is often the key that unlocks many other helpful insights. As soon as the listeners were granted the insight that their own salvation was purchased for them apart from deeds of the law, they were then granted the insight needed to happily rejoice in these reports of the salvation of others.

15:13-17

And after they had become silent, James answered, saying, "Men and brethren, listen to me: Simon has declared how God at the first visited the Gentiles to take out of them a people for His name. And with this the words of the prophets agree, just as it is written: 'After this I will return and will rebuild the tabernacle of David, which has fallen down; I will rebuild its ruins, and I will set it up; so that the rest of mankind may seek the LORD, even all the Gentiles who are called by My name, says the LORD who does all these things.'"

The Holy Spirit now confirms Peter's testimony by reminding the church through James of the words of Scripture from Amos 9:11-12. The Pharisee believers had contended that it was disobedient to God's Word to allow non-Jewish followers into God's family. James' insight suddenly helped everyone see that, far from being disobedient to Scripture, Paul and Barnabas' experience with the Gentiles actually fulfilled the words of the Lord in the Old Testament. God, Himself, declared in Amos 9:12 that the day was coming when there would be Gentiles who would be "called by My name." The arrival of the Gentiles into God's family would not be the result of the efforts of misguided men, it would be the Lord God who would do "all these things."

15:18

Known to God from eternity are all His works.

The admission of the Gentiles into the congregation of God's people was not a strange novelty as some supposed. It was not an abrupt change in God's plan. He had set this effort in motion since the dawn of time. "From eternity" He had begun "all His works" to draw all peoples to Himself. The message of salvation through faith in Jesus is a message of "good tidings of great joy" that is intended to bless "all people" (Luke 2:10). God told Abraham His intention to bless "all the families of the earth" (Genesis 12:3). God told Moses that "all the earth shall be filled with the glory of the LORD" (Numbers 14:21). And He said through David, "All nations whom You have made shall come and worship before You, O Lord, and shall glorify Your name" (Psalm 86:9). The entrance of the Gentiles into the kingdom of heaven was not a sudden aberration from God's intended plan. Their arrival into the fold of the Good Shepherd was not a surprise event. God had been working toward this end "from eternity" and He had made "known" this intention "from eternity." And though it took some of the Pharisee believers by surprise, the testimonies of Paul, Barnabas, Peter, and James all confirmed this intention of God that He had already made known.

15:19-21

"Therefore I judge that we should not trouble those from among the Gentiles who are turning to God, but that we write to them to abstain from things polluted by idols, from sexual immorality, from things strangled, and from blood. For Moses has had throughout many generations those who preach him in every city, being read in the synagogues every Sabbath."

God had clearly called these Gentile believers to Himself. Seeing people from foreign nations stream to God with a heart to worship Him and serve Him was good cause for celebration. James felt that God's people should rush to welcome these new believers and do everything possible to encourage them in their new faith. They should make every effort to "not trouble" these Gentiles who were turning to God. At the same time, knowing their pagan background, James wanted to encourage them to demonstrate their new faith with lifestyles that honored God and would not needlessly offend their Jewish brothers. God's first commandment to His people in Exodus 20:3 was for them to have no other gods in their life except the Creator God who delivered them from Egypt. His second command to them charged them to have no idols among them. Idolatry and admiration for multiple gods were expressly forbidden by God and were rightly repulsive to the Jewish believers. But the new believers from polytheistic, idolatrous backgrounds likely did not feel such a natural loathing for these things, so James thought it prudent to grant them this appeal.

Secondly, the Greek and Roman backgrounds of these new believers likely affected their views on sexuality. They were prone to hold the ungodly belief that yielding to sexual cravings was not wrong. So, next to his appeal for the new believers to avoid idolatry, James also emphasized the need for sexual purity.

Then, thirdly, James urged the new Gentile believers to refrain from eating blood, or even from eating animals that were strangled, and so still had blood in the meat. In Genesis 9:4 God commanded Noah and his family, "You shall not eat flesh with its life, that is, its blood." All life is created by God, and it is essential that man recognizes that since he has no power

175

to create life, he has no authority to take life, except where God grants him that authority as He did in Genesis 9:3. Peter had just declared that believers in Christ were free from following the ceremonial laws of Moses (Acts 15:10), but perhaps James felt that God's command for us to acknowledge His authority over all life by avoiding the consumption of blood predated Moses' law and so urged the Gentile believers to submit to this counsel as well.

The Jews who had come to faith in Christ would not have required this exhortation from James. They had heard the laws of God from the Old Testament "read in the synagogues every Sabbath" since their childhood. But these new Gentile believers would have had no such opportunity to study the heart of God written into His laws, so James wished to strengthen their discipleship with these three fundamental matters.

Even today, the first two of James' exhortations are still basic essentials to walking rightly with God. The matter of eating blood is now considered by many to be among the ceremonial/symbolic laws that Jesus fulfilled (Matthew 5:17) and are thus no longer required, but it is easy to see why James would include this instruction in his communication with the fledgling group of Gentile believers in Antioch.

James' words remind us that it is the good work of mature Christians to urge and inspire holy, God-honoring lifestyles in new believers and to "not trouble" brand new Christians with criticisms or requirements that might discourage them in their new-found faith.

15:22-29

Then it pleased the apostles and elders, with the whole church, to send chosen men of their own company to Antioch with Paul and Barnabas, namely, Judas who was also named Barsabas, and Silas, leading men among the brethren. They wrote this letter by them: The apostles, the elders, and the brethren, To the brethren who are of the Gentiles in Antioch, Syria, and Cilicia: Greetings. Since we have heard that some who went out from us have troubled you with words, unsettling your souls, saying, "You must be circumcised and keep the law" – to whom we gave no such commandment – it seemed good to us, being assembled with one accord, to send chosen men to you with our beloved Barnabas and Paul, men who have risked their lives for the name of our Lord Jesus Christ. We have therefore sent Judas and Silas, who will also report the same things by word of mouth. For it seemed good to the Holy Spirit, and to us, to lay upon you no greater burden than these necessary things: that you abstain from things offered to idols, from blood, from things strangled, and from

sexual immorality. If you keep yourselves from these, you will do well. Farewell.

Confirming their support for the new believers in Antioch, James and the leaders of the church in Jerusalem sent a letter. The letter was addressed to "the brethren." The greeting alone must have blessed the hearts of the readers. For centuries the Jews had held Gentiles in disdain. But now, through the testimonies of the Gentile believers and through the affirmation of the Holy Spirit, Jewish believers in Jerusalem embraced the Antioch believers as family members. They were brothers and sisters in Christ, adopted into the family of God. The letter says that Barnabas and Paul, leaders in the Antioch church are "beloved," and acknowledged their Christ-honoring devotion by "risking their lives for the name of our Lord Jesus Christ." This, too, must have blessed the letter's readers in Antioch, assuring them that they and their leaders had been fully accepted by their fellow believers in Jerusalem. "It seemed good to us," the Jerusalem church wrote, to write this letter of encouragement and acceptance to the saints in Antioch, because they saw that the Holy Spirit of God had accepted the saints in Antioch. And since "it seemed good to the Holy Spirit" to grant the Antioch believers the full measure of His power and presence without requiring them to obey the ceremonial laws of Moses, "it seemed good to us" to accept them without requiring strict adherence to those things as well. Physical and spiritual purity were required to maintain unity between these fellowships, but "no greater burden than these necessary things" would be required of the Gentile believers.

When controversy arises among us in the church today, may we use these same parameters for establishing unity and fostering mutual admiration for one another in the body of Christ. Let us communicate proper appreciation for those who sacrifice and risk their own well-being for the cause of Christ (verse 26). Let us recognize the fruits of the Spirit in the lives of our fellow believers (verses 8, 12, 28). And let us keep the Word of God central to our discussion (verses 15-17). If we will do this, we "will do well."

15:30-33

So when they were sent off, they came to Antioch; and when they had gathered the multitude together, they delivered the letter. When they had read it, they rejoiced over its encouragement. Now Judas and Silas, themselves being prophets also, exhorted and strengthened the brethren with many words. And after they had stayed there for a time, they were sent back with greetings from the brethren to the apostles.

And so this early controversy was laid to rest with rejoicing, encouragement, preaching, and strengthening one another with "many words." The godly service and manifestations of the presence of the Holy Spirit in the Gentile believers had blessed the Jewish believers, and now the preaching, teaching, and loving acceptance of Judas and Silas from Jerusalem blessed the saints in Antioch. May it always be so. May God's people always be "mutually encouraged" (Romans 1:12 ESV) by the faith and efforts of one another.

15:34-35
However, it seemed good to Silas to remain there. Paul and Barnabas also remained in Antioch, teaching and preaching the word of the Lord, with many others also.

The matter is briefly described, but we sense that we would be blessed to hear more of Silas' story in detail. Silas was selected along with Judas to accompany Paul and Barnabas back to Antioch with words of encouragement and affirmation from the church in Jerusalem. We are told that Silas "exhorted and strengthened the brethren (in Antioch) with many words" (verse 32), and now it seems that Silas was so moved by his encounters with the Antioch believers that he chose to "remain there." The bonds of Christian love with these new believers became so strong, so quickly, that they overwhelmed his natural desire to return home. Jesus said that blessed are those who leave "house or parents or brothers or wife or children for the sake of the kingdom of God" (Luke 18:29), and so we find that Silas was richly blessed by his fellowship with the believers in Antioch, and doubly blessed by the Lord who promises gifts on earth and eternal life in heaven (Luke 18:30) to those who sacrifice the pleasures of home, family, and the familiar for the sake of caring for and expanding Christ's kingdom of believers far away. I have often seen the "Silas experience" reproduced here in Thailand. Godly men and women come to help with the ministry for a short time and find themselves quickly drawn by the Spirit to invest their lives in the work here in Thailand and elsewhere overseas. Encounters with saints in cross-cultural settings often stir the soul and enliven our spirit's drive to devote oneself to Christian service. We will see that soon the direction of Silas' life will be altered completely by his short-term mission to Antioch.

15:36
Then after some days Paul said to Barnabas, "Let us now go back and visit

our brethren in every city where we have preached the word of the Lord,
and see how they are doing."

The imagined distinction between evangelism goals and discipleship
efforts is too often magnified. Paul was clearly not content with evangelizing
strangers and then leaving them to their own devices. And neither should
missionaries be content to disciple already mature believers that were won
to Christ through the hard labors of others. Proper discipleship demands
modeling the concepts described so that others might imitate the life of
the discipler (I Corinthians 11:1). This means that those who rightly disciple
others must necessarily be engaged in evangelism efforts themselves. It is
also just as necessary that those who work to bring the lost to Christ have
no less passion to disciple those who are saved. Our Lord commanded us to
go and make disciples (Matthew 28:19), not simply to go into all the world
and make converts.

Here we see Paul's heart for nurturing and discipling believers. The Lord
had used his efforts to bring many to saving faith in Christ. But not content
with that, the heart of Paul compelled him to revisit the many believers
spread out over many cities to "perfect what is lacking in your faith"
(I Thessalonians 3:10). Paul the Evangelist was ever Paul the teacher, ad-
visor, nurturer, friend and father of those he brought to faith. As a parent
can never stop loving and caring for their child, so the true evangelist will
never stop seeking to bring their children in the faith ever closer to the Lord.
Paul longed to see their faces and see that their doctrine was still true, their
knowledge of the Lord had greatly advanced, their love for one another was
ever deepening, their strength was holding in the face of persecution, and
they were passing on to others the great things of God that Paul had shared
with them. The adage says that a mother's work is never done, and this
holds true for evangelists too. Let us seek to see men saved. But then let
us continue to hold them and care for them, visit them and pray for them,
as "a mother cherishes her own children" (I Thessalonians 2:7), so that we
might imitate the heart of Paul who was "well pleased to impart to you not
only the gospel of God, but also our own lives, because you had become
dear to us" (I Thessalonians 2:8).

15:37-38
Now Barnabas was determined to take with them John called Mark.
But Paul insisted that they should not take with them the one who had
departed from them in Pamphylia, and had not gone with them to the
work.

Let there be no misunderstanding: quitting has severe repercussions for the Christian. God's words in Hebrews 10:38 are ominous. If anyone starts well with God, but doesn't stay the course, God says, "My soul has no pleasure in him." God's desire for us to endure until the task set before us is completed includes both matters of great import as well as tasks that are seemingly of lesser significance. "Let us not grow weary in doing good" is the exhortation from Galatians 6:9, "for in due season we shall reap if we do not lose heart." Mark grew weary of the work in Pamphylia and went home (Acts 13:13). His departure from the work stirred distrust in Paul and created a rift between Paul and Barnabas. Failure to complete God-given assignments will always have negative effects on our Christian efforts. Blessedly, forgiveness and restoration are attainable. We find Paul and Mark reconciled in II Timothy 4:11. But here we see the deleterious effects of Christians quitting their post. We are called to "run with endurance the race that is set before us" (Hebrews 12:1). Proverbs 24:10 says, "If you faint in the day of adversity, your strength is small," and you fail to reveal the power of God within you. Let us walk in our Lord's strength and not our own so that we will not faint when the task assigned to us is difficult.

15:39-41

Then the contention became so sharp that they parted from one another. And so Barnabas took Mark and sailed to Cyprus; but Paul chose Silas and departed, being commended by the brethren to the grace of God. And he went through Syria and Cilicia, strengthening the churches.

Colossians 4:10 tells us that Mark was the cousin of Barnabas (or his nephew, depending on your translation), and that likely played a large role in Barnabas' willingness to overlook his failure in Pamphylia. But there is a price to pay when Christians fail to carry out their God-given assignments, and part of the price Mark paid was the loss of Paul's trust (at least for a time). We are led to believe that the argument between Paul and Barnabas was long and not always friendly (the "contention" was "sharp"). And in the end, their opposing views simply could not be reconciled. Unable to find common ground, Barnabas took Mark and went one way, while Paul chose Silas as his partner and went another. Modern readers are often grateful for Barnabas' forgiveness and willingness to give Mark a second chance, but it appears from the wording here that it was Paul that was "commended by the brethren to the grace of God." Paul's work will continue to be central to the expansion of Christ's kingdom on earth, and Barnabas' work is not again mentioned in Scripture. So we can see that it was not a simple matter of Barnabas being graciously forgiving and Paul being stern and uncompromising. Paul was not willing to overlook a character flaw that Barnabas was quick to forgive, but we see that it was Paul's work that was "commended by the brethren" and blessed by the Holy Spirit to an incredible degree. It is best not to wrestle with whether Paul was right or Barnabas was right in their handling of this matter, but to see that Mark was wrong, and his failure to endure and finish his job in Acts 13:13 eventually led to this falling out of two godly men.

Sin and character flaws in Christians very often lead to collateral damage. It is not just the sinner that suffers the effects of his sin. So many good wives are broken by the sins of their husbands. So many churches are wracked with dissension while dealing with the character flaws of their leaders. One man sins and two better men become angry with each other over their differing opinions on how to best deal with that sin. Let us recognize that this is the case and seek to minimize the collateral damage of sins and flaws among our church body. May the guilt of one not incite disharmony among the innocent.

Acts 16

16:1-3

Then he came to Derbe and Lystra. And behold, a certain disciple was there, named Timothy, the son of a certain Jewish woman who believed, but his father was Greek. He was well spoken of by the brethren who were at Lystra and Iconium. Paul wanted to have him go on with him. And he took him and circumcised him because of the Jews who were in that region, for they all knew that his father was Greek.

The narrative of Paul's second missionary journey begins here in Derbe and Lystra. He finds there a young man named Timothy who was a faithful "disciple" and was "well spoken of" by the believers in two cities. II Timothy 1:5 tells us that his mother, Eunice, was a faithful believer, but we are told here that "his father was Greek," and the wording suggests that he was not a believer. So many children are raised in homes like this, with godly mothers and unbelieving fathers. We are rightly saddened by the lack of godly fathers in many homes, but we are encouraged here by the reminder of how wonderful a godly mother's influence can be.

We are struck by Paul's decision to circumcise Timothy. We just read the decision by the Jerusalem council in chapter 15 which declared that Gentile believers did not have to be circumcised and become Jews to follow Christ. Yet now, fresh off his efforts to declare circumcision unnecessary, Paul circumcised Timothy! Although Paul's work emphasized delivering the Good News to the Gentiles, he still had a tremendous heart for bringing Jews to faith in Christ, and discipling Jews in their early faith. It would be a significant hindrance to Timothy's effectiveness in Jewish ministry if he did not embrace Jewish customs. So, for the sake of his work among the Jews, Timothy was circumcised. In I Corinthians 9:20 Paul said, "To the Jews I became as a Jew, that I might win Jews," and here, Timothy literally does the same. Timothy's action lived out the sentiment of Paul to "become all things to all men, that I might by all means save some" (I Corinthians 9:22).

May we be found equally as willing to give up all things that might impair our communication of the gospel with those that we have been called upon to reach.

16:4-5
And as they went through the cities, they delivered to them the decrees to keep, which were determined by the apostles and elders at Jerusalem. So the churches were strengthened in the faith, and increased in number daily.

Paul and Silas "went through the cities" and "delivered to them the decrees to keep." They taught God's Word and they taught the apostles' mandates regarding Gentile believers – and in so doing "the churches were strengthened" and the believers "increased in number daily." Let us be reminded that teaching is the primary means by which we see new believers come to faith. Teaching is the primary means by which we strengthen our churches. Fellowships, community service, and the many and varied ministries of the church all have value, but it is by teaching others all the things that God has commanded us that we will have the greatest impact in strengthening our church and seeing new believers won to faith in Christ.

16:6-7
Now when they had gone through Phrygia and the region of Galatia, they were forbidden by the Holy Spirit to preach the word in Asia. After they had come to Mysia, they tried to go into Bithynia, but the Spirit did not permit them.

God does not affirm all our ideas. Not even all our good ideas meet His approval. Certainly, the plan to preach the gospel of God in Asia and Bithynia was born out of holy desires. But interestingly, and instructively, we find the Lord disapproving of their godly designs. Let us be humbly cautious about steamrolling our altruistic plans through dissenters and questioners in our church. We are reminded here that it is not possible for one person to know all the will of God, even if that person is Paul the Apostle. Sometimes our godly ideas must be put on hold for a time when the Spirit of God and the voice of His saints advise us to adjust our plans. Ellicott's Commentary for English Readers says, "The verse describes very vividly the uncertainty produced day by day by this conflict between human plans and divine direction."

The gospel would certainly be preached in Asia. But God had other plans for Paul first. When the voice of God's Spirit speaks to us directly, or speaks to us through His Word, or speaks to us through His saints and tells us to hold off on our plans for a time, let us be sensitive and obedient to His leading. Some matters that we see as God's will, are, indeed, God's will, but must be delayed for a time before implementation.

16:8-10

So passing by Mysia, they came down to Troas. And a vision appeared to Paul in the night. A man of Macedonia stood and pleaded with him, saying, "Come over to Macedonia and help us." Now after he had seen the vision, immediately we sought to go to Macedonia, concluding that the Lord had called us to preach the gospel to them.

We are reminded here that people that are far from Jesus need help. The man of Macedonia stood before Paul in the vision and "pleaded" with him to help. Those without Jesus are in urgent need. And those whose heart is awakened to their spiritual need will plead in desperation for help. The Benson Commentary says that the Macedonian cried out for help "against Satan, ignorance, and sin." Like a lion, Satan mauls and scars and sometimes completely devours (I Peter 5:8) those who are defenseless against him. The lost need our help to stand up against him. Like Satan, ignorance is also a great enemy of man which causes men and women to be "alienated from the life of God" (Ephesians 4:18). We must rush to help those who suffer from "blindness of heart" (Ephesians 4:18) as a result of that ignorance so that they might have their understanding enlightened and be rescued from the tragic separation and alienation from the life of God that ignorance brings. And thirdly, Benson's Commentary reminds us that people need us to help them in their war against sin. Sin separates us from God and hides His face from us. Sin disallows our prayers from reaching His ear (Isaiah 59:2) – and what hope does a man have if God will not hear his prayers? People without Jesus are in darkness, and they are pleading with God's people to "help us" see the light. They battle with Satan, and ignorance, and sin and can find no hope for victory over these things unless someone helps them. As Paul responded to the vision granted him, let us tune our spiritual ears to the unspoken cries of the lost for us to "come over (to them) and help."

16:11-13
Therefore, sailing from Troas, we ran a straight course to Samothrace, and the next day came to Neapolis, and from there to Philippi, which is the foremost city of that part of Macedonia, a colony. And we were staying in that city for some days. And on the Sabbath day we went out of the city to the riverside, where prayer was customarily made; and we sat down and spoke to the women who met there.

How do you start a church where there are no Christians? Up to this point, when Paul entered a city, he would begin by teaching the God-fearing Jews in the city synagogue (Acts 13:5, 13:14, 14:1, etc.). In Philippi, however, there was no synagogue, so in his effort to find spiritually awakened people, Paul went to the riverside "where prayer was customarily made." Those who are devoted to prayer will always be the greatest allies of those who are devoted to godly service. It is interesting to note that the first group that Paul addresses, and the first group which comes to God by faith is a group of women. How often this has been reproduced in our efforts to begin new work in unreached places here in Thailand. In our efforts here, it has not been uncommon to find that the only people spiritually attuned to the things of God, the only ones seeking forgiveness of sin and seeking to be reconciled with their Creator are women. In his effort to begin the first church in Philippi, Paul did not seek out the leading men of the city. He did not seek out the powerful, influential men of the city. He sought those who were aware of their spiritual needs. And since God had drawn only women to seek His blessings, Paul addressed only women in his initial presentations of the great things of God. Let us pray for men to be saved. But let us not be surprised when our churches have many more women than men coming to God in prayer. The work in Philippi reminds us that it has long been this way. God gives no preferential treatment based on gender. But we are told that He grants the meek the privilege of inheriting His blessings on earth, He allows those who are poor in spirit the privilege of inheriting His blessings in heaven, and He grants the pure in heart the joy of seeing His face (Matthew 5:3,5,8). And in those places where only women are meek, poor in spirit, and pure in heart, God will continue to call only women even now.

16:14-15

Now a certain woman named Lydia heard us. She was a seller of purple from the city of Thyatira, who worshiped God. The Lord opened her heart to heed the things spoken by Paul. And when she and her household were baptized, she begged us, saying, "If you have judged me to be faithful to the Lord, come to my house and stay." So she persuaded us.

Epaenetus was a "beloved" friend to Paul, because he was the first one to come to faith in Achaia. And now we see Lydia's beloved name etched forever in the Scriptures, because, like Epaenetus, she was the first one to come to faith in Philippi.

In Romans 16:5, Paul greets his "beloved" Epaenetus. Epaenetus was the very first person Paul was blessed to see reconciled to the Father through his ministry in that area. Working to see Christ praised where He has never been praised before is exhilarating work. The soul loves it! It is also daunting work, however. The effort to start a church where no one knows Jesus begins on your knees, pleading with the Lord to call people to Himself, and imploring Him to lead you to those that He has prepared to hear His gospel. Finally, after rising from your knees, the church planter begins to preach. You preach to complete strangers, not knowing if anyone will believe this new message, or even if anyone will listen to what you are saying. But the supreme importance of the work drives you to persevere! Oh, that the Son of God and Savior of man might be worshiped in this city as He deserves! Oh, that the souls of men and women in this city might be saved from hell and reconciled to their Creator! Such are the thoughts that drive and inspire the hearts of church planters from Paul's day to ours. The work is so great! Souls eternally saved and Christ finally glorified where He has never been honored before! And so, since the work is so great, the joy of seeing the work begin is exhilarating, and those who first believe are forever precious in the heart of those devoted to seeing Christ praised where He has never been praised before.

16:16-18

Now it happened, as we went to prayer, that a certain slave girl possessed with a spirit of divination met us, who brought her masters much profit

by fortune-telling. This girl followed Paul and us, and cried out, saying, "These men are the servants of the Most High God, who proclaim to us the way of salvation." And this she did for many days. But Paul, greatly annoyed, turned and said to the spirit, "I command you in the name of Jesus Christ to come out of her." And he came out that very hour.

We are reminded here of the seemingly widely varying encounters that can be had with the demonic. In Mark 5, the demons torment the man in the country of the Gadarenes. In Mark 9, a demon tries to destroy a young boy. But here, this girl and her masters accrue "much profit" through the activities of this deceitfully benevolent demon. And, perhaps most surprising of all, we find Paul willing to work right alongside the girl and her indwelling demon for days! Finally, as always, the demon is submissive to the name of Jesus that is invoked by Paul. But why wouldn't Paul cast out the demon on the first day, rather than wait <u>days</u> later? We are reminded that casting out demons is not a soul saving event and not the highest priority of God's servants. When the apostles were flushed with the success of casting out demons in Luke 10, Jesus gave them this admonition: "Do not rejoice in this, that the spirits are subject to you, but rather rejoice because your names are written in heaven" (Luke 10:20). Jesus' stated purpose for coming to earth was to "save sinners" (I Timothy 1:15, Luke 19:10), and casting out demons is not a soul-saving event. Jesus called His apostles and calls us today to His great work of saving souls, and we are to rightly rejoice when new names are written in heaven's book of life. But we are not to overly rejoice over the thrill of casting out demons, because we are saved "through faith" (Ephesians 2:8), not through the departure of the demonic. In fact, Jesus taught that casting demons out of those who do not have saving faith can actually make them worse off than they were before (Luke 11:26)! This account from Acts is of significant practical importance to those of us who work in areas of the world where the demonic influence in the lives of men and women is still much the same as it is here presented in Acts 16. It is the intent of the devil and his demonic angels (Revelation 12:7-9) to steal and to kill and to destroy (John 10:10). But their murderous plans for men and women are not always carried out through open assaults of terror as with the boy with the mute spirit in Mark 9. Often, they seek to destroy the lives of men and women by giving people what they want. And until men and women turn from their sin and cling to Jesus, casting out their pet demon will likely not move them closer to faith in God, but to resentment of and a heightened opposition to God's will, just as we will soon see exemplified in the verses to come.

16:19-24

But when her masters saw that their hope of profit was gone, they seized Paul and Silas and dragged them into the marketplace to the authorities. And they brought them to the magistrates, and said, "These men, being Jews, exceedingly trouble our city; and they teach customs which are not lawful for us, being Romans, to receive or observe." Then the multitude rose up together against them; and the magistrates tore off their clothes and commanded them to be beaten with rods. And when they had laid many stripes on them, they threw them into prison, commanding the jailer to keep them securely. Having received such a charge, he put them into the inner prison and fastened their feet in the stocks.

The Philippian "masters" seized Silas and Paul and dragged them off to inflict pain on them because "their hope of profit was gone." Whatever pretended complaints these vile men made later against Paul and Silas, Luke makes it clear here that the real reason for their violent attack was because the deliverance of the girl from demon possession cost them money. The love of money is the root of so much evil (I Timothy 6:10). These men did not care that a young girl was freed from the torment of demonic oppression. All they cared about was protecting their money.

They claimed that the teachings of Paul and Silas "exceedingly trouble our city." The gospel does indeed "trouble" the conscience of its listeners. The gospel calls men to repent of sins they may enjoy. The gospel urges men to love neighbors and even love enemies that they may prefer to hate. The gospel demands that all men turn their back on idols and gods whose requirements are less demanding regarding personal holiness. God's servants call all men and women to repent of sin and submit to the lordship of Christ, and this call will "trouble" those with a working conscience. Matthew Henry writes, "Those who do good by drawing men from sin, may expect to be reviled as troublers of the city. While they teach men to fear God, to believe in Christ, to forsake sin, and to live godly lives, they will be accused of teaching bad customs."

The great disparity between how God views His servants and how the world views His servants is highlighted here. In Mark 12:1-12, Jesus told the parable of the wicked vinedressers, which might also be called the parable of the martyred saints. In the parable, the Master sends out one servant after another as his personal emissaries to the caretakers of His vineyard. These servants are trusted, obedient servants who are serving their master well. But the caretakers of the vineyard view them with scorn and hatred, "beating some and killing some" (Mark 12:5). Just as in that parable, Paul and Silas are sent by the Lord as His emissaries to Philippi, and just like those wicked vinedressers, the magistrates and others of the city beat God's servants and place them in a jail, likely with the intent to do them more evil on the following day. As servants of the Lord, we have no guarantees regarding how the world will treat us. We are only guaranteed that He will be with us, "even to the end of the age" (Matthew 28:20). May the promise of His presence sustain us should we be called upon to face anything like the persecution leveled at Paul and Silas. And let us be sure to take our self-esteem from how God views us, not on how the world views us.

16:25
But at midnight Paul and Silas were praying and singing hymns to God, and the prisoners were listening to them.

Paul and Silas were stripped, beaten with rods, thrown in prison, and had their feet fastened in the stocks so that they were left all night in a most uncomfortable position. And in the midst of this severe trial, we find them singing praises to God in prayer, praying to God in songs of praise. Ellicott's Commentary for English Readers quotes Tertullian's words to the martyrs of his day, stating, "The leg feels not the stocks when the mind is in heaven. Though the body is held fast, all things lie open in the spirit." Barnes' Notes on the Bible reminds us, "The Christian has the sources of his happiness within him. External circumstances cannot destroy his peace and joy. In a dungeon he may find as real happiness as on a throne. On the cold earth, beaten and bruised, he may be as truly happy as on a bed of down. The enemies of Christians cannot destroy their peace. They may incarcerate the body, but they cannot bind the spirit, they may exclude from earthly comforts, but they cannot shut them out from the presence and sustaining grace of God."

16:26-28
Suddenly there was a great earthquake, so that the foundations of the prison were shaken; and immediately all the doors were opened and everyone's chains were loosed. And the keeper of the prison, awaking from sleep and seeing the prison doors open, supposing the prisoners had fled, drew his sword and was about to kill himself. But Paul called with a loud voice, saying, "Do yourself no harm, for we are all here."

Paul and Silas prayed out loud, praising God for His lovingkindness toward them and exalting God for His power to deliver them from sin – and from the trial before them. Verse 25 made it clear that their fellow prisoners "were listening to them" as they prayed. Suddenly, even as Paul and Silas were praising God for His power and love, perhaps immediately after thanking God in advance for delivering them, the prison is shaken apart by an earthquake, "and everyone's chains were loosed." The miracle of the sudden release from bondage was so earthshaking, that no one thought to run to freedom. Everyone chose listening more to God's spiritual truths over gaining physical freedom. As Paul and Silas prayed, the presence of the Lord permeated the prison, captivating those held captive so that even when escape was possible, they felt no impulse to seek it. The presence of the Lord made personal freedom seem menial by comparison.

For those of us who have knelt in the presence of God, we can understand the prisoners' disinterest in escaping. When the power and love of our Lord fill us as we pray, we can hardly think of leaving Him to do something else. The joy of the awareness of His love, basking in the wonderful truths in His Word makes minutes flow into hours as we dwell on His truth and His mercies that hold our soul spellbound. And we see here that the presence and protection of the Lord is held dear not only by His godly children, but even hardened criminals are enraptured by the greatness of God when He draws near. In John 6:68, after Jesus asked His disciples if they wanted to leave Him, Peter said, "Lord, to whom shall we go? You have the words of eternal life." The presence of the Son of God was overwhelming, the truths of eternal life that He taught were riveting. The apostles could not imagine leaving Him. And here we find the same sentiment expressed by Peter demonstrated by a group of imprisoned criminals. The presence of God and the truths of His glory displayed before them made their prison the finest place to be on earth.

The earthquake awakened the keeper of the prison who ran out to find the prison doors wide open. He assumed that the prisoners had escaped and that he would be held accountable. In rash despair he intended to kill himself. Likely, the prisoners were all hidden from his sight in the darkness of the prison chambers, but they could see him clearly as he stood in the light at the prison's entrance. Paul intervened as the jailer drew his sword. "Do yourself no harm, for we are all here." In Luke 9:56 Jesus said, "The Son of Man did not come to destroy men's lives but to save them." And with that mindset Paul saved the life of the man that had just so recently brought him pain.

16:29-30
Then he called for a light, ran in, and fell down trembling before Paul

and Silas. And he brought them out and said, "Sirs, what must I do to be saved?"

After being led away from Asia and Bithynia, Paul and Silas came to Philippi to "preach the word" as they had done in so many other cities before (verse 6). The Word which they preached was affirmed by the unlike-liest of sources – a demon possessed slave girl who publicly acknowledged, "These men are the servants of the Most High God, who proclaim to us the way of salvation" (verse 17). It seems that the jailer was not initially convinced of his need of this "way of salvation," but we see here that now he is suddenly swept away with the weight of his guilt, the glory of God, and his desperate need "to be saved." The singing and prayers of Paul and Silas revealed a source of joy that the jailer did not know. How could men in pain and in prison sing songs of praise to an unseen God? The earthquake convinced him of the power and displeasure of God. The earthquake had to be God's doing, for what natural earthquake opens doors and loosens chains, but leaves buildings otherwise undamaged? And finally, the jailer was overwhelmed with amazement that the prisoners did not run away when the doors swung open. What was it about this unseen God that made sitting in His presence preferable to escaping to freedom? These questions moved the jailer to ask the most important question of all, "Sirs, what must I do to be saved?" The demonic presence in the slave girl confirmed Paul's message. The jailer's own conscience confirmed Paul's declaration that he needed to be reconciled to his Creator. And now the earthquake and the inspiring demeanor of the prisoners continued to confirm Paul's message, at last breaking the will of the jailer, who "fell down trembling" before Paul and Silas and begged to be granted salvation from sin from the Most High God.

"What must I do to be saved?" It has been a deep joy to hear this question asked by many here in Thailand. The truth of the gospel over-whelms the listener, breaking their willpower to resist. Just as the songs of Paul and Silas in the dungeon, the earthquake, and the serenity of the prisoners all confirmed the powerful truth of the gospel for the eternal benefit of the Philippian jailer, so today, the power of the gospel itself (Romans 1:16) and the power of Christian witnesses (John 4:39), as well as "their conscience also bearing witness" (Romans 2:15), all serve to confirm the powerful truth of God's message to man, and compel hearers even now to trust in Him.

16:31

So they said, "Believe on the Lord Jesus Christ, and you will be saved, you and your household."

Scripture grants us here a perfect summary of the gospel, a perfect summary of what is required to be made right with God and gain the promise of eternal life in heaven. "Believe on the Lord Jesus Christ, and you will be saved." It is good to ponder and discuss what it means to rightly "believe." It is good to ponder and to discuss what it is about the Lord Jesus Christ that makes belief in Him salvific for the soul. But in response to the jailer's straightforward, simple question in verse 30, Paul and Silas provide him with a straightforward and very simple answer.

God has created us with a conscience. And He has created us with the mandate to be holy in obedience to that conscience (Leviticus 11:44). He has created us with the mandate to seek His presence and seek His favor (Acts 17:26-27). He has created us to honor Him with our lives (Colossians 1:16). And when we fail to obey our conscience in any or all of these areas, our life is forfeit. We forsake the reason for our existence, the purpose for living, and God holds us accountable, stating very clearly that the penalty for failing to live up to His standard for living is death (Romans 6:23). But for those of us like the Philippian jailer who are broken by the realization that we are in desperate need for God's favor, there is great hope! A means has been provided for us to return to right standing with our Creator. "Believe on the Lord Jesus Christ, and you will be saved." Trust in personal merit will not save us. Trust in any other god except the Lord Jesus Christ will not save us. But trusting in the Lord Jesus Christ's provision for us through the sacrifice of His own life on the cross restores us to a right relationship with God and saves us from the penalty of our sin.

The decision to "believe on the Lord Jesus Christ" is a highly personal one. No one can prevent us from believing, and no one can believe for us. At the same time, however, we see the Lord's heart to call families to Himself, not just individuals. "You will be saved, you and your household." Not that one person's faith can save someone else, but that the example of one can inspire many to place saving faith in the Lord Jesus Christ just the same.

16:32-34

Then they spoke the word of the Lord to him and to all who were in his house. And he took them the same hour of the night and washed their stripes. And immediately he and all his family were baptized. Now when

he had brought them into his house, he set food before them; and he rejoiced, having believed in God with all his household.

Paul and Silas began their presentation of the gospel with an ultra-quick summary, "Believe on the Lord Jesus Christ and you will be saved." But here we find them following up on that summary with further details regarding "the word of the Lord." They likely explained to him how God, the Creator of all things, requires His creation to be holy. But we are not holy. We have all sinned and thus fallen short of His purposes for us. The punishment for that sin is death and hell. Religious efforts are incapable of restoring us to a right relationship with God, so Jesus, the Son of God, came to earth and exemplified for us a life that is truly God-pleasing. Then He willingly offered His own life to pay the penalty for our sins. On the third day He rose from the dead, proving His power over death and sin. And now, if we will confess our sinfulness and cling to Him as our Savior and our Lord, He will forgive us our sins, make us right with our Creator, and reserve a place for us in heaven for eternity. Though the jailer may not have ever heard this gospel before, it would not have taken Paul and Silas long to explain this lifesaving "word of the Lord" to him and his family. It did not take long for Paul and Silas to set the gospel clearly before him, and it took the jailer even less time to decide to embrace it. "Immediately" he and his entire family placed their faith in Christ and were baptized.

The effects of their faith in Christ and the promptings of the Holy Spirit in their souls were equally as immediate. At once, the jailer brought Paul and Silas into his home! He washed and tended to their wounds and set food before them. One minute he was guarding prisoners. The next minute he was enjoying fellowship with brothers in Christ. And the "prisoners" and the "brothers" were the same men! Oh, the remarkable transformation that overtakes the souls of those who come to Christ by faith! Just hours ago he was filled with scorn for these law-breakers, just minutes ago he was so distraught that he contemplated suicide. But now, with Jesus in his heart and Christ's children at his side, the jailer "rejoiced." He suddenly "believed in God." And that sudden belief filled his soul with joy. The Lord has designed the soul of man to love knowing the truth. The soul delights in knowing who his Creator is, and what the Creator wants from him. When we know God's truths regarding who He is, why He made us, and what we can do to know His favor, the soul rejoices, just as the jailer's soul does here.

16:35-37
And when it was day, the magistrates sent the officers, saying, "Let those

men go." So the keeper of the prison reported these words to Paul, saying, "The magistrates have sent to let you go. Now therefore depart, and go in peace." But Paul said to them, "They have beaten us openly, uncondemned Romans, and have thrown us into prison. And now do they put us out secretly? No indeed! Let them come themselves and get us out."

It is likely that the magistrates had a restless night. They had beaten and imprisoned two strangers without any effort to hear solid evidence against them. Then the earthquake shook their home in the middle of the night, again stirring their conscience awake. Barnes' Notes on the Bible says of this passage: "An earthquake is always suited to alarm the guilty; and among the Romans it was regarded as an omen of the anger of the gods, and was therefore adapted to produce agitation and remorse." The earthquake produced a tremor in their conscience that caused them to call a rushed meeting together as soon as it was light. Each man affirmed the other man's concern that they had seriously mistreated Paul and Silas and so sent word immediately to have the two men released.

It was not their estrangement from Paul and Silas, however, that was their greatest danger. Their sin had separated them from God, and this was a far greater concern. Paul would not have them quietly reconcile with him, but remain alienated from Christ. So he took the liberty of his undeserved captivity to force one last meeting with the magistrates that would grant them one parting opportunity to reconcile, not with Paul and Silas, but with their Creator.

16:38-40
And the officers told these words to the magistrates, and they were afraid when they heard that they were Romans. Then they came and pleaded with them and brought them out, and asked them to depart from the city. So they went out of the prison and entered the house of Lydia; and when they had seen the brethren, they encouraged them and departed.

Having been exonerated by the magistrates, it was not necessary for Paul and Silas to sneak out of the city and leave the new believers without another encouraging visit. In full view of the people that had just perse-cuted them severely, Paul and Silas met with the brand-new believers in the house of Lydia and encouraged them with their testimony of how God had been present with them in the prison and had saved the jailer's family through their hardship. After the new believers were "encouraged" by Paul's testimony and by his continued instructions from God's Word, Paul and Silas said their goodbyes "and departed," entrusting the new believers to the protection and instruction of the Holy Spirit.

They could trust that the Spirit of God that had buoyed their spirits in prison, freed them with an earthquake, and saved the souls of the jailer's household, would work just as powerfully in the lives of the fledgling believers of Philippi. The departure of Paul and Silas, their fathers in the faith, would have been painful for these new believers. But Paul's willingness to leave them reminds us that although godly leadership is a dear blessing to new believers, it is not a necessity. Followers of Christ require God's Word and they require the presence of the Holy Spirit. Constant contact with godly leaders who love us is very helpful, but it is not vital to Christian growth. The early believers in Philippi were denied Paul's continued fellowship and leadership, but they had the Word of God and the presence of His Holy Spirit in full measure. The Holy Spirit anoints His children so that even without Paul's continued instruction the believers in Philippi could "know all things" (I John 2:20). Paul's continued presence would have been a joy to the new believers, but I John 2:27 reminds us that "you do not need that anyone teach you" because the Holy Spirit grants understanding to those who devote themselves to His instruction. Paul and Silas planted the gospel in the hearts of the believers in Philippi. But "the Spirit gives life" (II Corinthians 3:6). It is the Spirit of God, not the hand of man that breathes life into the soul of the believer. Let us neither minimize the importance of godly leadership, nor miss the essentialness of the presence and guidance of the Holy Spirit in the advancement of Christ's church.

Acts 17

17:1-4

Now when they had passed through Amphipolis and Apollonia, they came to Thessalonica, where there was a synagogue of the Jews. Then Paul, as his custom was, went in to them, and for three Sabbaths reasoned with them from the Scriptures, explaining and demonstrating that the Christ had to suffer and rise again from the dead, and saying, "This Jesus whom I preach to you is the Christ." And some of them were persuaded; and a great multitude of the devout Greeks, and not a few of the leading women, joined Paul and Silas.

Paul and Silas left Philippi, but they did not leave the work of going into all the world and preaching the gospel. They came to the towns of Amphipolis and Apollonia, but finding neither a synagogue nor God-fearers there, they pushed on to Thessalonica. "As his custom was" Paul went to the synagogue and "reasoned with them from the Scriptures." We can assume that Paul's personal testimony of what God had done for and through him would have been a powerful tool to draw unbelievers to the Lord. The miracles that the Holy Spirit carried out through Paul we could also assume would have incentivized people to place their faith in Jesus. But here, at the onset of Paul's ministry in Thessalonica, we find him using neither of those methods of drawing hearts to Christ. Instead, we find him reasoning with his hearers "from the Scriptures." Paul was certain that the Word of God was more powerful and carried more weight with the souls of lost men and women than even miracles or his personal testimony. In Romans 1:16 he teaches what he exemplifies here in Thessalonica: "I am not ashamed of the gospel of Christ, for it is the power of God to salvation for everyone who believes." The presentation of the words of God in His Scriptures will always be our most powerful means of drawing lost souls to saving faith in Jesus.

Paul explained that Jesus "had to suffer." God taught long before, "The life of the flesh is in the blood, and I have given it to you upon the altar to make atonement for your souls; for it is the blood that makes atonement for the soul" (Leviticus 17:11). "Without shedding of blood there is no remission" of sins (Hebrews 9:22).

Paul also taught that Jesus must "rise again from the dead." Just as Jesus explained the prophecies of His death and resurrection to Cleopas and his friend on the road to Emmaus in Luke 24, so Paul does here. Psalm 16:10 foretold the resurrection: "For You will not leave my soul in Sheol, nor will You allow Your Holy One to see corruption." Our salvation required His resurrection: for if "Christ is not risen, (our) faith is futile; (we) are still in (our) sins!" (I Corinthians 15:17).

As Paul anticipated, his presentation of the truths of God from the Scriptures persuaded "a great multitude" to place saving faith in Jesus Christ. They immediately "joined" Paul and Silas in the pursuit of holy living and the advancement of Christ's kingdom. When we present the gospel of Jesus Christ, we do not call our listeners to do anything that we are not doing ourselves. We call them to "join" us, to "join in following my example" (Philippians 3:17). The heart of making disciples is not just teaching Christ's commandments, it is exemplifying obedience to Christ's commandments. We do not send people off on their own to obey Jesus, we invite them to "join" us in following Him.

17:5

But the Jews who were not persuaded, becoming envious, took some of the evil men from the marketplace, and gathering a mob, set all the city in an uproar and attacked the house of Jason, and sought to bring them out to the people.

It is fascinating to see how enraged evil men become when they see their peers repent of sin and endear themselves to Christ. Here, we are told that envy was the root of the seething rage that catapulted the disbelievers against Paul and Silas. They were envious because their own disciples became fewer when the disciples of Jesus grew. They were envious that others' hearts were made pure, while their own heart remained stained with sin. And they were envious that others were gifted with a new compass by which they could now chart a course of abundant living that was infinitely more fulfilling than their own. Envy is a terrible source of action. Here we see that because of envy, the Jews partnered with "evil men," "set all the city in an uproar," and "attacked" an innocent man in his home. Similar outcomes can be expected any time envy is the trigger for our behavior. "For where envy and self-seeking exist, confusion and every evil thing are there" (James 3:16). Let us be happily content with what our Lord chooses to provide for us and do with us. Envying what others have or what others do places us in very poor company, and sets us up to say and do extremely vile things.

17:6
But when they did not find them, they dragged Jason and some brethren to the rulers of the city, crying out, "These who have turned the world upside down have come here too."

In Acts 16:20 Paul and Silas were accused of coming to "exceedingly trouble our city," and here, they are accused of not just troubling cities, but of turning the world upside down. The gospel does, indeed, turn worlds upside down. I have seen happy businessmen suddenly lose their love for money and sell all to devote themselves to serving Christ. I have seen happy families leading pleasant lives suddenly find themselves overpowered by the glory of God and abandon their life of ease and trade it for a life weighted by the (joyous) burden of the cross. I have seen so many who had given their lives to sin, find forgiveness in the blood of Jesus and then suddenly detest the sin they once reveled in. It is not a good sign when Christians can work beside unbelievers, live next door to unbelievers, and attend family gatherings with unbelievers and have no one feel the spiritual vertigo of having the Holy Spirit begin to tip their world upside down. We are called upon to be salt (Matthew 5:13) and light (Matthew 5:14). Salt stings the wounds of guilt and light stings the eyes of the conscience. Manifestation of the presence of the Holy Spirit in the lives of His people will compel a response from those nearby. They will either repent and turn their lives upside down in happy devotion to Christ, or they will turn themselves inside out in an effort to silence the voice of conviction calling them to reconcile with their Creator. Either way, wherever the gospel goes, worlds are turned upside down.

17:7-9

"Jason has harbored them, and these are all acting contrary to the decrees of Caesar, saying there is another king – Jesus." And they troubled the crowd and the rulers of the city when they heard these things. So when they had taken security from Jason and the rest, they let them go.

Jason "harbored" Paul and Silas while the two were sharing the gospel in his town. And because of his support of Paul's ministry, he was "attacked" in his home (verse 5), "dragged" from his home by an angry mob (verse 6), and fined by the city officials (verse 9). As followers of Christ and leaders of men, we must come to terms with the fact that our call for men and women to follow Jesus may well lead to trouble for them, sometimes serious trouble. We cannot be blind to the fact that Jason's decision to "join" Paul in following Christ (verse 4) brought him significant physical harm, Silas' decision to partner with Paul caused him to be whipped and thrown into prison (Acts 16:24), and Timothy's decision to follow Paul led him to an adult circumcision (Acts 16:3). Our soul's desire must be to see God's name praised and the souls of men saved. If we harbor any lesser goals, we will set ourselves up for anxiety and disillusionment when those who follow us suffer pain. "Christ had to suffer" in order to save our souls (verse 3), and to this same life of suffering we also have been called "because Christ also suffered for us, leaving us an example, that you should follow His steps" (I Peter 2:21). We call on men and women to follow us as we follow Christ, not so that they can avoid pain and suffering, but because Christ is worthy of all our worship, and He is worthy of any suffering that we might endure for the sake of His great name.

17:10-11

Then the brethren immediately sent Paul and Silas away by night to Berea. When they arrived, they went into the synagogue of the Jews. These were more fair-minded than those in Thessalonica, in that they received the word with all readiness, and searched the Scriptures daily to find out whether these things were so.

Just as they were forced to leave Philippi, we find Paul and Silas again forced to leave Thessalonica. Those who insist on going to Hell will insist on taking others with them and so we see the Thessalonian unbelievers persecuting and opposing Paul's ministry to lead people to saving faith in Christ. Jesus taught His disciples, "When they persecute you in this city, flee to another" (Matthew 10:23). So, in obedience to Jesus' instruction and to avoid the violent opposition in Thessalonica, the two men fled to Berea. Once again, we find that although they left Thessalonica, they did not leave the work of drawing men to Jesus. Without hesitation, or consideration of personal safety, they "went into the synagogue of the Jews" and taught again the great truths of the gospel of Jesus Christ.

The Bereans are described wonderfully. They are said to be "noble" (ESV). Literally, the word translated as "fair-minded" in the NKJV here means "well-born" – of noble birth, or in this case, noble character. The same word is used in I Corinthians 1:26 when Paul says that "not many *noble*" are called into the kingdom of God. What character traits make men and women appear "noble" in the eyes of heaven? Verse 11 tells us: "They received the word with all readiness, and searched the Scriptures daily." Let us be noble believers! Let us search the Scriptures daily to see what the Lord would say to us. Let us listen to sermons, participate in Bible studies, and read God's Word "with all readiness." The "noble" believer drinks in God's Word when he hears it preached, listens to it taught, and when he reads it alone at home. He is always ready to hear God speak to him when the Bible is presented before him. Noble believers are not those who daydream of other things while God's Word is taught. They do not cynically analyze the preacher's words. They sit on the edge of their seat "with all readiness" to hear God speak to their listening soul. Such were the people of Berea. It is a dear joy to me to see all my children grow to be "noble" men and women of God. Gary, Jonathan, Becky, and Sandi, all four of you bless me with how you love to drink in God's Word with "all readiness." When you were young it was my joy to teach you God's Word, and now that you are grown it is my joy to see you reverently handle the Scriptures and pass them on to others. May our family forever prove to be "noble" in this same regard.

17:12-15

Therefore many of them believed, and also not a few of the Greeks, prominent women as well as men. But when the Jews from Thessalonica learned that the word of God was preached by Paul at Berea, they came there also and stirred up the crowds. Then immediately the brethren sent Paul away, to go to the sea; but both Silas and Timothy remained there. So those who conducted Paul brought him to Athens; and receiving a command for Silas and Timothy to come to him with all speed, they departed.

In Matthew 23:13 Jesus leveled this scathing criticism on the Pharisees: "Woe to you, scribes and Pharisees, hypocrites! For you shut up the kingdom of heaven against men; for you neither go in yourselves, nor do you allow those who are entering to go in." Here we find the unbelieving Jews illustrating Jesus' point as they travel to the next city over just to prevent Paul's listeners from gaining a relationship with Christ. They were too late, though. "Many" Bereans had already believed. Their threats of violence could not keep people out of the kingdom of heaven, but they were successful in driving Paul away once again. The experience in Lystra in Acts 14:19 had a lasting effect on Paul's missionary band. After seeing Paul nearly stoned to death by an angry mob, they learned that you cannot reason with unreasonable men and that violent harm can come even to the purest of heart. So then, from Acts 14 on we find Paul fleeing violent persecution rather than confronting it.

We also note here the benefit of not being the center of attention. Paul's fame made it impossible for him to continue ministry in Berea, but Silas and Timothy were able to remain there because they were not so well known. Almost paradoxically, their anonymity made them more beneficial for Christian service. Their personal insignificance permitted a ministry of tremendous significance. May it always be our aim to make the name of Jesus known, not our own.

17:16
Now while Paul waited for them at Athens, his spirit was provoked within him when he saw that the city was given over to idols.

Paul waited for his friends to return to him from Berea, but he did not sit idle as he waited. As he walked through the city of Athens, looking for what the Lord would have him do, he became "provoked," he was "deeply troubled" (NLT), "grieved and roused to anger" (Amplified), he was "greatly distressed" (NIV) by the sight of the great city of Athens being "given over to idols." Seeing lost people grope around in the dark for the truth should provoke us to action. Seeing needy people praying to gods that cannot help them should greatly distress us. We should be grieved and roused to anger when we see that there are cities in the world where no one in the entire city gives glory to God. The thought of so many people doomed to hell because of misplaced devotion should deeply trouble us. May the vision of so many people being "given over to idols" provoke us to action just as it did Paul. May the present plight and ultimate doom of all who trust in idols provoke our souls to do something to rescue the perishing and care for the dying. May the tragedy that awaits idol worshipers stir us to give our lives to missions and the proclamation of the gospel in places that are given over to idols today. Let us go on mission trips, let us give of our finances to see the gospel go where we cannot, and let us pray fervently, vehemently, caringly that God would call people to Himself in these places of darkness so that He might be glorified as He deserves and that souls would be saved from the sin and hopelessness of false-god worship.

17:17
Therefore he reasoned in the synagogue with the Jews and with the Gentile worshipers, and in the marketplace daily with those who happened to be there.

It is our happy responsibility as servants of our Lord to "reason" with people regarding mankind's *reasonable* (Romans 12:1) response to God's greatness. Our calling is not to an unpleasant task of berating people for their past failures, nor is our calling to attract disciples with a fluffy emotional appeal that excites the ears and eyes but provides no substance for the soul. No, ours is the thoroughly pleasant duty to reason with people. It is reasonable to honor one's omnipotent Creator. It is reasonable to listen to your own conscience which cries out to be cleansed. It is reasonable to defer to the omniscient God's mandates when His judgments differ from your own opinions. It is reasonable to respond to our loving God's provisions for us with a loving, devoted response of our own. We cling to God by faith, but it is certainly not blind faith. We have excellent reasons for believing in Him, trusting Him, obeying Him, and devoting ourselves to His purposes. We find Paul approaching complete strangers in a foreign country -- and yet he is perfectly comfortable with delivering his message to them. He is confident in his presentation, because the gospel is reasonable. It is reason-based and can be defended with excellent reasons. Paul anticipates that his message will move strangers in a foreign land to repent of their sin and reconcile with their unseen Creator because the gospel that he preaches is not far-fetched. It is reasonable. And if properly considered by reasonable people with an awakened conscience, God's message to man will draw hearers to respond with repentance and submission to God's will. Samuel felt this way too. In I Samuel 12:7 Samuel sought to use reason to persuade his countrymen to walk rightly with God. "Now therefore, stand still, that I may reason with you before the LORD concerning all the righteous acts of the LORD which He did to you and your fathers." In fact, God, Himself, uses reason to set His message before us! "'Come now, and let us reason together' says the LORD,

'Though your sins are like scarlet, they shall be as white as snow; though they are red like crimson, they shall be as wool" (Isaiah 1:18). Yes, we come to God by faith. But it is not blind faith. We have very good reasons for believing and serving God like we do. And it is good for us to pass along those reasons for the sake of others, that they might find proper cause to reconcile with their Creator as well.

17:18
Then certain Epicurean and Stoic philosophers encountered him. And some said, "What does this babbler want to say?" Others said, "He seems to be a proclaimer of foreign gods," because he preached to them Jesus and the resurrection.

Paul had to overcome a number of obstacles in order to communicate his message. Here we see that many of his hearers viewed him negatively because they erroneously believed that he was "a proclaimer of foreign gods." God is not a foreign god. No matter what continent we stand on when we proclaim Him, He will never be a foreign entity. The earth is His footstool (Matthew 5:35). He has a furnished living room in every nation on earth. God is never a foreigner. God is not a visitor who comes to call on nations from afar, He is the One who formed the nations (Psalm 86:9). When we preach His message to distant peoples, we can be so confident that we are not proclaiming a foreign god to them. He is not a Toyota that must be imported. He is not even a Maserati or Porsche that is a deluxe import. Long before Jesus was born in Bethlehem, Our Lord has forever been Immanuel, God with us (Matthew 1:23). God is with all His creation all the time. He does not need to be imported or smuggled into obscure nations. He is Immanuel and has lived with and moved among the peoples that He has made since the dawn of time.

17:19-21
And they took him and brought him to the Areopagus, saying, "May we know what this new doctrine is of which you speak? For you are bringing some strange things to our ears. Therefore we want to know what these things mean." For all the Athenians and the foreigners who were there spent their time in nothing else but either to tell or to hear some new thing.

Paul's message was new and "strange" sounding to the Athenians, but blessedly, they did not discount it right away. Their natural interest in "either to tell or to hear some new thing" induced them to take Paul to the Areopagus which provided a more convenient venue for hearing him out. The Athenians' spiritual curiosity did not help them believe Paul's message, but it did, at least, encourage them to listen to Paul's message, which granted them a significant benefit. In Jesus' parable of the sower, He taught us that some who hear the gospel are like "the wayside." As soon as the gospel reaches their ears "Satan comes immediately and takes away the word that was sown in their hearts" (Mark 4:15). The Athenians spoken of here were not like that. The interest of some was truer than the interest of others, but at least Paul was granted an audience which would lead to several men and women finding new life in Christ (verse 34). We have good cause for increased hope for our hearers when, like the Athenians, they greet the gospel message with a readiness to listen. "Faith comes from hearing" (Romans 10:17). So we can rightly rejoice every time the Spirit provides us the opportunity to present the gospel to a crowd who is willing to hear.

17:22-23

Then Paul stood in the midst of the Areopagus and said, "Men of Athens, I perceive that in all things you are very religious; for as I was passing through and considering the objects of your worship, I even found an altar with this inscription: TO THE UNKNOWN GOD. Therefore, the One whom you worship without knowing, Him I proclaim to you:

In one sense, we can present the truths of the gospel without mention, or even without knowledge of our hearer's spiritual understanding. We can have quiet confidence that the gospel itself is fully capable of convicting sinners of their need to be reconciled with God. We can present to our hearers the essential truths that: God made the world. He designed us to be holy and to give Him His due glory. But we have all sinned and failed to give Him the glory He deserves. The penalty for our sin is death and hell. No meritorious actions on our part can erase our sins. But Jesus the Son of God came to pay the penalty for our sins by His death on the cross. On the third day He arose from the dead, proving His power over death and sin. And if we will trust in His provision to cover our sin, He will cleanse us from our sin, make us as His child, and prepare a place for us in heaven when our time has come.

This gospel of Jesus Christ is fully capable of convicting hearts of sin and compelling listeners to place saving faith in Jesus. We can know that all our listeners have sinned and fallen short of God's purposes for their lives. We already know that no meritorious acts on their part have been sufficient to erase their sins or reconcile with God. No further insights into our hearers' spiritual understandings are required of us. At the same time, however, having such insights into our hearers' background and beliefs can be extremely helpful. Here, Paul uses his recent observations to provide a powerful prelude to the gospel. Paul says, I see from my time in your city that "you are very religious." His hearers would have nodded in agreement. And I see that you have been worshiping "THE UNKNOWN GOD." Again, his hearers would have nodded in agreement. Then, with tremendous wisdom, Paul uses his observation of their spiritual understanding to bridge to the gospel. "The One whom you worship without knowing, Him I proclaim to you." They had thought that Paul had come to proclaim to them stories of a foreign god (verse 18). But Paul points out that God is no foreigner. He has been among them all along, they have sensed His presence and His existence and have sensed that He was worthy of their worship, even though they did not know His name. But now, the Lord God Creator was providing the people of Athens the opportunity to know Him more fully. They had already sensed His greatness, but now they could know Him personally.

God is our Creator; He is worthy of our praise. This most basic of truths is "clearly seen" by observing all that God has made in the world (Romans 1:20). Although many do not respond rightly to this innate understanding of the origins and purpose of the universe, we are reminded here that God's revelation of His truths allows men and women to sense His presence even before they are introduced to the gospel. This fact facilitated Paul's presentation of the Good News in Athens and continues to provide an advantageous starting point for missionary efforts today.

17:24-25
God, who made the world and everything in it, since He is Lord of heaven and earth, does not dwell in temples made with hands. Nor is He worshiped with men's hands, as though He needed anything, since He gives to all life, breath, and all things.

The beginning is a good place to start things. So Paul begins his call for his hearers to repent of sin and reconcile with God by discussing the beginning of all things. God is the One "who made the world and everything in it." Understanding that God is our Creator provides a compelling reason for us to comply with His commands. Then, the further understanding that God not only made all things, but He also provides "all things" that sustain our life, beautify our life, and grant us a fulfilling life gives us further cause to honor Him and happily live in submission to Him.

In contrast to the idols that filled Athens, God needs nothing from the human race. The idol gods of Athens needed someone to carve them, paint them, and prop them up. But the Creator needs nothing from us. In Psalm 50:12-13 God says, "If I were hungry, I would not tell you; for the world is Mine, and all its fullness." The world belongs to God. Heaven belongs to Him as well. And it is our happy task to join Paul's effort to remind people of these essential matters of understanding. If God made and sustains all things on earth, He is worthy of our gratitude and worship. And if God rules over heaven and decides who enters in, we must be sure to submit to His decrees or our eternal destiny is in peril.

17:26-27

And He has made from one blood every nation of men to dwell on all the face of the earth, and has determined their preappointed times and the boundaries of their dwellings, so that they should seek the Lord, in the hope that they might grope for Him and find Him, though He is not far from each one of us;

In just a few words, Paul provides us here with a remarkable instruction on the origins and purpose of all the nations on earth, which carries tremendously significant implications for each one of us. God has formed "every nation" from "one blood." On an individual level this is terribly important to understand and put into practice. There is no superior race. There is no race of man that is inferior to another. We must be little affected by the differences of skin and very affected by the fact that we all share common blood – given to us by our Creator. God made all people "from one blood." Any racial prejudices that arise in the hearts of men are artificially conceived and must be volitionally quelled if we are to view our fellow man with the eyes of God.

Paul insists that we understand that all men were created from the same blood by the same God for the exact same purpose. God has "determined," He has "preappointed" the rise of the nations of the world. He has predetermined the "times" – the timing of when each nation would rise, and when that nation would fall. He has appointed the boundaries of the nations' borders – determining both the size of their physical borders and the extent of their worldwide influence. This is true on a personal level as well as on the national level. God has "determined" when we would be born, where we would be born, and the borders of our influence. And He has ordained all these great matters of international and interpersonal relations with a single magnificent purpose behind it all: "that they might grope for Him and find Him." God has formed nations and peoples and individuals so that each of us might find Him. "He is not far from each one of us" and "He has put eternity in (our) hearts" (Ecclesiastes 3:11) so that we might know within ourselves our need to seek out and relate rightly with our Creator. He has established nations and created people for the great purpose of seeking God. And although some nations are so spiritually dark that people must "grope" for Him in semi-blindness, He has promised that we will not seek Him in vain. "You will seek Me and find Me, when you search for Me with all your heart" (Jeremiah 29:13).

My time here in Thailand has been filled with inspiring fellowship with people that illustrate Paul's words here – people that sought God in the dark and found Him in miraculous ways. God has formed the world and everyone in it for the glorious purpose of calling His creation to seek Him and know Him. And God promises that everyone who will lift their eyes to look for Him and stretch out their hands to hold on to Him will find Him, and find Him wonderfully worthy of their search.

17:28
For in Him we live and move and have our being, as also some of your own poets have said, "For we are also His offspring."

Once again, we see Paul countering the argument presented by people in verse 18 claiming that he was presenting information about a foreign god. God is not foreign to anyone. He is not far from any of us. We live in Him. We move about in Him. Our being is sustained by Him. Even Paul's Greek listeners had some sense of this, acknowledging that humanity is "His offspring."

By alluding to the writings of the Greek poets, Paul again demonstrates his study of his listeners' background, just as he did in verse 23. Paul was apparently well read in his host city's literature, and rather than argue against what they believed, he focused on the matters of belief in their background that were true, or that bridged to gospel truths. "God is not far from each one of us" (verse 27). He lives among us, moves among us, and provides everything we require for our spiritual well-being. Even lost people in desperately dark places, as in ancient Athens here, are granted spiritual insights by their Creator that are intended to draw them to seek Him. Even in the darkest settings, we can present the gospel with the confidence that God has gone before us alerting our listeners to His truths that compel us to rightly respond. We are all the "offspring" of God. Like a good father, He has provided for us and has taught us the right way to live. We, then, are to be good children and obey all that He commands. On some level, the pagan Greeks listening to Paul already knew this to be true, even before Paul taught them. No matter who it is we are sharing the gospel with, we can be confident that the Lord began calling them to Himself well before we arrived on the scene.

17:29
Therefore, since we are the offspring of God, we ought not to think that the Divine Nature is like gold or silver or stone, something shaped by art and man's devising.

God's Word says: "God created man in His own image; in the image of God He created him" (Genesis 1:27). The thinkers of Athens expressed their acknowledgement of that fact: "we are His offspring" (verse 28). "Since we are the offspring of God" and made in His image, it is not reasonable to believe that man-made, inanimate objects are proper representations of God. "We ought not to think" that an idol that is made of "gold or silver or stone" can reflect "the Divine Nature" in any way. No one who desired an audience with the king would be satisfied with a moment spent in the presence of the king's picture. The thought would be ridiculous. Even more ridiculous would be for the person requesting an audience with the king to be offered a ceramic toad in his place. But that is exactly what is offered to idol worshipers when they are given a carved replica of something not God in the place of an audience with the true God. Worshiping "art" and things of "man's devising" cannot meet the spiritual needs of man and Paul tells his audience in Athens that "we ought not to think" that it can.

17:30
Truly these times of ignorance God overlooked, but now commands all men everywhere to repent,

The worship of idols and false gods of all types is the result of "ignorance." God "overlooked" this sinful display of ignorance insofar as He did not destroy humanity outright as soon as they picked up a stick and made it an object of deceitful worship. But let no one mistake the patience of God and the grace of God for the approval of God. Paul declares that God is hereby calling on all men and women everywhere to "repent." They must repent of sins against their conscience and repent of a life that has never honored its Maker. Their worship of false representations of God and their failure to honor the one true God has alienated themselves from Him, and to reconcile with Him, they must repent and turn away from their God-dishonoring religious acts.

This call to repentance remains the mainstay of missionary endeavor. We preach and demonstrate the love of Christ. We preach and demonstrate the power of God. But at the core of what we do is this call on our hearers to repent. We cannot be right with God and continue in our sin. We cannot be right with God and fail to honor Him with our lives. We must repent of our past failures and embrace a life that lives for the purpose of honoring and obeying our Lord. This is the message which Paul preached, and which we continue to preach today.

17:31

Because He has appointed a day on which He will judge the world in righteousness by the Man whom He has ordained. He has given assurance of this to all by raising Him from the dead.

One day, Jesus will "judge the world." "For He is coming, for He is coming to judge the earth. He shall judge the world with righteousness, and the peoples with His truth" (Psalm 96:13). If every man was judged by his own personal standard, or his own religion, or his own god, then everyone the world over could feel safe in their religious preferences. But there will not be multiple options for judgment when our life on earth is over. Jesus is "the Man" that the Creator God has appointed to bring judgment on everyone in the world. Jesus is not the god who judges Christians while other gods judge their subjects. No, Jesus is the God who judges everyone – everyone! The world must see their need for reconciling with their Judge!

Paul says that Jesus' resurrection from the dead provides us with evidence, it gives us "assurance" that He is our judge for eternity, and that His approval will grant us an eternal pardon. Because Christ is risen from the dead, our faith in Him is well placed, for our eternity is no longer determined by the sins we have committed (I Corinthians 15:17). Death is coming for us all. Judgment is coming for us all. Those who are wise will never allow this fact to slip from their thoughts. But Jesus is our Judge and Jesus has conquered death, so all who trust in Him as Savior will be rewarded by Him with rescue when that day of death and judgment arrives.

17:32-34

And when they heard of the resurrection of the dead, some mocked, while others said, "We will hear you again on this matter." So Paul departed from among them. However, some men joined him and believed, among

them Dionysius the Areopagite, a woman named Damaris, and others with them.

"The message of the cross is foolishness to those who are perishing" (I Corinthians 1:18), and we see the men of Athens "mocked" Paul after they heard him speak of Jesus rising from the dead. The message of Jesus rising from the dead sounds far-fetched to many, but the Greeks in Paul's day found it especially foolish to believe in (I Corinthians 1:23). Let us not be shocked or discouraged when lost people scoff at our message and mock us for believing things they find outlandish. "The natural man does not receive the things of the Spirit of God, for they are foolishness to him; nor can he know them, because they are spiritually discerned" (I Corinthians 2:14). The scoffing of gospel mockers will prove to be their own punishment, however. Because they loved to debate novel concepts (verse 21), they joked of hearing Paul "again on this matter." But they would be granted no such opportunity to better respond to God's Truth through the words of Paul. They scoffed at his message, so "Paul departed from among them." Although God promises divine help to worms (Isaiah 41:14), He does not throw His pearls before swine (Matthew 7:6). There will always be some who will mock the message of Christ's cross, but it is the Lord who has the last laugh (so to speak). Psalm 2:4 says, "He who sits in the heavens shall laugh; the LORD shall hold them in derision."

We are encouraged to see that despite the skepticism of the mocking crowd, God's Word did not return void. Dionysius and Damaris along with a few others turned a deaf ear to the mockers' protests, believed Paul's words to be true, and placed saving faith in Jesus. The salvation of these souls in response to Paul's preaching is in keeping with God's stated intention in Isaiah 55:10-11: "For as the rain comes down, and the snow from heaven, and do not return there, but water the earth, and make it bring forth and bud, that it may give seed to the sower and bread to the eater, so shall My word be that goes forth from My mouth; it shall not return to Me void, but it shall accomplish what I please, and it shall prosper in the thing for which I sent it."

Paul's time in Athens was short, and he found himself there out of necessity, not out of advanced planning. But his time there led to the eternal salvation of several precious souls. May our itinerary, no matter how planned or how thrust upon us by circumstance, also lead to God's words being spoken, God's purposes being carried out, and the souls of men being brought closer to Him.

Acts 18

18:1-4
After these things Paul departed from Athens and went to Corinth. And he found a certain Jew named Aquila, born in Pontus, who had recently come from Italy with his wife Priscilla (because Claudius had commanded all the Jews to depart from Rome); and he came to them. So, because he was of the same trade, he stayed with them and worked; for by occupation they were tentmakers. And he reasoned in the synagogue every Sabbath, and persuaded both Jews and Greeks.

Here we are introduced to the means by which Paul supported himself as he worked tirelessly for kingdom purposes. Paul exemplified the life of the bivocational minister. Even as he devoted his life to the high calling of expanding God's kingdom of heaven, his hands were busy making tents so that he could pay the bills on earth. Paul, himself, championed the virtues of the full-time laborer for Christ, teaching that it was proper, perhaps even preferable for pastors to be supported by the church so that they might spend all their time in the service of God and His people. In I Corinthians 9:14 he wrote, "The Lord has commanded that those who preach the gospel should live from the gospel." And in I Timothy 5:17-18 he wrote, "Let the elders who rule well be counted worthy of double honor, especially those who labor in the word and doctrine. For the Scripture says, 'You shall not muzzle an ox while it treads out the grain,' and, 'The laborer is worthy of his wages.'"

Paul was clearly a proponent of church elders, at least church elders "who rule well" receiving full-time wages in return for their full-time labors for the cause of Christ. Even so, Paul exemplifies for us the great value to the church of those who support themselves with a trade even as they devote themselves to Christian service. Later, while writing to God's people right here in Corinth, Paul called on them to "imitate me, just as I also imitate Christ" (I Corinthians 11:1). So much of discipleship is mentorship and modeling, living out the Christian life and inspiring others to imitate our example. This model for discipleship whereby the church provides godly leaders who demonstrate the Christian walk so that new believers might imitate their lifestyle is only enhanced when the godly role models provided for the laymen of the church are laymen themselves. Those who, like Paul, work to support themselves outside the church, even as they devote their full energies to the ministries of the church, are uniquely suited to inspire new believers to do the same.

18:5-6

When Silas and Timothy had come from Macedonia, Paul was compelled by the Spirit, and testified to the Jews that Jesus is the Christ. But when they opposed him and blasphemed, he shook his garments and said to them, "Your blood be upon your own heads; I am clean. From now on I will go to the Gentiles."

Paul was "compelled" by the Spirit of God, he was "occupied" (CSB, ESV) with the task of preaching the word of God to the Jews first and also to the Greeks (Romans 1:16). Paul was consumed by his devotion to God's Word. May it always be so for us as well.

We are struck by how God's Word compelled Paul to preach it to others, while at the same time, that same Word convulsed many others to oppose it and try to prevent it from being preached. The same Word of God that in-spired Paul to preach it, incited others to oppose it – "they opposed him and blasphemed." The Word of God is sharp (Hebrews 4:12). It stabs our soul with such a piercing sensation that we cannot ignore it. The Word of God demands a response. It incites a response. Any soul that it touches will be either stirred to life by the sharpness of the message, or it will be prodded to lash out in counterattack as a dog lashes out at a goading stick. There can be no unimpassioned response to the entrance of God's Word into the soul. When the word of God penetrates the soul of man, he will either be compelled to obey it and teach it to others, or he will be goaded to lash out in opposition and blasphemy. If anyone claims to be a follower of Christ and yet demonstrates no stirring to pass on to others the truths that he finds in God's Word, we have good cause to have grave concern that God's Word has never really entered his soul. In MacLaren's Expositions he writes, "If a man has never felt that he must let his Christian faith have vent, it is a very bad sign." In Isaiah 30:21 and again in Isaiah 50:4, God promises to speak His Word to our ear, and in Matthew 10:27 Jesus gives the command, "What you hear in the ear, preach on the housetops." So if anyone in our churches are not similarly "compelled" to preach to others what God is whispering in their ear, we have cause for concern that they are not hearing Him speak.

18:7-10
And he departed from there and entered the house of a certain man named Justus, one who worshiped God, whose house was next door to the synagogue. Then Crispus, the ruler of the synagogue, believed on the Lord with all his household. And many of the Corinthians, hearing, believed and were baptized. Now the Lord spoke to Paul in the night by a vision, "Do not be afraid, but speak, and do not keep silent; for I am with you, and no one will attack you to hurt you; for I have many people in this city."

Paul was distressed by the poor response to the gospel shown by some of his countrymen. But not all responded so poorly. Crispus, Justus, and "many of the Corinthians" exhibited a more noble response (17:11) to Paul's gospel message.

Paul had seen this many times before. In so many cities over the previous years a similar pattern emerged. A small group of men and women believed the gospel and devoted their life to Christ, but a large and violent crowd of unbelievers always chased Paul away quickly. For some divine reason, however, Corinth was to be different. The Lord spoke to Paul and told him not to fear the persecution that had plagued him in Thessalonica, Philippi, and Berea. The Lord said to him, "Do not be afraid...for I am with you." The fact that God promised to be with Paul would not have caught him by surprise. He had promised that very thing to all his teaching servants in Matthew 28:20. But Paul may well have found the final phrase of the vision to be a delightful surprise: "I have many people in this city." God has allies for us in places we may not anticipate. He reserved 7,000 fellow believers for Elijah in I Kings 19:18. He prepared Aquila and Priscilla to join forces with Paul upon his arrival in Corinth, and now He tells Paul that He has raised up many more than just Aquila and Priscila to help him. God owns the cattle on a thousand hills (Psalm 50:10), and He has many good people situated in many strategic places as well. May the promised presence of God and the blessed bonus of the company of His precious saints continue to be the mainstays of our ability to endure, just as they were for Paul.

18:11

And he continued there a year and six months, teaching the word of God among them.

Paul served in Philippi for a matter of days (16:12), he was in Thessalonica for three weeks (17:2), and he did not remain in Berea or Athens for an extended length of time either. But in Corinth, Paul stayed 18 months. In Philippi he taught by the river (16:13), in Thessalonica he taught in the synagogue (17:1-2), and in Athens he taught in the marketplace and on Mars Hill (17:17, 17:19). Where he taught and how long he taught varied from place to place during Paul's ministry, but this was constant: "teaching the word of God among them." Teaching the Word of God is our ministry on earth. It is by this means that we raise up new generations that are fully capable of doing everything that God requires of them. Teaching God's Word allows God's people to be "complete, thoroughly equipped for every good work" (II Timothy 3:17). Preaching and teaching God's Word is essential to raising up a new generation of believers in our own house or in foreign lands. The apostles found that all other ministries were subservient to their work of prayer and the teaching of God's Word (Acts 6:4), and Paul's impassioned appeal to Timothy in II Timothy 4:2 highlights the significance, the essentialness of this work: "Preach the word!"

18:12-16

When Gallio was proconsul of Achaia, the Jews with one accord rose up against Paul and brought him to the judgment seat, saying, "This fellow persuades men to worship God contrary to the law." And when Paul was about to open his mouth, Gallio said to the Jews, "If it were a matter of wrongdoing or wicked crimes, O Jews, there would be reason why I should bear with you. But if it is a question of words and names and your own law, look to it yourselves; for I do not want to be a judge of such matters." And he drove them from the judgment seat.

In verse 10 the Lord told Paul in a vision that "no one will attack you to hurt you; for I have many people in this city." And here we see that one of those people that was in the Lord's grip was an unbeliever – the proconsul Gallio. The unbelieving Jews "rose up against Paul" just as they had done in so many cities before. But this time, the outcome of their animosity was vastly different than before. As Paul was about to speak in his own defense, Gallio spoke up for him! Just as the Lord had promised in verse 10, He had prepared allies for Paul in unexpected places. The Lord prepared Ebed-Melech, the Ethiopian, to rescue Jeremiah in Jeremiah 38. He prepared the foreigner Ittai to defend David in II Samuel 15, and here, God once again uses a foreigner to defend His servant in an unexpected way.

It is good for us to devote our life's work to carrying out the works of God. If we submit to His sovereign hand, we will find ourselves under His protective wing. If we will work to declare His name, we will find that "the name of the LORD is a strong tower," and those who defend His name "are safe" (Proverbs 18:10).

18:17
Then all the Greeks took Sosthenes, the ruler of the synagogue, and beat him before the judgment seat. But Gallio took no notice of these things.

The story of Sosthenes, pieced together from several Scriptures, is fascinating. My rendition here is by no means certain – there are other possible narratives. But I think we have ample cause to put forward this storyline and good cause to be encouraged by it. When Paul arrived in Corinth, Crispus was the ruler of the synagogue (verse 8). But he became a follower of Christ through Paul's preaching and so Sosthenes was apparently made ruler of the synagogue in his place. In contrast to Crispus' acceptance of Paul's message, Sosthenes violently opposed Paul and riled up "the Jews with one accord" (verse 12) to arrest Paul and drag him to the judgment seat of Gallio. Gallio, however, found Sosthenes' accusations of Paul to be completely without merit and beneath his dignity to even listen to (verses 15-16). Sosthenes' accusations against Paul so incensed Gallio's Greek attendants that, not only did Gallio throw his case out of court, but his men beat him up before he could get out the door! Apparently, this beating did him a great deal of good, however. With bruises to help him reconsider his ways, Sosthenes eventually becomes a follower of Christ as well. In Paul's letter back to these believers in Corinth his opening line reads: "Paul, called to be an apostle of Jesus Christ through the will of God, and Sosthenes our brother..." Apparently, the old adage, "If you can't beat 'em, join 'em" applied to Sosthenes. When his opposition to the cause of Christ failed so miserably, and his persecution of God's servants brought him personal pain, he found just cause to rethink his position.

Let us remember that people who cause us trouble are certainly guilty of no unforgivable sin. The Lord may, in fact, use their harshness toward us to awaken their conscience to their guilt before God. With this in mind, let us "pray for those who spitefully use you and persecute you" (Matthew 5:44). Sometimes the voice of criticism from unbelievers is loudest just before the Lord saves their soul.

18:18

So Paul still remained a good while. Then he took leave of the brethren and sailed for Syria, and Priscilla and Aquila were with him. He had his hair cut off at Cenchrea, for he had taken a vow.

We are not told what it was that Paul vowed, but we are reminded by his vow that God is worthy of our full attention, and that sometimes it is appropriate for us to publicly present demonstrations of our intent to live holy lives in His service. If we vow to abstain from alcohol, or vow to keep ourselves from other physical or visual intoxicants, or vow to fast from food for a certain period, or vow to devote ourselves to prayer and the study of His word for a certain period, we are reminded that our Lord is worthy of such vows. We should not make such vows lightly, and if we make them we must keep them, for it is "better not to vow than to vow and not pay" (Ecclesiastes 5:5).

18:19-23

And he came to Ephesus, and left them there; but he himself entered the synagogue and reasoned with the Jews. When they asked him to stay a longer time with them, he did not consent, but took leave of them, saying, "I must by all means keep this coming feast in Jerusalem; but I will return again to you, God willing." And he sailed from Ephesus. And when he had landed at Caesarea, and gone up and greeted the church, he went down to Antioch. After he had spent some time there, he departed and went over the region of Galatia and Phrygia in order, strengthening all the disciples.

In so many cities previously, Paul was forced to leave before he was ready because his audience was uninviting. Here, however, we find his hearers captivated by his message and hungry to hear more. But we must remain always faithful to God's itinerary, not our own, and not that of others. Paul felt that he "must by all means keep this coming feast in Jerusalem."

Perhaps this had to do with the vow he took that was mentioned in verse 18, or perhaps this was tied to some other unmentioned commitment, but for whatever reason, Paul was compelled to join God's people in Jerusalem for the "coming feast," perhaps the Passover. Interestingly, although Paul felt an urgency and a necessity to return for a time to Jerusalem, Luke provides no details of what Paul did when he got there. We are told only that he spent time with the saints in Jerusalem and Antioch and then immediately returned to the mission field.

The missionary tends to love his homeland forever. There are comforts, precious relationships, and familiar sights that gladden his heart. But that same heart that is cheered by his homeland is also compelled to return to the distant work that the Holy Spirit has called him to carry out. Paul's heart is urged to return to Jerusalem and Antioch. But as soon as "he had spent some time there" the Spirit compelled him to leave home for the Lord's sake "and the gospel's" (Mark 10:29, Mark 8:35). The entirety of his time on "furlough" in Jerusalem and Antioch was summarized in a single phrase: he "greeted the church." And when his short greeting was finished, he returned to the missionary task that the Lord had called him to carry out years before.

18:24-28

Now a certain Jew named Apollos, born at Alexandria, an eloquent man and mighty in the Scriptures, came to Ephesus. This man had been instructed in the way of the Lord; and being fervent in spirit, he spoke and taught accurately the things of the Lord, though he knew only the baptism of John. So he began to speak boldly in the synagogue. When Aquila and Priscilla heard him, they took him aside and explained to him the way of God more accurately. And when he desired to cross to Achaia, the brethren wrote, exhorting the disciples to receive him; and when he arrived, he greatly helped those who had believed through grace; for he vigorously refuted the Jews publicly, showing from the Scriptures that Jesus is the Christ.

We are introduced here to the wonderful character of Apollos. So many commendable things are said about him! May Luke's description here inspire us to strive to be like him. We are told that he was "an eloquent man and mighty in the Scriptures." Eloquence is a gift given to us from the Lord, but what we choose to speak about, and how to use our eloquence is of even greater significance. Moses felt that he was a terrible speaker, stating plainly, "I am not eloquent" (Exodus 4:10), and yet his hearers found him to be "mighty in words" (Acts 7:22). Speaking the words of God will cause our words to move powerfully in the hearts of our hearers. So even if we do not consider ourselves to be "an eloquent man," let us work to become "mighty in the Scriptures" so that God's words on our lips might have great impact with or without the aid of an eloquent tongue.

Apollos was blessed with the opportunity to be "instructed in the way of the Lord," and his learning inspired him to be "fervent in spirit." Just as Apollos' mightiness in the Scriptures empowered his ministry more than his eloquence, so, too, his fervent spirit – his fervent, driven, dedicated response to what he had learned, empowered his ministry even more than his opportunity to receive excellent spiritual training. Some men hear good Bible teaching but do nothing to act upon what they learn. But as Timothy learned from his mother and grandmother, and as Apollos learned from the teachings of John the Baptist, let us take full advantage to learn from godly instructors in the faith. And then, let us rise from our seat of learning and go out with a glowing fervor to obey and serve our Lord.

We also find that Apollos was teachable. Although he was a powerful speaker and was accustomed to drawing large crowds to hear him speak, he was laudably willing to listen to Aquila and Priscilla and embraced their "accurate" teachings. Often the best teachers of God's Word are the best learners and best listeners to God's people. Let us always be "ready to preach the gospel" (Romans 1:15). But let us always be just as ready to listen and learn.

We are also told that Apollos "greatly helped" the believers around him. A holy life lived out in view of others greatly helps God's people. Teaching God's Word to the saints and expressing God's Word to the lost is also a blessing to everyone. The church is "greatly helped" by those who, like Apollos, are teachable, fervent in serving the Lord, and eloquently teach His truths to the saints and to the lost. May our family always 'greatly help' our church in these ways.

Acts 19

19:1-5

And it happened, while Apollos was at Corinth, that Paul, having passed through the upper regions, came to Ephesus. And finding some disciples he said to them, "Did you receive the Holy Spirit when you believed?" So they said to him, "We have not so much as heard whether there is a Holy Spirit." And he said to them, "Into what then were you baptized?" So they said, "Into John's baptism." Then Paul said, "John indeed baptized with a baptism of repentance, saying to the people that they should believe on Him who would come after him, that is, on Christ Jesus." When they heard this, they were baptized in the name of the Lord Jesus.

As he promised in Acts 18:21, Paul returns now to Ephesus. He finds a group of disciples there, and we find him making two assumptions about them that are instructive to us. First, he assumes, since they are disciples of Jesus Christ, that they will be filled with the Holy Spirit. Soon after "finding" these disciples, Paul noticed that they did not appear to be filled with God's Spirit and so he asked them pointedly about it. They honestly answered that they hadn't even heard of the Holy Spirit. People who have been saved by

God will be infused by the presence of the Spirit of God. Paul assumes this to be so and is concerned when he did not find evidence that these disciples were filled with the Spirit. There are many manifestations of the Spirit that confirm His presence. The Spirit of God grants His children "diversities of gifts," "differences of ministries," and "diversities of activities" (I Corinthians 12:4-7), all of which reveal His presence in the lives of those who follow Him. The gifts, ministries, and activities that the Holy Spirit allocates to Christ's disciples will differ from person to person, but Paul's assumption reminds us that all God's children will be filled with His Spirit. The absence of Spirit-endowed gifts, ministries, and activities in the life of a church member is highly concerning and should alert us to the need to address the issue as Paul does here.

Secondly, Paul assumes that they have all been baptized. Since baptism is for the public declaration of repentance of sin and faith in Jesus, Paul asks them what kind of baptism they were given since they did not know Jesus and did not appear to be filled with the Spirit of God. Paul was somewhat pleased with their answer, because their testimony involved a "baptism of repentance" that John the Baptist preached. Repentance is a manifestation of the Spirit's work in the heart of the believer, so their answer reassured Paul that they did possess the true beginnings of saving faith. They simply needed further instruction regarding the One that John the Baptist foretold "would come after him."

Paul assumes that all disciples of Christ will be baptized, and that all baptized believers will show evidence of the presence of the Holy Spirit in their lives. May these assumptions of Paul be instructive to us as we train up disciples of our Lord today.

19:6-7

And when Paul had laid hands on them, the Holy Spirit came upon them, and they spoke with tongues and prophesied. Now the men were about twelve in all.

Paul's concern that there was no manifestation of the Spirit of God in these disciples was quickly cured when the Lord answered his prayer and suddenly filled the 12 men with His Spirit. Immediately, the Spirit confirmed His presence in all 12 when they "spoke with tongues and prophesied." Some might suppose that this indicates that all who are filled with the Spirit will speak in tongues, but I Corinthians 12:30 adequately dispels that notion. The point is not what particular gifts are granted, the point is that the Holy Spirit endows His children with spiritual gifts that reveal His presence. These are given to bless the whole body of Christ, not just the one granted the gift: "The manifestation of the Spirit is given to each one for the profit of all" (I Corinthians 12:7).

19:8-9
And he went into the synagogue and spoke boldly for three months, reasoning and persuading concerning the things of the kingdom of God. But when some were hardened and did not believe, but spoke evil of the Way before the multitude, he departed from them and withdrew the disciples, reasoning daily in the school of Tyrannus.

Paul went into the synagogue and boldly taught the truths of Jesus Christ. He was granted a much better opportunity here in Ephesus than he had encountered in many cities and took full advantage of three good months to reason with the people there and persuade them to follow Christ. Eventually, however, "some were hardened" and not only refused to believe Paul's message but became more and more agitated in their opposition to him. The Lord has not called us to argue with people. "God has called us to peace" (I Corinthians 7:15). We are granted a wonderful message of God's power, love, forgiveness, holiness, and His wonderful plan for our eternity. But our ministry of presenting these truths is a ministry of "reasoning and persuading." It is not a ministry of arguing or hostility. In Matthew 12:15, when the Jews plotted against Jesus because He healed a man in the synagogue on the Sabbath, we are told that Jesus "withdrew from there." He did not battle His opposition. He quietly withdrew from His antagonizers in fulfillment of Isaiah's prophecy that He "will not quarrel nor cry out" (Matthew 12:19). He will be gentle with people – so gentle that "a bruised reed He will not break, and smoking flax He will not quench" (Matthew 12:20). In keeping with Jesus' example, therefore, we find that rather than argue his points with incorrigible people, Paul "withdrew his disciples" to a more peaceful atmosphere. He and his followers found a satisfactory meeting place in the school of Tyrannus, turning that secular institution into a holy shelter for the saints.

19:10
And this continued for two years, so that all who dwelt in Asia heard the word of the Lord Jesus, both Jews and Greeks.

The result of Paul's next two years in Ephesus is remarkable. "All who dwelt in Asia heard the word of the Lord Jesus, both Jews and Greeks." Paul writes of this experience in I Corinthians 16:8-9, stating, "I will tarry in Ephesus until Pentecost. For a great and effective door has opened to me, and there are many adversaries." With his efforts based in the school of Tyrannus (verse 9), Paul was able to "daily" discourse with a steady stream of visitors who were drawn by the Spirit to hear the message that he preached.

"All who dwelt in Asia heard the Word of the Lord Jesus." What a wonderful goal to set before us – that everyone around us would hear the Word of the Lord. "Faith comes by hearing" (Romans 10:17), so let us make it our aim that everyone might hear. Whether the centerpiece of our service be through our church, a school, a Baptist Clinic, or our own home, may the Spirit bless our fervor to see Christ's name made known. May it be our desire for the gospel of Jesus Christ to be wonderfully widespread around us just as it was around Paul, so that everyone who lives in our vicinity might hear the Word of the Lord.

19:11-12

Now God worked unusual miracles by the hands of Paul, so that even handkerchiefs or aprons were brought from his body to the sick, and the diseases left them and the evil spirits went out of them.

The Word of God alone, without any accompanying miracles, is powerful (Romans 1:16). The Spirit requires no physical manifestations of His authority to convince men and women of the truth of the gospel or convict them of the evils of their sin. Even so, it is our Lord's good will to confirm the Word of truth with works of power. Mark 16:20 says that after the Lord Jesus ascended into heaven, His apostles "went out and preached everywhere, the Lord working with them and confirming the word through the accompanying signs." Jesus pleaded with His listeners to see that even if their heart was hardened by their sin and stubbornness, that their eyes should tell them that His words were true. He said in John 14:11, "Believe Me that I am in the Father and the Father in Me, or else believe Me for the sake of the works themselves." The opportunity to both hear the truths of God and see the works of God holds man to an even higher accountability. In John 15:24 Jesus said, "If I had not done among them the works which no one else did, they would have no sin; but now they have seen and also hated both Me and My Father."

God's Word is powerful. It cuts to the center of the soul convincing us of its veracity and convicting us of our sin. God's works are also powerful, confirming for us the truthfulness of the message preached. Together, God's Word and His works powerfully present the imperative for men and women to repent of sin and reconcile with their Creator. We are held accountable if we respond poorly to our Lord's provisions that are designed to spur us to belief.

19:13
Then some of the itinerant Jewish exorcists took it upon themselves to call the name of the Lord Jesus over those who had evil spirits, saying, "We exorcize you by the Jesus whom Paul preaches."

The society that abandons Jesus or who has never known Jesus leaves its people unprotected from the attacks of Satan who comes to "steal, and to kill, and to destroy" (John 10:10). Demonic oppression and outright demonic possession can become so commonplace that significant numbers of the people can fall under the destructive dominion of the devil and his demonic henchman. Here we see that demonic disturbances were so common in Paul's day that people could make their living by traveling from place to place and working to cast demons out of people. Jesus seems to indicate that some of these who cast out demons were working for God's glory and for His purposes (Matthew 12:27 and Luke 9:49-50). But in Matthew 7:22 Jesus taught that not all of those "itinerant Jewish exorcists" were working for God's purposes, and many of them would suffer the same eternal doom as those demons that they sought to cast out.

Having heard of Jesus, and perhaps having even witnessed Paul casting out demons in the name of Jesus, this group of Jewish exorcists "took it upon themselves" to use the name of Jesus in their interaction with demons as Paul did. But just as the presence of the Ark of God provided no protection to the ungodly Israeli army in I Samuel 4, so we will see that the name of Jesus uttered in an unholy incantation provides no protection to the unholy mutterers in this case just the same.

19:14-15
Also there were seven sons of Sceva, a Jewish chief priest, who did so. And the evil spirit answered and said, "Jesus I know, and Paul I know; but who are you?"

It is helpful for us to be aware of what demons know and what they don't know. They know Jesus (Luke 4:34). They know His power, His ultimate victory, and their ultimate fate (Matthew 8:29). And here we see that they know who His children are. They know how to scare people, how to hurt people, and how to gang up on people (Matthew 12:45). At the same time, however, neither Satan, nor his demonic legions are omniscient. There is much that they don't know. Satan and his demons know how people usually act when they come to frighten or tempt us, but they are not sure how we will respond to their attacks. They suspect that we will be frightened like most of their targets, but if we boldly resist them, they will run away (James

4:7). If Satan had known how Job's godly response to his attacks would inspire God's people for thousands of years, he would certainly have left Job alone. If Satan had known that killing Jesus would save the souls of billions of people, he would have done all in his power to prevent the crucifixion.

If we feel that the evil one is tempting us or oppressing us, let us cling to the Lord and adamantly assert that we will not turn from our resolve to bring glory to God in all facets of our life. If Satan senses that he has found a weakness in us that he can exploit, he may keep at us for some time. But if he sees that we are determined to resist him, James tells us that he will flee. He knows who Jesus is. He knows who belong to Jesus. And he has no desire to fight battles that he cannot win.

19:16-17

Then the man in whom the evil spirit was leaped on them, overpowered them, and prevailed against them, so that they fled out of that house naked and wounded. This became known both to all Jews and Greeks dwelling in Ephesus; and fear fell on them all, and the name of the Lord Jesus was magnified.

Attempting to confront the demonic without the Spirit of God within you is a frightful proposition. Empowered by the love of Christ, "we are more than conquerors" (Romans 8:37). Without Christ filling us, however, we cannot stand up to even the weakest of Satan's pawns. This realization filled the believers in Ephesus with fear. We can fool people into thinking we are godlier than we are. But it is sobering to realize that the state of our spiritual armor is very visible in the spiritual realm. It is likely that many in the church felt that Sceva and his sons were powerful spiritual people. But the beating they endured at the hands of the evil spirit showed that they actually possessed no spiritual power at all. The incident brought "fear on them all" as each one assessed his own spiritual state, suddenly aware that pretended religion has no value for our soul. "God is not mocked" (Galatians 6:7), He can see right through pretended devotion. Apparently, Satan, too, can see straight through to the heart of the Christless soul. The experience of Sceva's sons reminds us that the naked truth of our spiritual state is fully visible to everyone in spiritual places. We, therefore, have good cause to join the Ephesians in solemnly considering the state of our walk with the Lord and renewing our vigor to see the Lord Jesus "magnified" both in our actions that men can see and in our deep inner affection for our Savior that they cannot.

19:18-20
And many who had believed came confessing and telling their deeds. Also, many of those who had practiced magic brought their books together and burned them in the sight of all. And they counted up the value of them, and it totaled fifty thousand pieces of silver. So the word of the Lord grew mightily and prevailed.

Seeing the Christless state of Sceva's sons laid bare in front of everyone moved the whole church to examine their own hearts to see "if there is any wicked way in me" (Psalm 139:24). The failures of others ought to have this effect on us. We are not to mock the spiritual failures of others. We are to learn from them and use their failure as our lesson to walk rightly with our God. Seeing a demon-powered man overwhelm the sham faith of Sceva's family caused the Ephesian church to make sure their faith was pure and sure. Seeing the uselessness of magic remedies and powerless incantations made the Ephesian believers do what they should have already done – completely reject their old infatuation with the occult, and publicly cut their ties with all spiritual powers that did not come from God. They could have sold their books of witchcraft and magic, but they preferred not to profit from evil works that opposed God's purposes.

The debacle of the Sceva family's duel with the devil led to a revival among the believers in Ephesus. "The word of the Lord grew mightily and prevailed." God's Word prevailed in the hearts of the Christians, moving them to repent of sin and turn from all associations with the arts of the occult. And God's Word "grew mightily," compelling those who heard of the event to study "the word of the Lord" rather than study books that clearly held no authority over the powers of darkness.

19:21-22
When these things were accomplished, Paul purposed in the Spirit, when he had passed through Macedonia and Achaia, to go to Jerusalem, saying, "After I have been there, I must also see Rome." So he sent into Macedonia two of those who ministered to him, Timothy and Erastus, but he himself stayed in Asia for a time.

We are ambassadors for Christ. We are servants of the risen Lord. It is not our desire to establish our own kingdom of followers on earth. Paul did not think to build a cathedral and preach to an ever-expanding throng of followers. Here, we find him sending his trusted ministers into Macedonia to tend to the Lord's work there, even as he remained to serve the Lord in Asia. We are moved to find Paul virtually alone at the end of his days

(II Timothy 4:9-12). Even in his last days, Paul was still doing just as we find him doing here – sending away those he loved the most so that they might serve the Lord in places of need. It was God's kingdom that Paul sought to expand, not his own.

19:23-27

And about that time there arose a great commotion about the Way. For a certain man named Demetrius, a silver-smith, who made silver shrines of Diana, brought no small profit to the craftsmen. He called them together with the workers of similar occupation, and said: "Men, you know that we have our prosperity by this trade. Moreover you see and hear that not only at Ephesus, but throughout almost all Asia, this Paul has persuaded and turned away many people, saying that they are not gods which are made with hands. So not only is this trade of ours in danger of falling into disrepute, but also the temple of the great goddess Diana may be despised and her magnificence destroyed, whom all Asia and the world worship."

For two years, Paul taught the people of Ephesus the truths of God. His words stirred many to save their soul. Sadly, his words stirred others to save their money. Many who worshiped idols were moved to throw those idols away. But those who crafted those idols felt threatened and offended rather than humbled and repentant. MacLaren's Expositions on this passage says: "Probably Demetrius and the rest were more frightened than hurt; but men are very quick to take alarm when their pockets are threatened." They claimed that their offense was on behalf of "the great goddess Diana," but they admitted that "we have our prosperity by this trade," and we suspect that their devotion was more to their wallet than to their goddess.

Paul taught that idols that are man-made "are not gods." And though both logic and conscience confirmed Paul's words, their love for money outvoted both reason and integrity and incited a riot in their minds and in their city. Demetrius claimed that "all Asia" and the entire world worshiped Diana. But that was simply exaggerated nonsense. It is a common malady of sinful men to fool themselves into thinking that everyone thinks just like they do. And here, Demetrius was emboldened to oppose the Christians because he wrongly believed that his view was shared by "all Asia and the world." "The love of money is a root of all kinds of evil, for which some have strayed from the faith in their greediness, and pierced themselves through with many sorrows" (I Timothy 6:10). The actions of Demetrius remind us of Paul's warning to Timothy. His love for money moved him to exaggerate the popularity of his false religion and miss the essentialness of reconciling with

God. His fear of losing income moved him to defend his profession and his prosperity rather than embrace the opportunity to secure the treasure of heaven for eternity.

19:28-29
Now when they heard this, they were full of wrath and cried out, saying, "Great is Diana of the Ephesians!" So the whole city was filled with confusion, and rushed into the theater with one accord, having seized Gaius and Aristarchus, Macedonians, Paul's travel companions.

Demetrius said that his quarrel was with Paul, but here we see the mob grab Aristarchus and Gaius simply because they were "Paul's travel companions." Their association with Paul put them in physical danger. It will not be the last time this happens. In Colossians 4:10 Paul calls Aristarchus his "fellow prisoner." We must be prepared to see our friends in the faith suffer hardship for the cause of Christ. We call on all God's people to surrender themselves to God's purposes, and well we should. But we cannot guarantee that their devotion to God will not bring them danger and sacrifice and pain. Jesus said in John 15:20, "If they persecuted Me, they will also persecute you." If we imitate Christ and call on others to imitate us as we do so (I Corinthians 11:1), we must anticipate that since "it was necessary for the Christ to suffer" (Luke 24:46), that those who follow us in our imitation of Him will also find times when it is "necessary" to suffer. It is one thing to put yourself through hardship for the cause of Christ, but it requires a much tighter grip on the Savior's hand to endure the sight of suffering in your children in the faith because they are your "travel companions" in the pursuit of Christ.

19:30-31
And when Paul wanted to go in to the people, the disciples would not allow him. Then some of the officials of Asia, who were his friends, sent to him pleading that he would not venture into the theater.

It is hard on the soul to see others inconvenienced, or endangered, or even in pain on our account. We feel Paul's inner turmoil as he saw his friends in the hands of an angry mob as a result of his actions. He "wanted to go in to the people" but the believers would not allow it. His arrival would only fan the flames of the meritless rage that already burned out of control.

Our Lord gave Paul (and us) the high calling of "reasoning" with people (verse 8). But you cannot reason with unreasonable people. You cannot find common ground with people who have lost their mind. Paul's stoning in Lystra (14:19) provided the disciples an essential experience. From that point on when violent men rose up to oppose Paul, we find that "they sent Paul and Silas away by night" from Thessalonica (17:10), "sent Paul away" from Berea (17:14), and now protect him from an unnecessary exposure to this mob in Ephesus.

Solomon wrote that it is safer to fight a bear than to fight with a fool: "Let a man meet a bear robbed of her cubs rather than a fool in his folly" (Proverbs 17:12). In keeping with that wisdom, we find the believers seeking to protect Paul from doing battle with the angry fools of Ephesus. Paul's desire was to explain the way of salvation to the belligerent mob so that they might yet be saved. Sadly, we are advised not to waste our words on this sort of crowd. Proverbs 23:9 advises us, "Do not speak in the hearing of a fool, for he will despise the wisdom of your words."

Let us always be on the cusp of sharing the good news of Jesus Christ. Let us generously sow the seed of the gospel on good soil and hard soil alike. At the same time, however, let us seek wisdom to discern the difference between those who are ignorant and need to be taught, and those who are violently foolish and need to be avoided.

19:32-34

Some therefore cried one thing and some another, for the assembly was confused, and most of them did not know why they had come together. And they drew Alexander out of the multitude, the Jews putting him forward. And Alexander motioned with his hand, and wanted to make his defense to the people. But when they found out that he was a Jew, all with one voice cried out for about two hours, "Great is Diana of the Ephesians!"

We can see why the disciples did not want Paul to go speak to the mob. No one was listening. The crowd grabbed Alexander and made him the focus of their anger. Perhaps he was known for being a Christian (although this is not certain), but when he tried to speak on his behalf, their shouts drowned him out. They put him forward, as if on trial, but had no interest in hearing his defense. The crowd was so enraged that for two hours they cried out, "Great is Diana of the Ephesians!" – two hours!

"Most of them did not know why they had come together." They were "confused." This is the sad state of so many unbelievers. They reject the gospel and vehemently oppose it because "they are confused." Just as the mob demonstrates here, too many people reject and oppose the gospel of Jesus Christ simply because everyone else seems to be doing so. Mob rule is a dangerous thing. It tears apart cities and devastates souls. For two hours the people stood and shouted the same line over and over. Joining the mob had made them out of their mind. If the only reason we do what we do is because others are doing it, the mind and the conscience are both smothered. When people relinquish control of their actions to the soul-less decisions of the mob, we find no limit to the evil and insane things people will discover themselves doing.

Paul wanted to turn hearts to God, but his words would have gained no better hearing than Alexander's. The conscience is horrifyingly silenced while mob rule or popular opinion reigns.

19:35-37

And when the city clerk had quieted the crowd, he said: "Men of Ephesus, what man is there who does not know that the city of the Ephesians is temple guardian of the great goddess Diana, and of the image which fell down from Zeus? Therefore, since these things cannot be denied, you ought to be quiet and do nothing rashly. For you have brought these men here who are neither robbers of temples nor blasphemers of your goddess."

We have a great story to tell the nations – and it does not require us to desecrate temples or malign false goddesses while we tell it. Let us tell the truth: God made the world. Our sin separates us from God. Jesus died and rose again to take away our sin, and those who trust in Him will have an eternal home in heaven. The Message is wonderful, and we can tell it without cursing other gods as we discuss its essential truths. In Acts 24:12 Paul defended his actions before his accusers saying, "They didn't find me disputing with anyone or causing a disturbance among the crowd, either in the temple complex or in the synagogues or anywhere in the city." Demetrius had incited a riot in opposition to Paul's preaching. But the city clerk found no basis for his complaint against the Christians. The presentation of the gospel in Ephesus was carried out courteously with the desire to see God's blessings flow on the people there. The well-mannered actions of Paul and the Christians gave "no reason" (verse 40) for anyone to treat them poorly in return. Paul's example is helpful to us. Let us seek to inspire people, persuade people, even plead with people to follow Christ. It is a far greater work to describe the greatness of God than it is to malign the failures of false religions.

19:38-41

"Therefore, if Demetrius and his fellow craftsmen have a case against anyone, the courts are open and there are proconsuls. Let them bring charges against one another. But if you have any other inquiry to make, it shall be determined in the lawful assembly. For we are in danger of being called in question for today's uproar, there being no reason which we may give to account for this disorderly gathering." And when he had said these things, he dismissed the assembly.

Just as the unbelieving Gallio protected Paul in Corinth (Acts 18:14), so the city clerk now comes to the defense of Paul's friends here in Ephesus. The Lord raised up Cyrus to restore God-directed worship in Jerusalem in Ezra chapter 1. He used the pagan king Ahasuerus to protect the Jews in Esther chapter 8. And here He used an unnamed city clerk in Ephesus to protect His servants. The Lord delights in providing His children with friends in unexpected places and in times when we need them the most. He can make children out of stones (Matthew 3:9) and He is able to make friends for us out of anyone who passes by.

Acts 20

20:1-3
After the uproar had ceased, Paul called the disciples to himself, embraced them, and departed to go to Macedonia. Now when he had gone over that region and encouraged them with many words, he came to Greece and stayed three months. And when the Jews plotted against him as he was about to sail to Syria, he decided to return through Macedonia.

Paul made plans to set sail for Syria. But apparently, his plans were made known to his enemies who "plotted against him" either to attack him as he was boarding the ship or to attack the ship after it set sail. Let us make our plans and trust in the Lord's protective blessings, but let us also be "wise as serpents" (Matthew 10:16) and be willing to adapt our plans when unforeseeable events confront us. May the Lord grant us discernment to know when it is better to plow ahead heedless of the minefield of dangers before us, and when we should follow discernment to safer pathways.

20:4-6
And Sopater of Berea accompanied him to Asia – also Aristarchus and

Secundus of the Thessalonians, and Gaius of Derbe, and Timothy, and Tychicus and Trophimus of Asia. These men, going ahead, waited for us at Troas. But we sailed away from Philippi after the Days of Unleavened Bread, and in five days joined them at Troas, where we stayed seven days.

We suddenly find Paul surrounded by a large number of travel companions from different areas of his ministry. II Corinthians 8:19-21 tells us why. Paul was entrusted with a large sum of money to take from these churches to the saints that were undergoing hard times in Judea. Paul wanted to assure everyone that their gifts to God's people would arrive safely to their desired recipients. He wanted to avoid the possibility "that anyone should blame us in this lavish gift which is administered by us" (II Corinthians 8:20). It is not enough for godly men to be honest and pure as we serve our Lord and His church. We must be able to prove that we are walking honestly and purely with the Lord. We must not only overcome temptation, we must also strive to avoid any opportunity to be tempted. We must not only handle money honestly and keep ourselves sexually pure, we must also make all possible effort to see to it that we have no opportunity to fail in these areas. We must be honorable in all things, "not only in the sight of the Lord, but also in the sight of men" (II Corinthians 8:21).

20:7-12

Now on the first day of the week, when the disciples came together to break bread, Paul, ready to depart the next day, spoke to them and continued his message until midnight. There were many lamps in the upper room where they were gathering together. And in a window sat a certain young man named Eutychus, who was sinking into a deep sleep. He was overcome by sleep; and as Paul continued speaking, he fell down from the third story and was taken up dead. But Paul went down, fell on him, and embracing him said, "Do not trouble yourselves, for his life is in him." Now when he had come up, had broken bread and eaten, and talked a long while, even till day break, he departed. And they brought the young man in alive, and they were not a little comforted.

We are provided here with the remarkable story of Eutychus, whose untimely death and prompt resurrection grant us some practical reminders. We first see Paul preaching until midnight. We find this noteworthy since in our day we find criticism leveled on preachers of God's Word if they speak beyond 20 minutes. The great things of God are worthy to be discussed. They are worthy to be discussed in detail. And they are worthy to be discussed over great stretches of time. It is not our modern mind that causes us agitation when the preacher continues his discourse for longer than 30 minutes – it is spiritual weakness. Paul preached until midnight because his subject matter provided his listeners with the keys to abundant living now and eternal bliss in heaven hereafter. The delivery of the words of God is a task worthy of our time! It is worthy of our listeners' time! Though Eutychus slept himself to death because his poor body wore out in his holy pursuit, Paul was not only unapologetic regarding the length of his sermon, as soon as Eutychus was healed, he continued preaching until day break! Preaching God's Word until the break of dawn is a task worthy of God's choicest servants. It is right for us to dedicate hours on end to the study of God's truths. This in no way gives us license to drone on for an hour without making a point. This does not excuse poor preaching, dull preaching, or preaching that is not mindful of the time. Paul's actions remind us of the richness of God's Word. We are reminded that God's Word grants us the essential truths that save men's souls, restore hope to those who are desperate, and teach us of the purpose behind all created things. It is worthy to be preached and pondered for hours at a time.

Eutychus' story reminds us of the glory of God's Word and of the imperative to preach it. But it also reminds us of the frailty of man. God's Word is worthy to be preached and studied and lived out in the world for hours and days and years on end. But our bodies are frail things that wear out. Let us be patient with ourselves and even more gentle with others when physical limitations grant us less endurance in holy service than we would prefer. When God's people struggle to stay awake during Bible study or even during prayer, it may not be a sign of spiritual weakness, but merely a display of physical fatigue. Saints get tired, and it brings them no discredit.

20:13-16

Then we went ahead to the ship and sailed to Assos, there intending to take Paul on board; for so he had given orders, intending himself to go on foot. And when he met us at Assos, we took him on board and came to Mitylene. We sailed from there, and the next day came opposite Chios. The following day we arrived at Samos and stayed at Trogyllium. The next day we came to Miletus. For Paul had decided to sail past Ephesus, so that he would not have to spend time in Asia; for he was hurrying to be at Jerusalem, if possible, on the Day of Pentecost.

Paul had much love for the saints in Ephesus. The rest of chapter 20 will be devoted entirely to documenting Paul's final words to the church leaders of Ephesus that traveled down to meet with him in Miletus. But as much as he loved the people in the Ephesian church, he felt a higher calling to rush to Jerusalem for the Day of Pentecost. There would be Jews traveling to Jerusalem from all over the world. This would provide a unique opportunity to bear witness to the cause of Christ to a vast number of Jewish leaders. Paul's heart to enjoy fellowship with friends was overcome by his burden to share the gospel of salvation through Christ with the lost. Hebrews 12:1 calls on us to "lay aside every weight, and the sin which so easily ensnares us, and let us run with endurance the race that is set before us." We are called on to lay aside both "weight" and "sin." And we are reminded here that not all things that hinder our completion of the God-given task set before us are sins. Paul longed to see his friends in the faith in Ephesus. But the "weight" of traveling to see them would put his mission in Jerusalem at risk – a risk he could not bear to take. He was "bound in the spirit" to hurry to Jerusalem (verse 22), and he would allow no weight to hinder his progress toward that goal, regardless of how pleasant that weight might be. May the thirst to see God glorified in us always make us quick to throw off weights of diversion, weights of amusement, and certainly weights of sin, so that we may run the race that God has called us to run unhindered.

20:17-21

From Miletus he sent to Ephesus and called for the elders of the church. And when they had come to him, he said to them: "You know, from the first day that I came to Asia, in what manner I always lived among you, serving the Lord with all humility, with many tears and trials which happened to me by the plotting of the Jews; how I kept back nothing that was helpful, but proclaimed it to you, and taught you publicly and from house to house, testifying to Jews, and also to Greeks, repentance toward God and faith toward our Lord Jesus Christ."

How did Paul serve in Asia? May his example provide us with inspiration to serve where we serve just as he served the Lord in Asia. Paul served the Lord "with all humility." Pride cripples our ministry and destines our spiritual successes to be short lived. The desire to see oneself exalted in the eyes of others puts us at odds with God even as our soul longs to be in His service. If we try to take credit for the works of God in His church, we are prone to incur the same wrath that Moses incurred when he struck the rock in Numbers 20:10-11. Insisting that others honor us with open respect and feeling miffed when they fail to grant us that respect is to turn a blind eye to our Lord's example before the cross and communicate that we feel worthy of more respect than He was granted. Let us serve the Lord "with all humility." Our Lord intentionally "humbled Himself" (Philippians 2:8). Moses "was very humble," more humble "than all men who were on the face of the earth" (Numbers 12:3). And John the Baptist noted that it was essential that he be abased if Christ was to be exalted. "He must increase, but I must decrease'' (John 3:30). It is apparent that there is a direct relationship between humility and utility in the kingdom of God. When Nebuchadnezzar thought otherwise, God humbled him to the point of making him sleep on the ground like an ox until he woke up to the understanding that God is great and we are not. Let us seek to make God's name great, not our own. Let us seek to see Him honored and not ourselves. And let us long for God to be glorified in the eyes of all men and take no offense at all when others show us no respect. Paul served the Lord with all humility. Father, please help me serve you like that.

Paul also served the Lord "with many tears and trials." Jesus promised to give us His peace (John 14:27). But the peace that Christ gives is the peace forged in the Garden of Gethsemane and tempered with the tears of agony (Luke 22:44). Psalm 126:5 reminds us that our work of sowing and reaping in the Master's field is a work of tears. We are encouraged knowing that "those who sow in tears shall reap in joy." (Psalm 126:6). But let us not fool ourselves into thinking that we need only endure a few moments of tears before good times roll. Psalm 126 further warns us that the servant of God "continually goes forth weeping" before seeing the happy fruits of his labor.

In his work in Asia, Paul also "kept back nothing that was helpful." He taught those who were helped by instruction. He rebuked those who were helped by admonishment. He healed those who were helped by restored health. He showed compassion to those who were helped by a kind word. He was generous to those who were helped by his provision. And he made tents when that was a help to the work. Whatever people needed, Paul helped provide. He held nothing back. He gave his time, his love, his instruction, his mentorship, and his prayers. He held nothing back. His example is inspiring.

And lastly, Paul taught. He taught "publicly" to large crowds in public venues, and he taught privately "house to house." He taught Jews and Greeks. His teaching was without prejudice. He retained his deep love for his own countrymen (Romans 10:1) even while embracing God's call for him to reach those of different ethnicities (Romans 11:13). And importantly, we are told the heart of Paul's subject matter. He taught repentance from sin and wrongful worship, and he taught the need for faith in the Lord Jesus Christ. "Repentance from dead works" and "faith toward God" provide "the foundation" of our return to right standing with our Maker (Hebrews 6:1) and "the foundation" of our service to the Lord on the behalf of others. Teaching to crowds large and small, teaching people like us and unlike us, and teaching the need for repentance and faith in Jesus Christ is the ministry that Paul personified and remains at the core of the missionary task today.

In just a few words, this description of Paul's ministry in Asia provides us with a wonderful summary of Spirit-directed ministry. May our work today stay true to Paul's example presented here.

20:22-24

"And see, now I go bound in the spirit to Jerusalem, not knowing the things that will happen to me there, except that the Holy Spirit testifies in every city, saying that chains and tribulations await me. But none of these things move me; nor do I count my life dear to myself, so that I may finish my race with joy, and the ministry which I received from the Lord Jesus, to testify to the gospel of the grace of God."

Translators are divided on the proper rendering of Paul's words in the first phrase, whether they should read "bound in the spirit," or "bound by the Spirit" (NLT, ESV, etc.). But the meaning is clear, Paul was "impelled by a constraint felt to be irresistible" (MacLaren's Expositions). MacLaren goes on to say that Paul was carried by "the supreme determination to do what Jesus had given him to do. He knew that his Lord had set him a task, and the one thing needful was to accomplish that. We have no such obstacles in our course as Paul had in his, but the same spirit must mark us if we are to do our work. Consciousness of a mission, fixed determination to carry it out, and consequent contempt of hindrances, belong to all noble lives, and especially to true Christian ones." MacLaren then adds this powerful reflection: "Perils and hardships and possible evils should have no more power to divert us from the path which Christ marks for us than storms or tossing of the ship have to deflect the needle from pointing north."

When I arrived on the mission field in 1992, Tom Williams, who was leading our efforts in Thailand at the time, said to our group of new missionaries, "We are bound here by the will of God." His words echoed Paul's sentiments here and profoundly affected me. My early days in Thailand brought all my immaturities, insecurities, and inadequacies to center stage. I was good at nothing that was required of me. I missed the familiarities of home. But despite the weight of being inadequate at every endeavor, it was not possible for me to sink into discouragement. I was buoyed by the assurance that I was not here of my own choosing. I had been led here and was now bound here by the will of God. The chains of God that bind us to His calling also link us to His life-giving power and His peace-giving presence which sustain us and inspire us to continue in the work that He has compelled us to do. God binds us to His work, and He sustains us in that work, so that no number of "tribulations" can dissuade us from continuing with delight in the work that He has assigned to us.

Clearly, Paul's preoccupation was not self-preservation. His pure and holy passion was to finish the "race" that God had assigned to him, and to finish it "with joy." He was determined to complete the "ministry" that Jesus gave to him and give testimony to "the gospel of the grace of God."

Paul compared his service to the Lord to a race. The Christian life is not lived out from a lounge chair. It requires bursts of energy and a competitive drive. It is a race, but it is not a sprint. We must "run with endurance the race that is set before us" (Hebrews 12:1). We do not stroll through life. We run. We do not jog. We run. We run because our Lord is at the finish line holding up the prize that He bestows on all who finish – and we want that prize! The prize of God's approval is not granted to everyone just for showing up in life. We must win His approval. "Do you not know that those who run in a race all run, but one receives the prize? Run in such a way that you may obtain it" (I Corinthians 9:24). It was Paul's final satisfaction for his soul, that at the end of his days he could say, "I have fought the good fight, I have finished the race, I have kept the faith" (II Timothy 4:7). May our arrival at the finish line of life bring us equal satisfaction.

Paul finished his race, and he carried out to completion "the ministry which I received from the Lord Jesus"(Acts 20:24). In Acts 13:2 we read, "As they ministered to the Lord and fasted, the Holy Spirit said, 'Now separate to Me Barnabas and Saul for the work to which I have called them.'" Paul received from the Lord the specific task of carrying the gospel to the Gentiles. And he was determined to carry out that ministry regardless of the dangers and trials required to do so. Paul's words are inspirational. "None of these things move me; nor do I count my life dear to myself." Paul did not hold personal safety as a thing to be prized. He similarly disregarded physical comfort and personal enjoyments. His goal was not to protect his health; his driving ambition was to carry out the purposes of God on earth. The prospect of facing "chains and tribulations" did not dissuade Paul from his service to the Lord in the least. When our service to the Lord brings us sleepless nights, stressful decisions, or even risks of danger, may this example steel our nerve and strengthen our resolve.

20:25-27

"And indeed, now I know that you all, among whom I have gone preaching the kingdom of God, will see my face no more. Therefore I testify to you this day that I am innocent of the blood of all men. For I have not shunned to declare to you the whole counsel of God."

In Ezekiel 3 and again in Ezekiel 33, God appoints Ezekiel as His watchman for the sake of His people. Ezekiel's responsibility is to "give them warning from Me" (Ezekiel 3:17). If Ezekiel fails to warn the people of God's imminent judgment, God will hold Ezekiel accountable for the death of those who die in their sins. If, however, Ezekiel faithfully warns those around him of God's coming judgment, Ezekiel will be considered innocent – he will deliver his soul (Ezekiel 3:19), even if his listeners refuse to obey the Lord.

Here, as if responding to the same responsibility that God gave to Ezekiel, Paul declares his innocence. He has faithfully declared to all in Asia "the whole counsel of God." If anyone in Paul's vicinity goes to hell, they will have to climb over his preaching body to get there.

Let us preach the Word! Let us faithfully, persuasively preach "the whole counsel of God" so that no one within earshot of us will remain separated from the Lord due to ignorance. If anyone remains apart from God because of a heart of rebellion or an addiction to sin, so be it. But their blood is on their own hands. Like Paul, we have been called as watchmen to look out for the souls of men. It is our blessed responsibility to instruct and warn everyone regarding the "whole counsel of God." Let us leave none of His words out of our teaching, and let us strive to see that none are left without the knowledge of His counsel.

20:28

"Therefore take heed to yourselves and to all the flock, among which the Holy Spirit has made you overseers, to shepherd the church of God which He purchased with His own blood."

Paul calls on these leaders of the church in Ephesus "to shepherd the church of God." These men were not made leaders of the church because of their personal talents or their deep pockets. They were made leaders because "the Holy Spirit has made you overseers." And when the Holy Spirit calls His saints to leadership in the church, He does so, not to bless the leader, but to bless His church with the provisions provided by the one He has called to "shepherd" them.

Church members are like sheep in that they are weak, prone to injury, prone to wander, and are of great value to the owner (more on that in a moment). So then, church leaders are compared to shepherds because they are called to lead the sheep, feed the sheep, tend to the injured and ill, and protect the sheep from harm. Jesus calls Himself "the good shepherd" (John 10:13), and He calls us to join Him in tenderly shepherding His lambs just as He does. "The good shepherd gives His life for the sheep" (John 10:11), because they are precious to Him. We have been entrusted with the care of those that our Lord holds very dear. He loves His sheep. He loves them! And He entrusts their well-being into our hands. Let us be faithful to the task. Our Lord "purchased" these sheep in our church "with His own blood." The saints in our fellowship could not possibly be more valuable. They were bought with the very blood of Christ. Let us love them as He does. Let us "shepherd the church of God" with all the strength in our back and all the love that we can summon.

20:29-30
"For I know this, that after my departure savage wolves will come in among you, not sparing the flock. Also from among yourselves men will rise up, speaking perverse things, to draw away the disciples after themselves."

Church leaders are like shepherds because they protect the flock. The church of God has many enemies – inside and out. "Savage wolves" come from the world and threaten persecution and temptation. Also, "from among yourselves" enemies arise from within the church that threaten to weaken the flock with false teaching and tolerance of sin. Pride and "perverse things" will invade the church and try to "draw away the disciples after themselves." The church is ever at risk of perverse and prideful men rising up and seeking glory for themselves rather than allowing themselves to remain in the shadows while God is praised. Good shepherds must guard the flock from all these various enemies. We must provide warm loving fellowship so that our lambs will be less infatuated with the world's offer of friendship. We must provide sound teaching that stirs their soul to search the Scriptures for themselves so that they will not be deceived by the wolves of false doctrine. We must help them hold their shield of faith so that they can withstand the attacks of persecution and tribulation. The Lord's lambs have many "savage," wolf-like enemies, and Paul would have us join these Ephesian leaders in protecting the flock from these monstrous, but defeatable enemies.

20:31-32

"Therefore watch, and remember that for three years I did not cease to warn everyone night and day with tears. So now, brethren, I commend you to God and to the word of His grace, which is able to build you up and give you an inheritance among all those who are sanctified."

For three years Paul worked faithfully among the believers in Ephesus to build up their faith and "warn everyone" to look out for the "savage wolves" (verse 29) that would attack their flock of believers. He gave continual, emotional pleas to them to cling to God and cling to His Word so that they would be protected from the various enemies of the Christian life. He warned them to flee sin, turn away false teachers, and stand strong before persecution. But now he was leaving them and would no longer be able to provide the warnings and teachings and comforting friendship that he had given them for the past three years. Paul knew that the great work that was done in Ephesus through his efforts was not the result of his own personal merits. "This was the LORD's doing" and it was marvelous in his eyes (Psalm 118:23). But now, even more aware of the fact that he could do nothing more for the spiritual benefit of these saints that he loved so much, he "commends" them to God and to God's Word. Paul could not carry these believers on his back and make them mature followers of Christ. But he was fully confident that God would continue the work that he had begun in Ephesus (Philippians 1:6), and that His Word, "the word of His grace," would guide them successfully through all the trials and challenges ahead.

Paul's comfort here was a great comfort to me as my children left my home. Much of me would have preferred for us to never be apart. But I was forced to recognize that I had never been the one that had secured spiritual maturity for my children. My Lord called them to Himself, and His Word grew them in the knowledge of Him. My children did not need my constant presence, they needed my Lord's constant presence and constant access to His Word. And so, it was a pleasant sorrow to commend my children to the Lord and to His Word, just as Paul commended the saints of Ephesus to the Lord here. I cannot always be with my children. They cannot have constant access to my words of counsel and comfort. But my Lord is always with them, and they do have constant access to His words of counsel and comfort. As Paul experienced here with the leaders of Ephesus, so it is our pleasant sorrow to commend those we love to the sustaining care of our Lord when the time comes for us to be set apart.

20:33
"I have coveted no one's silver or gold or apparel."

The Lord delights in giving gifts. His gifts vary from person to person, for there are "diversities of gifts" (I Corinthians 12:4). His gifts are not always dependent on our personal character qualities, for He gives gifts to both the evil and the good (Matthew 5:45). But the godly man who has been gifted by God finds no cause to be jealous of what God gives to others. The gifts of God enjoyed in the presence of God under the smiling approval of God fills godly men and women with the highest possible sense of satisfaction. The Lord may grant others more money, more clothes, or less troubles, but the child of God who has experienced the presence and approval of God finds cause to envy no one. He would trade places with no one. Here, Paul makes note of his complete satisfaction with how the Lord has reimbursed him for his labors. Others may have more money and more things. Paul is not jealous. He covets nothing that anyone has, for the joy of looking up into the face of his approving Savior completely satisfies his soul (Psalm 63:5).

20:34-35
"Yes, you yourselves know that these hands have provided for my necessities, and for those who were with me. I have shown you in every way, by laboring like this, that you must support the weak. And remember the words of the Lord Jesus, that He said, 'It is more blessed to give than to receive.'"

Paul quotes an adage from Jesus that had not been recorded by any of the gospel writers, "It is more blessed to give than to receive." This was the reason that Paul worked at his trade of tentmaking rather than take support from other believers. It is a blessing to receive timely gifts from loving people when in need. But Paul writes that there are greater blessings granted those who give to those in need. Proverbs 22:9 says, "He who has a generous eye will be blessed, for he gives of his bread to the poor." And Proverbs 11:25 says, "The generous soul will be made rich, and he who waters will also be watered himself." Jesus takes careful note of every kind gesture and every generous act on our part (Matthew 10:42) and intends to bless those He sees providing for others. So, in order to help provide for others, Paul worked hard to earn his own keep, and to keep something extra on hand to give to those in need. In his letter to these same Ephesians Paul wrote, "Let him who stole steal no longer, but rather let him labor, working with his hands what is good, that he may have something to give him who has need" (Ephesians 4:28). The Christian life that honors God and grants blessings on the believer is the life that strives to "have something to give him who has need." By "laboring like this," Paul sought to grant us an example to live by: work hard and meet needs. Paul's example may be easy to comprehend, but it is difficult to live up to.

20:36-38

And when he had said these things, he knelt down and prayed with them all. Then they all wept freely, and fell on Paul's neck and kissed him, sorrowing most of all for the words which he spoke, that they would see his face no more. And they accompanied him to the ship.

Matthew Henry writes, "It is good for friends, when they part, to part with prayer." It is the Lord that brings us our friends and fathers in the faith, and so it is right to thank Him for them and commend them to His blessings when we are separated. Even self-centered people appreciate friends, and Christ-centered men and women find good cause to be even more grateful for the companionship of those who bless us with their friendship as we carry out God's purposes. We are shown here that it is appropriate for us to mourn the loss of friends. We do not mourn "as others who have no hope" (I Thessalonians 4:13), for we know that we will see our friends in Christ again. But the world offers few delights that compare to the holy joy of sitting with, talking with, and working with godly friends, so the loss of beloved godly company on earth, even for a time, is a godly sorrow. Paul's friends "accompanied him to the ship." Their time together would soon end, but they stayed with Paul as long as they possibly could. Our abilities to bless our friends and fellow believers have many limitations. But may everyone see that we stay with them as long as we possibly can, we give to them all we possibly can, and that we remain good company from the start to the finish of all our times together.

Acts 21

21:1-4
Now it came to pass, that when we had departed from them and set sail, running a straight course we came to Cos, the following day to Rhodes, and from there to Patara. And finding a ship sailing over to Phoenicia, we went aboard and set sail. When we had sighted Cyprus, we passed it on the left, sailed to Syria, and landed at Tyre; for there the ship was to unload her cargo. And finding disciples, we stayed there seven days. They told Paul through the Spirit not to go up to Jerusalem.

Luke provides for us Paul's itinerary for his trip to Jerusalem. "Finding disciples" in Tyre, Paul and his group stayed with them for a week before continuing their journey. "Through the Spirit" the group of disciples urged Paul to change his intentions and avoid Jerusalem. This merits our consideration. The Holy Spirit inspired Paul to travel to Jerusalem, and the Holy Spirit also inspired these saints in Tyre to warn Paul not to go. Let us be cognizant of the fact that godly men can disagree and neither party be in the wrong. Sometimes the Spirit will guide His saints in a certain course of action – but then use the counsel of others (that He has also inspired) to warn them to tread very carefully.

We must not discount the words of God's people when they disagree with us. We cannot follow everyone's advice, for often the advice of the saints will not agree, and their advice may conflict with what the Spirit has commanded us to do. But neither should we disrespect godly disagreement. Paul could not submit to this counsel which was at odds with his God-given assignment, but their words provided a helpful warning signal so that the troubles he was soon to face in Jerusalem did not take him by surprise.

21:5-6

When we had come to the end of those days, we departed and went on our way; and they all accompanied us, with wives and children, till we were out of the city. And we knelt down on the shore and prayed. When we had taken our leave of one another, we boarded the ship, and they returned home.

Just as the Ephesian leaders had accompanied Paul all the way to his ship to see him off (Acts 20:38), so we see the saints in Tyre accompany Paul all the way out of the city on his final day with them as well. Shakespeare wrote that "parting is such sweet sorrow," and Paul's departure from both Tyre and from the Ephesians seems to indicate that this is especially true for those who are bound by the bonds of love in Christ. Parting moves us to recall our precious times together, moan over the prospect of being separated, and fill us with joy in the anticipation of being reunited – a hope that is guaranteed for all who trust in Jesus. The Derbyshire goodbye is founded on this Biblical model.

21:7-9

And when we had finished our voyage from Tyre, we came to Ptolemais, greeted the brethren, and stayed with them one day. On the next day we who were Paul's companions departed and came to Caesarea, and entered the house of Philip the evangelist, who was one of the seven, and stayed with him. Now this man had four virgin daughters who prophesied.

Philip was a man "of good reputation, full of the Holy Spirit and wisdom" (Acts 6:3-5). Acts chapter 8 is devoted to providing us with a sketch of Philip's remarkable ministry. The chapter ends with Philip coming to Caesarea, and here we find Paul joining him there and staying at his home. As foretold in Joel 2:28, Philip's four grown daughters were all known for joining in their father's work as they served God's people and "prophesied." It is a dear blessing to the church when families serve the Lord together.

Philip was used by the Holy Spirit to meet the needs of the church's poor (Acts 6:1-7), to display the miraculous power of God (Acts 8:5-7), and to lead the lost to faith in Christ (Acts 8:26-40). Men like Philip are hard to find, and are a dear blessing to the church. But men like Philip who serve the Lord <u>and</u> who are blessed to see their children serve Him in the same way are even harder to find and are a rich blessing to their church indeed.

God's people love to see families serving Him together. The sight moved Luke to make note of it because it is such an encouragement to see and because it is all too hard to find. Abigail was a saintly follower of God, but her husband was not. Timothy was a faithful servant of the Lord, but his father was not. Job was "blameless and upright in heart" and approved by God, but his wife was not. David's heart was knit to God's, but his sons' were not. And on and on the list goes.

It remains my prayer for our family that we might be like Philip's family – that all who take note of us (as Luke did of Philip) would have the joy of seeing not only our faith, but seeing the faith of our children as well.

21:10-14

And as we stayed many days, a certain prophet named Agabus came down from Judea. When he had come to us, he took Paul's belt, bound his own hands and feet, and said, "Thus says the Holy Spirit, 'So shall the Jews at Jerusalem bind the man who owns this belt, and deliver him into the hands of the Gentiles.'" Now when we heard these things, both we and those from that place pleaded with him not to go up to Jerusalem. Then Paul answered, "What do you mean by weeping and breaking my heart? For I am ready not only to be bound, but also to die at Jerusalem for the name of the Lord Jesus." So when he would not be persuaded, we ceased, saying, "The will of the Lord be done."

Paul did not puff himself up into thinking he did not need to listen to others. He did not discount the concerns of his fellow believers with a wave of his hand. Their words of alarm and pleas for him not to go to Jerusalem broke his heart (verse 13). Paul was deeply moved by the concerns expressed by the saints, but he could not submit to their wishes and obey his conscience at the same time.

The church needs godly leaders. The church is blessed by leaders, like Paul, who powerfully articulate the great truths of God for the salvation of the lost and for the edification of the saints. It is right for the church to stand up and try to protect their leaders as Agabus and the saints try to do for Paul here. It is good for the church to help shoulder their leaders' burdens so that they do not wear out. It is good to pray for their protection and to pray for their health and their family, so that nothing prevents them from continued service in the church. Godly leaders are an invaluable blessing to the church. But the church needs the obedience of its leaders far more than it needs the talents of its leaders. Here we see the saints exhibit proper concern and protective efforts for the sake of Paul. But Paul was adamant. He must obey the Spirit of God's command to his heart. He must travel to Jerusalem even if it means imprisonment or death. In doing so, Paul richly blessed the church. For as much as his powerful presence could bless the church, his submissive obedience blessed God's people even more.

21:15-19

And after those days we packed and went up to Jerusalem. Also some of the disciples from Caesarea went with us and brought with them a certain Mnason of Cyprus, an early disciple, with whom we were to lodge. And when we had come to Jerusalem, the brethren received us gladly. On the following day Paul went in with us to James, and all the elders were present. When he had greeted them, he told in detail those things which God had done among the Gentiles through his ministry.

The work of the missionary is not completed with his presentation of the gospel, the discipleship of new believers, and the formation of churches. Upon Paul's return to Jerusalem, he "told in detail those things which God had done among the Gentiles through his ministry." Our work is to go into all the world and "make disciples of all the nations" (Matthew 28:19), and then our continued work is to return home and tell our home churches "in detail" all that we have seen God do. After Paul's first missionary journey he and Barnabas did the same thing. Promptly after returning to Antioch from their missionary efforts, Acts 14:27 says that the duo "gathered the church together" and "reported all that God had done with them, and that He had opened the door of faith to the Gentiles."

The Lord has called all His people to be engaged in His task to reconcile the world to Himself. Everyone is to have a heart to see God open "the door of faith" to the nations. So then, since everyone is called to play a part in bringing the nations to Christ, but not everyone is able to travel to distant lands, it is the responsibility of the church and the missionary to provide this forum for missionaries to report in vibrant, pulsating detail the works of God on the mission field. The Spirit-filled account of the Lord's distant work richly blesses the Spirit-filled souls of saints who actively seek to see God glorified and souls saved in every nation on earth.

21:20-21
And when they heard it, they glorified the Lord. And they said to him, "You see, brother, how many myriads of Jews there are who have believed, and they are all zealous for the law; but they have been informed about you that you teach all the Jews who are among the Gentiles to forsake Moses, saying that they ought not to circumcise their children nor to walk according to the customs.

Disharmony and distrust among believers sting the church like an open sore. But communication and face to face meetings can cure even the deepest wounds of discord. Here we see that Paul's missionary efforts overseas had created quite a stir among the believers in Jerusalem – but, sadly, the miraculous, glorious works of God through him were not presented in a good light. It is amazing how often faithful service to God can be "rewarded" with suspicion and criticism. Without good communication this distrust and disapproval can billow up to destroy relationships in the church even between those who have devoted themselves to the cause of Christ. That was the case here in the church of Jerusalem – until the church had the opportunity to hear Paul speak in person. As soon as they heard the voice of the Lord speak through him, and felt his heart beat in unison with theirs "they glorified the Lord."

Let us be slow to critique the efforts of our fellow believers if we have not had the opportunity to listen to their testimony with our own ears. And let us seek to enhance the opportunity for our church members to hear one another's heart and be blessed by one another's testimony. Suspicion and criticism abound when believers are separated by distance or poor communication.

21:22-25
What then? The assembly must certainly meet, for they will hear that you have come. Therefore do what we tell you: We have four men who have taken a vow. Take them and be purified with them, and pay their expenses so that they may shave their heads, and that all may know that those things of which they were informed concerning you are nothing, but that you yourself also walk orderly and keep the law. But concerning the Gentiles who believe, we have written and decided that they should observe no such thing, except that they should keep themselves from

things offered to idols, from blood, from things strangled, and from sexual immorality.

Paul taught the Gentile believers that they were free from the regulations of the ceremonial Jewish laws. But we will find him here freely willing to subject himself to both the laws and the advice of his fellow believers. This plan will not work, and this suggestion set out by well-meaning people will actually turn out to cause violent persecution to fall on Paul. But we find Paul guiltless in it all. There is nothing that we can do that will guarantee us the approval of others. Paul's righteous character should have won over his critics, but it did not. The report of the miraculous ways that God used Paul to bring salvation to countless souls should have won over his detractors, but they were unmoved by that testimony as well. So the church leaders came up with this plan whereby Paul would take part in this Old Testament ceremony and thereby prove his allegiance to the traditions handed down by Moses. This, however, will also fail. Some people cannot be won over no matter what we do. Even so, our desire to please our Lord will allow us to win over some, and our meek submission to one another will please our Lord, even if it fails to please others.

21:26-29

Then Paul took the men, and the next day, having been purified with them, entered the temple to announce the expiration of the days of purification, at which time an offering should be made for each one of them. Now when the seven days were almost ended, the Jews from Asia, seeing him in the temple, stirred up the whole crowd and laid hands on him, crying out, "Men of Israel, help! This is the man who teaches all men everywhere against the people, the law, and this place; and furthermore he also brought Greeks into the temple and has defiled this holy place." (For they had previously seen Trophimus the Ephesian with him in the city, whom they supposed that Paul had brought into the temple.)

Violence and false accusations, these are the things which epitomized the Jews' persecution of Paul just as they epitomized their persecution of Jesus. They claimed that Paul taught against the things they held dear – that he fought against the people of Israel, the law of Moses, and the temple of God. Paul came to Jerusalem with money collected overseas to give to the people of Israel, so clearly that accusation was false. And these people grabbed Paul while he was in the temple carrying out the very acts of worship that were intended to prove his submission to Moses' law. So clearly their second and third accusations were false as well. "And fur-thermore," they accused Paul of desecrating the temple by bringing Greeks inside. But this was absolute nonsense. Paul never did any such thing.

False accusations and violent opposition. These are the weapons of those who are far from the heart of God. Instead of these weapons, Jesus calls on us to fight, instead, with tenderness, kindness, humility and longsuffering (Colossians 3:12). And though it may seem that the weapons aimed at Paul are better suited than ours to defeat opposition, we are promised that our gentle weapons are "mighty in God for pulling down strongholds" (II Corinthians 10:4). Let us guard our choice of weapons when dealing with those we disagree with. Let us be "gentle" and "not quarrelsome" (I Timothy 3:3) even when we deal with those that we find blameworthy. And let us be careful not to bring false accusations against a child of God. I Timothy 5:19 warns us not to "receive an accusation against an elder except from two or three witnesses" so that we might avoid the sin of Paul's accusers here.

21:30-32
And all the city was disturbed; and the people ran together, seized Paul, and dragged him out of the temple; and immediately the doors were shut. Now as they were seeking to kill him, news came to the commander of the garrison that all Jerusalem was in an uproar. He immediately took soldiers and centurions, and ran down to them. And when they saw the commander and the soldiers, they stopped beating Paul.

With no attempt to listen to Paul's defense, the villainous people dragged Paul from the temple with the intention of beating him to death. We are troubled by the extent of the evil that men are capable of doing – especially since these violent, evil intentions are carried out by those actively wor-shiping God! Those who were seemingly worshiping God one minute are now foaming at the mouth to murder an innocent man a single moment later.

The crowd intended to beat Paul to death, but here, just as He did in Ephesus (Acts 19), the Lord brought secular leaders to his rescue. Claudius Lysias, with a contingent of armed soldiers "ran down to them," arriving in time to save Paul's life. It is comforting to recognize that God can raise up rescuers for us even in those situations that seem most hopeless. God used ravens to rescue Elijah in I Kings 17. He sent an angel to rescue Daniel in Daniel 6:21. And He came Himself to rescue Shadrach and friends in Daniel chapter 3. There are no hopeless situations for children of God. God has rescuers for us hidden in unseen places. Even pagan garrison commanders are at His beck and call. And they will all come running to help us when He says the word. What a pleasant thought.

21:33-36

Then the commander came near and took him, and commanded him to be bound with two chains; and he asked who he was and what he had done. And some among the multitude cried one thing and some another. So when he could not ascertain the truth because of the tumult, he commanded him to be taken into the barracks. When he reached the stairs, he had to be carried by the soldiers because of the violence of the mob. For the multitude of the people followed after, crying out, "Away with him!"

The commander's first action was to bind Paul with two chains. He did not come to rescue Paul, he came to quiet the unrest. But his effort to keep the peace turned out to save Paul's life. One right effort often leads to many good results. The commander listened to the crowd, but "he could not ascertain the truth" from their testimony. Even to his unbiased ear, the crowd's accusations sounded suspect. False accusations against our character can be a sore trial for godly men and women. We want so badly to reflect positively on our Savior, and we may be burdened by the fear that if our name is tarnished that God's name may be less revered as well. But heaven knows the truth and guards our reputation there. And even people with limited insight will see right through false accusations made against godly men and women. Pilate saw through the baseless accusations against Jesus, but was too timid to protect our innocent Savior. The garrison commander, however, shows no such cowardice here. In a short moment, the commander went from chaining Paul to saving him from the "violence of the mob." Even without hearing Paul's side of the story, the commander could discern that the accusations made against him were untrustworthy. If we are called upon to endure false accusations, let us willingly commit our souls and entrust our reputation to our "faithful Creator" (I Peter 4:19), assured that our name is secure with Him.

21:37-40

Then as Paul was about to be led into the barracks, he said to the commander, "May I speak to you?" He replied, "Can you speak Greek? Are you not the Egyptian who some time ago stirred up a rebellion and led the four thousand assassins out into the wilderness?" But Paul said, "I am a Jew from Tarsus, in Cilicia, a citizen of no mean city; and I implore you,

permit me to speak to the people." So when he had given him permission, Paul stood on the stairs and motioned with his hand to the people. And when there was great silence, he spoke to them in the Hebrew language, saying,

Paul was rescued and escorted off to safety. But we are inspired to see that it was not his safety that was his chief concern! Rather than breathe a sigh of relief for the protective custody of the soldiers, Paul sought to use this unique opportunity to present the gospel truths to the gathered crowd. The crowd had gathered to kill him, but somehow Paul was undistracted by that. His only concern was their salvation and Christ's glory. And with these two great motivators before him, he overlooked his personal danger to see only an opportunity to preach the gospel of Christ which is infused with the power to save men's souls (Romans 1:16). May the Lord grant us Paul's discernment to recognize opportunities to teach God's truths when they are granted to us – especially when those opportunities are disguised as personal dangers.

Acts 22

22:1-3
"Brethren and fathers, hear my defense before you now." And when they heard that he spoke to them in the Hebrew language, they kept all the more silent. Then he said: "I am indeed a Jew, born in Tarsus of Cilicia, but brought up in this city at the feet of Gamaliel, taught according to the strictness of our fathers' law, and was zealous toward God as you are today."

In chapter 21, just moments before Paul began this speech, the crowd refused to listen to him, assuming false accusations against him to be true. But now, "when they heard that he spoke to them in the Hebrew language" they quieted their irrational criticism and listened to his defense. "The sound of their holy mother tongue awed them into deeper silence" (Jamieson-Fausset-Brown Bible Commentary). When faced with undue criticism, let us seek to speak the language best suited to communicate with our detractors. Often, humble words will win over critics who appreciate our meek response to their concerns. Others need us to speak to them with firm tones that snap them out of the folly of their ways. Some need us to give them clear directives to follow, while others will chaff under such leadership and do better when spoken to with gentle requests and frequent encouragement.

There are some who will criticize our efforts no matter what we do or say. But many others can be won over if we can speak to them in their language – the language of gentleness to the tender, with intellectual arguments to the scholarly, with cordial responses to those who value personal relation-ships, and so on. Lord willing, we will not be harassed and threatened by an angry mob as Paul is here. But we very well may be called upon to face criticism and opposition. Let us not apologize for doing the right thing. Let us not give in on matters of conscience simply because our critics are angry and make life difficult for us. Instead, let us seek to speak their language, and explain the truths that guide us, using ways and words that are selected to best communicate our motivations to the open minded. We cannot hope to win over those enemies that gnash at us without reason and without altruism. But speaking the truth in a language our hearers can appreciate may win over some of even our harshest critics.

22:4-5
"I persecuted this Way to the death, binding and delivering into prisons both men and women, as also the high priest bears me witness, and all the council of the elders, from whom I also received letters to the brethren, and went to Damascus to bring in chains even those who were there to Jerusalem to be punished."

When testifying to the saving power of Jesus it is good to do as Paul does here and confess to our hearers the faults that characterized us before Jesus made us new. At one time Paul had arrested and murdered followers of Jesus just as the angry mob sought to do to him now. Paul and those who sought to murder him were not so different as the Jews supposed. They were unified by a common language and also by this common venom that once poisoned him against Christians just as it poisoned them. Paul recounted for his listeners how he "persecuted this Way to the death." But now, "this Way" had brought him life. It was Paul's hope that God's work in him would provide evidence to incite faith in others. Paul's words remind us that we can prepare our hearers to be changed by Christ by picturing for them how Jesus changed us. The testimony of a transformed soul is the match-flame that the Spirit often uses to ignite the fires of belief in the souls of those who witness their change.

22:6-11

"Now it happened, as I journeyed and came near Damascus at about noon, suddenly a great light from heaven shone around me. And I fell to the ground and heard a voice saying to me, 'Saul, Saul, why are you persecuting Me?' So I answered, 'Who are You, Lord?' And He said to me, 'I am Jesus of Nazareth, whom you are persecuting.' And those who were with me indeed saw the light and were afraid, but they did not hear the voice of Him who spoke to me. So I said, 'What shall I do, Lord?' And the Lord said to me, 'Arise and go into Damascus, and there you will be told all things which are appointed for you to do.' And since I could not see for the glory of that light, being led by the hand of those who were with me, I came into Damascus."

Paul recalls his encounter with Jesus on the road to Damascus. The crowd had just tried to kill him, the soldiers had just bound him with chains and dragged him away – and yet he is not at a loss for words. God had called Paul to be "His witness" (verse 15) and the work of a witness is remarkably simple. We need not memorize long phrases of dogma; we need not conjure up clever presentations of religious truisms. We simply need to recount for others "that which we have seen and heard" (I John 1:3). The work of an eyewitness is not taxing. He simply tells what he has seen and heard with his own eyes and ears. This is what Paul does here. In a trial, a witness's objective is not to impress the jury. His duty is to retell what he has seen and heard. Whether the jury is swayed by him or not is not his responsibility. His duty is to faithfully retell the events he has witnessed. Paul provides an example of this here. His opportunity to share the gospel came suddenly and unexpectedly. But he needed no preparation. He immediately and fluidly told his audience what God had done for him.

May we be likewise found always ready to give testimony to what God has done for us, that we may "always be ready to give a defense to everyone who asks you a reason for the hope that is in you" (I Peter 3:15).

22:12-16

"Then a certain Ananias, a devout man according to the law, having a good testimony with all the Jews who dwelt there, came to me; and he stood and said to me, 'Brother Saul, receive your sight.' And at that same hour I looked up at him. Then he said, 'The God of our fathers has chosen you that you should know His will, and see the Just One, and hear the voice of His mouth. For you will be His witness to all men of what you have seen and heard. And now why are you waiting? Arise and be baptized, and wash away your sins, calling on the name of the Lord.'"

Paul continues his testimony of the miraculous events that moved him to repent of his opposition to Jesus. Paul does not call Ananias a Christian, but rather, "a devout man according to the law." Along that same line, he also mentions that Ananias had "a good testimony with all the Jews." Paul's wording was intentional. His desire was to build a bridge between the gospel and his unbelieving Jewish listeners. He did not wish to use terms that would offend his audience unnecessarily, and he wanted to "suggest his great principle that a Christian was not an apostate but a complete Jew" (MacLaren's Expositions).

Ananias prophesied that Paul would "be His witness to all men of what (he had) seen and heard," and in partial fulfillment of that prophecy Paul was granted this remarkable opportunity to declare the great acts of God in front of a large crowd, under the protection of Roman soldiers.

Paul's testimony declared what God had done for him, but it was also an invitation to call all his hearers to allow Jesus to reign in their hearts just as He reigned in Paul's. Such is the value of all such testimony. Hearing what God has done in and for us moves the hearts of listeners to sense their similar need. The gospel message and the testimonies of transformed souls are a powerful combination that our Lord has used to draw men and women to Himself from Paul's day to ours.

22:17-21

Now it happened, when I returned to Jerusalem and was praying in the temple, that I was in a trance and saw Him saying to me, 'Make haste and get out of Jerusalem quickly, for they will not receive your testimony concerning Me.' So I said, 'Lord, they know that in every synagogue I imprisoned and beat those who believe on You. And when the blood of Your martyr Stephen was shed, I also was standing by consenting to his death, and guarding the clothes of those who were killing him.' Then He said to me, 'Depart, for I will send you far from here to the Gentiles.'"

Paul continues to give his testimony to the gathered crowd. After his encounter with Jesus on the road to Damascus, Paul says that while he was praying in the temple, Jesus again spoke to him. The Lord said that Paul needed to leave Jerusalem because the Jews there "will not receive your testimony concerning Me." Paul thought that this meant that he was to teach the Christian Jews, but he felt that this was not possible either. The unbelieving Jerusalem Jews would not receive him because of his conversion to Christ, and Paul feared that the Christian Jews would not receive him because of his previous persecution of Christ's followers. But none of those matters disqualified Paul from the shocking ministry that the Lord was calling on him to carry out. Paul's new faith may have banned him from reaching out to the tradition-bound Jews in Jerusalem, and his past may have rendered him ineligible for a ministry among the Jewish Christians in the city, but none of these things precluded him from reaching Gentiles – the groundbreaking ministry that the Lord had called him to carry out.

Let us always be properly humbled and troubled by our past sins and present weaknesses that impede our aspirations for godly service. But let us be reminded by Paul's testimony that the Lord's calling on our lives springs from His vision for us, not from our limited vision for ourselves. And our ability to serve Him arises from His work in us and His presence in us, not from any imagined powers or prowess that we suspect we possess.

22:22
And they listened to him until this word, and then they raised their voices and said, "Away with such a fellow from the earth, for he is not fit to live!"

Filled with the sin and prejudice of Jonah, Paul's Jewish listeners could not bear the thought of Paul offering God's blessings to the Gentiles that they despised. In Jonah 4:4, the prejudiced prophet, in a fit of temper, cried out that he would rather die than see God's mercies extended to the Gentiles in Nineveh. The crowd here shows a similar mindset and immediately determines that it would be better to murder Paul than allow him to carry out his plan to see Gentiles reconciled to God. It is sobering to see how far personal prejudice can carry us from the heart of God. It seems none of us are immune from the possibility of hating certain groups of people with such a passion that it blinds us to the heart of our beloved Savior. Even the apostles failed in this same matter. In Luke 9, James and John asked for the power to call down fire from heaven to destroy the Samaritans at hand. Their request troubled their Lord: "You do not know what manner of spirit you are of. For the Son of Man did not come to destroy men's lives but to save them" (Luke 9:55-56).

I Corinthians 2:16 tells us that we have "the mind of Christ." If so, let us be sure to keep our thoughts in line with His and recognize that it is God's will to save men's souls – even the souls of men and women that we really do not like.

22:23-25
Then, as they cried out and tore off their clothes and threw dust into the air, the commander ordered him to be brought into the barracks, and said that he should be examined under scourging, so that he might know why they shouted so against him. And as they bound him with thongs, Paul said to the centurion who stood by, "Is it lawful for you to scourge a man who is a Roman, and uncondemned?"

There were so many things that the commander did not know! He makes multiple mistakes right in a row – and all because of ignorance. Paul spoke to the crowd in Hebrew, so the commander had no idea what he was saying. But when the crowd suddenly turned rabid, he (incorrectly) assumed it was Paul's fault. He didn't know what Paul said but assumed that he had instigated the tumult. Assumptions based on ignorance lead to actions we are liable to regret. Furthermore, the commander was ignorant of the fact that Paul was a Roman citizen – which made it unlawful to chain and scourge him without a trial. Once again, the commander's ignorance made him vulnerable to carrying out blameworthy actions that could well cause him dire repercussions.

Let us guard ourselves from charting courses and choosing actions that are mired in ignorance. Some matters demand prompt action. But as best we can, let us listen before we speak, learn before we lead, study before we are examined, and at least check the winds before we set sail. Let us be mindful of the commander's error here. When we hear criticism heaped on someone, let us be sure to hear their side of the story before pronouncing judgment. Proverbs 19:2 says, "It is not good for a soul to be without knowledge." In matters great and small, let us do our homework. Failure to do so may place us and others in harm's way.

22:26-30
When the centurion heard that, he went and told the commander, saying, "Take care what you do, for this man is a Roman." Then the commander came and said to him, "Tell me, are you a Roman?" He said, "Yes." The commander answered, "With a large sum I obtained this citizenship." And Paul said, "But I was born a citizen." Then immediately those who were about to examine him withdrew from him; and the commander was also afraid after he found out that he was a Roman, and because he had bound him. The next day, because he wanted to know for certain why he was accused by the Jews, he released him from his bonds, and commanded the

chief priests and all their council to appear, and brought Paul down and set him before them.

Jesus called Paul to Himself on the road to Damascus, but He had been preparing Paul for this unique ministry since his birth. By divine providence, Paul had been born a Roman citizen, and never had that privilege been more useful than right here. Rather than being consigned to a dark cell in isolation, Paul's citizenship would afford him a public hearing where he would be granted the opportunity to present the gospel of Jesus Christ to a great number of civic and religious leaders that Claudius Lysias "commanded" to come and hear! Let us pay proper attention to and give God proper praise for the privileges, abilities, and opportunities that He has granted us. He has provided these things, not for our selfish enjoyment, but for His purposes. May every strength and every privilege afforded us be useful for kingdom purposes. Paul's Roman citizenship will prove to be the means by which he is able to preach the gospel to many. May all benefits granted us be similarly useful for the purposes of Christ.

Acts 23

23:1
Then Paul, looking earnestly at the council, said, "Men and brethren, I have lived in all good conscience before God until this day."

Paul spoke frequently of the role of the conscience in guiding men and women in the pursuit of living rightly. In Romans 2:15 he writes, "Their own conscience and thoughts either accuse them or tell them they are doing right" (NLT). Here, Paul confesses before the council that his conscience tells him that his faith in Jesus is right. He asserts that he has strived to live with a pure conscience all his life right up "until this day."

A pure conscience is a wonderful thing. Paul is not saying that he has never slipped into error. In fact, even while he states that he lives with a pure conscience, he mourns over his past grievous mistakes that make him the "chief" sinner of all (I Timothy 1:15). But he strives to obey the voice of his conscience continually. When his conscience tells him to alter course, he changes his direction. When his conscience tells him to do that which is difficult, he does not fail to comply. And when his conscience tells him he has sinned, he repents with sorrow and amends his ways. A "good conscience" requires both obedience and quick repentance when obedience is missed.

The conscience of man is not perfect. Some people have a conscience that is weak (I Corinthians 8:12). Some have their conscience "seared with a hot iron" (I Timothy 4:2). And others develop "an evil conscience" (Hebrews 10:22) that is so badly disfigured that it mistakes wrong for right and evil for good. But by design, the conscience is God's precious gift to man that allows us to hear Him speak to our spiritual ear even when our flesh may be sending us entirely different signals.

Here, Paul asserts that his conscience is pure. He is a follower of Christ because God has spoken to his conscience and instructed him to do so. It was not rebellion against Old Testament law, nor rejection of Jewish traditions which moved him to follow Christ, but his commitment to maintaining a "good conscience before God."

23:2-5

And the high priest Ananias commanded those who stood by him to strike him on the mouth. Then Paul said to him, "God will strike you, you whitewashed wall! For you sit to judge me according to the law, and do you command me to be struck contrary to the law?" And those who stood by said, "Do you revile God's high priest?" Then Paul said, "I did not know, brethren, that he was the high priest; for it is written, 'You shall not speak evil of a ruler of your people.'"

For our own protection, the Lord has gifted us with a variety of reflexes. When our fingers touch a hot surface, our hand reflexively moves away. When something touches an eyelash, our eyes reflexively close. These reflexes protect us from injury. We have emotional reflexes as well. And although they are designed to be protective, the intrinsic swiftness and thoughtlessness of the reflex can cause hurt. Here we see Paul reflexively respond to a slap in the face with an immediate verbal slap in return. His response shocked his violent, yet religious accusers who accused him of "reviling" God's high priest. After coming to his senses and bringing himself under control, Paul is humble and apologetic, admitting that he did not realize he was rebuking the high priest when his reprimand somewhat involuntarily flew from his lips.

Let us benefit from Paul's example. Let us be understanding when others give us a verbal slap when they are offended or injured as Paul is here. Even the godliest of men and women may say things they do not mean to say when reflexively responding to a burn or a stinging wound. And if we are the one who has spoken rashly in response to an offense or a wound, let us follow Paul's example and apologize quickly as soon as we are made aware that our knee-jerk response was hurtful to our hearers. The high priest's actions were blameworthy, but his position demanded respect – respect that Paul's impulsive response failed to demonstrate. Reflexes, both physical and emotional, are involuntary responses to noxious stimuli. Let us be understanding of others when their reflex response makes them sound harsh. And let us train our tongue to quickly soften its tone as soon as we realize that our words were spoken without proper constraint.

23:6-10

But when Paul perceived that one part were Sadducees and the other Pharisees, he cried out in the council, "Men and brethren, I am a Pharisee, the son of a Pharisee; concerning the hope and resurrection of the dead I am being judged!" And when he had said this, a dissension arose between the Pharisees and the Sadducees; and the assembly was divided. For Sadducees say that there is no resurrection – and no angel or spirit; but the Pharisees confess both. Then there arose a loud outcry. And the scribes of the Pharisees' party arose and protested, saying, "We find no evil in this man; but if a spirit or an angel has spoken to him, let us not fight against God." Now when there arose a great dissension, the commander, fearing lest Paul might be pulled to pieces by them, commanded the soldiers to go down and take him by force from among them, and bring him into the barracks.

By all appearances, Paul's situation appeared desperate. A large coalition of violent accusers were gathered to renew their assault on him. Claudius Lysias had provided a reprieve from their physical attack, but they would see him dead one way or another, and if they could see Paul executed by legal means, they would be so much the happier. We can imagine Paul, holding his cheek in one hand as he embraced the sting of the high priest's slap, and then looking up to gaze upon his accusers seated before him. He saw some old friends, perhaps – Pharisees that had partnered with him in God-directed service in years past. And he also saw, perhaps, some old enemies – Sadducees, whose unbiblical views he had opposed even before becoming a Christian. In Luke 12:11-12, Jesus promised that when His children were hauled before "magistrates and authorities" that they need not fear, the Holy Spirit would reveal to them the words to say before their accusers. And here, in fulfillment of that promise, the Holy Spirit inspires Paul with the perfect words to say. He does not begin his defense by declaring that Jesus is the Son of God. Certainly, that would have unified his enemies against him. No, he introduces himself as a Pharisee – zealously devoted to God's Word. And he begins his defense of the gospel by asserting his conviction that God's Word teaches the resurrection of the dead. It is the promise of the resurrection and the assurance of spending eternity in the presence of God that is "the hope" of all who diligently study and obey God's Word.

Paul's words incited immediate "dissension" among his enemies. II Chronicles 20:23 tells how the Lord delivered his people from a powerful army raised up against them. As the troops of Ammon, Moab, and Mount Seir gathered around Judah, on the cusp of victory, the Lord defeated them all in a flashing moment. "For the people of Ammon and Moab stood up against the inhabitants of Mount Seir to utterly kill and destroy them. And when they had made an end of the inhabitants of Seir, they helped to destroy one another." And so here, God repeats that method of protection for His people by turning Paul's accusers against themselves. Matthew Henry writes, "There is no true friendship among the wicked, and in a moment, and with the utmost ease, God can turn their union into open enmity." The alliance between the Sadducees and Pharisees was as pretend as their devotion to God, and it quickly disintegrated after a single salvo from Paul's arsenal of truth.

23:11
But the following night the Lord stood by him and said, "Be of good cheer, Paul; for as you have testified for Me in Jerusalem, so you must also bear witness at Rome."

Paul had asked the garrison commander for the chance to present the truths about Jesus to the people of Jerusalem (21:39) and he had been granted, not one, but two remarkable opportunities. His further desire, however, was to preach the gospel to the people in Rome (19:21). Likely, on this night, as he lay in the protective, yet restrictive confines of his cell, Paul could not help wondering if his captivity would be prolonged, and if he would be denied the opportunity to preach in Rome as he desired. His concerns were heard in heaven and the Lord Jesus came personally to encourage him. "Be of good cheer, Paul; for as you have testified for Me in Jerusalem, so you must also bear witness at Rome."

It is our Father's good will to give His children glimpses of His plans for our future. An entire book in our Bible is devoted to His intentions in this regard, and great parts of other books are given to foretelling our future state as well. The route that Paul would take to reach Rome was certainly unforeseeable. He would be imprisoned in Caesarea for two years. Later, his ship would be lost at sea for 14 days until it was finally wrecked on Malta. He would be bitten by a deadly viper. There would be plenty of opportunity for Paul to doubt that his vision to preach the gospel in Rome would ever be realized. The Lord graciously preempted Paul's cause to doubt or worry, however, by encouraging him in advance that he would certainly realize his vision to "bear witness at Rome."

It is true that not all the details of our future are clear. "Now we see things imperfectly, like puzzling reflections in a mirror" (I Corinthians 13:12 NLT). But even if our Lord has not dealt with us exactly as He did here for Paul, He has plainly revealed for us some things about our future, with this same intent: that we would be "of good cheer" in hard times, and that we might "bear witness" to His glorious truths before those who do not know Him.

23:12-14
And when it was day, some of the Jews banded together and bound themselves under an oath, saying that they would neither eat nor drink till they had killed Paul. Now there were more than forty who had formed this conspiracy. They came to the chief priests and elders, and said, "We have bound ourselves under a great oath that we will eat nothing until we have killed Paul."

In John 16:2 Jesus taught His disciples, "The time is coming that whoever kills you will think that he offers God service." Who could imagine that the human conscience could become so twisted that a man could think that killing God's children would please Him? Yet we find Jesus' warning clearly fulfilled here as this group of 40 men conspire with priests of God's law and elders of God's people to murder one of God's choicest servants. Zealots, priests, and elders. Those who should do a society the most good are seen here conspiring to commit murder. Let us be reminded that neither passion, nor religion, nor leadership – none of these things – has ever shielded anyone from sin. Far from it. In fact, these seeming virtues are often described in God's Word as liabilities rather than assets.

-Proverbs 19:2 states "Zeal is not good without knowledge" (Proverbs 19:2 CSB).

-Hosea 6:9 explains that religion mixed with hypocrisy moves priests to murder those they are supposed to teach.

-James 3:1 teaches that leaders are held to a higher standard which makes their faults even more glaring.

-And we find here in Acts 23:12-14, zealots, priests, and elders misuse passion, religion, and leadership, the attributes that should have most blessed their society, in a conspiracy to commit murder.

Sadly, man is capable of polluting even the Lord's purest gifts, making them plagues on society rather than blessings.

23:15-16

"Now you, therefore, together with the council, suggest to the commander that he be brought down to you tomorrow, as though you were going to make further inquiries concerning him; but we are ready to kill him before he comes near." So when Paul's sister's son heard of their ambush, he went and entered the barracks and told Paul.

Psalm 64:2 says, "Hide me from the secret plots of the wicked." And here we see the Lord answer this prayer for Paul. Though these men made their plans in secret, nothing they said or did was hidden from God. "For there is nothing hidden which will not be revealed, nor has anything been kept secret but that it should come to light" (Mark 4:22). Our Lord "reveals deep and secret things; He knows what is in the darkness" (Daniel 2:22). We do not know how Paul's nephew came to hear of this plot, (though we would enjoy hearing the details), but we do know that nothing these vile men did in their secret thoughts or in their secret hideouts was hidden from God's view. Some hurtful matters may catch us by surprise, but it is comforting to be confident that nothing at all catches our Lord by surprise. He saw the zealot's plans well before they even set their ambush in place. God can never be ambushed. He always knows where His people are and where His enemies are. Let us heed His warnings of impending troubles (as Paul will do here), and if anything does catch us by surprise, let us quickly take counsel with our Lord, knowing that He saw it coming all along.

23:17-22

Then Paul called one of the centurions to him and said, "Take this young man to the commander, for he has something to tell him." So he took him and brought him to the commander and said, "Paul the prisoner called me to him and asked me to bring this young man to you. He has something to say to you." Then the commander took him by the hand, went aside and asked privately, "What is it that you have to tell me?" And he said, "The Jews have agreed to ask that you bring Paul down to the council tomorrow, as though they were going to inquire more fully about him. But do not yield to them, for more than forty of them lie in wait for him, men who have bound themselves by an oath that they will neither eat nor drink till they have killed him; and now they are ready, waiting for the promise from you." So the commander let the young man depart, and commanded him, "Tell no one that you have revealed these things to me."

In Acts 21:33 the commander bound Paul with two chains before he even knew if Paul was guilty of a crime or not. In 22:24 he commanded that Paul be scourged and interrogated – again, even before he charged Paul with any crime. But somewhere between Acts 22:24 and Acts 23:19, much changed in their relationship. Somehow, a great deal of trust developed between Paul and Claudius Lysias, the commander of the Roman garrison in Jerusalem. Paul suddenly trusts the commander enough to send his nephew to him with information regarding his personal danger. Likewise, the commander trusts Paul enough to take his information seriously and then displays tender concern for Paul's family by keeping the information secret, lest the Jews take revenge on Paul's nephew.

We are reminded that the friends who help us tomorrow may be disguised as enemies that are a pain to us today. Humble responses to offenses can provide the warmth that melt enemies into friends. Good answers, communicated without malice, can win over detractors and critics. And Jesus gave us His divine plan for how to reconcile with our foes: "love your enemies, bless those who curse you, do good to those who hate you, and pray for those who spitefully use you and persecute you" (Matthew 5:44). Our prime motivation for treating antagonists in this way is not to win them over, it is to please our Father in heaven (Matthew 5:45). But humility, respect, solid answers, and loving responses can turn detractors into supporters and foes into friends, just as we see done between Paul and Claudius Lysias in our passage here.

23:23-24
And he called for two centurions, saying, "Prepare two hundred soldiers, seventy horsemen, and two hundred spearmen to go to Caesarea at the third hour of the night; and provide mounts to set Paul on, and bring him safely to Felix the governor."

Forty men vowed to murder Paul. That news could be anxiety provoking even in the heart of the godliest of men. But then Claudius Lysias gives Paul a horse and surrounds him with hundreds of soldiers. His enemies remained, but suddenly, their power to harm him appeared insignificant. Our Lord does not promise us a life without enemies. He does, however, promise us that "whoever trusts in the LORD shall be safe" (Proverbs 29:25). At times, our Lord's provision of safety is palpable, even visible, as were Paul's armed bodyguards. At other times we may need our spiritual eyes opened to fully appreciate His army of protectors around us, as Elisha taught his servant in II Kings 6:17. Either way, let us be mindful that our Lord is a (very) good shepherd (John 10:11). His love is certain, and so our safety is assured.

23:25-30
He wrote a letter in the following manner: Claudius Lysias, To the most excellent governor Felix: Greetings. This man was seized by the Jews and was about to be killed by them. Coming with the troops I rescued him, having learned that he was a Roman. And when I wanted to know the reason they accused him, I brought him before their council. I found out that he was accused concerning questions of their law, but had nothing charged against him deserving of death or chains. And when it was told me that the Jews lay in wait for the man, I sent him immediately to you, and also commanded his accusers to state before you the charges against him. Farewell.

The contents of the commander's letter to Governor Felix are recorded for us here. We raise an eyebrow at his rendition of his first encounter with Paul. Luke wrote that the commander arrested Paul and "commanded him to be bound with two chains" (21:33). But Claudius Lysias describes the event as his rescue of a Roman citizen. Intentional or not, however, we agree that the commander's arrival did rescue Paul from death at the hands of the mob. He admits that Paul had done nothing "deserving of death or chains," but for the sake of the Jewish leaders, he does not free Paul, he simply passes him on to the authority of Felix. In so doing, Claudius Lysias closely follows the pattern of Pontius Pilate, who found Jesus likewise innocent of wrongdoing, but lacking the courage to release Him, tried to refer Him to Herod for sentencing (Luke 23:7). Jesus seems to grant some tenderness to Pilate in John 19:11, and so it may be reasonable for us to extend some level of understanding to Claudius Lysias for his actions in this predicament too. He did not free Paul, but at least he provided protection to him, and made some attempt to provide a fair trial for him as well.

23:31-35
Then the soldiers, as they were commanded, took Paul and brought him by night to Antipatris. The next day they left the horsemen to go on with him, and returned to the barracks. When they came to Caesarea and had delivered the letter to the governor, they also presented Paul to him. And

when the governor had read it, he asked what province he was from. And when he understood that he was from Cilicia, he said, "I will hear you when your accusers also have come." And he commanded him to be kept in Herod's Praetorium.

Paul is delivered to Governor Felix safe and sound. He is not free, which must have been a sore trial for him, but he was safe from violence from his Jewish persecutors. Felix agrees to hear Paul's case, but keeps him in Herod's Praetorium until Paul's accusers arrive, which will take a full five days (24:1). History finds little virtue in Felix. The Cambridge Bible for Schools and Colleges says of Felix: "The character of Felix, as gathered both from Roman and Jewish historians, is that of a mean, profligate, and cruel ruler, and even the troublous times in which he lived are not sufficient to excuse the severity of his conduct." This was the man that was given charge of Paul's case. Blessedly, Paul had the assurance that it only appeared as though his fate was in the hands of Felix. Paul's future was safely held in his Father's hands. The eternal God is our refuge. We are in His "everlasting arms" (Deuteronomy 33:27), not in the hands of any other.

Acts 24

24:1-4

Now after five days Ananias the high priest came down with the elders and a certain orator named Tertullus. These gave evidence to the governor against Paul. And when he was called upon, Tertullus began his accusation, saying: "Seeing that through you we enjoy great peace, and prosperity is being brought to this nation by your foresight, we accept it always and in all places, most noble Felix, with all thankfulness. Nevertheless, not to be tedious to you any further, I beg you to hear, by your courtesy, a few words from us.

The high priest arrives, but he does not bring the charges against Paul himself. No, the dirty work falls to Tertullus, "a certain orator." He was not called upon to testify against Paul because he was an eyewitness to any crimes Paul committed. He was not there because he was injured by Paul's actions. No, he was there because he was a good talker. He flatters Felix with smooth speech and buttery accolades. He is not a witness, he is a tongue for hire, and we are naturally repulsed by his words. He sounds like a snake. We feel the barely concealed evil shadowed behind the sinister sweetness of his speech. Tertullus was entrusted with a grotesquely evil duty – to bring injury to a godly man. "A false witness who speaks lies" is one of the 7 things that God hates (Proverbs 6:16-19), and although being falsely accused, as Paul is here, is as painful as an attack by "a club, a sword, and a sharp arrow" (Proverbs 25:18), we can rest assured that our Lord does not allow people like Tertullus to get away with their sinister plans. Proverbs 19:9 says, "A false witness will not go unpunished, and he who speaks lies shall perish." Tertullus had his day in court, but he will answer for it. False accusations sting, but only for a moment. We are rightly repulsed by silver tongues in wicked people. But we are encouraged by the reminder from Proverbs 6 that God hates Tertullus-tongues too.

24:5-9

"For we have found this man a plague, a creator of dissension among all the Jews throughout the world, and a ringleader of the sect of the Nazarenes. He even tried to profane the temple, and we seized him, and wanted to judge him according to our law. But the commander Lysias came by and with great violence took him out of our hands, commanding his accusers to come to you. By examining him yourself you may ascertain all these things of which we accuse him." And the Jews also assented, maintaining that these things were so.

Tertullus summarizes three accusations against Paul. He prefaces his remarks by calling Paul "a plague" (on society). This was not so much an accusation as it was simple slanderous name-calling. Matthew Henry writes: "Let not Christians value the applause, or be troubled at the revilings of ungodly men." Those far from God "cannot discern between their right hand and their left" (Jonah 4:11), they cannot distinguish evil men from good men. They can't even tell who is a plague on society and who is a gift to society. We must not be troubled by the insults of men like Tertullus.

Tertullus then accuses Paul of being "a creator of dissension among all the Jews throughout the world." The charge was a serious one, since Rome severely punished those who stirred commotion and incited rebellion among the masses. Tertullus was attempting to show that Paul was a threat to Roman rule and national security by stirring unrest among the people. In fact, Paul actively taught his followers to obey Roman rule (Romans 13:1, Titus 3:1, etc.), and not cause dissension (I Thessalonians 4:11), so this accusation was without merit. Secondly, Paul is accused of being "a ringleader of the sect of the Nazarenes." Although followers of Jesus were soon called Christians in Antioch (Acts 11:26), they were called "Nazarenes" by the Jews in Jerusalem. Paul is accused, accurately, of being a Nazarene, but since the Nazarenes were guilty of no crime, this accusation was hardly incriminating. And thirdly, Paul is accused of trying to "profane the temple." This accusation was simply slanderous nonsense. Paul never did any such thing.

Paul will answer these charges effortlessly and succinctly in the following verses.

24:10-13

Then Paul, after the governor had nodded to him to speak, answered: "Inasmuch as I know that you have been for many years a judge of this nation, I do the more cheerfully answer for myself, because you may ascertain that it is no more than twelve days since I went up to Jerusalem to worship. And they neither found me in the temple disputing with anyone nor inciting the crowd, either in the synagogues or in the city. Nor can they prove the things of which they now accuse me."

Paul is accused in verses 5 and 6 of profaning the temple and creating dissension, but Paul highlights the fact that no eyewitness was brought to the stand to testify against him, because he was guilty of none of those things. No one had ever seen him "inciting the crowd." No one had ever found him "disputing with anyone," because he had never been involved in such actions. No, his intention was to worship God. And it was while he was in the very act of worship that these accusers accosted him.

The Jews charged Paul with "being a ringleader of the sect of the Nazarenes." Paul does not deny this central charge against him and begins his defense by asserting that he entered Jerusalem twelve days before "to worship." If they are going to find fault with Paul, their accusations will have to center on his devotion to God, for it is his service to God, his obedience to God, and his worship of God which provides the framework from which all his actions flow. Such was also the case with Daniel. When his enemies sought to accuse him, they, too, acknowledged that "we shall not find any charge against this Daniel unless we find it against him concerning the law of his God" (Daniel 6:5). May our life be so filled with acts of obedience and acts of worship that no accusation against us can miss the fact that everything we do is done with the intention of honoring our Savior.

24:14

"But this I confess to you, that according to the Way which they call a sect, so I worship the God of my fathers, believing all things which are written in the Law and in the Prophets."

Paul continues to address the central charge against him that he was a leader of the "sect of the Nazarenes" (verse 5). Rather than denying the charge, he embraces the charge and explains that the so called "sect of the Nazarenes" was dedicated to the worship of "the God of my fathers" and the obedience of "all things which are written in the Law and in the Prophets." His Pharisee accusers claimed to be devoted to these same Scriptures and the same Creator God as well. Paul's point is that he cannot possibly be charged with a crime, since his teachings stemmed from his devotion to God and God's Word – the very God that his accusers claimed to follow as well.

24:15-16

"I have hope in God, which they themselves also accept, that there will be a resurrection of the dead, both of the just and the unjust. This being so, I myself always strive to have a conscience without offense toward God and men."

Paul was on trial, but he reminds his hearers that at the resurrection of the dead everyone will be placed on trial and judged by God. "This being so," Paul, himself, sought to prepare for that coming day of judgment by living "without offense toward God and men." Far from being a rebel-rouser as his accusers claimed, Paul says that he endeavored to live in harmony with God and men so that he would be able to stand before God on judgment day with a clear conscience – "a conscience without offense."

If we ever stand accused by men, may we be able to withstand the accusations, as Paul does here, with a clean conscience. People may "twist (our) words" to make it sound like we said things we did not say (Psalm 56:5). They may "hate (us) without a cause" (Psalm 35:19). But let us "strive to have a conscience without offense toward God and men" so that when false friends and false accusations rise up against us, our inner peace is preserved within the protections of a clear conscience.

24:17-19

"Now after many years I came to bring alms and offerings to my nation, in the midst of which some Jews from Asia found me purified in the temple, neither with a mob nor with tumult. They ought to have been here before you to object if they had anything against me.

Tertullus accused Paul of trying to "profane the temple" (verse 6). Paul shows here that this charge was ridiculous. He was "purified" in the temple, observing all the temple laws concerning preparation of oneself for entrance to this holy place. And he came to the temple "to bring alms and offerings" to his nation. In stark contrast to the accusation against him that he was a "creator of dissension among all the Jews" (verse 5), Paul was engaged in an effort to bring financial relief to his people at the time that "some Jews from Asia" attacked him in the temple (verse 18). Paul highlights the fact that not a single eyewitness was among his accusers before Felix. If anyone had a complaint against him, it should have been those who saw him in the temple – "they ought to have been here before (Felix)" to state their claims. But, no, not a single eyewitness was present. It is hard to imagine a shoddier indictment effort, or a more disgraceful display of slanderous, baseless accusations against a godly man.

24:20-21

"Or else let those who are here themselves say if they found any wrongdoing in me while I stood before the council, unless it is for this one statement which I cried out, standing among them, 'Concerning the resurrection of the dead I am being judged by you this day.'"

Paul was accused of being a "creator of dissension" (verse 5). Paul refutes that claim, stating that he was not found "disputing with anyone," nor was he "inciting the crowd" (verse 12). Neither was he found in the temple "with a mob" or with "tumult" (verse 18). But Paul has no desire to absolve himself of guilt by forsaking his defense of the gospel – he does acknowledge that some tumult and dissension arose from his declaration concerning the resurrection of the dead. Jesus did die and rise again to save us from our sins. And we will die and be judged by our Creator and Judge, so we must reconcile with Him while we have opportunity. If dissension was created as a result of Paul's message of man's need to reconcile with the eternal Judge of all mankind, so be it. Paul was not a troublemaker. He did not incite riots or spur people to violence. He did, however, preach that Christ Jesus was the Judge of both the living and the dead and that He decides the eternal fate of everyone on earth. Paul was well aware that the message of the cross and the resurrection is a "stone of stumbling and a rock of offense" (Isaiah 8:14). If Paul's accusers make the claim that Paul incited tumult and sedition among the people, he maintains his innocence. If, however, he is on trial because his message regarding the cross and the resurrection offends his listeners, then he is happy to stand behind his words.

24:22-23

But when Felix heard these things, having more accurate knowledge of the Way, he adjourned the proceedings and said, "When Lysias the commander comes down, I will make a decision on your case." So he commanded the centurion to keep Paul and to let him have liberty, and told him not to forbid any of his friends to provide for or visit him.

After listening to the accusations of Tertullus and Paul's words in his own defense, Felix opts to make no immediate decision. Felix had a significant understanding of Christianity, "having more accurate knowledge of the Way," which would have informed him that Christians were not prone to the seditious activity that Paul was accused of. So, suspecting that Paul was innocent, but unwilling to enrage the influential Jews in the case, Felix "commanded the centurion to keep Paul and to let him have liberty." Felix' decision to hear the testimony of Lysias appears laudable, but we are hardly impressed with his decision to "keep Paul" imprisoned even as he found him worthy of being granted "liberty." Paul's Christian friends could come and go to provide for his needs and keep him company, but Paul could not come and go as he pleased, which we might consider to be no "liberty" at all.

24:24-25

And after some days, when Felix came with his wife Drusilla, who was Jewish, he sent for Paul and heard him concerning the faith in Christ. Now as he reasoned about righteousness, self-control, and the judgment to come, Felix was afraid and answered, "Go away for now; when I have a convenient time I will call for you."

Here we find the Lord drawing Felix to Himself. He moves Felix to bring his wife Drusilla to come with him to listen to a word from Paul. Their visit to Paul had nothing to do with Paul's case in court. They came to hear a message for their soul's well-being. Paul preached to them the need for "righteousness" and "self-control," and warned them of "the judgment to come." The adulterous relationship that bound Drusilla and Felix together is well documented in history, and Paul's message wounded their conscience – at least it did so for Felix, who "was afraid" of the judgment that awaited him because of his sin. His conscience was pricked, but sadly, he does not cry out in repentance as his conscience was compelling him to do. All too often, men and women are warned by a stinging conscience to repent of their ways, but they cannot bear the thought of giving up the sinful pleasures that they have become addicted to. Matthew Henry writes of this passage, "Many are startled by the word of God, who are not changed by it.

Many fear the consequences of sin, yet continue in the love and practice of sin. In the affairs of our souls, delays are dangerous. Felix put off this matter to a more convenient season, but we do not find that the more convenient season ever came. Behold now is the accepted time; hear the voice of the Lord today."

24:26-27
Meanwhile he also hoped that money would be given him by Paul, that he might release him. Therefore he sent for him more often and conversed with him. But after two years Porcius Festus succeeded Felix; and Felix, wanting to do the Jews a favor, left Paul bound.

Here we find the corrupt motivations that moved Felix to keep Paul imprisoned: he wanted bribe money from Paul, and he wanted to court the favor of evil, yet influential people. He sat as judge over a case in court, but justice was nowhere in his thinking. His motivations were completely dominated by the pursuit of personal gain. He wanted bribes from Paul and favors from the Jews, so for two years – think of it – two years, he kept an innocent man in prison!

Using our position at work, in the community, or at church for our own personal advantage is disgraceful. May Felix' reprehensible behavior provide sufficient inspiration for us to never follow his example. Let us use all opportunities afforded us by the Spirit and society to advance Christ's kingdom, never our own.

And if we are called upon, like Paul, to spend a season of life seemingly behind the front lines of service, let us bear this trial patiently, seeing that even Paul was not spared this difficulty. No one is indispensable to Christ's kingdom and no small opportunity for service is insignificant in Christ's kingdom efforts. Whether we are called upon to preach the gospel to thousands, or we are called upon to sit with only small children or a rare visitor in an otherwise empty home, let us serve Him faithfully and joyfully, knowing that all our works, small or great are not in vain (I Corinthians 15:58).

Acts 25

25:1-5
Now when Festus had come to the province, after three days he went up from Caesarea to Jerusalem. Then the high priest and the chief men of the Jews informed him against Paul; and they petitioned him, asking a favor against him, that he would summon him to Jerusalem – while they lay in ambush along the road to kill him. But Festus answered that Paul should be kept at Caesarea, and that he himself was going there shortly. "Therefore," he said, "let those who have authority among you go down with me and accuse this man, to see if there is any fault in him."

Because of his many faults, Felix was at last replaced, and Festus comes now to take his office. Upon his arrival, Festus is introduced to the high priest and "chief men" of Jerusalem who quickly turn the topic of discussion to Paul. Two years after Paul was arrested at the temple, we find his enemies still embroiled in bitterness against him! We are grateful for the prudence and sound judgment that Festus immediately shows regarding Paul's case. He does not give in to their request to summon Paul to Jerusalem, instead he summons them to Caesarea to present their accusations there.

Already, he does not trust the high priest and the other religious leaders around him. It is a sad day, and a blot on society when a nation's religious leaders are so notoriously untrustworthy. <u>Gill's Exposition of the Entire Bible</u> says that this scene "shows the malice of these men, the badness of their cause, the indefatigableness and diligence to attain their end, the danger the apostle was in, and the care of Providence over him." Yes, for although these powerful enemies were determined to murder Paul, yet "the care of Providence" provides for us further evidence that "the name of the Lord is a strong tower; the righteous run to it and are safe" (Proverbs 18:10).

25:6-8

And when he had remained among them more than ten days, he went down to Caesarea. And the next day, sitting on the judgment seat, he commanded Paul to be brought. When he had come, the Jews who had come down from Jerusalem stood about and laid many serious complaints against Paul, which they could not prove, while he answered for himself, "Neither against the law of the Jews, nor against the temple, nor against Caesar have I offended in anything at all."

Once again Paul is on trial and once again, he insists on his innocence of these baseless charges against him. He had never broken "the law of the Jews," in fact, he was a strict adherent to the Old Testament law. He had not desecrated the temple, having entered the temple "purified" according to the law (Acts 24:18). Nor was he guilty of sedition against Caesar, having instructed his followers that every soul must be "subject to the governing authorities" (Romans 13:1). Matthew Henry writes, "It becomes those who are innocent, to insist upon their innocence." False accusations were made against Jesus (Matthew 26:59 etc.), and Jesus has warned us that as the world treated Him, so it will treat us. John 15:20 says, "A servant is not greater than his master. If they persecuted Me, they will also persecute you." The godly believer should not be taken by surprise by false accusations. We should prepare for them with holy living that is "above reproach" (Colossians 1:22) and with a "steadfast, immovable" (I Corinthians 15:58) spirit of devotion to our Lord's work that is undaunted by harsh criticism or false accusations.

25:9-12

But Festus, wanting to do the Jews a favor, answered Paul and said, "Are you willing to go up to Jerusalem and there be judged before me concerning these things?" So Paul said, "I stand at Caesar's judgment seat, where

I ought to be judged. To the Jews I have done no wrong, as you very well know. For if I am an offender, or have committed anything deserving of death, I do not object to dying; but if there is nothing in these things of which these men accuse me, no one can deliver me to them. I appeal to Caesar." Then Festus, when he had conferred with the council, answered, "You have appealed to Caesar? To Caesar you shall go!"

Festus did not have to ask for Paul's permission before sending him back to Jerusalem for trial, but we can sense his inner conflict. His desire to keep the peace and placate the volatile Jews made him willing to send Paul back to Jerusalem. But the desire of his conscience to protect the innocent moved him to take counsel with his guiltless prisoner before doing so. The Lord had promised Paul that he would bring the gospel to Rome (Acts 23:11), and now through the unlikeliest of all pathways, Paul will be guaranteed safe passage there. His enemies would have him returned to Jerusalem, but the Lord has plans for him in Rome, and His plans cannot be thwarted. "The desire of the wicked shall perish" (Psalm 112:10), "but the Lord's plans stand firm forever; his intentions can never be shaken" (Psalm 33:11 NLT). So many of Paul's plans were opposed by this group of vile Jewish leaders. But we are reminded by Psalm 14:6 that "the wicked frustrate the plans of the oppressed, but the Lord will protect his people" (NLT).

25:13-16
And after some days King Agrippa and Bernice came to Caesarea to greet Festus. When they had been there many days, Festus laid Paul's case before the king, saying: "There is a certain man left a prisoner by Felix, about whom the chief priests and the elders of the Jews informed me, when I was in Jerusalem, asking for a judgment against him. To them I answered, 'It is not the custom of the Romans to deliver any man to destruction before the accused meets the accusers face to face, and has opportunity to answer for himself concerning the charge against him.'"

King Agrippa now arrives on the scene with his sister Bernice. The two lived together in an infamous, incestuous union. It is a dark blot on society when those entrusted with leadership in a nation live without attention to any moral compass. After "some days" of meeting together, Festus began relating to Agrippa the facts involving Paul's case. Festus probably felt that since Agrippa and Bernice were Jews, they would take interest in the matter, and may even have some helpful insights on Paul's situation. So we see Paul surrounded by wicked, violent accusers, and the judge in his case (Festus) takes counsel from a famously amoral king. Without Paul's confidence being well grounded in the fact that his life was in the hands of his omnipotent Savior, he would have had excellent cause to despair. But Paul knew well that his destiny did not lie in the hands of these spiritually depraved men of rank. In I Corinthians 4:3 Paul wrote, "It is a very small thing that I should be judged by you or by a human court." Paul could face his unholy accusers without despair because his innocence was not decided by this trio of unrighteous judges. Paul appealed to a much higher authority than theirs or even Caesar's. Men without merit reviewed Paul's case, but they did not decide his fate. "He who judges me is the Lord" (I Corinthians 4:4).

25:17-21

"Therefore when they had come together, without any delay, the next day I sat on the judgment seat and commanded the man to be brought in. When the accusers stood up, they brought no accusation against him of such things as I supposed, but had some questions against him about their own religion and about a certain Jesus, who had died, whom Paul affirmed to be alive. And because I was uncertain of such questions, I asked whether he was willing to go to Jerusalem and there be judged concerning these matters. But when Paul appealed to be reserved for the decision of Augustus, I commanded him to be kept till I could send him to Caesar."

Festus continues to narrate Paul's story from his perspective. It seems clear that Festus knew nothing of the background of either Paul or Jesus. The accusations of the Jews against Paul took him by surprise. They had no legal complaint against him at all! They simply "had some questions against him about their own religion." But Festus did successfully discern that Jesus was central to the discussion. The Jews' dispute with Paul was his claim that Jesus was alive, and that by the power of His resurrection, He reigned supreme and superior to "their own religion." Festus could not see how Paul's affirmation that Jesus was alive could be considered a crime by any standard. Paul appeared to be innocent of any misdeeds from Festus' point of view, but the vehemence of Paul's accusers and the completely religious nature of the complaints against him made Festus "uncertain" of his proper course of action. As Festus weighed his options, Paul appealed to Caesar for judgment rather than be given over to the Jews for certain condemnation. This provided Festus with the straightforward decision he was looking for. Festus could "send him to Caesar" and not have to make a decision concerning Paul's claims regarding the life and resurrection of Jesus. Before Festus, Felix had kept Paul at arm's length, waiting for a more "convenient time" to talk to him (Acts 24:25). Soon, Agrippa will be "almost persuaded" to believe Paul's testimony of the supremacy of Jesus (Acts 26:28), and here we see Festus struggling with the same dilemma of how to respond rightly to the truths of this "certain Jesus, who had died, whom Paul affirmed to be alive." There are "some questions" regarding "a certain Jesus" that must be rightly answered by everyone on earth. Paul's imprisonment and trial provided Felix, Festus, and Agrippa with the opportunity to hear the answers to these questions regarding Jesus – and they all responded poorly to the opportunity afforded them. Felix "was afraid" (Acts 24:25), Festus was "uncertain" (verse 20), and soon, Agrippa will be "almost" persuaded. Let us pray that as we present the certain truths of Jesus today, our hearers will respond more appropriately.

25:22-27

Then Agrippa said to Festus, "I also would like to hear the man myself." "Tomorrow," he said, "you shall hear him." So the next day, when Agrippa and Bernice had come with great pomp, and had entered the auditorium with the commanders and the prominent men of the city, at Festus' command Paul was brought in. And Festus said: "King Agrippa and all the men who are here present with us, you see this man about whom the whole assembly of the Jews petitioned me, both at Jerusalem and here, crying out that he was not fit to live any longer. But when I found that he had committed nothing deserving of death, and that he himself had appealed to Augustus, I decided to send him. I have nothing certain to write to my lord concerning him. Therefore I have brought him out before you, and especially before you, King Agrippa, so that after the examination has taken place I may have something to write. For it seems to me unreasonable to send a prisoner and not to specify the charges against him."

There is little cause to believe that Agrippa's desire to hear Paul arose from anything more than idle curiosity. There are many noble and less-than-noble intentions that move men to listen to God's people declare the gospel. There are many intentional and unintentional actions that move men to a place where they can hear God's Word. Blessedly, the Lord can use all these venues to present His truths to the ears of men that are knowingly or unknowingly desperate to hear them.

By this time, Paul had been in prison for over two years. The limitations placed on him must have been difficult for him to bear, except that he knew that he did not require personal freedom to serve His Lord and to share the gospel. God's precious servants may be confined, but the gospel cannot be restrained. In II Timothy 2:9 Paul wrote, "I suffer trouble as an evildoer, even to the point of chains; but the word of God is not chained." Here, even in chains, we find Paul set before a king, the commanders of the army, and the prominent men of the city. It was an opportunity to proclaim God's truths to an audience that he could never have reached as a free man. The Benson Commentary writes: "We have reason to think that his sermon, contained in the next chapter, though it might not be so instrumental as some other of his sermons for the conversion of individual persons, yet redounded as much to the honor of Christ and Christianity as any sermon he ever preached."

We are awed by this remarkable opportunity for the gospel to be preached to the most prominent men in Caesarea's society. We further marvel at the fact that this opportunity only availed itself after Paul endured seemingly service-restricting imprisonment for over two years. May this re-markable experience remind us that the power of the gospel is independent of our personal well-being. Writing from yet another prison, Paul wrote, "I want you to know, brethren, that the things which happened to me have actually turned out for the furtherance of the gospel, so that it has become evident to the whole palace guard, and to all the rest, that my chains are in Christ; and most of the brethren in the Lord, having become confident by my chains, are much more bold to speak the word without fear" (Philippians 1:12-14).

Acts 26

26:1-3

Then Agrippa said to Paul, "You are permitted to speak for yourself." So Paul stretched out his hand and answered for himself: "I think myself happy, King Agrippa, because today I shall answer for myself before you concerning all the things of which I am accused by the Jews, especially because you are expert in all customs and questions which have to do with the Jews. Therefore I beg you to hear me patiently."

After two years of improper imprisonment based on false accusations, Paul is brought before King Agrippa and a crowd of important people and granted his most prominent stage ever to present the gospel. He is granted the opportunity to defend himself, but that is not his imminent concern – he is much more concerned with defending the gospel. He has been jailed for over two years, yet he is "happy" because he has been granted this forum to speak of "the promise made by God" (verse 6), and call his listeners to "repent, turn to God, and do works befitting repentance" (verse 20). Let us likewise turn all opportunities to talk about ourselves into opportunities to discourse on the great things of God just as Paul will do in the following verses.

26:4-8

"My manner of life from my youth, which was spent from the beginning among my own nation at Jerusalem, all the Jews know. They knew me from the first, if they were willing to testify, that according to the strictest sect of our religion I lived a Pharisee. And now I stand and am judged for the hope of the promise made by God to our fathers. To this promise our twelve tribes, earnestly serving God night and day, hope to attain. For this hope's sake, King Agrippa, I am accused by the Jews. Why should it be thought incredible by you that God raises the dead?"

The Jews accused Paul of betraying their religion (Acts 25:19). But Paul immediately refutes that claim, maintaining that he could provide multiple eyewitnesses who could confirm that "according to the strictest sect of our religion I lived a Pharisee." Paul was no betrayer of the Jews' religion; he was a devoted adherent to it. He obeyed Jewish law and he trusted in the promises given to the Jews from God that were written down in their Scriptures. Specifically, Paul trusted in God's "promise" to Israel to send them a Savior, the Messiah, who would deliver His people from death. Paul points out that this is the crux of the accusations against him – not that he incited sedition, not that he desecrated the temple – he was innocent of these things. Paul was persecuted because he believed in "the promise made by God to our fathers" that the Messiah would come and deliver His people from death and sin. If Paul was to stand trial, he wanted to be sure the trial highlighted the glories of Jesus. Jesus grants all men "hope" to have sin forgiven and a heavenly resurrection assured. Paul's defense rests, not on his own innocence, but on this essential truth.

26:9-11

"Indeed, I myself thought I must do many things contrary to the name of Jesus of Nazareth. This I also did in Jerusalem, and many of the saints I shut up in prison, having received authority from the chief priests; and when they were put to death, I cast my vote against them. And I punished them often in every synagogue and compelled them to blaspheme; and being exceedingly enraged against them, I persecuted them even to foreign cities."

Before he begins to tell of his powerful, personal encounter with Jesus that he relates in verses 12-18, Paul here identifies with his audience. Are his listeners Jews? So is he (verse 5). Are his listeners hostile to Jesus? So was he. In fact, he violently, aggressively fought against Jesus-followers right up to the moment he met with Jesus on the road to Damascus (verse 12). In identifying with his listeners, Paul strips away their first line of defense in their unbelief. They cannot say that their rejection of Jesus stems from their Jewish background. Paul's Jewish background brought him to Jesus. Neither can they maintain that they have hated Jesus too long to change now. Paul hated Jesus and His followers more than anyone, but he was living proof that the truths of God and an experience with Jesus can change the heart of even the most spiteful enemy of the cross. Paul's method of communication has been instructive to me in my effort to communicate the truths of the gospel in both the U.S. and in Thailand. It is helpful for me to identify with my audience, anticipate their objections, and recognize common ground between us that can provide a bridge to help them cross the canyon of unbelief.

26:12-15
"While thus occupied, as I journeyed to Damascus with authority and commission from the chief priests, at midday, O king, along the road I saw a light from heaven, brighter than the sun, shining around me and those who journeyed with me. And when we all had fallen to the ground, I heard a voice speaking to me and saying in the Hebrew language, 'Saul, Saul, why are you persecuting Me? It is hard for you to kick against the goads.' So I said, 'Who are You, Lord?' And He said, 'I am Jesus, whom you are persecuting.'"

Paul hopes to awaken his listeners to the truth just as he was awakened. On the road to Damascus, he and his company were struck down to the ground by the brilliance of a supernatural light and the sense of the presence of Almighty God. When the voice spoke, Paul knew immediately that it was the voice of God which spoke. He knew it was God, but he was thoroughly confused by the Lord's upbraiding question: "Saul, Saul, why are you persecuting Me?" Paul was devastated by the accusing question, but he was blessedly moved by the Lord to ask the right question, "Who are You Lord?" Heaven's answer transformed Paul's life: "I am Jesus, whom you are persecuting."

Jesus regards it as a personal attack when the world persecutes His children. When Paul persecuted His people, the Lord felt that he was "persecuting Me." The Voice from heaven admonished Paul, saying, "It is hard for you to kick against the goads." It is hard to avoid personal injury when kicking the point of a spear. If Paul continued to battle against God's people, he would inevitably wound himself severely. Perhaps it was not Paul's intention, but his words served as a subtle warning to his listeners. Those with reasonable insight in the crowd would have seen their need to cleanse their hands quickly of any involvement in the persecution of Paul, having no desire to enrage the Creator who claimed Paul as His own.

26:16
"But rise and stand on your feet; for I have appeared to you for this purpose, to make you a minister and a witness both of the things which you have seen and of the things which I will yet reveal to you."

In the light of God's glory, Paul had fallen to his face on the ground. But the Lord did not approach Paul to punish him, He came to commission him to a great work: to "minister" and to bear "witness." The Lord stood in glory before Paul and declared: "I have appeared to you for this purpose, to make you a minister." Paul was faithful to this task to which the Lord called him. In Romans 15:25 Paul wrote, "I am going to Jerusalem to minister to the saints." The Lord called Paul to minister to His people, to care for their needs, encourage the downcast, strengthen the weak, comfort the hurting, visit the lonely – to bear the burdens of God's people. Jesus gave Peter the same charge: "Feed My sheep" (John 21:17). This mandate to Peter and Paul has now been extended to us all. Galatians 6:2 says, "Bear one another's burdens, and so fulfill the law of Christ." Let us join Paul in this great work as a "minister" to God's people. The needs of God's people are many. Ministering to their needs will require divine strength, discernment, and wisdom that are beyond us, and will require the capacity to comfort others when our own heart feels like it is barely able to beat. But our Lord abounds in all those things, and He endows His ministers with all these things in colossal quantity so that they will be able to do this great work of a minister. The Lord "gives strength and power to His people" (Psalm 68:35); He "gives wisdom" to His servants (Proverbs 2:6); and He "comforts us in all our tribulation that we may be able to comfort those who are in any trouble, with the comfort with which we ourselves are comforted by God" (II Corinthians 1:4). The Lord calls us to minister to His people and He provides all the strength, wisdom, and comfort that we need to carry out this great task.

Secondly, the Lord called Paul and now calls us to bear "witness" to the things that He has done for us and bear "witness" to the things that He has revealed to us in His Word. John the Baptist was given this same charge: "This man came for a witness, to bear witness of the Light, that all through him might believe. He was not that Light, but was sent to bear witness of that Light" (John 1:7-8). We are not required to write a doctoral thesis on the attributes of God. We are simply called upon to give testimony to the mighty things He has done before us as "eyewitnesses of His majesty" (II Peter 1:16). We do not pass on to others ideas about God that we have imagined ourselves. We bear witness to what He has revealed about Himself in the Scriptures.

Jesus appeared to Paul on the road to Damascus and called him to be a minister to His people and a witness to His many glories. Here, even in captivity, we find Paul faithful to that task. May we also be found faithful to the similar calling our Lord has extended to us.

26:17-18

"I will deliver you from the Jewish people, as well as from the Gentiles, to whom I now send you, to open their eyes, in order to turn them from darkness to light, and from the power of Satan to God, that they may receive forgiveness of sins and an inheritance among those who are sanctified by faith in Me."

Jesus further details the work that He has called Paul to carry out. The Lord sent Paul to the nations to "open their eyes, in order to turn them from darkness to light." God soundly refutes the notion that all religions are good. All men and women who worship any god other than the Creator God who called Abraham to Himself are in "darkness." They are immersed in ignorance and doom awaits them. It is not their personal autonomy that empowers them to choose their own religion, it is the "power of Satan" that deceives men into trusting in God-less beliefs.

Paul is sent by the Lord to tell the nations that they can find "forgiveness of sins" in Jesus and only in Jesus; and that once forgiven, their faith in the Lord will grant them access to His persistent work to sanctify them – to make them holy day-by-day. And finally, those who are forgiven and sanctified will win "an inheritance." They will be granted an eternal home in heaven and "always be with the Lord" (I Thessalonians 4:17). This is the glorious work that Jesus called Paul to carry out among the nations: to turn people from darkness and Satan toward the light of Jesus, to teach them that sin must be hated, but that it can be forgiven, and that stained hearts with a penchant for sinning can be transformed into sanctified souls destined for an eternity in heaven. What a marvelous calling. What a fabulous duty. David summarized the responsibility entrusted to him with the same descriptors that we find appropriate for the work given to Paul: "the work is great" (I Chronicles 29:1).

This work that was given to David to see God praised and this work that was assigned to Paul to see souls saved and God's truths revealed to the nations has now been passed on to us. Let us give all possible devotion to these sacred responsibilities. "The work is great."

26:19-20

"Therefore, King Agrippa, I was not disobedient to the heavenly vision, but declared first to those in Damascus and in Jerusalem, and throughout all the region of Judea, and then to the Gentiles, that they should repent, turn to God, and do works befitting repentance."

Having detailed "the heavenly vision" when the Lord commissioned him to godly service, Paul now summarizes his obedient response to the directives he was given. Paul's message to the nations was that men and women must "repent." They must "turn to God." And they must "do works befitting repentance."

Paul's first task (and our task today) was to call people to repent. Romans 3:23 says that "all have sinned." And since all have sinned, all must repent. We must not excuse away our sin, we must not minimize sin as a trifle. And we certainly must not persist in sinning. If we are to reconcile with God and reserve for ourselves a place in heaven, we must repent of our sin. We must grieve over our past sins, put a sudden stop to present sins, and turn our life around in such a way that we protect ourselves from temptations that will put us in danger of committing further sins.

Paul was also commissioned by the Lord to call on the people of the nations to "turn to God." We do not simply call people to good behavior. We do not call them to be more devoted to the religion of their choice. Paul called the nations to "turn to God" – to turn to God for provision of need, turn to God for the purpose of living, turn to God for comfort, guidance, and hope. And, of course, turn to God for forgiveness of sin. In Acts 14:15 we found Paul faithful to this calling when he called on his listeners in Lystra to "turn from these useless things" (idols and God-less religion) "to the living God, who made the heaven, the earth, the sea, and all things that are in them." Like Paul, we are all the more encouraged to call people to turn to God, seeing that He has promised such all-encompassing blessings to those who "turn to the LORD your God will all your heart and with all your soul" (Deuteronomy 30:10).

In addition, Paul was to call on his hearers among the nations to "do works befitting repentance." Repentance that shows no indebted gratitude for the Savior is not true repentance. Repentance that fails to forgive others as God forgave us is likewise not "befitting repentance." Repentance that does not ignite in us an excitement and fervor to love on and serve God's people in His church is also an improper outcome of true repentance. And, of course, returning to sin after voicing repentance of sin is clearly not "befitting repentance." Paul was to call on the peoples of the world to repent, turn to God, and then produce works befitting repentance. May we display lives consistent with a repentant heart, even as we join Paul and call on others to do the same.

26:21-23

"For these reasons the Jews seized me in the temple and tried to kill me. Therefore, having obtained help from God, to this day I stand, witnessing both to small and great, saying no other things than those which the prophets and Moses said would come – that the Christ would suffer, that He would be the first to rise from the dead, and would proclaim light to the Jewish people and to the Gentiles."

The Jews accused Paul of desecrating "their own religion" (25:19), but Paul once again maintains that he taught "no other things" except that which "the prophets and Moses" taught in the Jewish Scriptures. It was Paul's joyful duty to witness "both to small and great" of the things that were taught by God's prophets in the Old Testament. Paul was happy to preach to the poorest of the poor, and he was unashamed to preach before kings and governors of this message that would bring light to the souls of both Jews and Gentiles alike. The controversy was not that Paul blasphemed his Jewish religious roots – he did no such thing. The controversy was that he preached the message that Jesus was the light of the world, and the Jews rejected that light because their deeds were evil. The Jews' response to Paul's teaching illustrated the words of John: "And this is the condemnation, that the light has come into the world, and men loved darkness rather than light, because their deeds were evil. For everyone practicing evil hates the light and does not come to the light, lest his deeds should be exposed" (John 3:19-20).

Paul was no criminal. He broke neither civil nor religious laws. What he did do, however, was proclaim that Jesus was "the first to rise from the dead" and that He was the light of the world, illuminating the (only) way to live rightly and enter heaven. The Jews' complaints were not really against Paul at all, but against the teachings and authority of Jesus Christ.

26:24

Now as he thus made his defense, Festus said with a loud voice, "Paul, you are beside yourself! Much learning is driving you mad!"

"The fool has said in his heart, 'There is no God'" (Psalm 53:1). Fools think that God is not real and that all who devote themselves to Him are mad. Those close to Jesus, but far from God said of Jesus, "He is out of His mind" (Mark 3:21). Those who were far from both the Father and the Son said the same thing: "He has a demon and is mad. Why do you listen to Him?" (John 10:20). It is not surprising, then, that Festus' foolish unbelief moved him to treat Paul with the same scorn that was directed toward Jesus. His spiritual discernment was amputated by the "willful ignorance" (II Peter 3:5) of his unbelief.

Let us stand strong, unmoved by the ridicule of those who think we are out of our mind to devote ourselves to Jesus. Jesus and Paul were similarly ridiculed. We do not envy the blind when they cannot see what we see. We do not envy the deaf when they cannot hear what we hear. Let us likewise pity those who think us crazy because we are devoted to the Jesus that they have not yet met.

26:25

But he said, "I am not mad, most noble Festus, but speak the words of truth and reason."

It is a privilege and a joy to speak to others "the words of truth and reason." We do not call others to Jesus simply because our experience with Jesus has been positive. We call people to Jesus because "(His) word is truth" (John 17:17). In fact, "The entirety of (His) word is truth" (Psalm 119:160). People may try to "suppress the truth" (Romans 1:18) that God punishes sin, so it is of crucial importance for us to remind them of the truth so that they will not be duped into hell by the deceitfulness of sin. Some choose to exchange the truth for the lie that the worship of inanimate idols is a viable religious option (Romans 1:25). But this, too, has horrifying eternal consequences and these are in desperate need of having the truth set before them as well. Still others are presented with the truth, but then "do not believe the truth" (II Thessalonians 2:12), or "resist the truth" (II Timothy 3:8), "turn from the truth" (Titus 1:14), or "wander from the truth" (James 5:19). We are not held accountable for these unwise and culpable responses to the truth. Our work is simply to do as Paul does here: "to speak the words of truth and reason," and pray that our listeners will rightly alter the course of their life in proper response to it. We are not embarrassed to call others to Jesus even if they have never heard of Him, staunchly believe in a different religion, possess a keen intellect, or are offended by what we say. None of these things dissuade us, none of these things intimidate us because the message that we bring to them is the truth. Knowing the truth sets us free from the chains of ignorance and deception (John 8:32). So, with boldness and hopefulness we eagerly present the truths of Jesus before the hearts and minds of our listeners.

In addition to speaking the words of truth, Paul also tells Festus that he speaks the words of "reason." We come to God by faith, that is true. But our reasons for coming to Jesus are excellent. We abandon neither logic nor reason when we devote ourselves to the cause of Christ. We have excellent reasons for the hope that is in us and are prepared to share those reasons with all who are willing to listen (I Peter 3:15).

Truth and reason. These provide the powerful framework for our presentation of man's need to reconcile with his Creator. Paul's confidence before the presence of kings and governors sprang from the fact that what he presented was the truth and that men with sound reason would leap to embrace it. May the truth of the gospel and the many wonderful reasons for obeying the truth of the gospel continue to anchor our faith and embolden our speech as we make known to others what God has made known to us.

26:26-28

"For the king, before whom I also speak freely, knows these things; for I am convinced that none of these things escapes his attention, since this thing was not done in a corner. King Agrippa, do you believe the prophets? I know that you do believe." Then Agrippa said to Paul, "You almost persuade me to become a Christian."

Many scholars, perhaps most of them, argue against the rendering of Herod's response to Paul here. They maintain that in the Greek, Agrippa's wording is more sarcastic and sneering. The CEV says, "In such a short time do you think you can talk me into being a Christian?" In contrast, the NKJV here makes him seem to struggle with his decision to reject Christ. He seems to be moved by Paul's words and "almost" persuaded to repent of his sin and put his faith in Jesus. His statement in verse 32 certainly does not sound sarcastic, but sounds more like he is favorably moved by Paul's testimony. Ultimately, the difference is minor. In either case, King Agrippa rejects Paul's call to submit to the lordship of Christ. Whether he mockingly, scornfully rejects Jesus, or painfully wrestles with the decision, the result is the same: King Agrippa departs from Paul still estranged from Jesus and still in his sin (I Corinthians 15:17). Matthew Henry calls it a "fatal hesitation."

Our eternal destiny hinges on this single decision. Will we repent of our sin and submit to Jesus as Lord of our life, or will we refuse? Whether we wrestle with the decision or sneer at the decision is of little eternal consequence. No matter what our reason is for rejecting Christ, there is no acceptable means for rejecting Jesus. There is no polite rejection, no earnest rejection, no good-intentioned rejection of Jesus that the Almighty God will find acceptable. Agrippa was granted the opportunity to hear the gospel truth of God's provision to save the world from sin through the death and resurrection of Jesus. Agrippa heard the truth and rejected it. Whether his rejection was sinister and sneering or emotionally troubling is immaterial. Let us pray that as we present the gospel today, our listeners will respond with prompt repentance and submission to the Lord – for any other response is condemning.

26:29
And Paul said, "I would to God that not only you, but also all who hear me today, might become both almost and altogether such as I am, except for these chains."

Despite appearances, Paul did not stand before the king, the governor, and this court of important leaders with the intention of defending himself. His desire was to defend the gospel and to call all his hearers, small and great, to follow his example and become "altogether such as I am." Chains notwithstanding, Paul's life was a glorious, enviable life. He was forgiven of sins and made pure by the blood of Jesus. He was reconciled with his Creator and privileged with the opportunity to enter the very presence of God in prayer. He was granted access to the Holy Scriptures – the very words of God which taught him the way to live a fulfilling, purpose-filled, abundant life of joy. Paul's joy was so complete, his confidence in God so certain that he encouraged his rich, influential listeners to exchange their life for his. From Paul's perspective – even from his jailed perspective – no one in the world had it better than he did. He was experiencing an abundant life (John 10:10) that was overflowing with joy, purpose, and a clean conscience. No one had it better than he did, and he invited his listeners to join them if they dared.

26:30-32

When he had said these things, the king stood up, as well as the governor and Bernice and those who sat with them; and when they had gone aside, they talked among themselves, saying, "This man is doing nothing deserving of death or chains." Then Agrippa said to Festus, "This man might have been set free if he had not appealed to Caesar."

At the close of Paul's remarks, the king stood up, putting an immediate end to the proceedings. There was no need for cross examination. There was no need to hear again from Paul's accusers. Agrippa had heard enough. Paul was innocent. The king required no further counsel and no prolonged deliberation to see it plainly: "This man is doing nothing deserving of death or chains."

Paul longed to present the gospel in Rome (Romans 1:8-15) and the Lord promised that he would be enabled to do that very thing (Acts 23:11). And now, the next leg of the unforeseeable route that would take Paul to Rome is set in motion. Paul would travel to Rome in the custody of, under the protection of, and with the favor of Roman captors. It is hard to imagine a set of circumstances filled with more contrasts – Paul is granted the security of his Roman guards, while enduring the confines of captivity, while enjoying the favor and good will of his captors. Certainly, the Lord's ways are "past finding out" (Romans 11:33).

Acts 27

27:1-3

And when it was decided that we should sail to Italy, they delivered Paul and some other prisoners to one named Julius, a centurion of the Augustan Regiment. So, entering a ship of Adramyttium, we put to sea, meaning to sail along the coasts of Asia. Aristarchus, a Macedonian of Thessalonica, was with us. And the next day we landed at Sidon. And Julius treated Paul kindly and gave him liberty to go to his friends and receive care.

Paul had been imprisoned for over two years by the time his ship finally sailed for Rome. But here we are reminded of some of the precious comforts that our Lord provided him during these difficult years. We see that Julius "treated Paul kindly" and allowed him "liberty" – a temporary pass of some sort to visit his friends in Sidon. Unexpected kindness can provide a wealth of comfort to the recipient. Let us imitate Julius and seek to treat everyone "kindly" – everyone – especially strangers, so that we might be the conduit by which the Lord encourages the hurting with His love. Our Lord "comforts us in all our tribulation, that we may be able to comfort those who are in any trouble, with the comfort with which we ourselves are comforted by God" (II Corinthians 1:4).

We also find the Lord comforting Paul through the company of Aristarchus (and Luke, the writer). Aristarchus had accompanied Paul to Jerusalem as a representative from the church of Thessalonica (Acts 20:4). Rather than return home after Paul was arrested, Aristarchus continued to minister to Paul's needs in prison for two years! And now we find him loyally committed to remaining at Paul's side on the voyage to Rome. It is God's good will to "comfort the downcast" (II Corinthians 7:6), and one of His most precious means of comforting His downcast saints is through blessed friendships with other believers. Those who love God, love those who love God. And there is no greater encouragement to the downcast saint than the love that is shown to us by God's people who seem to be remarkably perceptive to our needs.

Paul's ministry was restricted. But God's grace toward him that buoyed his spirits knew no limits. Even in captivity, the kindness of strangers and the company of the saints channeled to him constant reminders of God's compassion. May these constant reminders of God's love for us buoy our spirits as well.

27:4-8

When we had put to sea from there, we sailed under the shelter of Cyprus, because the winds were contrary. And when we had sailed over the sea which is off Cilicia and Pamphylia, we came to Myra, a city of Lycia. There the centurion found an Alexandrian ship sailing to Italy, and he put us on board. When we had sailed slowly many days, and arrived with difficulty off Cnidus, the wind not permitting us to proceed, we sailed under the shelter of Crete off Salmone. Passing it with difficulty, we came to a place called Fair Havens, near the city of Lasea.

Luke works to provide some detail of the early challenges of the voyage in order to set up the shipwreck that is soon to come. We are told that they "sailed slowly," traveled "with difficulty," and encountered winds that did not permit them to proceed as they had planned. Perhaps verse 4 summed it up best, "the winds were contrary."

Let us be on our guard when the winds of change, and the whims of those in charge, and adversaries large and small become "contrary." Leviticus 26:23-24 says, "If by these things you are not reformed by Me, but walk contrary to Me, then I also will walk contrary to you, and I will punish you yet seven times for your sins." Sometimes, difficulties arise because something we are doing is contrary to what God wants done. Let us examine ourselves when the winds of life are contrary to be sure that we are not harboring disobedience within us. Here, however, Paul's journey faced difficulty when he was walking obediently in the perfect will of God. The Lord's way is often a difficult way and serving Him may cause us to face much opposition that arises from our obedience, not our faults. In I Corinthians 16:9 Paul wrote of "a great and effective door" of ministry that had opened to him, and in that open door for godly service, as he obeyed God and served Him faithfully, he faced "many adversaries." God's way provides us with peace during storms. His way does not guarantee clear skies.

27:9-12

Now when much time had been spent, and sailing was now dangerous because the Fast was already over, Paul advised them, saying, "Men, I perceive that this voyage will end with disaster and much loss, not only of the cargo and ship, but also our lives." Nevertheless the centurion was more persuaded by the helmsman and the owner of the ship than by the things spoken by Paul. And because the harbor was not suitable to winter in, the majority advised to set sail from there also, if by any means they could reach Phoenix, a harbor of Crete opening toward the southwest and northwest, and winter there.

Paul advises the centurion and ship's captain that they should not proceed. The Spirit of the Lord had revealed to Paul the imminent danger that awaited if they ventured further on their course. The centurion, however, was naturally "more persuaded by the helmsman and the owner of the ship than by the things spoken by Paul." Paul's warning came from spiritual insight, the mariners' insights arose from personal experience and expertise. Let us be very reticent to follow the advice of experts when it conflicts with the counsel of those who walk closely with God.

This time, those in charge do not listen to Paul. Two weeks later, however, when yet another storm threatens to drown them all, they will remember that Paul proved right here. Their failure here will help them to trust Paul's advice in verses 30-36, and their trust in Paul's advice at that time will save their life. Christians have very good cause to be patient. God's Word and God's ways will always prove to be best. If people do not believe us as we teach them God's messages today, let us bear with them with contented, kind-hearted patience, knowing that eventually, everyone will be convinced by the truths of God.

27:13-20

When the south wind blew softly, supposing that they had obtained their desire, putting out to sea, they sailed close by Crete. But not long after, a tempestuous head wind arose, called Euroclydon. So when the ship was caught, and could not head into the wind, we let her drive. And running under the shelter of an island called Clauda, we secured the skiff with difficulty. When they had taken it on board, they used cables to undergird the ship; and fearing lest they should run aground on the Syrtis Sands, they struck sail and so were driven. And because we were exceedingly tempest-tossed, the next day they lightened the ship. On the third day we threw the ship's tackle overboard with our own hands. Now when neither sun nor stars appeared for many days, and no small tempest beat on us, all hope that we would be saved was finally given up.

Luke does not say specifically that Paul had also given up hope that he would survive the storm, but it seems implied that everyone onboard the ship, to one degree or another, resigned themselves to the likelihood that death was imminent. "Neither sun nor stars appeared for many days." This would certainly be fear-provoking for anyone on the open sea even in our day, and in the days before the compass was invented, it would have been even more terrifying. What will be our reaction when we stare in the face of death?

Our verses here tell us that the sailors worked feverishly with their hands to save themselves. They did everything physically possible to improve their hope of survival. Verse 33 says that they fasted for days in an attempt to do everything spiritually possible to improve their hope of survival as well. But it appeared, at least for a time, that their efforts would fail. "All hope that we would be saved was finally given up." Like the sailors, let us do all within our means to extend our life so that we may use our time on earth to serve and bless our fellow man (Philippians 1:24). And when the day appointed for us to enter into our heavenly rest comes to greet us in the form of a storm, or a cancer, or in old age, let us commit our souls to our faithful Creator (I Peter 4:19), anticipating a wondrous reception when we reach heaven's door.

Blessedly, for God's children, our hope that we will be saved will never need to be abandoned. Our ship may be lost. Our life may be lost. But our eternity is secure in heaven, and our hope for our resurrection there will not disappoint (Romans 5:5).

27:21-26

But after long abstinence from food, then Paul stood in the midst of them and said, "Men, you should have listened to me, and not have sailed from Crete and incurred this disaster and loss. And now I urge you to take heart, for there will be no loss of life among you, but only of the ship. For there stood by me this night an angel of the God to whom I belong and whom I serve, saying, 'Do not be afraid, Paul; you must be brought before Caesar; and indeed God has granted you all those who sail with you.' Therefore take heart, men, for I believe God that it will be just as it was told me. However, we must run aground on a little island."

The storm continued to rage around them, but we imagine that the Lord now instilled a slight break in the deafening roar of the wind and waves so that the men on the ship could hear Paul speak. As a prisoner, yet with Spirit-given authority, Paul stands before the 276 people onboard the ship and tells them what God had said to him. He begins with a holy I-told-you-so. His intention was not so much to make them regret their failure to listen to him the first time, as it was to help protect them from failing to listen to him now. Their survival will depend on their obedience to his instructions, and Paul does not want them to miss their opportunity for rescue. By reminding them that he was right the first time, he was helping them to be confident that what he said to them was true.

He then instills his listeners with hope. People with hope listen to counsel much better than those without it. Without the hope of an improved outcome, all counsel, instruction, loving advice, and direction sound like useless drivel. Those who have lost hope that they will survive tomorrow have little interest in bettering their lot today. Paul, however, fills them with hope: "I urge you to take heart, for there will be no loss of life among you."

Paul concludes his talk with a glimpse of the future: "We must run aground on a little island." This prophetic word is granted to Paul to further help people believe in the power of God and trust in Paul's revelation. Soon, the ship will run aground on the small island of Malta, and all will see that Paul's prophecy proved true.

In addition to the word of hope and the prophecy of the events to come, the angel also granted Paul this further encouragement: "God has granted you all those who sail with you." Goodness, what a precious promise. In answer to Paul's prayer, and as a blessing to him personally, God promises to rescue everyone that is on Paul's ship. Matthew Henry says about this verse, "There is no greater satisfaction to a good man than to know he is a public blessing." Because of His love for Job, God forgave his three friends

(Job 42:8). Because God loved David, He rescued an entire city (Isaiah 37:35). And here we see that because of God's love for Paul, He answered Paul's request and saved the lives of 276 people that otherwise would have perished. "Sometimes God saves a nation, a city, a body of men, even of ungodly men, for the sake of a few that fear his name, who are among them" (Gill's Exposition of the Entire Bible). It would be a point of eternal joy for us should the Lord find our family sufficient reason to save those that we live among. Let us live lives pleasing to the Lord. So many lives depend on it.

27:27-32

Now when the fourteenth night had come, as we were driven up and down in the Adriatic Sea, about midnight the sailors sensed that they were drawing near some land. And they took soundings and found it to be twenty fathoms; and when they had gone a little farther, they took soundings again and found it to be fifteen fathoms. Then, fearing lest we should run aground on the rocks, they dropped four anchors from the stern, and prayed for day to come. And as the sailors were seeking to escape from the ship, when they had let down the skiff into the sea, under pretense of putting out anchors from the prow, Paul said to the centurion and the soldiers, "Unless these men stay in the ship, you cannot be saved." Then the soldiers cut away the ropes of the skiff and let it fall off.

See what remarkable confidence the centurion now has in Paul! The centurion did not listen to Paul in verse 11, but he will not make that mistake again! In the middle of the night, Paul tells the centurion that everyone must remain on the ship or "you cannot be saved." Taking that advice to heart, the centurion orders his soldiers to "cut away the ropes of the skiff and let it fall off." He would rather lose the lifeboat completely than tempt men to escape to their own demise. It seems a shame, for the skiff would have been valuable when the ship ran aground a few hours later. But in MacLaren's Expositions he writes, "Misused good things have sometimes to be given up in order to keep people from temptation." In Matthew 18:8 Jesus said, "If your hand or foot causes you to sin, cut it off and cast it from you. It is better for you to enter into life lame or maimed, rather than having two hands or two feet, to be cast into the everlasting fire." Here, the centurion instantly assessed that this skiff was a hand and foot that was tempting his men to sin, so he cut it off, just as Jesus directed.

27:33-38

And as day was about to dawn, Paul implored them all to take food,

saying, "Today is the fourteenth day you have waited and continued without food, and eaten nothing. Therefore I urge you to take nourishment, for this is for your survival, since not a hair will fall from the head of any of you." And when he had said these things, he took bread and gave thanks to God in the presence of them all; and when he had broken it he began to eat. Then they were all encouraged, and also took food themselves. And in all we were two hundred and seventy-six persons on the ship. So when they had eaten enough, they lightened the ship and threw out the wheat into the sea.

Fasting has value to us. Our Lord invites us to draw near to Him, and there are times that fasting helps focus our attention on Him as we do. Joel 2:12 says, "Turn to Me with all your heart, with fasting, with weeping, and with mourning." But we must not neglect the strength of our body and mind even as we seek to draw near to God and guard our spiritual health. Jonathan bemoaned his father's unwise fast in I Samuel 14:24-30 because it weakened the soldiers when they needed their strength for battle. Similarly, Paul now invites those on the ship to break their fast. They will need their strength to battle the storm and then swim to shore in just a few hours. It is true that without the Lord's blessings we cannot be saved, but the apostle Paul also instructs those on the ship (and us) that taking "nourishment" is also essential for "survival." Paul prayed and fasted, interceding for the lives of all those on the ship. And when it was time to eat, he thanked the Lord for his food and ate – and Luke thought that it was important enough to record for us that Paul ate a meal in a storm. In mercy, our Lord delights to save our soul; and in kindness, God delights to give us our daily bread. It is right to take joy in thanking Him and being "encouraged" by all His gifts, large and small.

27:39-44

When it was day, they did not recognize the land; but they observed a bay with a beach, onto which they planned to run the ship if possible. And they let go the anchors and left them in the sea, meanwhile loosing the rudder ropes; and they hoisted the mainsail to the wind and made for shore. But striking a place where two seas met, they ran the ship aground; and the prow stuck fast and remained immovable, but the stern was being broken up by the violence of the waves. And the soldiers' plan was to kill the prisoners, lest any of them should swim away and escape. But the centurion, wanting to save Paul, kept them from their purpose, and commanded that those who could swim should jump overboard first and get to land, and the rest, some on boards and some on parts of the ship. And so it was that they all escaped safely to land.

Dangers continue to assault Paul. From the onset of his missionary efforts in Acts 13, through the plot to kill him in Jerusalem, the trials before Felix and Festus, the storm, the shipwreck, and now the soldier's plan to kill all the prisoners, the Lord continually protected His servant. Here, the Lord moves the centurion to once again keep Paul safe. Let us not seek to live a safe life. Let us seek to live a life in our Father's hands. His protection and His favor in dangerous waters grant us far greater security than the pretended safety of comfortable surroundings.

Acts 28

28:1-6

Now when they had escaped, they then found out that the island was called Malta. And the natives showed us unusual kindness; for they kindled a fire and made us all welcome, because of the rain that was falling and because of the cold. But when Paul had gathered a bundle of sticks and laid them on the fire, a viper came out because of the heat, and fastened on his hand. So when the natives saw the creature hanging from his hand, they said to one another, "No doubt this man is a murderer, whom, though he has escaped the sea, yet justice does not allow to live." But he shook off the creature into the fire and suffered no harm. However, they were expecting that he would swell up or suddenly fall down dead. But after they had looked for a long time and saw no harm come to him, they changed their minds and said that he was a god.

The people on Malta demonstrate for us the spiritual understanding that God has revealed to all of humanity. They also demonstrate for us man's tendency to warp these God-given spiritual insights and twist them into unhealthy and God-dishonoring directions. First, they express the God-given understanding that human beings should be holy, and that death is the penalty for sin. "No doubt this man is a murderer, whom, though he has escaped the sea, yet justice does not allow to live." The people of Malta did not know God. But they knew "justice," the reflection of His heart in theirs. They knew, without anyone telling them, that "the wages of sin is death" (Romans 6:23). They knew that "righteousness and justice are the foundation of Your throne" (Psalm 89:14). They did not know the Person behind the rule of justice, but they knew that justice reigns.

Sadly, without the Holy Spirit reigning in our hearts, men and women are terribly prone to distort their spiritual understandings. The people of Malta felt that every mishap was an indication of personal sin – which is not always the case (John 9:1-3). And they thought that Paul's good fortune was proof that "he was a god." Riches, health, and fortunate events do not prove that God favors us, and certainly do not show that we are gods ourselves.

The denizens of Malta also illustrate how fickle the hearts of men can be. One minute they accuse Paul of being a murderer – with no evidence at all against him – and moments later they acclaim him as a god. In so doing they unknowingly mimicked the impulsiveness and untrustworthiness of the people of Lystra who hailed Paul as a god one minute, and then moments later stoned him in murderous contempt (Acts 14). Let us not be overmoved by the praises of men. The hearts of men are not trustworthy. Their praise can turn into scorn in an instant (John 2:23-25).

28:7-10
In that region there was an estate of the leading citizen of the island, whose name was Publius, who received us and entertained us courteously for three days. And it happened that the father of Publius lay sick of a fever and dysentery. Paul went in to him and prayed, and he laid his hands on him and healed him. So when this was done, the rest of those on the island who had diseases also came and were healed. They also honored us in many ways; and when we departed, they provided such things as were necessary.

Paul was chained, but he felt complete freedom to do good works and bless those around him. When troubled by seemingly unhelpful limitations, let us follow Paul's example and overlook our personal discomforts and obey the godly yearning within us to never stop blessing others. With amazing selflessness, Paul remains undistracted by his personal troubles, and focuses, instead, on glorifying God and ministering to the needs of people. His immediate rewards were of some comfort. He was "honored" in some small way by the people, and they provided for him "such things as were necessary." His kindness to others, however, did not win his freedom. Let us abandon all desire for personal reward in this life. Let us use all the strength the Lord places within us to bless those that He places in our path. And let us not be discouraged by the dearth of immediate rewards. Our reward in heaven is very sure.

28:11-16

After three months we sailed in an Alexandrian ship whose figurehead was the Twin Brothers, which had wintered at the island. And landing at Syracuse, we stayed three days. From there we circled round and reached Rhegium. And after one day the south wind blew; and the next day we came to Puteoli, where we found brethren, and were invited to stay with them seven days. And so we went toward Rome. And from there, when the brethren heard about us, they came to meet us as far as Appii Forum and Three Inns. When Paul saw them, he thanked God and took courage. Now when we came to Rome, the centurion delivered the prisoners to the captain of the guard; but Paul was permitted to dwell by himself with the soldier who guarded him.

The arrival of fellow believers gave Paul "courage." When the brethren heard that Paul had arrived in Italy, groups of them traveled from far away to show their support and encourage him in the knowledge that he was prayed for and loved by God's people. Let us be inspired by this picture of Christians visiting a beloved believer for the mutual edification of them all. Those who love God are blessed by the company of others who love Him too. Let us be especially mindful of those who are enduring trials of any kind, as Paul endured his captivity. Even those endowed with the power of Paul are thankful and are encouraged by the visits of fellow believers. We might surmise that those who are weak in the faith, or new in the faith may benefit from the visits of their brothers and sisters in Christ even more. The visitors were unable to remove Paul's trial. He was just as much a captive after their visit as he was before they arrived. Even though his circumstances did not change, however, he "took courage" and "thanked God" for their visit. If we can relieve the cause of someone's pain, let us relieve it. If we can help bear the burden of a heavy-laden saint, let us do that too. But if we can do nothing more than sit close by their side so that the Spirit in us might uplift their troubled heart, let us rush to do so, having reason to hope that the Lord might use us to do for others what these Italian visitors did for Paul.

28:17-20

And it came to pass after three days that Paul called the leaders of the Jews together. So when they had come together, he said to them: "Men and brethren, though I have done nothing against our people or the customs of our fathers, yet I was delivered as a prisoner from Jerusalem into the hands of the Romans, who, when they had examined me, wanted to let me go, because there was no cause for putting me to death. But when the Jews spoke against it, I was compelled to appeal to Caesar, not that I had anything of which to accuse my nation. For this reason therefore I have called for you, to see you and speak with you, because for the hope of Israel I am bound with this chain."

The "hope of Israel" was the coming of Christ the Messiah. In Luke 2 we find Simeon in the temple buoyed each day by the hope that he would see "the Lord's Christ" who was "the Consolation of Israel." In John 4 we find the woman at the well expecting that one day her spiritual needs and spiritual questions would be answered by the arrival of "that Messiah." In Paul's day, all those with any spiritual insight at all awoke each day with the expectant hope that the Messiah would come and be their Deliverer. The "hope of Israel" was that the Messiah would come "beautiful and glorious" (Isaiah 4:2). They hoped that the Messiah would come and "(pour) out His soul unto death" that He might "(bear) the sin of many, and (make) intercession for the transgressors" (Isaiah 53:12). The "hope of Israel" was the Messiah, who would come and "save His people from their sins" (Matthew 1:21). Paul met the Messiah on the road to Damascus and was eternally changed by his encounter. And once changed, Paul dedicated his life to the service of the Messiah and the proclamation of His teachings. It was this effort, his service to the Messiah, that caused Paul to fall into disfavor with influential Jews, that ultimately led to his arrest. Furthermore, it was this "hope of Israel" which enthused and empowered Paul to call for "the leaders of the Jews" to visit him, so that even in captivity he might bear them witness to the gospel of Jesus Christ who is able to save men's souls. Paul was "bound with this chain." But he was also bound with a hope. It was for this hope that he was unjustly held captive, it was by this hope that his soul was sustained in his captivity, and it was the source of this hope that gave him vision to overcome his constraints and proclaim this gospel of hope to as many people as he possibly could, so that they, too, might be saved and transformed by "the hope of Israel."

28:21-23

Then they said to him, "We neither received letters from Judea concerning you, nor have any of the brethren who came reported or spoken any evil of you. But we desire to hear from you what you think; for concerning this sect, we know that it is spoken against everywhere." So when they had appointed him a day, many came to him at his lodging, to whom he explained and solemnly testified of the kingdom of God, persuading them concerning Jesus from both the Law of Moses and the Prophets, from morning till evening.

Once again, we find the Lord opening opportunity for Paul to discuss the great things of God with a new gathering of hearers. Though he was a stranger to them and his confinement in chains gave him no place of honor from which to deliver his gospel truths, yet the Lord called people to Himself, and called them to listen to Paul, despite his unglorified condition. We are reminded that the glory of God shines even when we do not. Our honor does nothing to add any luster to God's glory, and the brilliance of His glory does not shine any less when we are humbled.

Paul used the Scriptures as the heart of his message to the gathered crowd. Paul's testimony of his conversion on the road to Damascus is a remarkable story. But he did not simply talk about his personal experiences –- as compelling as they were. The Word of God is even more persuasive to the awakened conscience than any personal testimony. Jesus taught through His parable of the rich man and Lazarus that God's Word has more power to convince the human soul of the truth than any other force on earth. Luke 16:31 says, "If they do not hear Moses and the prophets, neither will they be persuaded though one rise from the dead." In his letter to these same Romans, Paul wrote that the gospel message regarding Jesus Christ "is the power of God to salvation" (Romans 1:16). Paul's opening experience with Christ was a remarkable event. His further encounters with Christ, when he was allowed to see the glories of Paradise (II Corinthians 12), were also glorious. But he does not spend all day talking of these things. "From morning till evening" he taught his listeners the truths about Jesus from "both the Law of Moses and the Prophets." Paul taught the Bible. He brought people the saving knowledge of Jesus Christ by teaching them God's Word. His example provides us an obvious lesson. Those who are taught and well-grounded in the Word of God are "complete, thoroughly equipped for every good work" (II Timothy 3:17). When our Lord blesses us with precious experiences with Him, let us share those experiences with others that they may be encouraged. But may the mainstay of our ministry always remain the proclamation of God's Word. Let us devote ourselves to teaching God's Word, for it is "the Holy Scriptures, which are able to make you wise for salvation" (II Timothy 2:15).

28:24
And some were persuaded by the things which were spoken, and some disbelieved.

A group of religious men gathered to hear truths presented by the apostle Paul regarding Jesus. He told them about the prophecies regarding Jesus that were written in the Scriptures that they themselves revered. He told them of the life and teachings of Jesus. He told them how Jesus died to pay the penalty for our sins, how He rose from the dead to prove His power over death and sin, and how He returned to heaven some weeks later. He taught them that Jesus will return to judge all mankind and that our eternal fate rests in His hands. And when he had finished his presentation of the truths regarding Jesus, "some were persuaded by the things which were spoken, and some disbelieved."

This short summary statement of the effect of Paul's discourse to the Roman Jews reminds us of both the joy and the sorrow, the opportunity and the limitations of the preacher of God's Word. We rejoice over the souls who hear us and believe to the saving of their soul; and we groan over the souls who hear us preach but remain lost in their unbelief. We grieve over them, knowing that they are "condemned who did not believe the truth" (II Thessalonians 2:12).

Paul preached, and "some were persuaded" and "some disbelieved." The same preacher preached the same message at the same time to the same subset of people – and the results widely varied from one hearer to the other. We must see from this that our personal giftings and our sundry strategies for ministry have extremely limited impact on the fruitfulness of our kingdom efforts. Paul's amazing giftedness did not move everyone to turn to Jesus, nor did his shortcomings drive everyone away. When our service to the Lord yields great results, we cannot take personal credit. We must humbly give all glory to the Lord for calling people to Himself. And when our efforts fall on hard ground and the fruit of our labors seems minimal, we cannot allow ourselves to be discouraged or plagued with doubt. It is the Lord who builds the house (Psalm 127:1). He calls people to Himself. Everyone is called upon to respond to His invitation. And His invitation is so compelling that the personal attributes of His messengers add or subtract very little from the forcefulness of His call.

Today, when we present these same truths, we have good cause to trust that some of our listeners will likewise be persuaded by the message we present and place their faith in Jesus "to the saving of the soul" (Hebrews 10:39). If our mouth speaks the words of God, we can hope that God's assertion to Isaiah will hold true for us just as it did for Paul: "For as the rain comes down, and the snow from heaven, and do not return there, but water the earth, and make it bring forth and bud, that it may give seed to the sower and bread to the eater, so shall My word be that goes forth from My mouth; it shall not return to Me void, but it shall accomplish what I please, and it shall prosper in the thing for which I sent it" (Isaiah 55:10-11).

28:25-27
So when they did not agree among themselves, they departed after Paul had said one word: "The Holy Spirit spoke rightly through Isaiah the prophet to our fathers, saying, 'Go to this people and say: "Hearing you will hear, and shall not understand; and seeing you will see, and not perceive; for the hearts of this people have grown dull. Their ears are hard of hearing, and their eyes they have closed, lest they should see with their eyes and hear with their ears, lest they should understand with their hearts and turn, so that I should heal them."'"

Paul preached for his Roman hearers, and we are told that many did not agree with what he said. Though they heard the gospel truths from one of God's finest servants, they did not believe. Unless God opens our eyes, we are so spiritually uninsightful that we will not believe the truth even if we hear God speak with His own voice (Exodus 20:18-21/Exodus 32:1), or even if we see Jesus raise the dead right in front of us (John 11:45-53). Of this passage, Gill's Exposition of the Entire Bible says, "It appears that the Gospel preached in the clearest and most powerful manner, and even miracles wrought in confirmation of it, are insufficient for conversion; and nothing will effect it, but efficacious grace." It is God who builds the house, and it is God who opens the eyes and ears of His people that we might believe that what He tells us is true. Just as Paul does here, Jesus also quoted these words from Isaiah 6, saying that the reason that He taught in parables was so that these words might be proven true, that men would see and hear the truth, but their "dull" heart would not understand. John also quoted these words in John 12 to explain how it was possible for the people to see "so many signs before them" (John 12:37) and yet not believe in Jesus.

Oh, the eyes of men are so blind! What hope do we have that anyone can be saved when people hear the gospel but can't understand it, they see the truth but can't perceive how to respond to it, and the truths of the gospel pierce their soul, but their heart is too dull to turn from their former ways? The eyes of men are blind, but blessedly, our Lord came for this very purpose, "to open blind eyes" (Isaiah 42:7). Let us join David and pray, "Open my eyes, that I may see wondrous things from Your law" (Psalm 119:18). And then let us join Elisha and pray that the Lord would open the eyes of those around us that they too, might see the truth and rightly discern how they should respond (II Kings 6:17).

28:28

"Therefore let it be known to you that the salvation of God has been sent to the Gentiles, and they will hear it!"

Paul's final words are both a condemnation of his unbelieving listeners and a promise of the marvelous days to come when the nations of the earth will happily accept God's salvation from sin. Isaiah foretold the arrival of this wonderful day, the day when God's offer of salvation from sin would be extended "to the ends of the earth" (Isaiah 49:6). Paul was grieved by the hardness of the hearts of those who came to hear him speak, but this grief was salved by the knowledge that the Lord would rescue many others from every nation under heaven. The rejection of Christ by unbelievers rightly saddens the heart of God's servants, but we are consoled by the knowledge that the rejection of one will not stop saving faith from coming to many others.

In Paul's letter to the Romans, he expounds for three chapters (9-11) on this very matter that is summarized here in a single verse. In Romans 10:1 Paul writes, "My heart's desire and prayer to God for Israel is that they may be saved." And when Paul's countrymen reject the gospel, Paul says he has "great sorrow and continual grief in my heart" (Romans 9:2). But even as he grieves over the lostness of his countrymen, Paul rejoices that those who were once far from the promise of heaven are now "called sons of the living God" (Romans 9:26) and that God is pleased to "call them My people who were not My people, and her beloved, who was not beloved" (Romans 9:25).

The Jews reject Paul and the gospel message that he presented to them. But their rejection is not the end of the story. Paul repeats here his same response that he gave to the unbelieving Jews in Corinth in Acts 18:6 – "When they opposed him and blasphemed, he shook his garments and said to them, 'Your blood be upon your own heads; I am clean. From now on I will go to the Gentiles.'" Let us be faithful to share the gospel truths to everyone that our Lord places in our path. Let us mourn over those who reject the Truth. But let us not brood over them. If persecution or unbelief give us an unholy welcome in one place, let us find joy in the privilege of serving our Lord, and find further joy in the prospect of delivering the Good News to the next soul that God sends our way. When Jeremiah faced ridicule and unbelief as he proclaimed God's message to the Jews, he considered, for a moment, that it might be time to protect himself from further abuse and stop declaring God's truths. But as soon as he considered that possibility, the power and excellence and delight of God's words welled up within him until he was unable to keep silent even for a moment. Jeremiah contemplated keeping God's Word to himself and told himself, "I will not make mention of Him, nor speak anymore in His name." But as soon as the thought came to his mind, he dismissed it instantly. He could not keep God's Word to himself because "His word was in my heart like a burning fire shut up in my bones; I was weary of holding it back, and I could not" (Jeremiah 20:9).

28:29-31
And when he had said these words, the Jews departed and had a great dispute among themselves. Then Paul dwelt two whole years in his own rented house, and received all who came to him, preaching the kingdom of God and teaching the things which concern the Lord Jesus Christ with all confidence, no one forbidding him.

Paul had already endured over two years of imprisonment in Caesarea (Acts 24:27), and now he is forced to endure two more years of unjust confinement in Rome. Somehow, however, Paul is able to consider his time in captivity a "furtherance for the Gospel" (Philippians 1:12). A steady stream of visitors "came to him" in his "rented house." The house was a jail, limiting Paul's movements. But by God's design, it also became a pedestal upon which we find Paul continually "preaching the kingdom of God and teaching the things which concern the Lord Jesus Christ." Let us willingly tolerate much in this life that limits our liberties and conflicts with our personal preferences. Many matters that are personally humiliating may actually serve to enhance our service to God. Fetters on the outside and frailties from within may hinder our secular affairs. Paul demonstrates for us here, however, that many matters that cause us discomfort and inconvenience prove to be no hindrance at all to our efforts to carry out our Lord's purposes.

Author's Note

It is the longing of everyone at Tell the Kids publishing that all their published works include a reminder of God's plan for how we can be freed from the penalty of sin and made right with the God who made us. These pages of Acts that we have just read together are filled with this same desire of the apostles to see their listeners reconciled with God. Sometimes that call is expanded into a lengthy sermon as we see from Stephen in Acts chapter 7. And sometimes the plan for reconciliation is summarized succinctly in a single sentence as we see in Peter's words in Acts 2:38 and again in Acts 3:19 when he says, "Repent therefore and be converted, that your sins may be blotted out, so that times of refreshing may come from the presence of the Lord."

Repentance is at the heart of our reconciliation with God. Acts 17:30 says that God "now commands all men everywhere to repent." We must repent of our false hopes in false gods. We cannot be right with God and maintain allegiances to or confidence in other gods. Additionally, we must repent of our sins and turn to obedience to all God's will and all His commandments. We cannot be right with God and persist in those things which He calls sin. We must repent of these things if we are to be right with our Creator.

The remarkably wonderful news for modern man is that salvation from sin and reconciliation with the holy, Creator God is possible! But the path to a right relationship with Him requires a faith in Jesus that is demonstrated by a heart of repentance. For the reader that still holds divided loyalties between the God who created all things and another, lesser god as well, may this serve as a reminder of the need to repent of those divided loyalties. And for those who have long claimed faith in God, yet persist in sin against Him, may the call to repent from the book of Acts likewise serve as a call for us to repent of all attitudes and actions which our Creator Lord calls sin.

May the words of the apostles throughout this wonderful book of Acts inspire all of us to a greater thirst to repent of anything that interferes with a right relationship with Jesus, the Prince of life (Acts 3:15). "For there is no other name under heaven given among men by which we must be saved" (Acts 4:12).

-Doug Derbyshire MD